online
consumer behavior

theory and research in
social media, advertising, and e-tail

online consumer behavior

theory and research in
social media, advertising, and e-tail

edited by

angeline g. close

The University of Texas at Austin

Routledge
Taylor & Francis Group
New York   London

Routledge
Taylor & Francis Group
711 Third Avenue
New York, NY 10017

Routledge
Taylor & Francis Group
27 Church Road
Hove, East Sussex BN3 2FA

© 2012 by Taylor & Francis Group, LLC
Routledge is an imprint of Taylor & Francis Group, an Informa business

Printed in the United States of America on acid-free paper
Version Date: 20120323

International Standard Book Number: 978-1-84872-969-8 (Hardback)

Library of Congress Cataloging-in-Publication Data

Online consumer behavior : theory and research in social media, advertising, and e-tail / editor, Angeline G. Close.
    p. cm.
  Includes bibliographical references and index.
  ISBN 978-1-84872-969-8 (hbk. : alk. paper)
    1. Consumer behavior. 2. Internet marketing. 3. Electronic commerce--Psychological aspects. I. Close, Angeline.

HF5415.32.O547 2012
381'.142--dc23   #754734005   2012005630

Visit the Taylor & Francis Web site at
http://www.taylorandfrancis.com

and the Psychology Press Web site at
http://www.psypress.com

To my Facebook friends

Contents

SECTION III   Online Advertising and Online Search Behavior

SECTION IV   e-Tail Consumer Behavior and Online Channels

Foreword

The Beginnings of a New Research Domain

In many respects, the study of consumer behavior is relatively new in the scheme of things. Prior to the 1960s, the topic of consumption was primarily an area of inquiry and interest in the economics discipline. With the emphasis on consumption, the area of analysis was the household and how households managed their budgets as well as how they expended their incomes. In fall 1963, I was in my first semester of the doctoral program at the University of Illinois. In one course, the term requirement was to develop and write a marketing paper that featured a model of a marketing phenomenon. (This was at a time when business schools were trying to add quantitative methods to their curricula.) I thought that I would develop a model of consumer behavior. When I approached the course professor with this idea, he was somewhat perplexed as he did not know of any previous model of consumer behavior. He nonetheless directed me to go to the library and ask the librarian to order a recent dissertation by Franco Nicosia who had completed his doctoral dissertation in 1962 at the University of California, Berkeley. Franco had developed a conceptual model of individual consumer behavior that was later published in a landmark book, *Consumer Decision Processes: Marketing and Advertising Implications* (Prentice Hall, 1966). Also in 1966, Alan Andreasen published an essay, "Attitudes and Customer Behavior: A Decision Model," in *New Research in Marketing*, edited by Lee E. Preston.

In 1968, James Engel, David Kollat, and Roger Blackwell published the first *Consumer Behavior* textbook in which they developed a comprehensive model of consumer behavior. At the same time, John Howard was developing his ideas about individual buyer behavior and, in 1969, published a book with Jagdish Sheth titled *The Theory of Buyer Behavior*. These two books sparked considerable interest and led to many attempts to study consumer behavior from a more comprehensive perspective. New courses were being developed in marketing to describe and explain how individual consumers made purchase decisions and how they might be influenced by multiple factors. In the same year, Engel organized a symposium at The Ohio State University on consumer behavior research and that meeting led to the decision to form the Association for Consumer Research (ACR). The initial ACR conference was held at the University of Massachusetts in August 1970. It was my privilege to attend that conference and meet scholars with interest in doing consumer research.

The New Research Domain Established

During the next several years, consumer research rapidly developed as a legitimate area of research. Sparked by developments in psychology, it grew rapidly. New courses were added to the marketing curricula of business schools and considerable research was produced and submitted to the two marketing journals of the American Marketing Association, the *Journal of Marketing* and *Journal of Marketing Research*. Unfortunately, there was limited space in these two journals to publish many articles on consumer research. Frustrated by the limited space available to address consumer research, a move was made to start a new journal. The first issue of the *Journal of Consumer Research* (*JCR*) was published in June 1974. The journal was labeled as a new interdisciplinary quarterly and was co-sponsored by 10 scholarly associations: the American Association for Public Opinion Research, American Council on Consumer Interests, American Economic Association, American Home Economics Association, American Marketing Association, American Psychological Association (Division 23), American Sociological Association, American Statistical Association, Association for Consumer Research, and the Institute of Management Sciences.

In his introductory editorial, the first *JCR* editor, Ronald Frank, indicated that the journal's objective was to be the first journal to which professionals with an interest in consumer behavior across disciplines sent their research papers. Furthermore, he stated that consumer behavior was to be broadly construed to consider a wide range of behaviors and decisions including family planning, occupational choices, attitudes toward products and services, the purchase, consumption, and uses of products and services such as financial services and medical care as well as other responses to marketing variables.

During these first years in the 1970s, ACR became firmly established as a scholarly professional association and its annual conferences rapidly grew in attendance, surpassing 400 in 1980. (Today, the attendance at the annual ACR conferences each fall numbers over 1,000!) Beginning with the 1973 fall conference proceedings entitled *Advances in Consumer Research*, this annual quickly gained acceptance and recognition for the quality of the papers presented at the conferences and published in the proceedings.

Turmoil in Consumer Research

During the 1980s, considerable concern arose over the philosophical foundations of studies in consumer research. Debates arose in journal pages and in conferences over the merits of logical positivism, critical realism, and interpretive consumer research. Unfortunately, some of this debate was reduced to quantitative versus qualitative research methods. At times, the debates were bitter and there was a feeling that journal space for traditional consumer research might be limited by this newer approach to studying consumer behavior. Indeed, soon after I assumed the editorship of *JCR* in 1990, I was queried about the composition of the editorial review board. The question put to me concerned the seven consumer researchers known to favor qualitative research methods. I quietly responded that the board that appeared at that time on the *JCR* masthead was from the previous editor, Richard Lutz. I did not inform the questioner that the next issue which would list my editorial review board would have 15 qualitative researchers as I expanded the editorial review board by an additional 20+ people. Eventually, the controversy abated in the early 1990s, and acceptance of multiple philosophical and methodological approaches to consumer research has occurred.

Recent Shifts in Consumer Behavior Research

Since the early 1990s, interest in consumer behavior research has expanded and has become truly a global research interest. The Association for Consumer Research began to hold conferences in late spring or early summer in Europe and in the Asia–Pacific region. These conferences led to a growing roster of consumer researchers in these areas of the world. An important consequence of these conferences is that even the so-called national ACR conference saw researchers from Europe, Asia, and Australia attending and presenting their research. Also, in 1990 the Society for Consumer Psychology (Division 23 of the American Psychological Association) began publishing the *Journal of Consumer Psychology* (*JCP*).

The content of consumer research as exemplified by the articles now appearing in *JCR*, *JCP*, and other research journals has shifted to put more emphasis on psychological factors such as cognitive processes and goals, motivation, cross-cultural issues, and behavioral decision theory including judgment and decision making. Issues of public policy, consumer welfare, and family decision making do not seem to attract many consumer researchers. Experimentation has become the dominant research methodology and less attention is placed on studying the more "traditional" marketing influences on consumer behavior such as advertising and promotions. Triggered by the development of the World Wide Web, the globalization of consumer research mentioned above, and the increasing rate of consumers shopping on the Internet, there is growing attention on the Internet as an area needing careful study. Research relative to e-commerce, computing, and the Internet now appears in the journals and in presentations at the conferences.

Online Consumer Behavior Research

Today, consumers purchase products and services in brick-and-mortar stores, and through online Web sites as well as other venues. They share information readily and instantaneously via multiple social media outlets. Consequently, in many respects, researchers have had to rethink how to study consumer behavior. Indeed, one of the effects of the World Wide Web is to make available to consumers throughout the world products and services at any time of the day or night. Initially, it was thought that online access would return the economies to those approaching the economic model of perfect competition. Alas, we have not witnessed such a result as individuals are not able to process all of the information that is available from the many sources online. Moreover, the social media have made it possible for consumers and buyers to provide information to others on a worldwide basis about how the products and services they have acquired meet their expectations and needs. Consequently, it behooves researchers to think carefully through the assumptions that were made about how consumers would search, buy online, and communicate with other consumers and with sellers as well.

Buying and selling online also introduce a number of stimulating questions, some of which will require that researchers think about issues related to public policy, consumer welfare, and family decision making. Foremost are the concerns of security and privacy. Can consumers be protected from unscrupulous sellers and hackers? Will the threat of security breaches make consumers hesitant to shop and purchase online? Can they trust the online sellers to protect their private information and not provide access to that information to others without the knowledge and consent of consumers? Can public policy be framed to protect consumers and therefore the marketplace? Why do consumers abandon their shopping carts before completing a transaction? Are the online reviews ostensibly by other consumers believable and reliable? What is the future of online selling and will it replace the traditional retail store? There is also a need for consumer research to become more multimethod as well as more multidisciplinary. Although it is convenient to conduct experiments using college students, nevertheless relying primarily on this approach raises strong concerns of validity.

These and other relevant research issues concerning online consumer behavior are addressed in this book. It is important that we now have such a volume not only to raise critical research questions but also to begin suggesting solutions and to gain understanding of this phenomenon. This timely book is an essential reference for helping us understand the implications of online consumer behavior.

Kent B. Monroe
J.M. Jones Distinguished Professor of Marketing Emeritus
University of Illinois at Urbana-Champaign
Champaign, Illinois
Distinguished Visiting Scholar
University of Richmond
Richmond, Virginia

Preface

You've Been Poked

Friend me. Social media. Facebook. Tweet that. LinkedIn. Groupon. Retweet that. Buzz marketing. Face-time tonight? Un-friend him. These online terms and brands have changed online consumer behavior, advertising, and branding. It is crucial to understand how consumers think, feel, and act regarding social media, online advertising, and online shopping. Business practitioners are looking for answers and solutions as to how to understand online consumer behavior so that they can maximize their online customers' experiences to help instill brand loyalty. Nonprofit managers or politicians, in a similar fashion, seek an understanding of online consumer behavior so that they can raise awareness and make online giving easy. Scholars have produced only the beginning stages of theory that can systematically explain and predict online consumer behavior, and this book continues that objective.

Online advertisers know the importance of not just incorporating but also embracing consumer blogs, Facebook, Twitter, LinkedIn, MySpace, Digg, HowSocial, Groupon, and other social media to enhance their online presence. Yet questions remain as to how to synergistically leverage these online branding tools to increase the online consumer experience and hence the value of their Web sites. Some of the world's leading brand visionaries such as Apple, as well as emerging brands such as Trader Joe's, align their corporate site and social media objectives to enhance online return on investment.

This theory-driven, research-based book helps address important questions for scholarship and practice, such as

- What are some industry best practices for measuring social media impact and brand visibility?
- How can social media channels help funnel more qualified leads and lessen online cart abandonment rates?

- What is the role of user-generated content in today's online marketplace?
- How do consumers envision their online identity (e.g., via avatars), and how does their online identity relate with their offline identity?
- What is the role of trust and authenticity in an online presence?
- How do different groups, such as adolescents, men, or even politicians, use and embrace social media?

By the end of this book, readers will understand more about online consumer behavior to help unify a Web site's business or nonprofit goals with social media or e-commerce knowledge to maximize the return on investment of both channels.

This book has four fun sections. The first section covers "Consumers' Online Identity." Online identity, in the virtual world and in the on-ground world, is increasingly an important pseudo-image for today's connected consumer. Interestingly, we explore the role of avatars and how these consumer-generated online images accurately coincide with consumers' "real identity." In my dissertation research on e-dating (circa 2005), I found startling evidence that consumers' online identity in some drastic cases was highly exaggerated from their "real identity." People may do such exaggerations to enhance their sense of self-concept (perhaps even lying to themselves), or more drastically to lure an unknowing potential dating partner. It is of note that similar findings of dissimilarity are presented in this volume, outside the context of e-dating photographs and profiles, and in the context of avatars, or cartoon-based pictorial representations of the image an online consumer wishes to portray. In some cases, such avatars are brands, designers, sports teams, or other nonhuman images. Although depersonalized compared to an avatar that is purported to look like the consumer, these nonhuman avatars, such as the Nike swoosh or the University of Texas Longhorn, are attractive and represent an image transfer from the brand to the person adopting that image.

It is unhealthy to fully understand online identity without considering the notion that there is more than one world in today's consumer's mind. There is the real world, which, for many, consists of working, family, social activities, and shopping at brick-and-mortar stores and service providers. Some of this is difficult, if not impossible to do online. Until someone invents an application that can put gas in one's car, or bring one's child to daycare, such interactions in the real world are necessary. A consumer has her real-world image. The twist is that this image is not necessarily congruent with her image in the virtual world. Behind the screen, a consumer may create a new identity, a new attitude, and in a sense, become a different person while online. As scholars, it is our duty to understand consumer identity in virtual worlds, and to delve into the important questions that can help us understand that virtual identities are indeed real. Understanding such can help consumer-minded businesses and organizations cater better to customer wants.

Having an overview of the online identity and virtual worlds set, Section II, "Social Media, Blogs, and Privacy Issues," makes the necessary link to social media and privacy issues. One cannot have an intelligent conversation about social media without discussing the role of privacy, security, and related fears about one's personal and financial information. The thought of cyber-identity theft is enough to inhibit some consumers from shopping and banking online. It is key for us to explore consumer perception of both privacy and security. Doing so can help e-tailers make sure that they are accurately addressing the concerns their customers have that could be preventing them from completing online transactions. Establishing the highest standards for privacy and security is important for online brand managers.

Today's brand managers have a wealth of resources at their fingertips to help establish their brand's identity and to connect with their customers (and their friends) via social networking. That said, Facebook, Twitter, LinkedIn, and other social networking sites are not just tools for consumers to connect with each other (C2C). Instead, we must look at social networks as a brand management tool. Just as touch points with the brand are key at live events (e.g., sponsor signage at a sporting event), virtual touch points are a tool to help leverage those on-ground consumer relationships. Social networking can never replace the authenticity of a handshake and personalized service; however, these virtual touch points can reinforce extant relationships, or spark a new interest.

Now, the question becomes, "Do we as consumers actually want those online touch points with brands on our social networks?" I bring this question up as it has much relevance to the issues investigated in Section II, as well as in our own social networking experiences. I believe that there is some market resistance demonstrated (or at least at the attitudinal level) here. For some consumers, myself included, we feel that social networks are designed as a vehicle that connects us with people who have at one point graced our lives. Be it old high-school pals, current colleagues, or, yes, even your parents, it is this constant connection with people that draws consumers to log on for hours on end to social networking sites. In fact, as noted in Chapter 4, Facebook.com is the most visited site in America. Make these vehicles another way to market to us and sell to us, and we may resist. There could be the perception that marketers and advertisers are stomping on consumers' sacred territory. That said, if done correctly (i.e., precise targeting in a nonintrusive manner), there can be some nice subtle synergies from online advertisers that can actually enhance one's social networking experience. For example, after I changed my Facebook status from "in a relationship" to "engaged," a sidebar on the social media site appeared from a wedding dress vendor. Life stage marketing at its finest, the online advertiser understood psychologically what many women feel—that there are two important dresses in a woman's life—the prom dress and the wedding dress. So, yes, the dress is one of the first things on the newly engaged woman's mind, and Facebook and their advertisers were right there to assist in the search. (In case you are wondering . . . although I checked out the ad, I stayed local and gave my business to the dress shop in Las Vegas, because a girlfriend, also a Facebook friend, raved about their top-notch service.) Somehow, the platforms change, but the role of (electronic) word-of-mouth and relationships remains a stronghold for effective business.

This leads us right to the role of such online advertising and how it affects consumer attitudes, cognitions, and behaviors. Section III, "Online Advertising and Online Search Behavior" covers these timely topics. In many ways, online awareness and social media tactics are means to enhance online advertising effectiveness and consumer search. This section includes hot topics such as online political advertising, invertising, and how men use the Internet to search and shop. With respect to political advertising, authors consider how online videos and ads can influence voter assessment. A political candidate's image is one of his most important assets; thus, it is consequential to consider his online image. Next, the invertising chapter examines the influence of business to consumer (B2C) communication in social media on consumers' relationships with brands. The final chapter in this section considers male consumers' motivations to use the Internet to shop for their preferred brands, and how their online consumer behavior is distinct when seen through a gender lens. Whoever said males were not born to shop must have lived prior to the e-commerce revolution, because males do like to shop, online especially.

To culminate the book, the final section (IV) is on "e-Tail Consumer Behavior and Online Channels." This section is last because many of the aforementioned topics are precursors to getting consumers to e-tail sites, into virtual shopping carts, and, it is hoped, converting cart placements into sales turned relationships. For any relationship, online or offline, trust is a key asset, for politicians and businesses alike. In this section, authors uncover the conditions under which trust makes a consumer repatron-ize or stay loyal to an e-tailer. That said, it is important to consider what drives consumers to hybrid channels; thus, we explore hybrid channels from the consumer perspective. This culminates in the hybrid consider-ations of brick-and-mortar retailers with e-tailers. We uncover how and why consumers use and abandon their virtual shopping carts. This gets our field one step closer toward a theory of consumer electronic shopping cart behavior.

It has been a pleasure to work with this group of authors. I have worked with the contributors to this project since 2008, when we put our minds together for a symposium about online consumer behavior preceding an American Marketing Association conference. Since that time, the authors have worked very hard on their respective chapters, so please join me in thanking them for their ideas and time. You may even wish to friend them on Facebook. I sincerely hope that this book "pokes you" toward new ideas that will serve as a platform for scholars and for companies/organizations that wish to understand online consumer behavior to enhance consumer-based business in this ever-changing (virtual) marketplace.

Angeline G. Close, PhD
Assistant Professor
The University of Texas at Austin

About the Editor

Angeline G. Close, PhD
The University of Texas at Austin

Professor Close researches, teaches, and serves in the marketing community. A main interest is in event marketing, namely, how consumers' experiences at sponsored events influence attitudes and consumer behavior. This research explains engaging consumers with events, uncovering drivers of effective event sponsorships, how entertainment affects events/ purchase intention toward sponsors, the role of sponsor–event congruity, and why consumers may resist events. A scholarly book edited with Lynn Kahle, PhD, *Consumer Behavior Knowledge for Effective Sports and Event Marketing* (Routledge, 2011), synthesizes thinking in the area of sports and events.

Synergistically, Professor Close researches consumer experiences with electronic marketplaces and online experiences, and how they interplay with on-ground events. One of the goals of this current volume is to bring forward new thoughts on this topic. Her research ties theory with implications for consumers, society, or consumer-focused business practice. Professor Close has contributed over a dozen peer-reviewed research publications and book chapters. These appear in the *Journal of the Academy of Marketing Science*, *Advances in Consumer Research*, *Journal of Advertising Research*, and *Journal of Business Research*, among others. This research has been featured on CBS, and in *The New York Times*, *The Los Angeles Times*, *New Scientist*, *The St. Petersburg Times*, and *The Las Vegas Review-Journal*.

Where creating knowledge via research is important, Professor Close believes that disseminating knowledge is crucial to move the field forward and to inspire young minds. She is currently teaching integrated communication management, and she has taught MBA market opportunity analysis, marketing management, advertising, integrated marketing communication, international marketing, strategy, and sales/promotions courses. A goal of this teaching is to spark student interest in the fields of advertising and marketing by involving students with research projects, co-collaborating on new ideas, and hosting esteemed marketing executives. She takes pride in engaging students' thinking in marketing theories and applications, especially in the local entertainment and technology economies.

For community service, Professor Close serves the local and national marketing and academic communities. Nationally, she is president of the American Marketing Association's Consumer Behavior division (CBSIG. org). Involved with doctoral education, she serves on the board of directors to current doctoral students in AMA's doctoral student group. She also takes various leadership roles for the American Marketing Association, Society for Marketing Advances, and Academy of Marketing Science.

Professor Close brings experience as a marketing research consultant, as she has contributed marketing research projects for Hallmark, Coca-Cola, Dodge, Ford, Cingular, New Media Institute, Harvey's Grocery, United Community Bank, AT&T, Fashion Show Mall, Suzuki, Tour de GA, Road Atlanta, Red Rock Country Club, and Lexus.

Prior to joining Texas Advertising, Professor Close served on the University of Nevada–Las Vegas's business faculty for five years. Prior to that, she studied advertising and marketing at the University of Georgia's Grady College of Journalism & Mass Communication (ABJ 1997; MMC 2000) and the Terry College of Business (PhD 2006).

Selected Research

Close, A. G. & Kukar-Kinney, M. (2010). Beyond buying: Motivations behind consumers online shopping cart use. *Journal of Business Research, 63*(10), 986–992.

Close, A. G. & Zinkhan, G. M. (2004). The e-mergence of e-dating. *Advances in Consumer Research, 31,* 153–157.

Close, A. G. & Zinkhan, G. M. (2006). A holiday loved and loathed: A consumer perspective of Valentine's Day. *Advances in Consumer Research, 33,* 1–10.

Close, A. G. & Zinkhan, G. M. (2007). Consumer experiences and market resistance: An extension of resistance theories. *Advances in Consumer Research, 34,* 256–262.

Close A. G. & Zinkhan G. M. (2009). Market resistance and Valentine's Day events. *Journal of Business Research, 62*(2), 200–207.

Close, A. G., Dixit, A., & Malhotra, N. (2005). Chalkboards to cybercources: The internet in marketing education. *Marketing Education Review, 15*(2), 81–94.

Close, A. G., Krishen, A., & LaTour, M. S. (2009). This event is me: How consumer event congruity leverages sponsorship. *Journal of Advertising Research, 49*(3), 271–284.

Close, A. G., Moulard, J. G., & Monroe, K. (2011). Establishing human brands: Determinants of placement success for first faculty positions in marketing. *Journal of Academy of Marketing Science, 39*(6), 922–941.

Close, A. G., Zachary Finney, R., Lacey, R., & Sneath, J. (2006). Engaging the consumer through event marketing: Linking attendees with the sponsor, community, and brand. *Journal of Advertising Research, 46*(4), 420–433.

Kahle, L. R. & Close, A.G. (2011). *Consumer behavior knowledge for effective sports and event marketing.* New York: Routledge.

Kukar-Kinney, M. & Close, A. G. (2010). The determinants of consumers' shopping cart abandonment. *Journal of the Academy of Marketing Science, 38*(2), 240–250.

Lacey, R., Close, A. G., & Zachary Finney, R. (2010). The pivotal roles of product knowledge and corporate social responsibility in event sponsorship effectiveness. *Journal of Business Research, 63*(9–10), 986–992.

Lacey, R., Sneath, J., Zachary Finney, R., & Close, A. G. (2007). The impact of repeat attendance on event sponsorship effects. *Journal of Marketing Communications, 13*(4), 243–255.

Sneath, J. Z., Zachary Finney, R., Lacey, R., & Close, A. G. (2006). Balancing act: Proprietary and non-proprietary event marketing. *Marketing Health Services, 26*(1), 27–32.

Sneath, J. Z., Zachary Finney, R., & Close, A. G. (2005). An IMC approach to event marketing: The effects of sponsorship and experience on customer attitudes. *Journal of Advertising Research, 45*(4), 373–381.

Zinkhan, G. M., Prenshaw, P., & Close, A. G. (2004). Sex-typing of leisure activities: A test of two theories. *Advances in Consumer Research, 31,* 412–419.

About the Contributors

Pia A. Albinsson, PhD (New Mexico State University) is an assistant professor of marketing at Appalachian State University's Walker College of Business, where she has been teaching integrated marketing communications, services marketing, and other marketing courses since 2009. Her research encompasses sustainable consumption practices, alternative disposition behavior, advertising effectiveness, on- and offline communities, and consumer activism. She has published her work in a number of journals including the *Journal of Consumer Behaviour, European Journal of Marketing, Journal of Public Policy and Marketing, Journal of Online Learning and Teaching*, and *Advances of Consumer Research*.

Anjali Bal is a PhD candidate at Simon Fraser University with particular focus on consumer behavior and the fine art industry. Bal's work has been published in such journals as *Business Horizons, Journal of Public Affairs, Journal of Marketing Education*, and *Journal of Consumer Behavior*. Bal has worked extensively in the financial services industry as well as theater production.

Timothy Kyle Benusa attended the College of Arts and Sciences at the University of Virginia, where he received his bachelor of arts in history. Benusa graduated early from the University of Virginia in December 2008. Benusa decided very shortly after graduation from UVA to pursue a graduate degree in business. In August 2010 Benusa entered the MBA program at the University of Richmond where he concentrates on finance.

Elsamari Botha completed her BCom, BCom (Hons), and master's degrees in communication management at the University of Pretoria. As a student she was selected as one of South Africa's 100 BYM's (Brightest Young Minds) and one of 20 students for Accenture's national leadership conference. Her academic career started as a research assistant at UNISA

(University of South Africa); thereafter she was appointed as a lecturer in the Department of Marketing and Communication Management at the University of Pretoria. She then moved on to teach marketing research at the University of Stellenbosch and shortly after was appointed to the University of Cape Town to teach marketing research in their business science and postgraduate diploma programs. During her time at these universities she has organized two international seminars (one on CSR and one on reputation) in conjunction with Hannover University and consulted on various research projects. Botha has published in various accredited journals and books where her area of specialization is in sales management, social network analysis, B2B networks, and employee affect.

Lilia Boujbel, PhD, has been a professor and researcher in marketing at the University of Quebec in Montreal (UQAM, Canada) since 2009. She holds a PhD in business administration from HEC Montreal (Canada). Her main research interests include consumption desires, voluntary simplicity, and coping strategies.

Adriana M. Bóveda-Lambie, PhD, is an assistant professor and researcher in marketing at the E. Philip Saunders College of Businesses, Rochester Institute of Technology. She holds a PhD in business administration from the University of Rhode Island. Her main research interests include social networks, collaborative communities, social media communication efforts, and cross-cultural marketing.

Colin Campbell, PhD, is a lecturer at Monash University in Melbourne, Australia. He completed his doctorate in marketing at Simon Fraser University. Dr. Campbell's research examines consumer-generated advertising, social media, and consumer engagement. His work has appeared in the *Journal of Advertising Research, Journal of Advertising*, and *California Management Review.*

Cuiping Chen, PhD, received a PhD from the University of Arizona–Tucson, in 2007. Currently she is an assistant professor of marketing at the University of Ontario Institute of Technology in Toronto, Canada. Her research centers on how information technologies such as the Internet, CRM systems, and e-procurement systems influence consumer behavior, B2B relationships, and retail management. Dr. Chen has presented her work at world-class marketing conferences including the American Marketing Association's summer and winter annual conferences, the

Academy of Marketing Science's annual conference, and the Marketing Management Association (MMA)'s annual conference. She won the MMA 2005 Annual Spring Conference's Firooz Hekmat Award for Best Paper in Consumer Behavior.

Peter Coleman is a graduate student pursuing an MBA and MSIMC duo degree in the Graduate School of Business at Loyola University Chicago. He received his bachelor of arts degree in international business from Westminster College in Salt Lake City, Utah and has several years' experience in the advertising industry. He is currently the executive vice president for the Graduate Marketing Association at Loyola University Chicago and is a collegiate member of the American Marketing Association.

Jenna Drenten, PhD (University of Georgia) is an assistant professor of marketing in the Boler School of Business at John Carroll University. Her research interests lie at the intersection of consumer culture and identity development, particularly focusing on adolescent consumers. This includes related concepts such as adolescent consumption rituals and rites of passage, benefits and consequences of self-presentation through technology, and adolescent risk-taking behaviors. She is also interested in advancing qualitative methods and uncovering ways to use emerging technologies in qualitative inquiry. She has published in *Sport Marketing Quarterly* and the *International Journal of Retail and Distribution Management*. Furthermore, she has presented research at internationally recognized marketing conferences, including the American Marketing Association Conference, Marketing and Public Policy Conference, Society of Consumer Psychology Conference, Transformative Consumer Research Conference, Society for Marketing Advances Conference, and Consumer Culture Theory Conference. Before pursuing her PhD, Dr. Drenten received a BS in integrated marketing communication from Winthrop University and interned with BMW Manufacturing Co. and Minyanville Publishing and Multimedia, LLC.

Leila El Kamel, PhD, is a professor and researcher in marketing in TÉLUQ (Canada). She holds a PhD in business administration from Laval University (Canada). Her main research interests include postmodern consumption, consumption in virtual worlds, and responsible consumption. She also has considerable experience in consulting and advertising.

Lin Guo, PhD, is currently an assistant professor of marketing at the Whittemore School of Business & Economics, University of New Hampshire. She earned her PhD from the University of Arizona–Tucson in 2010. Her research focuses on customers' responses to service failures and their evaluations of service recovery performance, management of customer relationships, customer retention, and management of service contact employees. She has published her work in the *Journal of Business Research* and presented at various national leading conferences, such as the Academy of Marketing Science's annual conference and the American Marketing Association's annual conference.

Neil Hair, PhD, is an associate professor and researcher in marketing at the E. Philip Saunders College of Businesses, Rochester Institute of Technology. He holds a PhD in management from Cranfield University (UK). His main research interests include the use of the Internet in enhancing customer service, particularly customer relationship management initiatives, virtual ethnography, brand equity, and personal branding. He also has considerable experience in consulting and advertising and is a chartered marketer.

Angela Hausman, PhD, is an associate professor of marketing at Howard University. She is currently working predominantly in the areas of Internet and social media marketing, healthcare, and international marketing. In addition, she is the associate editor of the *European Journal of Marketing*. Dr. Hausman is also the founder of Hausman & Associates, a full-service marketing firm operating at the intersection of marketing and social media. Dr. Hausman has written several books and e-books on marketing and social media. Dr. Hausman's Web sites provide free content in marketing, especially social media marketing (at http://hausmanmarketresearch.org), plus step-by-step instructions for creating a profitable blog (at http://LetsBlogforMoney.org). She holds a PhD from the University of South Florida and an MBA from the University of Pittsburgh. Her publications have appeared in a number of scholarly journals, including the *Journal of the Academy of Marketing Science*, *Journal of Business Research*, *Journal of Advertising Research*, *Journal of Business and Industrial Marketing*, *Industrial Marketing Management*, *Journal of Services Marketing*, and *Journal of Consumer Marketing*. In addition, she has made presentations at numerous international conferences and consulted with Fortune 500 corporations and major nonprofits.

Monika Kukar-Kinney, PhD, is associate professor of marketing at the University of Richmond, Robins School of Business, and visiting professor at the Faculty of Economics, University of Ljubljana, Slovenia. Dr. Kukar-Kinney obtained her PhD in marketing from Indiana University in 2003. Her research focuses on consumer shopping and purchase behavior across a variety of retail channels (traditional brick-and-mortar stores, Internet, catalogues, TV shopping channels), consumer response to price, and compulsive buying. Dr. Kukar-Kinney's work has been published in the *Journal of Consumer Research*, *Journal of Retailing*, *Journal of the Academy of Marketing Science*, and *Journal of Business Research*, among others.

Lauren Labrecque, PhD, joined the faculty of Northern Illinois University in 2010. She completed her PhD in marketing at the University of Massachusetts–Amherst and holds a master's degree in digital media studies from the University of Denver. Before pursuing her doctorate she worked in online communications, database systems, and Web development. Dr. Labrecque's research interests include interactive marketing, sensory marketing, and consumer information privacy. Dr. Labrecque's research is published or forthcoming in the *Journal of the Academy of Marketing Science*, *Journal of Interactive Marketing*, *Journal of Retailing*, *Marketing Letters*, *Journal of Consumer Affairs*, *Journal of Brand Management*, and *Journal of Advertising Education*. Her dissertation work on the importance of color in marketing won the Society for Marketing Advances Dissertation Award and placed second in the Academy of Marketing Science's Mary Kay Inc. Dissertation Award Competition. She also serves as vice president of Internet communications and social media for the AMA's Consumer Behavior Special Interest Group (CBSIG).

Ereni Markos, PhD, joined the marketing and advertising faculty at Quinnipiac University in August 2010. She completed her PhD in marketing at the University of Massachusetts–Amherst and also holds a master's degree in integrated marketing communications from Emerson College in Boston. Prior to pursuing her doctorate degree Dr. Markos worked as a media planner/executive at an international media agency in the Boston area. She went on to start up a distribution company servicing boutique hotels and high-end restaurants in New England. Dr. Markos conducts research in the areas of consumer privacy in online and offline contexts, international marketing, atmospherics, and social media. Her research is published in the *Journal of Interactive Marketing* and *International Journal* *of Advertising.* She is also vice president of scholarly and social programs for the AMA's Consumer Behavior Special Interest Group (CBSIG).

Adam J. Mills completed his BA (Hons) in sociology from the University of British Columbia and his MBA from Simon Fraser University and is currently a PhD candidate in marketing at Simon Fraser University. After more than a decade of professional marketing, brand management, CSR, and operations experience in the hospitality industry, as well as several years' experience as a personal business coach, Mills's areas of research interest include brand delivery and communication strategy in the service sector and brand engagement in social media. Mills has published in several peer-reviewed journals and currently teaches marketing strategy and services marketing at Simon Fraser University.

George R. Milne, PhD, has been on the faculty of the University of Massachusetts–Amherst since 1992. He has also held visiting positions at the University of North Carolina–Chapel Hill and University of Canterbury, Christchurch, New Zealand. The majority of Dr. Milne's research efforts have been focused on issues pertaining to consumer information privacy, database marketing, and interactive marketing. Also, he has written on marketing strategy, niche marketing, and sports marketing. Recently, Dr. Milne has started research in the areas of natural versus artificial consumption, mindful consumption issues, and multiple selves. Overall, Dr. Milne has published 51 articles in journals such as the *Journal of Marketing, Journal of Consumer Research, Journal of Public Policy and Marketing, Journal of Academy of Marketing Science, Journal of Interactive Marketing, Marketing Letters, Journal of Business Research, Journal of Consumer Affairs, Information Society,* and *Journal of Sport Management,* among others.

Kent B. Monroe, DBA earned his DBA from the University of Illinois in 1968. He received his MBA in 1961 from Indiana University and his BA from Kalamazoo College. Dr. Monroe is the J. M. Jones Distinguished Professor of Marketing Emeritus, University of Illinois, Urbana-Champaign and Distinguished Visiting Scholar, University of Richmond, Richmond, Virginia. Dr. Monroe has pioneered research on the information value of price and authored *Pricing: Making Profitable Decisions* (3rd edition), McGraw-Hill/Irwin, 2003 (Chinese edition 2005). Dr. Monroe has presented papers before various international associations in Asia, Europe, and North America. His research has been published in the *Journal of Marketing Research, Journal of Consumer Research, Journal of Marketing, Management Science, Journal of the Academy of Marketing Science, Journal of Retailing, Journal of Business, Journal of Economic Psychology,* and *Journal of Business Research.* He served as chair of the American Marketing Association's Development of Marketing Thought Task Force, 1984–1988, was the editor of the *Journal of Consumer Research,* 1991–1993, and is a fellow of the Decision Sciences Institute and of the Association for Consumer Research. He served as the first editor of *Pricing Practice and Strategy,* 1993–2003, was associate editor of the *Journal of Consumer Research,* 2001–2005, and is on the editorial review boards of the *Journal of Consumer Research* and *Marketing Letters.* He has been honored as the Pricer of the Year by the Pricing Institute of the International Institute for Research, April 1999; recognized for his contributions to behavioral pricing research by the Pricing Center, Fordham University, New York, October 2000; received the Marketing Pioneer Award for lifetime contributions to the development of pricing theory in marketing, Central Illinois Chapter of the American Marketing Association, April 2002; the American Marketing Association/Irwin/McGraw-Hill Distinguished Marketing Educator Award, February 2005; and the Converse award for contributions to marketing knowledge, April 2008. His research papers have been published recently in a seven-volume set entitled *Legends in Marketing: Kent Monroe* by Sage Publications. He has served as a consultant on pricing, marketing strategy, and marketing research, to business firms, governments, and the United Nations. He has conducted executive training programs for business firms, nonprofit organizations, and universities in North and South America, Europe, Asia, Australia, and Africa. He regularly conducts a pricing certification workshop for the Professional Pricing Society in the United States.

Matthew O'Brien, PhD, is currently an associate professor at Bradley University in Peoria, Illinois. He earned his PhD from the University of Oklahoma. His published research includes investigations into organizational and marketing channel change, retailer–consumer interactions, relationship marketing, interorganizational exchange, and control/coordination mechanisms, international joint venture topics, and retail management. He has published or had articles accepted in the *Journal of the Academy of Marketing Science, Journal of Retailing, Journal of Marketing Theory and Practice, Journal of Marketing Channels,* and *Journal of International Marketing,* among others.

Iryna Pentina, PhD, is an assistant professor of marketing at the University of Toledo. Her research focuses on Internet retailing, applicability of marketing theory to online sales situations, virtual communities, social media, and interactive marketing. Her publications have appeared in several scholarly journals, including the *Journal of Retailing, European Journal of Marketing, Journal of Consumer Behaviour, Journal of Customer Behaviour, Journal of Electronic Commerce Research, Journal of Marketing Communications, International Journal of Retail and Distribution Management,* and others. She holds a PhD from the University of North Texas. Dr. Pentina currently serves as faculty director of the University of Toledo Interactive Marketing Initiative that combines research activities, student involvement, and business outreach in the areas of Internet and electronic marketing.

B. Yasanthi Perera is a PhD candidate in management at New Mexico State University. Her research interests include social entrepreneurship, business–community partnerships, and consumer and corporate social responsibility. She has presented her work at numerous marketing and management conferences and has published in journals including the *Journal of Consumer Behaviour.*

Leyland F. Pitt, MCom, MBA, PhD (h.c.), is the Dennis Culver EMBA alumni chair of business and professor of marketing, Segal Graduate School of Business, Simon Fraser University, Vancouver, Canada. He has also taught executive and MBA programs at schools such as the Graham School of Continuing Studies (University of Chicago), Columbia University Graduate School of Business, Rotterdam School of Management, and London Business School. The author of over 250 articles in peer-reviewed journals, his work has been accepted for publication in such journals as *Information Systems Research, Journal of the Academy of Marketing Science, Sloan Management Review, California Management Review, Communications of the ACM,* and *MIS Quarterly* (which he also served as associate editor). In 2000 he was the recipient of the Tamer Cavusgil Award of the American Marketing Association for best article in the *Journal of International Marketing.* He has won many awards for teaching excellence, including the Dean's Teaching Honor Roll Simon Fraser University; best MBA Teacher, Copenhagen Business School; and Best Professor, Joint Executive MBA, University of Vienna, and Carlson School of Management, University of Minnesota. In 2002, he was awarded the Outstanding Marketing Teacher of the Academy of

Marketing Science. In 2006 he was named the TD Canada Trust award for outstanding teachers, and listed as one of Canada's top MBA professors in Canadian business, 2005. The Lulea University of Technology, in Sweden, also awarded him an honorary doctorate in philosophy in 2009.

David G. Taylor, PhD, is assistant professor of marketing in the John F. Welch College of Business at Sacred Heart University. His areas of expertise and interest include digital marketing, consumer–brand relationships, and online word of mouth. His research has been published in the *Journal of Business Research, Journal of Advertising Research, Electronic Commerce Research, Journal of Consumer Behaviour,* and others. He holds a PhD from the University of North Texas.

Shabnam Zanjani, PhD, is on the faculty of Northeastern Illinois University. She did her PhD work at the University of Massachusetts–Amherst and holds a master's degree in marketing and e-commerce from Lulea University of Technology, Sweden. Her research interests include online communication, online consumer experience, and procrastination. Dr. Zanjani's research on advertising effectiveness in electronic magazines is published in the *Journal of Advertising.* Additionally, she has presented research at the American Marketing Association Summer Educators' Conference and the Academy of Marketing Science's Annual Conference. Her dissertation consists of two essays on procrastinators' online experiences, and antecedents and consequences of consumer procrastination.

Linda Tuncay Zayer, PhD, is associate professor in the Graduate School of Business at Loyola University Chicago. She received a PhD from the University of Illinois at Urbana-Champaign, an MBA from the University of Notre Dame, and a BS from Indiana University. Her research interests include how cultural discourses, particularly gender, influence identity, persuasion, and shopping behavior. She currently serves as the vice president for communications for the Consumer Behavior Special Interest Group of the American Marketing Association. She has published in the *Journal of Consumer Research, Journal of Retailing,* and *Qualitative Market Research,* among others.

Section I

Consumers' Online Identity

1

Snapshots of the Self
Exploring the Role of Online Mobile Photo Sharing in Identity Development Among Adolescent Girls

Jenna Drenten
John Carroll University

Giggling and chatter come streaming through the dressing room door as three teenage girls stand inside, trying on dresses covered in rhinestones and beads. One of the girls pulls out her cellular phone and turns on the camera feature. Instinctively, the other two girls strike a pose alongside their camera-wielding friend as she snaps a digital photograph of their reflection in the dressing room mirror. With the touch of a button, the picture is uploaded from the girl's mobile phone to her Facebook profile. Almost simultaneously, her online friends begin posting comments: "Cute dress!" "Looks great—you should definitely get it!" Thus, a consumption experience that was once privy only to the girls physically inside the dressing room is now displayed for public viewing and feedback on the World Wide Web.

As the previous scenario demonstrates, by tapping just a few buttons on a cellular phone, a young consumer has the capability of sharing her small experience with the world. Mobile technology has become a primary tool with which teens act in the marketplace, capture their experiences, and construct their identities. The percentage of teens (ages 12–17) who own cell phones has risen steadily, from 45% in 2004 to 75% in 2009 (Lenhart, Purcell, Smith, & Zickuhr, 2010). Moreover, teenagers commonly use their cell phones to snap and share digital photographs, on both a small scale (e.g., peer-to-peer picture messaging) and a large scale (e.g., posting photographs on social network sites). Users have the capability to snap a photograph and upload it to the Web in real-time, regardless of location, as long as a satellite signal is available. Thus, adolescents today are not only connected, they are also connected everywhere quickly. The purpose of this study is to explore how teenage girls utilize ubiquitous technology (e.g., camera phones) and social media (e.g., Facebook.com) to develop their identities through shared consumption activities. To this extent, the study aims to answer the following three research questions: what types of consumption activities are shared, how are consumption activities shared, and why are adolescent girls motivated to share their consumption activities? I focus specifically on teenage girls because they are more likely to use social network sites than teenage boys (i.e., 86% of girls ages 15–17 versus 69% of teenage boys ages 15–17; Lenhart, 2009) and they commonly use the emerging technologies to experiment with their identities (Mazzarella, 2005).

First, I review the relevant literature on modern adolescent consumer culture; namely, I discuss online self-presentation and mobile photo sharing. Second, I describe the research design and data analysis methodology used in the study, which involves a multimethod approach of visual photograph analysis and auto driving interviews (Collier & Collier, 1986; Heisley & Levy, 1991; Kvale, 1996). Data analysis follows a grounded theory approach based on constant comparative coding, as outlined by Glaser and Strauss (1967). Third, I present findings from the data and discuss emergent themes and patterns as they relate to identity development and consumer behavior. Finally, I provide implications for consumer behavior research and marketing strategy.

Millennials in a Mobile Marketplace

Adolescence (i.e., ages 11–18) spans the interval between childhood and adulthood (Steinberg et al., 2009), a stage in which youths are highly motivated to manage their identities through consumption (Belk, 1988; Weale & Kerr, 1969; Wooten, 2006). Many names have been assigned to this group, including Millennials (Howe & Strauss, 1991, 2000), Generation Y, Echo Boomers (Alch, 2000), Generation Me (Twenge, 2006), iGeneration, Generation Next, Net Generation, and Digital Natives (Palfrey & Gasser, 2008). Howe and Strauss suggest that Millennials is the most fitting name given that the members of the generation themselves coined the term. Today's youth, or Millennials, are uniquely defined by their prolific use of mobile technologies and, generally speaking, are operating in a drastically different marketplace than that of their parents' or grandparents' generations (Palfrey & Gasser, 2008; Strauss, Howe, & Markiewicz,

2006; Twenge, 2006). In addition, today's young people represent a huge cohort (i.e., 76 million in 2000) and boast significant combined purchasing power (i.e., $600 billion; Kennedy, 2001); hence, understanding how this economically attractive youth market operates in an evolving mobile marketplace is critical.

Mobile technology plays a key role in the lives of modern adolescents. In contrast to their parents, children born in America after the mid-1990s have never known a world without digital technologies (e.g., computers, the Internet, mobile phones, MP3s; Lenhart, Madden, & Hitlin, 2005; Palfrey & Gasser, 2008). As an anecdotal example, phrases such as "Facebook me" and "Google it" have always been a part of Millennials' vernacular. A rise in personal technology (e.g., computer-based entertainments, television, mobile phones) mediates adolescents' social interactions (Lee, 2009). Emerging technologies distance adolescents farther from traditional socialization agents such as the family, and pull teens deeper into the modern youth culture where norms and trends are constantly shifting (Hawley, 2011; Lee, 2009). Thus, peer influence and one's social identity are increasingly important in the new technology-driven marketplace to which Millennials are accustomed. Furthermore, given the ubiquitous nature of mobile technology, most adolescents never leave the marketplace inasmuch as it travels with them. Adolescents turn to the Internet for everything from gathering information about a new product to downloading new music (Tapscott, 2009).

Social media, particularly social network sites (e.g., Facebook.com, MySpace.com), are changing the nature of how teenage consumers behave in the marketplace and communicate with one another (Boyd, 2008). Social network sites allow individuals to create unique online profiles and define a list of other users with whom they can connect and communicate, as well as view and traverse their list of connections and those made by others within the system (Boyd & Ellison, 2007). Companies are increasingly turning to social network sites to support their marketing efforts (e.g., Kaplan & Haenlein, 2010), such as creating brand communities (Muniz & O'Guinn, 2001), conducting ethnographic marketing research (Kozinets, 2002), and uncovering co-creation opportunities (Prahalad & Ramaswamy, 2004). Tech-savvy Millennial teens are a primary target for such digital marketing practices (Montgomery, 2009). In recent years, the percentage of teens using social network sites has steadily risen to 73% (Lenhart, Purcell et al., 2010). In addition, cell phone ownership has become standard among even the youngest teens, and teens are increasingly using their mobile phones to access the Internet and social network sites (Lenhart, Ling, Campbell, & Purcell, 2010). Computer-mediated communication liberates adolescents, particularly girls (Mazzarella, 2005), to experiment with social skills and identities (Maczewski, 2002; Turkle, 1995; Valkenburg, Schouten, & Peter, 2005). To that end, this review aims to extend our understanding of youth consumer culture and consumption by providing a link between teenage girls' identity development and mobile photo sharing practices.

Identity Performance Through Social Media

Teenagers are at a stage in which they are "about to crystallize an identity, and for this [they need] others of [their] generation to act as models, mirrors, helpers, testers, foils" (Douvan & Adelson, 1966, p. 179). They grapple with the question, "Who am I?" and often define themselves through their clothing choices, unique jargon, musical preferences, extracurricular activities, and possibly most important, their group associations. The Internet offers adolescents many opportunities to experiment with their identities (Subrahmanyam & Smahel, 2011; Turkle, 1995; Valkenburg & Peter, 2008). In particular, teenage girls are driven to the Internet because of relational and social factors, such as forming friendships and chatting with classmates.

The terms "identity" and "self-concept" are often used interchangeably yet without complete definitional agreement among scholars (Belk, 1988; Markus & Nurius, 1986; Turner, 1987). An important distinction is that one's "self" exists regardless of external cues or public demonstrations, whereas one's "identity" is based upon social relations and symbolic representations. Identity is often contextually dependent and validated through culturally shared meanings. For instance, when a teenager is at home with his parents, then his identity as a son is activated. He may watch what he says and keep to himself. In contrast, when he is in the school locker room with his peers, then his identity as a jock might be activated. He may joke around with his friends and use harsh language. Interestingly, adolescents' offline social networks are increasingly converging on online social networks. For example, two-thirds of teens on Facebook.com, a popular online social network, report that they are connected to their parents through the Web site. In fact, 16% of teens state that "friending" their parents online is a precondition of acquiring a Facebook account (Schaffer & Wong, 2011). Although social networks such as Facebook provide customized privacy options, the fact remains that the virtual world is becoming increasingly transparent. According to the same survey, 56% of teens give their parents full profile access (e.g., pictures, status updates, wall posts), and 34% deny their parents access by rejecting their friend requests.

Adolescents primarily develop their identities in the context of peer groups (Douvan & Adelson, 1966; Erikson, 1963; Sherif & Sherif, 1964; Sullivan, 1953). Teenage girls commonly look to others for guidance through social comparison. Social network sites extend one's social groups to the Internet and provide a more extensive range of social comparison opportunities. Previous research suggests that online communication often happens in social communities that are separate from those in real life (Turkle, 1995); however, modern social networks such as Facebook tend to be a reflection of existing social groups. In other words, teenagers are acquaintances in real life before they become friends online. In any type of social interaction, individuals have the desire to strategically manage the impressions that other people form of them (Goffman, 1959). Social network sites allow adolescents to signal their identities online by sharing personal information, including thoughts, feelings, behaviors, and preferences.

Social media (e.g., instant messaging, chat rooms) afford teenagers the opportunity to pretend to be someone else (Gross, 2004; Valkenburg et al., 2005). Fewer face-to-face communication social cues (e.g., auditory cues, visual cues) are present on the Internet, thus teens may be more likely to explore their identities online. Although there are no apparent gender differences in the frequency with which boys and girls experiment with their identity online, they do differ significantly in the types of online identities they choose (Valkenburg et al., 2005). In recent years, the sexualization and commodification of young girls has been at the center of debates and discussion about the role of the media and consumption in adolescent identity development (e.g., Linn, 2004; Durham, 2009; Oppliger, 2008).

Mobile Photo Sharing Through Facebook

Photographs are commonly used to recall memories, maintain social relationships, and express one's identity (Van House et al., 2004). Today's teenagers are increasingly turning to their mobile phones to access social network sites and upload photographs directly from their camera phones to the Internet (Lenhart, Ling, Campbell, & Purcell, 2010). Young people send and receive about twice as many mobile images per month compared with adults (Kindberg et al., 2005). By tapping a few buttons on a cellular phone, a teenage girl has the capability of sharing her small experience with the world. Mobile photograph uploading is fundamentally different from traditional digital photograph uploading in the dimensions of immediacy and mobility. Users have the capability to snap a photograph and upload it to the Web in real-time, regardless of location, as long as a satellite signal is available.

The popular online social network Facebook.com serves as the primary social network site of interest in this study. Other social network sites, such as Flickr and YouTube, feature mobile upload options for photographs and videos, however, Facebook was selected based on the high rate of use among young consumers, with 71% of young adults maintaining Facebook profiles (Lenhart, Purcell et al., 2010). Facebook's mobile upload feature is only available to consumers who own camera phones and additional cell phone data charges may apply. Users can upload photos from their mobile phones to their Facebook profiles in one of three ways: (1) by e-mailing photos to a personal unique Facebook e-mail (e.g., user@m.facebook.com), (2) by using the Facebook application available on smartphones (e.g., iPhone, BlackBerry, Android, Windows Mobile), or (3) by picture messaging (i.e., MMSing) photos to Facebook. These pictures are published in the "Mobile Uploads" album by default. Although the cost of each method may vary, mobile photograph uploading is available to any teenager owning a camera phone. Furthermore, Facebook users are able to post comments below their friends' photographs.

Self-generated photographs make visible different aspects of the self (Harrison, 2002); thus, identity is symbolically represented through visual images. Pictures capture significant life moments, portray important social relationships, and reflect people's cultural and contextual shared meanings (Harrison, 2002). Although identity and self-representations change over time, photographs are static in that each one captures a moment in time from the photographer's perspective (Lorraine, 1990). Compared with traditional photography, online photographs can be shared with a wide audience. Mobile uploads differ even further in that they can be shared immediately. Given that teenage girls are at a stage of identity transformation and development, this study aims to explore this role of mobile photo uploads in developing one's identity.

Methods

Given the discovery-oriented nature of this project, this study employs a combined qualitative approach of visual photograph analysis and depth interviews (Collier & Collier, 1986; Heisley & Levy, 1991; Kvale, 1996) in an analysis sequence of constant comparative method (Glaser & Strauss, 1967). This research aims to explore how and why teenage girls use mobile uploading in their everyday consumption as well as understand the role of online mobile photo sharing in identity development. Therefore, sample recruitment focused on active adolescent female users of the mobile upload function on Facebook.com. Active users were defined as individuals who uploaded an average of at least four photographs per month. Informants were initially recruited from a local church organization. Through the process of snowball sampling, the final sample of participants extended beyond the confines of the church group. Sampling continued until the range of informants' responses was no longer expanding, but became redundant and consistent with qualitative data collection practice.

In total, a convenience sample of 13 adolescent girls was obtained; this sample size exceeds the recommendation by McCracken (1986) for generating emergent themes in qualitative research. The informants ranged in age from 15 to 18. About half of the informants attended an urban high school in an economically wealthy area, whereas the remaining half of informants attended a rural high school in an economically challenged area. The informants represented varying Facebook mobile upload activity levels. Table 1.1 presents the mobile uploading frequency of each informant. To protect the privacy of the informants, all data are reported using pseudonyms. Because all of the informants were teenagers, informed

TABLE 1.1   Informant Demographics

Informant Pseudonym	Age	Date of First Mobile Upload	Total Number of Mobile Uploads	Uploading Frequency (per Month)	Total Number of Comments
Claire	15	November 2009	124	6.9	184
Kimberly	16	February 2011	33	8.3	27
Kenlyn	16	March 2010	135	9.6	202
Madison	16	September 2010	86	10.8	93
Caitlin	16	July 2010	128	11.6	96
Jayma	15	December 2010	86	14.3	134
Krissy	17	June 2010	184	15.3	192
Ellen	18	December 2009	295	16.4	340
Paige	16	November 2010	123	17.6	135
Alyssa	18	October 2010	166	20.8	159
Heather	16	April 2011	42	21.0	34
Sherie	16	November 2010	200	28.6	143
Anne	15	June 2010	453	37.8	617

consent was obtained from each informant and her parent or guardian before inclusion in the study.

Qualitative interviews are useful for understanding cultural meanings and personal experiences from the informant's point of view (Kvale, 1996); hence, in the spirit of Heisley and Levy's (1991) auto driving method, each informant participated in a depth interview centering around each girl's mobile upload album(s) on Facebook. The informants granted the researcher access to their Facebook mobile upload albums prior to the interviews, producing a total of $N = 2,055$ photographs and $N = 2,356$ comments. During each interview, the informant and the interviewer discussed the photographs together; thus, the teenage informants acted as "expert guides leading the fieldworker through the content of the pictures" (Collier & Collier, 1986, p. 106). This photograph-driven interview method allows informants to spontaneously tell stories about the photographs, explain the symbolic meanings of objects in the photographs, and provide a richer understanding of social, cultural, and contextual factors represented in the photographs (Collier & Collier, 1986; Hagedorn, 1996; Pink, 2003). A general semistructured interview protocol (e.g., Table 1.2) supplemented the free association photographic interviewing method.

The informants were probed where appropriate and were encouraged to elaborate whenever they were discussing their shared consumption experiences and identity processes represented in their online photographs. In line with the constant comparative nature of grounded theory, the interview process resulted in new questions being added to the interview process as new themes emerged. The data were documented via field notes and subsequently transcribed into electronic journals.

I analyzed the mobile upload albums to identify recurrent themes and compare findings across informants. In accordance with the grounded theory approach, several different categories and subcategories of data emerged during the open coding process, and axial coding linked these categories and subcategories to dimensions of adolescent consumer identity construction as defined in the literature. To achieve respondent validation, I went back to several informants with tentative results to refine and confirm the findings.

Findings

In the process of data analysis, themes emerged suggesting that social networks serve as a platform upon which adolescents are able to interact and

TABLE 1.2   Semistructured Interview Questions

Topic	General Interview Questions
Frequency	How often do you use your phone to take pictures?
	When did you first start using the mobile upload feature on Facebook?
	How often do you upload pictures to Facebook?
Subject	Where do you normally take pictures that you upload to Facebook?
	Who do you normally take pictures of (e.g., friends, family, coworkers)?
	What do you normally take pictures of (e.g., food, clothes)?
Experience	Describe a typical experience in which you might take a picture and upload it to Facebook.
	What kinds of things go on?
	Why do you use the mobile upload feature on Facebook?
	What is your most memorable mobile uploading experience?
	What is your worst experience with mobile uploading?
Reflections	Describe your interaction with friends on Facebook after you've uploaded a photo.
	What do you think you gain from uploading pictures on Facebook?
	How long do you leave your mobile uploads up on Facebook?
	Do you ever get your camera phone pictures printed as hard copies?
	How do your mobile uploads reflect who you are?
	Photograph Specific Interview Questions
Mobile Upload	Tell me a little about this photograph and what was going on when you took it.
	Why did you decide to upload this photograph?
	Who was involved in taking this picture with you?

negotiate their consumption experiences. Social networks enable image management and identity construction among adolescents. The data reveal that teenagers, both individually and collectively, display their identities and culturally shared meanings through mobile uploading. Here, I present the findings in two parts: identity-oriented characteristics of shared mobile photos and identity-oriented motivations for mobile photo sharing. The first part examines the identity-oriented characteristic of shared mobile photos: (1) edited self-presentation, (2) symbolic consumption, and (3) culturally situated social spaces. The second part proposes four primary motivations for adolescents to partake in mobile photo sharing: (1) audience feedback, (2) memory manufacturing, (3) relational reassurance, and (4) bounded rebellion. The findings are supported here with illustrative examples from the depth interviews and mobile photograph album analysis. Although these themes are presented as distinct ideas, it should be noted that informants more typically related information about the themes in a highly intermingled fashion.

Identity-Oriented Characteristics of Mobile Photo Sharing

Edited Self-Presentation

Teens take on various identities throughout adolescence. Social network sites provide platforms upon which teenage girls can act out those various identities. In this way, the social network is the stage and the adolescent is the actor. Through mobile photo sharing, girls get into character (e.g., gender bender, rebel, tough girl, sex kitten), edit their performances, use props and costumes (e.g., brands, products, clothing), and shoot the performances on selected sets (e.g., retail store, school, bedroom). When a girl is in character, she behaves in accordance with the given personality and plays to the expectations of the audience. Thus, mobile photo sharing allows adolescent girls to adopt character traits, follow scripts, and create scenarios as part of their identity experimentations.

Each photograph uploaded to the social network offers a glimpse into the ever-evolving adolescent self-concept. Informants in this study showed an overwhelming propensity for uploading self-portraits, normally taken by holding the cell phone at arm's length or by capturing one's reflection in a mirror. Whereas adults may commonly turn the camera toward external stimuli (e.g., their children and grandchildren, landscapes, and traveling), teenage girls appear to be the stars of their own shows on social networks. This supports previous scholarly work suggesting that adolescents are egocentric by nature (Elkind, 1969) and increasingly narcissistic (Twenge, 2006), particularly on social network sites such as Facebook (Mendelson & Papacharissi, 2010). For instance, Anne (age 15) points out that she takes multiple self-portraits, but uploads only the favorable ones. As she suggests, social desirability plays a role in the photos that she selects to upload. Mobile photo uploading offers a tool by which girls can strategically edit their social self-identities. Thus, she deliberately creates and controls her self-identity. Prior to uploading, teens further edit their pictures using photo-editing mobile applications (e.g., PicSay for Android, Mini Paint for BlackBerry, iCamera for iPhone), which contribute to purposefully creating an ideal self-image:

Lexi (age 15, comment): Beautiful!! Is it even possible for you to take a bad
    picture?
Claire (age 15, comment): Girl, I just airbrush all my pics into gorgeous-
    ness . . . you know I don't look this good in real-life. ;)
Lexi (age 15, comment): Ohh puuullease.

As Claire suggests, teenagers can create inauthentic or deceptive portrayals
of themselves through mobile photo sharing. Previous research corroborates
that individuals falsely portray their physical attractiveness online (Hancock
& Toma, 2009); however, an interesting finding from this study suggests that
teenage girls are likely to use editing applications to create less desirable mobile
photo uploads. For example, several of the informants posted pictures of
themselves or their friends, using FatBooth, a popular face-distorting mobile
application that adds a significant amount of weight to a person's headshot:

Kimberly (age 16, interview): Oh my God, I am obsessed with [FatBooth].
    I think it's hilarious to see what I'd look like if I ever got fat. I
    used it on my Grandma the other day. I could barely breathe
    it made me laugh so hard! I used it on my dog too. I don't get
    what's so mean about it. It's just meant to be funny. It's not like
    I'm going around taking pictures of strangers calling them fat.
    Oh, but my friend David actually did get written up because he
    took a picture of this really fat girl in our class and posted it on
    Facebook saying that it was a FatBooth picture.

Theories of social identity and social comparison suggest that one's
self-concept is derived from membership in a given social group (Tajfel &
Turner, 1986) and that people evaluate their own opinions and behaviors
through social comparison with other people (Festinger, 1954). Obesity is
viewed as a socially undesirable physical characteristic, and using applications like FatBooth reflect the in-group versus out-group prevalent during adolescence. One informant admonished the use of FatBooth saying
that it is "no different than making fun of someone who is overweight. It's
like saying, 'Thank God I don't look like you.'" Nonetheless, teenagers use
mobile uploading to stretch the boundaries of social identity and group
norms. For example, they use mobile uploading to experiment with their
gender identities and highlight gender stereotypes. Like the FatBooth
photos, the majority of gender bending photographs of themselves or their
friends appear to be taken in jest and the comments that follow each photograph tend to be derogatory in nature:

Kimberly (age 16, mobile upload): A teenage boy is holding two grape-
      fruits in front of his chest, suggesting female breasts.
Kenlyn (age 16, mobile upload): Two teenage boys posing shirtless. One
      is wearing a short jean skirt. The second is wearing pink plaid
      shorts.
Anne (age 15, mobile upload): Anne stands in front of the mirror wearing
      a team jersey and flexing her left bicep.
Madison (age 16, mobile upload): Two girls posing in a dressing room
      wearing men's boxer briefs.
Claire (age 15, mobile upload): Claire is buried up to her neck in sand at
      the beach. The sand covering her body is shaped to resemble the
      male physique.

Before the advent of digital cameras or camera phones, roll-film cameras were the standard of personal photography. In contrast, today's teenagers are growing up in a marketplace of digital technology. They have
been raised to view and critique their photographs immediately and, consequently they view and critique themselves. From a performance perspective, teens are essentially airbrushing and editing their own photos, which
ultimately reflect their identity expectations. The data reveal that teenagers use their camera phones and mobile uploading to practice and perfect
the physical presentation of their bodies. They practice facial expressions,
flex their muscles, and pose for the camera, in order to gain a mastery over
their bodies. On the one hand, a better understanding of which physical attributes are one's best may enhance self-esteem, however, a constant
critique of one's physical flaws may deflate that self-esteem. Despite technology's capability of creating unblemished photographs, many of the
informants posted pictures with self-deprecating captions and idealized
image portrayal. Examples of such captions are as follows:

Caitlin (age 16, photo caption): Seriously, I hate feet. My toes are totes
      (slang: totally) disgust (slang: disgusting).
Heather (age 16, photo caption): I am fully aware of how fat my arms look;
      it's cool.
Claire (age 15, photo caption): If only I were tan ♥
Jayma (age 15, photo caption): Besties (slang: best friends)!!! . . . I look
      rough but love you girls.

Girls use the social network as a platform upon which they can experiment with new identities and gauge audience reaction. They can upload a

self-portrait and immediately receive feedback, both solicited and unsolicited, from their peers. All of the previous captions were met with steadfast compliments and reassuring feedback (e.g., "omg, please! I wish I was as pretty as you on a 'rough' day!"). The characters that teenage girls portray on social networks are reflective of their emerging identities. Although family members, friends, and pets are also commonly featured in adolescents' mobile uploads, these characters are meant to play more of a supporting role to the individual lead performer. For example, Paige posted a picture of herself posing with four other girls in a mirror. Each of the girls had her own cell phone out to take her own picture. Even though the picture was meant to capture the collective group, each girl remained fixated on her own individual image, as captured with her own camera phone. Finally, echoing the technologically driven marketplace to which today's youth are accustomed, teenagers commonly use mobile uploading to post pictures of other digital media. In this way, teen's identity projects are meta-mediated through technology. For instance, Kenlyn's mobile upload album includes several photographs of her computer screen in which she captures a Facebook chat conversation with a friend or documents a Skype date with her boyfriend. Likewise, other informants uploaded mobile phone screen shots of text conversations and multiplayer mobile games.

Symbolic Consumption
Symbolic consumption is integral to the creation and continuation of a stable harmonious self-concept. Online social networks provide a platform upon which adolescents can present identity formation processes through symbolic consumption practices represented in their mobile uploads. In particular, girls use consumer products as props and costumes while exploring different aspects of their identities through mobile uploading. Evidence in the marketing literature suggests that consumer products reflect one's identity (Belk, 1988). Consumption and anticonsumption of particular products may reflect an emerging identity (e.g., makeup and cosmetics reflect femininity and womanly beauty) or loss of a past identity (e.g., ceasing to sleep with a baby blanket or stuffed animal associated with childhood). Furthermore, anticonsumption, or "a resistance to, distaste of, or even resentment of consumption," is symbolically related to self-concept factors (e.g., self-esteem, self-efficacy; Zavestoski, 2002, p. 121) and undesired self-states (Hogg, Banister, & Stephenson, 2009). Through mobile uploading, girls demonstrate anticonsumption practices by posting photos in mockery of particular brands, services, or ideals. For instance, Madison posted a photograph of a President Barack Obama chia pet with the caption,

"AFRObama. No you can't." The clear mockery of President Obama's former campaign slogan (i.e., "Yes we can!") suggests that Madison is symbolically disassociating from Obama supporters. Interestingly, Madison was
not old enough to vote in the 2008 presidential election.

In studying symbolic consumption, it is critical to take into account the
dynamic nature of the self-concept. Girls adjust their props and costumes
to mirror the characters they want to display. For instance, a teenager who
once enjoyed shopping at Justice, a fashion retailer catering to young girls,
may now view the store as immature and childish as she takes on a more
mature identity. The store itself does not change, but her evaluation of the
store changes to reflect her emerging identity. In this way, girls are torn
between their past childhood selves and their emerging adult selves. Their
mobile uploads reflect this state of liminality. For example, many of the
informants posted mobile photos of old photographs taken during childhood, thus incorporating their past selves into their emerging identities.
Mobile upload albums reveal an oscillation between a childlike identity
and a more mature, adult identity:

Alyssa (age 18, mobile upload): Alyssa posted a picture of chalk drawings
    that she and her boyfriend created on the sidewalk.
Alyssa (age 18, mobile upload): Alyssa posted a picture of herself carry-
    ing her 3-month-old nephew on her chest in a front-facing baby
    carrier.
Anne (age 15, mobile upload): Anne posted a picture of herself riding a
    rocking horse kiddie ride at Chuck E. Cheese.
Anne (age 15, mobile upload): Anne posted a picture of herself hanging
    upside down, provocatively wrapped around a metal lampost,
    referent of a dance pole.

In contemporary culture, the transition from childhood to adulthood
is not instantaneous; thus, as evident in the previous examples, teenagers
fluctuate back and forth between a youthful past identity and a mature
emerging identity. Props and costumes are used to symbolically demonstrate these identity transformations. The transition from childhood to
adulthood is largely marked by physical changes that adolescents experience as they go through puberty. Mobile uploading provides a platform
for teens to post evidence instantly of their physical transformations (e.g.,
breast development). Teenagers post mobile photos on social networks to
show off their developing bodies. For example, girls post pictures of themselves wearing cleavage-revealing bathing suits and clothing. In this way,

adolescents allow their online friends to take part in the transitional journey with them. Before, during, and after pictures remain posted so that the audience can easily watch the sequence of changes over time. From a consumption perspective, physical enhancements such as tattoos, piercings, haircuts, surgeries, and hair coloring are also shared through mobile photo uploading. For example, when Anne dyed her hair for the first time, she posted several pictures, including a picture of the hair color aisle at Target, a photo of the box that she chose, and before, during, and after pictures of her hair. In particular, getting one's braces removed seems to be a significant physical transformation in adolescence:

Interviewer: I see here you got your braces removed. (In reference to before and after pictures of Krissy on the day that she got her braces removed.)
Krissy (age 17, interview): Finally! I was so excited.
Interviewer: How long did you have them?
Krissy (age 17, interview): Four years. I had to have two surgeries, spacers, an expander, tongue spurs, and rubber bands—basically everything but headgear. It was awful. I took this picture while I was still at the orthodontist. I got them off in June so we weren't in school and I wanted all my friends to see.

Mobile photo sharing allows teens to instantly share their symbolic consumption with a wider network of friends. In many cases, products serve as the impetus for uploading a photograph in the first place. The data reveal that girls feel more justified in uploading photographs in which they are posing with an object. Even the most seemingly mundane objects can be transformed into meaningful props that the girls can use in their identity performances. Common props and costumes featured in adolescents' mobile uploads include awards (e.g., 4-H medal, pageant crown, MVP trophy) and achievements (e.g., earning a varsity letter, receiving a good report card), creative undertakings (e.g., playing guitar, baking a cake, practicing new makeup techniques, drawing a comic strip), cultural collectibles or celebrity promotions (e.g., SpongeBob SquarePants, Elmo, Justin Bieber), food and beverages (e.g., McDonald's Happy Meal, Monster Energy Drink, specialty cupcakes), and new or desired products and clothing (e.g., prom dress, nail polish). These props and costumes are used to symbolically convey one's identity while simultaneously drawing the attention back to the actor, in this case, the teenage girl posting the photograph.

Culturally Situated Social Spaces

Given that teenagers are not yet considered adults, they have less freedom to explore new locales; thus, they interact within a fairly limited set of social spaces. Adolescent girls act out their identity performances within the boundaries of culturally situated social spaces, which are evident in their mobile uploads. Much of their time is restricted to day-to-day school interactions (e.g., classes, lunch breaks, athletic team practices). The data reveal that other venues of importance include retail environments (e.g., department stores, the mall), restaurants, entertainment settings (e.g., movie theater, skating rink), community establishments (e.g., YMCA, church), and personal spaces (e.g., bedrooms, cars). Furthermore, dramatized shared identity performances appear to commonly take place in bathrooms: in school, at home, at the mall:

Krissy (age 17, interview): We're not supposed to have our phones out during school but everyone does it anyway. Most of the teachers are cool with it as long as you're not like texting during class or trying to cheat, but everyone has their phones out at lunch and between classes. We're allowed to sit outside for lunch at the picnic tables but if it's raining, my best friend and me always go pose for pictures in the bathroom mirror. It's just something fun to do because school is so freaking boring.

As evident in the previous quote, bathrooms play a particularly important role in setting the stage for mobile uploading among girls. A bathroom is a venue of choice given its relative level of privacy and its presence of mirrors. Mirrors and other reflective surfaces (e.g., Christmas ornaments, chrome automobile accents) appear to be a key component in the mobile uploading process, and it is important to note that mirrors physically reflect an individual's identity. In addition to inner identity transitions, adolescence is a period of immense physical transformation. As mentioned in the previous section, teenage girls embark on the often tumultuous and uncertain experience of puberty in which their bodies develop adult attributes. Mirrors allow girls to explore their physical self-images:

Interviewer: Tell me a little about this picture.
Sherie (age 16, interview): My friends were spending the night and we put on a ton of crazy makeup, like bright blue eye shadow and stuff. Then we just decided to dress up in kind of, like, skimpy outfits and

have a mini-photo shoot. We like to pretend we're on America's Next Top Model, so we do all these crazy poses and stuff.

Interviewer: Where were you in this picture?

Sherie (age 16, interview): We were in the bathroom. We took the picture in there so we could all see ourselves in the mirror. We took some in my bedroom mirror too, but I don't think I posted those.

As Sherie suggests, she and her friends enact adult consumption practices such as wearing makeup and donning more revealing clothing. Moreover, by taking the photos in the bathroom, they can see their reflections in the mirror, actively allowing themselves to dramatize their facial expressions and poses. Dressing rooms, like bathrooms, are common locales in which teenagers directly dramatize their consumption experiences, likely due to the prevalence of mirrors and the opportunity to experiment with new identities:

Interviewer: These few pictures seem to be at the same place. Tell me a little about them.

Anne (age 15, interview): My friend Lindsay and I were in the dressing room at Charlotte Russe, trying to find something to wear to the Katy Perry concert. I tried on this purple leopard tube top thing, but we couldn't decide if it was supposed to be a shirt or a dress.

Interviewer: Who made the comment on this picture? (In reference to the comment: "Put that tongue back in your mouth . . . wearing a skimpy thing like that!!")

Anne (age 15, interview): My dad. He's dumb. He would die if I wore that out in public.

Interviewer: So, I take it you didn't buy that outfit for the concert?

Anne (age 15, interview): God no! We were just trying stuff on for fun. We ended up making our T-shirts for the concert; they were amazing!

Interestingly, like Anne, many girls do not end up purchasing the items they try on or use in their mobile uploads. In this way, they can try on identities (e.g., try on a skimpy outfit or athletic gear) without actually committing to each possible role. Anne was able to try on an outfit that she ordinarily would not wear. She then received feedback from others (i.e., her dad) and did not purchase the outfit. Instead, she selected to create a new T-shirt and wear shorts from her existing wardrobe, representative of maintaining her existing self-conception. Interestingly, although

Anne recognizes her father's disapproval of wearing revealing clothing in public, she essentially circumvents this rule by posting it to her Facebook page where all of her friends can view it. Instead of telling his daughter to remove the picture, Anne's father joins in dramatizing the consumption experience by posting a comment on the photo.

Facebook provides a platform upon which girls can discuss their experiences, share consumption activities, and negotiate their identities. Mobile photographs taken in the marketplace can spark brand discussions and word-of-mouth among adolescent consumers. For example, in the following dialogue posted on one of Caitlin's mobile uploads, Caitlin and Sarah discuss their retail store preferences and shopping behaviors. Furthermore, Caitlin's Facebook friends can witness the interaction in real-time as it unfolds; thus, the conversation becomes privy to a wider audience than would ordinarily be included in traditional face-to-face communication:

Caitlin (age 16, mobile upload): Caitlin stands in dressing room wearing a casual sundress. (July 11, 2010)

> **(caption):** New fav [slang: favorite] dress. (:
> **(comments):**

Callie: cute dress(:
Brent: Beautiful dress
Tori: this is cute! (:
Sarah: I love ur dress!! :)
Caitlin: thanks! I do too! It's pretty great. Ha-ha. (:
Sarah: ha no prob. where did u get it?
Catlin: Aerie, in the mall of Georgia (:
Sarah: cool cool!! Yea I love that store lol [laugh out loud]. I have to go to mall of GA to get my new iPod Wednesday :)
Caitlin: I do too! I love American eagle also. They're basically the same. Ha-ha. That's cool.
Sarah: ha yea same here...but I loooove Hollister
Caitlin: ha-ha, I bet. I just love the mall in general. (:
Sarah: I just wish they weren't so expensive :/. But same here. I kinda like Mall of GA better tho, its bigger lol :)
Caitlin: that's what I meant. Ha-ha. They have every store you could think of. haha.
Sarah: for real lol...Just think about how big the Mall of America must be. haha we should go there!!

Caitlin: oh honey! I'd have a major heart attack if I went there! Ha-ha. We
           could totally take a road trip it. (:
Sarah: ha-ha same here!! And yes we definitely could :)
Caitlin: it really would be fun! When I turn 18, we should definitely try
           and go!

Finally, vacations (e.g., spring break, field trips), destinations (e.g., amusement park, college football game, concerts), and significant events (e.g., prom, 16th birthday, graduation) appear to prompt an increase in mobile uploads. These ritualized events and novel places embody the exciting potential identities to which teenagers may ascribe, the opposite of the mundane, day-to-day identities to which they are accustomed.

Identity-Oriented Motives for Mobile Photo Sharing

Audience Feedback

Girls are motivated to take part in mobile photo sharing because it carries an element of instant gratification: the audience can weigh in on the uploaded photograph as soon as it is posted. For instance, Karley posted pictures of her new pet pig and invited her friends to suggest names for him. Prior to the advent of camera phones and social media, personal photographs were printed as hard copies and placed in photo albums. Today's youth are growing up in a period in which consumption experiences can be shared with their network of friends as the experience progresses. From vacations and concerts to slumber parties and prom dress shopping, a wide range of consumption experiences are shared with a wider network of friends through social media. As such, teenage girls choose their mobile uploads purposefully, in anticipation of audience feedback, both positive and negative. Humor plays an evident role in mobile photo sharing. Teenagers upload pictures that they hope will be deemed entertaining and funny among friends. For example, Krissy posted a photo of a classmate drooling while asleep in class. She included a caption that mocked the classmate and encouraged her online friends to join in on the conversation. A camera in hand grants the young photographer an opportunity to be a cultural critic at the expense of others:

Heather (age 16, interview): I just take pictures of random people and
                                funny stuff that I see. Did you see the one I posted of the mullet

man at Wal-Mart? I still laugh every time I look at it. I got a little worried after I uploaded it though, 'cause I thought maybe he'd come hunt me down and attack me. I post a lot of embarrassing pictures of my friends too. They sometimes get pissed about it but I figure they can untag themselves if they want.

Mobile photo sharing grants immense social power to the photographer. As Heather suggests, she not only critiques the shortcomings of strangers; she also sets out to embarrass her friends. Interestingly, although some of her friends respond with cries to remove the incriminating photos, none of them untag themselves, as she suggests they could. Thus, from the adolescent perspective, all publicity is good publicity. In fact, Heather continued in her interview to say that she and her friends make a point of trying to upload embarrassing pictures of each other, particularly of the opposite sex. In this way, mobile uploading provides a method of flirtation. Moreover, through the comment feature on Facebook, teens are provided with a platform through which to publicly voice their ridicule of one another and their condemnation of certain products and services. This supports previous research that finds peer ridicule to be a key factor in shaping adolescents' consumption norms, social identities, and brand preferences (Wooten, 2006). Facebook is a social network in which users can communicate back and forth. By posting a photograph, the floor is open to critiques. For example, in her interview, Claire talks about a picture that she posted of herself in a bikini, which prompted a negative response (i.e., "eww, gross.") from a "friend" and subsequent back-and-forth online comments between the two of them:

Interviewer: I see here on this photo that you seemed to kind of get into an argument with a friend. What happened?

Claire (age 15, interview): Honestly, that girl was just jealous because I'm prettier than she is. She has some kind of secret problem with me and I am not all about playing those smart-ass sarcastic Facebook games so I deleted her after that. [Claire clicks through to a mobile upload photo of a Facebook screen shot.] See, I left her this message before I deleted her, then I uploaded a picture of it because I knew she'd delete it. [The message reads: "before I delete you, I thought I'd leave you a little message. I have never met anyone with the amount of immaturity you possess. You are a cruel, mean, manipulative girl. You use people and me. I appreciate that little comment you left me when you thought it was okay to blow up Facebook talking shit. Look in a mirror. Being a fake bitch won't get you anywhere in life. I know this comment will be deleted as soon as I press share because you have the balls to talk big when I can't see, but you can't take a dose of your own medicine. Have a nice life "princess" and don't ever contact me again. xoxoxo :D" (sic)]

Claire may have been hoping for positive feedback on her photograph. Instead, the picture stirred social drama. By posting photographs online, girls open the forum for others to discuss and comment on the pictures. Some girls even explicitly ask for feedback. For the most part, audience feedback on teens' mobile uploads are positive and reaffirming.

Ellen (age 18, mobile upload): Ellen posted a picture of herself trying on a long red evening gown.
> **(caption):** "Ahhh! I felt like a princess in this dress . . . and I LOVED it! ♥
> **(comments):**

Dawn: Awwwwwww girl u r beautiful!
Lizzy: work it :)
Sarah: Hot stuff!!! haha what is this dress for?!?!!?!?!?
Tyler: DAMN
Keeley: your soo pretty! I am jealous! :(
Brittany: OH EM GEE! [Ellen] this dress is GORGEOUS!
Ellen: dawn: thanks sweetie!!! love yaaa! ♥
Lizzy: OH YEAHHH! (:
Sarah: thankssss... and I was just trying them on. lol.
Tyler: thankkksss! (;
Kenzie: awwwwh... thanks! You're pretty too! (:
Brittani: haa. thankssss! :D
Renee: awwwwh. Thanks sweet peaa! ♥
Dawn: anytime babe: D love ya too
James: Anslee has a nice boo-tay ;) haha
Ellen: haha... you would say that! Thanks James.
Keeley: Awwh thanks [Ellen](:
Ellen: you're welcome sweetieee! (:

When asked about this photograph, Ellen mentioned that she and all of her friends, meaning her Facebook friends, loved the dress. She expanded her already positive opinion of the dress to include the others' feedback, which resulted in increased desire for the dress. Teenage girls post mobile uploads with the expressed intention of getting feedback from their friends. Moreover, this feedback loop appears to be reciprocal. As in Ellen's case, she thanked and complimented those who complimented her, whereas Claire struck back against the friend who disparaged her.

Memory Manufacturing
The data suggest that girls act out identity performances with the intention of creating memories, deliberately and purposefully. They foresee memories in the making. In other words, they create experiences for which they are already anticipating nostalgic feelings. By posting a photograph of a shared consumption experience, the individuals involved can immediately revel in the memory. Mobile uploads are typically uploaded immediately after the photographs are captured; in fact, evidence from the interviews suggests that photographs shared through mobile uploads on Facebook are taken for the sole purpose of uploading. In other words, the picture is taken with the deliberate motive of sharing it on the social network. Thus, to an extent, these captured memories are manufactured and mediated through technology:

Anne (age 15, interview): We about got kicked out of Party City the other day because we were putting on all the Halloween costume stuff they have in the back and the manager lady came back and yelled at us and told us that we need to stop treating the store like a playground. We just laughed. It was really funny.
Interviewer: Were you shopping for a costume?
Anne (age 15, interview): No. We had went over there to Old Navy and Rue 21 to look for clothes but we had to wait on my mom to come pick us up so we thought it would be funny to go take pictures of us dressed up at the party store.

As Anne suggests, the desire to take photographs was an initial impetus for the consumption experience. Mobile upload albums on Facebook act as instant scrapbooks, documenting the adolescents' idealized experiences. The data reveal that very few mobile uploads depict negative events. Rather, nearly all of the photographs show pleasant and enjoyable experiences:

Jayma (age 15, interview): In middle school, I guess I was in the preppy group or whatever, but when I started high school, all my friends started hanging out with seniors and going to parties and doing drugs and stuff. So I stopped hanging out with them as much, because I wanted to be good, but they are forever posting pictures of stuff they do together, and it's just kind of annoying to have to see it on Facebook 'cause you're like, "Oh awesome, all of my friends are at the mall without me. Thanks for the invite, guys." So yea, seeing other people's pictures, of like what they're doing, sometimes makes me frustrated because you realize that you were left out.

Interviewer: Well, it seems like you are having a lot of fun in your pictures.

Jayma (age 15, interview): I mean, I'm not going to post some picture of me like sitting at home alone, crying in a corner or something. I'm not that emo [slang: emotional]. I don't really care if they don't invite me, I just feel like—well really this one girl in particular, always posts pictures of all of them going to the movies or out to eat or something and I think she just does it on purpose sometimes.

Teenage girls desire to be portrayed as fun and exciting. To an extent, mobile uploads become a competition in which teens try to make their individual lives seem the most appealing, relative to their peers. It is worth noting that teens appear to be more likely to post negatively charged status updates (e.g., "fml" [slang: fuck my life]) on Facebook than they are to post negatively charged mobile photos. In general, the memories depicted in mobile uploads reflect generally happy and fun-loving adolescents. These photographs are almost immediately used to reflect collectively on teens' shared experiences (e.g., commenting on the picture, viewing the photo online). The girls reminisce about a moment captured in a photograph and develop a narrative understood only by those who were involved in the photograph. In this way, teenage girls upload mobile photographs to preserve their histories, share their stories, visually demonstrate their ideal identities, and entertain their friends.

Relational Reassurance

Relationships are paramount in adolescence. Peers and parents serve as the primary socialization agents in teenagers' lives. Mobile uploads are a reflection of these relationships. For example, Paige has a mobile upload album almost entirely devoted to her best friend. Moreover, teens' online friends comment with reaffirming statements (e.g., "I love us!" "OMG!!! We are soooo awesome :)" "Don't lie. You love me."). Mobile uploading allows teenagers to demonstrate the level of closeness they share with other individuals. Girls post pictures not only of the people who are important in their lives, but also of artifacts that represent those relationships (e.g., love notes, Valentine's Day gifts, matching best friend bracelets). Relationships are reaffirmed by posting pictures and commenting on them.

Kenlyn (age 16, mobile upload): Kenlyn uploaded in photo in which she and
        six of her friends are piled on top of one another on a small couch.
        (caption): "♥♥♥"
        (comments):

Ashley: Tim's face is a little too close to my crotch area ha-ha and his
        tongue is out which makes it so much worse
Tim: omg only you would notice that u dirty hoe bag jk [slang: just
        kidding]
Tim: and ur wearin my hat fool
Ashley: Ha-ha of course cause your nearest to me. . . . it's okay though we
        are besties so I can wear your hat:)
Tim: Ur right I totally forgot about that ur right lol but this is the snuggle
        train
Ashley: Hahaha If That's What You Call It
Tim: that is the cuddle train lol
Ashley: Hahah Okay Hooker Now Text Me Back!!
Tim: ok you dirty whore lol
John: CUDDLE TRAIN!!!!!!!!!!!!! Hell to the yeah
Kristen: ohh we all look so cute! :)

Interestingly, all of the above comments were posted the day after the photograph was uploaded, which supports the previous motive of manufactured memories. In this way, the teens immediately turned to Facebook to relive the events of the previous night and continue their bonding experience. Also, only individuals present in the photograph made comments on the picture; thus, the friends are reaffirming their social identity. The picture is important to each of them as members of a social group. Like the cuddle train mentioned in the previous quote, physical closeness (e.g., hugging, cuddling, kissing) documented in mobile uploads portrays the seriousness of relationships. This is particularly the case with romantic relationships, which begin to develop and take precedence during the adolescent years:

Interviewer: Have you ever deleted one of your mobile upload albums?

Claire (age 15, interview): No. Well not a whole album. I've deleted pictures before; like I posted a picture of my ex-boyfriend and I kissing and my mom made me take it down because she said it was "inappropriate," since I'm friends with a lot of my relatives on Facebook. She said she didn't want my Grandma seeing a picture of me making out. It really didn't matter anyway because we broke up like a week later so I deleted all of the pictures that I had posted of us together anyway. Guys get super jealous if you have pictures of old boyfriends and stuff on your Facebook, so you have to be careful what you leave up. It's stupid.

Ellen (age 18, interview): I was looking at this guy's profile and I see he still has pictures of him and his ex. I thought, "Hmm, okay. Why are they still there?" I'm not his girlfriend. We are only talking, so I can't really say anything, but if they have broken up, I don't really understand what he is holding onto.

Adolescence is a period in which young girls commonly begin to explore their sexualities, and, in a sense, teenagers use mobile uploading as currency in relationships. The frequency of appearance and nature of the content demonstrate how meaningful the relationship is. When the relationship ends, mobile uploads can be symbolically dissolved as well. From family and friends to love interests and even pets, mobile uploads reflect the significant relationships in a teenage girl's life. In and of itself, mobile uploading can establish the positive status of a given relationship, and relational bonds are solidified through commenting on the uploaded photograph.

Bounded Rebellion

Mobile uploading allows teenage girls an opportunity to test the waters of risk-taking and rebellion. Although Facebook began as a venture targeted toward college students, it now caters to a wider market of consumers. All of the informants said at least one of their parents was friends with them on Facebook, and many of them were friends with aunts, uncles, grandparents, school faculty, church pastors, coaches, and other adults; thus, many of today's young girls construct and deconstruct their identities in full view of both their parents and their peers. Sometimes they seek approval from authority and sometimes they rebel against it. Mobile uploading provides a platform upon which teens can act out rebellion within certain boundaries. For instance, teens use promotional products, such as a Marlboro hat or a Bud Light T-shirt, to symbolically represent their risky consumption behaviors:

Ellen (age 18, mobile upload): Ellen posted a picture of herself and her friends in the beer and alcohol aisle of the supermarket, despite being under the legal drinking age.

Claire (age 15, mobile upload): Claire posted a picture of the digital clock in her car as it read 4:20, which refers to the to cannabis consumption subculture.

Alyssa (age 18, mobile upload): Alyssa posted a picture of her friend playing Nintendo DS under the desk during their chemistry class.

Uploading photographs in which teenagers toe the line of rebellion allows them to experiment with their identities through bounded risk-taking. Madison (age 16) posted a picture of herself and a friend standing next to a restaurant sign, which read, "Now serving beer!" The photograph caption states, "Calm down, Mom. We are just kidding (sort of)." When asked about the photograph, Madison said that she just likes to mess with her parents. In fact, her dad commented on the photograph, saying, "ye root beer, ha ha." As in Madison's case, mobile uploading through social network sites may provide opportunity for parents and other adult role models to communicate with young people about their risky consumption behaviors. The social network site provides a captive audience for teens to perform such behaviors and receive positive or negative feedback from their web of friends.

Discussion

Drawing on previous research on adolescent identity and social media, the findings of this study provide a better understanding of the characteristics of and motivations for mobile photo sharing among adolescent girls. The social network site (e.g., Facebook) provides a platform upon which teens can publicly negotiate their identities through the mediated interface of the Internet. They engage in deliberate self-presentation, they symbolically portray their identities through consumption, and they capture the photographs in meaningful social spaces. The data reveal that teen girls actively take part in mobile photo sharing in order to gain audience feedback, manufacture memories, reaffirm relationships, and rebel within boundaries. The present study builds upon and extends previous research on adolescent identity and consumer behavior by identifying the process by which adolescents negotiate their identities through mobile uploading and the underlying motives for doing so.

The findings from this study lend support to the notion that ubiquitous technology and social media are fundamentally affecting the ways in which adolescent consumers interact in the marketplace. Social spaces that are traditionally thought of as private (e.g., bathrooms, bedrooms, dressing rooms) are willingly made public by teenagers eager to share their consumption experiences with their online friends. Young girls are using social media to gain feedback from their peers, and as evident in the findings, even from their parents. From an identity development perspective, adolescence is traditionally a period of life in which individuals begin to separate themselves from their parents and family and develop an identity that is more in line with that of their peers. This new age of mediated communication is creating a convergence of traditionally separate social groups. For instance, a teen girl may be Facebook friends with a wide range of individuals from varying social groups: her mom, her best friend from school, her science teacher, her soccer coach, her friend from summer camp, or her pastor. The traditional view of identity suggests that individuals will take on different identity characteristics depending upon their social setting; however, with all of their social groups converging online, teens who engage in mobile uploading through Facebook show evidence of using the Facebook platform to test-run identities regardless of the varied audience. In this way, Facebook provides a one-stop shop for identity feedback.

Consumption plays a key role in this online identity development process. Mobile uploading often occurs in marketplace settings (e.g., retail stores, restaurants) and consumer products serve as the justification or pretext for taking and sharing mobile photos. In this way, identity development on Facebook is performative in nature. For instance, a girl can try on a pair of high-heeled shoes at the store with the sole intention of taking a picture of the experience to share with her Facebook friends. Thus, the girl uses the product to create a memory of the experience without committing to the purchase of the product. It is important for marketers and retailers to understand how adolescents are interacting with their products for the purpose of identity construction in this new mobile marketplace. From a marketing perspective, if adolescents are simply using the marketplace as a stage upon which they can perform their identities through photo sharing, a challenge becomes whether to embrace the trend (e.g., encourage and provide photo sharing opportunities) or attempt to circumvent it (e.g., prevent instore photography).

Future Directions

This study represents a beginning understanding of how adolescent consumers use social media to construct their identities. Online photo sharing is only one tool with which adolescents can create, edit, and negotiate their identities. Future research should examine how other social media tools may be different or similar to online photo sharing in the context of identity development. Furthermore, although this study focused primarily on adolescent girls, that is not to say that boys do not use mobile photo sharing at all. Although they likely use it to a lesser degree, the nature of their use may differ, thus future studies should explore gender differences, and on a similar note, age differences (e.g., early adolescents versus emerging adults). Finally, given the transitional nature of identity over time, a longitudinal study is an imperative next step toward understanding how adolescents use online social media to negotiate their identities and to exploring the role of consumption and consumer products in this process.

References

Alch, M. L. (2000). The echo-boom generation: A growing force in American society. *The Futurist, 34*(5), 42–51.

Bamberg, M. & Andrews, M. (2004). *Considering counter narratives: Narrating, resisting, making sense.* Philadelphia: John Benjamins.

Belk, R. W. (1988). Possessions and the extended self. *Journal of Consumer Research, 15*(2), 139–168.

Boyd, D. M. (2008). Why youth (heart) social network sites: The role of networked publics in teenage social life. In *Macarthur Foundation Series on Digital Learning: Youth, Identity, and Digital Media Volume.* Cambridge, MA: MIT Press, pp. 119–142.

Boyd, D. M. & Ellison, N. B. (2007). Social network sites: Definition, history, and scholarship. *Journal of Computer Mediated Communication, 13*(1), 210–230.

Calvert, S. L. (2002). Identity construction on the Internet. In S. L. Calvert, A. B. Jordan, & R. R. Cocking (Eds.), *Children in the digital age: Influences of electronic media on development.* Westport, CT: Praeger.

Collier, Jr., J. & Collier, M. (1986). *Visual anthropology: Photography as a research method.* Albuquerque: University of New Mexico Press.

Douvan, E. & Adelson, J. (1966). *The adolescent experience.* New York: John Wiley.

Durham, M. G. (2009). *The Lolita effect: The media sexualization of young girls and what we can do about it.* New York: Overlook Press.

Elkind, D. (1967). Egocentrism in adolescence. *Child Development, 38*(4), 1025–1034.

Erikson, E. H. (1963). *Childhood and society.* New York: Norton.

Festinger, L. (1954). A theory of social comparison processes. *Human Relations, 7*(2), 117–140.

Glaser, B. G. & Strauss, A. (1967). *The discovery of grounded theory: Strategies for qualitative research.* Chicago: Aldine.

Goffman, E. (1959). *The presentation of self in everyday life.* New York: Overlook Press.

Gross, E. F. (2004). Adolescent Internet use: What we expect, what teens report. *Journal of Applied Developmental Psychology, 25*(6), 633–649.

Hagedorn, M. I. (1996). Photography: An aesthetic technique for nursing inquiry. *Issues in Mental Health Nursing, 17*(6), 517–527.

Hancock, J. T. & Toma, C. L. (2009). Putting your best face forward: The accuracy of online dating photographs. *Journal of Communication, 59,* 367–386.

Harrison, B. (2002). Photographic visions and narrative inquiry. *Narrative Inquiry, 12* (1), 87–111.

Hawley, P. H. (2011). The evolution of adolescence and the adolescence of evolution: The coming of age of humans and the theory about the forces that made them. *Journal of Research on Adolescence, 21*(1), 307–316.

Heisley, D. D. & Levy, S. J. (1991). Autodriving: A photoelicitation technique. *Journal of Consumer Research, 18*(3), 257–272.

Hogg, M. K., Banister, E. N., & Stephenson, C. A. (2009). Mapping symbolic (anti-) consumption. *Journal of Business Research, 62*(2), 148–159.

Howe, N. & Strauss, W. (1991). *Generations: The history of America's future, 1584 to 2069.* New York: William Morrow.

Howe, N. & Strauss, W. (2000). *Millennials rising: The next great generation.* Toronto: Vintage Books.

Kaplan, A. M. & Haenlein, M. (2010). Users of the world, unite! The challenges and opportunities of social media. *Business Horizons, 53*(1), 59–68.

Kennedy, L. (2001). The up & coming generation. *Retail Merchandiser, 41*(8), 66.

Kindberg, T., Spasojevic, M., Fleck, R., & Sellen, A. (2005). The ubiquitous camera: An in-depth study of camera phone use. *IEEE Pervasive Computing, 4*(2), 42–50.

Kozinets, R. V. (2002). The field behind the screen: Using netnography for market¬ing research in online communities. *Journal of Marketing Research (JMR), 39,* 61–72.

Kvale, S. (1996). *Interviews: An introduction to qualitative research interviewing.* Thousand Oaks, CA: SAGE.

Lee, S. J. (2009). Online communication and adolescent social ties: Who benefits more from Internet use? *Journal of Computer Mediated Communication, 14*(3), 509–531.

Lenhart, A. (April 10, 2009). Teens and social media: An overview. In *Pew Internet & American Life Project*. Washington, DC: Pew Research Center.

Lenhart, A., Ling, R., Campbell, S., & Purcell, K. (2010). Teens and mobile phones. In *Pew Internet & American Life Project*. Washington, DC: Pew Research Center.

Lenhart, A., Madden, M., & Hitlin, P. (July 27, 2005). Teens and Technology. In *Pew Internet & American Life Project*. Washington, DC: Pew Research Center.

Lenhart, A., Purcell, K., Smith, A., & Zickuhr, K. (2010). Social media & mobile Internet use among teens and young adults. In *Pew Internet & American Life Project*. Washington, DC: Pew Research Center.

Linn, S. (2004). *Consuming kids: The hostile takeover of childhood*. New York: New Press.

Lorraine, T. E. (1990). *Gender, identity, and the production of meaning*. Boulder, CO: Westview Press.

Maczewski, M. (2002). Exploring identities through the Internet: Youth experiences online. *Child and Youth Care Forum. 31*(2), 111–129.

Markus, H. & Nurius, P. (1986). Possible selves. *American Psychologist, 41*(9), 954–969.

Mazzarella, S. R., (Ed.) (2005). *Girl Wide Web: Girls, the Internet, and the negotiation of identity*. New York: Peter Lang.

McCracken, G. (1986). Culture and consumption: A theoretical account of the structure and movement of the cultural meaning of consumer goods. *Journal of Consumer Research, 13*(1), 71–84.

Mendelson, A. L. & Papacharissi, Z. (2010). Look at us: Collective narcissism in college student Facebook photo galleries. In Z. Papacharissi (Ed.), *The networked self: Identity, connectivity and culture on social network sites*. Boca Raton, FL: Routledge.

Montgomery, K. C. (2009). *Generation digital: Politics, commerce, and childhood in the age of the Internet*. Cambridge, MA: MIT Press.

Muñiz, A. M., Jr. & O'Guinn, T. C. (2001). Brand community, *Journal of Consumer Research, 27*(4), 412–432.

Noland, C. M. (2006). Auto-photography as research practice: Identity and self-esteem research. *Journal of Research Practice, 2*(1). Article M1. Retrieved September 18, 2009, from http://jrp.icaap.org/index.php/jrp/article/view/19/50

Oppliger, P. A. (2008). *Girls gone skank: The sexualization of girls in American culture*. Jefferson, NC: McFarland.

Palfrey, J. & Gasser, U. (2008). *Born digital: Understanding the first generation of digital natives*. New York: Basic.

Pink, S. (2003). Interdisciplinary agendas in visual research: Re-situating visual anthropology. *Visual Studies, 18*(2), 179–192.

Prahalad, C. K. & Ramaswamy, V. (2004). Co-creation experiences: The next practice in value creation. *Journal of Interactive Marketing, 18*(3), 5–14.

Schaffer, R., & Wong, C. (January 12, 2011). *Kaplan Test Prep Survey: 35% of teens with parents on Facebook aren't friends with them; Nearly 40% admit the reason is because they've ignored Mom or Dad's friend request.* New York: Kaplan Test Prep.

Schor, J. B. (2004). *Born to buy: The commercialized child and the new consumer culture.* New York: Scribner.

Sherif, M., & Sherif, C. W. (1964). *Reference groups: Exploration into conformity and deviation of adolescents.* New York: Harper and Row.

Steinberg, L., Graham, S., O'Brien, L., Woolard, J., Cauffman, E., & Banich, M. (2009). Age differences in future orientation and delay discounting. *Child Development, 80*(1), 28–44.

Strauss, W., Howe, N., & Markiewicz, P. G. (2006). *Millennials and the pop culture: Strategies for a new generation of consumers in music, movies, television, the Internet, and video games.* New York: LifeCourse Associates.

Subrahmanyam, K. & Smahel, D. (2011). *Digital youth: The role of media in development.* New York: Springer.

Sullivan, H. S. (1953). *The interpersonal theory of psychiatry.* New York: Norton.

Tajfel, H. & Turner, J. C. (1986). The social identity theory of intergroup behavior. In S. Worchel & W. G. Austin (Eds.), *Psychology of intergroup relations* (Vol. 2). Chicago: Nelson-Hall, pp. 7–24.

Tapscott, D. (2009). *Grown up digital: How the Net generation is changing your world.* New York: McGraw-Hill.

Turkle, S. (1995). *Life on the screen: Identity in the age of the Internet.* New York: Simon & Schuster.

Turner, V. (1987). Betwixt and between: The liminal period in rites of passage. In L. Carus Mahdi, S. Foster, & M. Little (Eds.). *Betwixt and between: Patterns of masculine and feminine initiation.* Peru, IL: Open Court, pp. 3–19.

Twenge, J. M. (2006). *Generation me: Why today's young Americans are more confident, assertive, entitled—and more miserable than ever before.* New York: Free Press.

Valkenburg, P. M. & Peter, J. (2008). Adolescents' identity experiments on the Internet: Consequences for social competence and self-concept unity. *Communication Research, 35*(2), 208–231.

Valkenburg, P. M., Schouten, A. P., & Peter, J. (2005). Adolescents' identity experiments on the Internet. *New Media & Society, 7*(3), 383–402.

Van House, N., Davis, M., Takhteyev, Y., Good, N., Wilhelm, A., & Finn, M. (2004). From "what?" to "why?": The social uses of personal photos. In *ACM Conference on Computer Supported Cooperative Work*, Chicago.

Walther, J. B. (1996). Computer-mediated communication: Impersonal, interpersonal, and hyperpersonal interaction. *Communication Research, 23*(1), 3–43.

Weale, B. W. & Kerr, J. R. (1969). Brand choices of teen-age "in-group" versus "out-group." *Journal of Retailing, 45*(4), 30.

Wooten, D. B. (2006). From labeling possessions to possessing labels: Ridicule and socialization among adolescents. *Journal of Consumer Research, 33*(2), 188–198.

Zavestoski, S. (2002). The social–psychological bases of anti-consumption attitudes. *Psychology and Marketing, 19*(2), 149–165.

2

Source Characteristics in Online Shopping
Do Avatar Expertise, Similarity, and Attractiveness Affect Purchase Outcomes?

David G. Taylor
Sacred Heart University

Iryna Pentina
The University of Toledo

In the 2009 motion picture *Avatar*, the consciousness of a paraplegic marine is transferred to a remotely controlled biological body that can survive in the lethal air of the sci-fi planet Pandora. In this fictional world, avatars are genetically engineered biological beings that walk, talk, and are essentially remote-controlled bodies. In the real world of the present, of course, the term "avatar" refers not to a living, three-dimensional body, but rather to a virtual representation of a user in a digital environment. In a very real sense, however, avatars have transcended their self-contained virtual worlds to interact with real people in the "real" world.

When, in 2004, you asked tech-savvy marketers about the potential for using avatars, you would inevitably receive a breathless description of the next business frontier: the virtual world of Second Life. In Second Life, an online virtual community created by Linden Labs in 2003, users create avatars and move through the electronic world meeting other avatars in a simulated environment. With millions of virtual users moving about in the world of Second Life, marketers were eager to create virtual versions of their brands and businesses. Calling Second Life "potentially a dream venue," *Harvard Business Review* reported that "instead of targeting passive eyeballs, marketers here have the opportunity to interact with engaged minds. Commerce is already an integral part of Second Life. . . .

Certainly, introducing new brands, in some form or another, is a logical next step" (Hemp, 2006, p. 49).

Although some marketers have experienced some moderate success in building brand awareness through Second Life, moving offline brands into the avatars' world has been, at best, an ancillary marketing technique. Arguably, the more interesting phenomenon has been the movement of avatars from their self-contained virtual environments into the wider world of the Web. Anecdotally, avatars have been used with some success in online advertising. For instance, rap musician 50 Cent created an avatar version of himself to promote one of his albums. Millions of fans downloaded, customized, and added the avatar to their social networking profiles (Hampp, 2007). Similarly, an avatar of sports commentator Greg Gumbel helped General Motors increase its click-through tenfold compared with similar advertisements with no avatar (Connelly, 2007).

However, avatars are not only relegated to the role of online ad pitchmen. Service providers such as Rovion, iNago, SitePal, and others offer the ability for marketers to use avatars—ranging from cartoonlike representations of humans to photorealistic animated avatars with humanlike voices and facial expressions—on their Web sites. An avatar is thus "an online communication source, a sales associate or customer service representative who assists Internet users in the information search process, providing product information and, if requested, advice about selecting from a set of product options" (Wood, Solomon, & Englis, 2005). McGoldrick, Keeting, and Beatty (2008) identified three preferred roles of avatars: (1) helping to solve problems or save time or effort; (2) sociable host; and (3) personal shopper or recommending agent.

In each of these roles, avatars interact with customers online, providing a human face and, presumably, a higher level of socialness in what is otherwise a human-to-machine interaction. Interestingly, social response theory suggests that in these types of interactions, people tend to react to computer-mediated communications not as they would with an inanimate object, but rather as they would in a similar interaction with a human (Moon, 2000). These types of responses appear to be unconscious reactions to the exhibition of human characteristics through electronic channels, which trigger scripts, labels, and expectations from the user's prior experiences (Langer, 1989). In other words, when online consumers unconsciously perceive social cues in the interaction, they subconsciously access and enact scripts for interactions with humans, as evidenced by their reactions and expectations.

Avatars and Social Cues

The behavior of a participant in any social interaction is determined by societal norms, roles, understandings, and customs based on past experiences (Berscheid, 1994). When one engages in an interaction, the relational schemas or performance scripts (based upon norms and experiences) are activated, and one behaves accordingly. The extent to which the "other" in a social interaction conforms to expectations largely determines whether one adheres, or continues to adhere, to the script. In other words, social cues in a human–computer interaction may activate a script that will continue as long as the computer reacts as expected in the interaction. The human will mindlessly continue to interact with the object as with a human unless expectations are violated, in which case the fact that she is interacting with a nonhuman "other" is made salient, and the human will allocate more mental resources to monitoring the interaction, that is, a mindful interaction (Bargh & Chartrand, 1999). Avatars, by closely simulating the reactions of a human in an interaction, may not only provide cues that trigger scripts in the interaction, but may also continue to exhibit cues that maintain the less mindful interaction. Possible cues include interactivity, voice capability, or a humanlike personality (Hayes-Roth, Sincoff, Brownston, & Lent, 1995; Reeves & Nass, 1996). These cues, as they relate to avatars, are detailed next, followed by a discussion of the impact of the cues on consumers interacting in a virtual space.

Interactivity

Although the exact definition of interactivity in the electronic marketplace has been debated, perhaps the most comprehensive version defines interactivity as "the degree to which computer-mediated communication is perceived by each of the communicating entities to be (a) bidirectional, (b) timely, (c) mutually controllable, and (d) responsive" (Yadav & Varadarajan, 2005). Bidirectionality (the ability of the consumer to both send and receive messages), timeliness (temporal proximity of messages and responses), and controllability (the ability of both sender and receiver to shape the nature of the interaction) are vital to a computer-mediated interaction, with or without an avatar. The avatar, however, provides added interactivity on the fourth dimension: responsiveness.

A responsive interaction has been described as one in which messages exhibit interconnectedness by building cumulatively on previous messages (Heeter, 2000; Steuer, 1992; Yadav & Varadarajan, 2005). However, avatars may improve the perception of responsiveness, and by extension, interactivity, by exhibiting interconnectedness through social cues, reacting to what the consumer is saying, by smiling when the consumer types, "Thanks," for example. But avatars can also exhibit interconnectedness by subtly reacting to what the consumer is doing. For example, the avatars available from SitePal have eyes that follow the cursor on the page when the consumer moves it. Previous research suggests that these types of eye movements and changes in the direction of gaze provide a strong social cue that increases the perception of realness during the interaction (Colburn, Cohen, & Drucker, 2000). One study found that, for photorealistic avatars, a gaze that follows the user resulted in that user being more attentive, less distracted, and more immersed in the interaction with the avatar (Cerezo, Baldassarri, & Seron, 2007). In addition to the eye movements, avatars may also display facial expressions of interest or anticipation while the consumer is typing in a chat window. These cues, although not necessarily consciously noticed by the consumer, provide an added level of interconnectedness that can enhance the perception of interactivity.

Voice Capability

Synthetic speech has come a long way since the metallic "Danger, Will Robinson" cadence of the old *Lost In Space* television series. Today's voice generation systems, although not quite perfect, are increasingly human-like. Most commercial avatar vendors have the capability to generate text-to-speech audio for Web sites, or voice actors can record scripted snippets of conversation. The text-to-speech audio tends to lack inflection resulting in a somewhat robotic cadence, however, it is becoming increasingly sophisticated. Emerging technology allows avatars not only to match facial expression and tone with what they are saying, but also to recognize speech and respond appropriately (DeMara et al., 2008). In fact, one form of cutting-edge technology allows avatars to simulate their own emotional states, which may vary depending on the avatar's relationship with the user and the modulation of its voice (Cerezo et al., 2007). Thus, by emulating the human voice, inflections, and expressions, avatars are able to dramatically enhance the level of interactivity and responsiveness.

Human Personality

The human personality is often defined as a dynamic and organized set of characteristics that uniquely influences cognitions, motivations, and behaviors in various situations (Ryckman, 2004). Extant research is rife with examples of consumers attributing these types of personality traits to nonhuman entities. As previously mentioned, computer users often infer human personality traits in computer interactions (Isbister & Nass, 2000; Moon & Nass, 1996; Nass & Moon, 2000; Nass, Moon, & Carney, 1996).

Consumers often imbue products and companies with a brand personality, defined as the set of human characteristics associated with a brand, including sincerity, excitement, competence, sophistication, and ruggedness (Aaker, 1997). With most types of online transactions, consumers perceive brand personality the same way they infer it offline. Personality is transferred from people who use the brand or are associated with the brand (McCracken, 1988), or through product attributes, brand name, logos, price, or distribution channels (Batra, Lehmann, & Singh, 1993). Thus, the personality of a Web site is an anthropomorphic culmination of the brand personality and the imagery and verbiage on the site. Social media sites have been shown to possess personalities inferred from attributes generally ascribed to their members, as well as the online activities in which they engage (Pentina, 2011).

The presence of an avatar, however, brings a more explicit dimension of personality to the interaction. In the virtual environment, the avatar is a projection of the company or brand, and users may interact with it as the anthropomorphic representation of the brand, that is, the company or brand in human form (Jin & Sung, 2010). However, there is a more explicit personality component in avatars. As electronic representations of humans, avatars can be designed to mimic any or all personality dimensions of humans. In psychology literature, human personality has been generally conceptualized along the "Big Five" dimensions of openness, conscientiousness, extraversion, agreeableness, and neuroticism (Digman, 1990). Because avatars are, in essence, artificial human beings, they not only replicate the appearance of actual persons, but also engage in humanlike behaviors, verbally (i.e., speech and text), as well as nonverbally (i.e., facial expressions, hand gestures, eye movements). These can be used to express Big Five personality traits such as extraversion, agreeableness, or openness. For example, a smiling avatar may demonstrate agreeableness, whereas an enthusiastic tone of voice may serve as a cue to indicate extroversion. In an experiment discussed later in this chapter, Pentina and Taylor (2010) manipulate the consumer's perception of the avatar's need for cognition by having the avatar explicitly describe behaviors that express either high or low levels of this trait.

In summary, avatars may possess an explicit personality that goes far beyond the symbolic personality of a product or brand. Although brand personality may be perceived as more feminine or masculine based on cues such as product category, fonts used in the logo, or imagery of the typical user, for example, an avatar often has an explicitly defined gender of either male or female. Indeed, the degree to which an avatar is perceived as having a unique and identifiable set of traits that influence its motivations, cognitions, and behaviors determines its level of human personality. Thus, when an avatar demonstrates a personality, it provides cues that trigger the relational scripts and schema in the human consumer.

The Effects of Perceived Socialness

People apply relational schema to interactions with computers when the computer possesses humanlike attributes or social cues (Reeves & Nass, 1996). Wang, Baker, Wagner, and Wakefield (2007) tested the veracity of this theory by conducting a pair of experiments to determine whether consumers respond positively to cues from an avatar portraying a representative of the firm. The researchers hypothesized that the social cues from the avatars would be perceived, triggering pleasure, arousal, and flow. Pleasure and arousal are, of course, a state of positive affect and heightened physical or cognitive response to stimuli. Flow is a multidimensional psychological state in which an activity is so intrinsically interesting that a person is engaged to the point of losing track of everything else (Csikszentmihalyi, 1988). In human–computer interactions, a state of flow is reached when the user feels a sense of control over the computer interaction, the user's attention is focused on the interaction, the user's interest is increased during the interaction, and the user's curiosity is evoked (Trevino & Webster, 1992). In brick-and-mortar retail stores, social cues from store employees and other customers have a positive effect on arousal and pleasure (Baker, Grewal, & Levy, 1992; Berry, Carbone, & Haeckel, 2002). Similarly, Csikszentmihalyi (1988) claims that the presence of others is a component of flow, so Wang and colleagues (2007) hypothesized that the social cues from avatars would increase the likelihood of consumers' arousal, pleasure, and flow.

In the first study, the researchers recruited a sample of 337 undergraduate students from a southwestern university to participate in a one-factor between-subjects experimental design. Participants were evenly split on gender (49% female and 51% male) ranging in age from 18 to 35 years old, with 80% having previously shopped online. The participants were randomly assigned to either a low-social or high-social Web site. Both Web sites were for a fictitious travel company named Caribbean Travel Net, or CTN, and provided travel information about islands in the Caribbean. The high-social Web site employed a female avatar as a virtual tour guide, using both written text and spoken language. The low-social Web site did not have a tour guide or voice, but instead just written text. As expected, the site with the avatar was perceived by users as being more social than the low-social Web site. Moreover, in a structural equation model, the paths from socialness indicated a significant ($p < .05$) relationship between socialness and arousal, pleasure, and flow.

In the second study, Wang and colleagues (2007) validated and extended the model with another between-subjects single-factor experiment. This time, the context was a window blind shopping site. Once again, the high-social Web site employed a female avatar as a shopping guide, using voice and spoken language, and the low-social Web site had only written text. The new sample consisted of 250 adults recruited from an online panel. The same measures were employed as in the first experiment, but in this study, involvement was measured as a potential moderator of the relationship between arousal and pleasure. Involvement is the relevance a person perceives for an object based on his or her needs, values, or interests (Zaichkowsky, 1985). The results of the second study were similar to those of the first. Once again, the site with the avatar was perceived as more social than the nonavatar site. Once again, the site with the avatar was perceived as more social than the nonavatar site, and the paths from socialness to arousal, pleasure, and flow were all significant. Interestingly, however, there was no interaction effect with involvement. Thus, Wang and colleagues (2007) found strong support for the notion that the social cues from avatars exert a positive influence on online customer behavior.

Avatar Expertise and Attractiveness

In another study, Holzwarth, Janiszewski, and Neumann (2006) explored how an avatar's characteristics—not just the presence of an avatar—influence the customer. Specifically, Holzwarth and colleagues investigated how the perceived attractiveness and expertise of an avatar salesperson affected the persuasiveness of their sales efforts. Among human communicators, the elaboration likelihood model theorizes that the consumer's level of involvement determines whether the consumer evaluates arguments using the central route (i.e., weighing the merits of the arguments) or the peripheral route (i.e., considering cues other than the actual arguments (Petty & Cacioppo, 1981). In a high-involvement situation, the consumer is more likely to consider the content of an argument, as well as the expertise of the communicator, in evaluating the argument (Petty, Cacioppo, & Heesacker, 1981). Conversely, in a low-involvement situation, peripheral cues such as the attractiveness of the communicator have a greater effect on the level of persuasion (Petty, Cacioppo, & Goldman, 1981). Holzwarth and associates hypothesized that this effect would be generalizable to communications between avatars and humans, that an expert avatar would be more effective in high-involvement conditions, whereas an attractive avatar would be more effective in a low-involvement condition.

To test their hypotheses, Holzwarth et al. (2006) conducted a pair of experiments. In the first, participants were asked to make a purchase of shoes on a simulated Web site. The experiment included three avatar conditions (no avatar versus attractive avatar versus expert avatar) two involvement conditions (moderate versus high). The 400 participants, all German consumers, were randomly assigned to one of the three avatar conditions, and involvement was a measured variable. As expected, the presence of an avatar resulted in significantly higher levels of satisfaction, attitude, and purchase intention. In addition, consistent with the predictions of the elaboration likelihood model (ELM), the attractive avatar was more persuasive for participants who were moderately involved in the purchase, whereas the expert avatar was marginally more persuasive when the participant was highly involved in the purchase.

To rule out alternate explanations, Holzwarth et al. conducted a second study in which a similar technique was used. This time, however, they used a two (attractiveness: low versus high) × two (expertise: low versus high) between-subjects design. Again using a sample of German consumers, 596 participants were recruited. Generally confirming the first experiment, the follow-up study found that moderately involved participants were influenced by the attractiveness of the avatar, but not the expertise. Consistent with the first study, high-involvement participants were influenced by the expertise of the avatar, but they were also unexpectedly influenced by the attractiveness of the avatar. In broad terms, however, Holzwarth et al. (2006) provided support for the more general proposition that human consumers not only react to avatars as they would in human-to-human interactions, but also perceive, and are influenced by, human traits such as expertise and attractiveness in avatars.

A subsequent study (Jin & Bolebruch, 2009) not only lent additional support to the effect of attractiveness in an avatar, but also provided a potential explanation for the unexpected results with regard to involvement. In their study, 116 college students participated in an experiment in which participants made a purchase inside the virtual Apple Store in the Second Life environment. The participants were randomly assigned to one of three conditions (no avatar, human avatar, or nonhuman avatar) and listened to a spokesavatar. The dependent variables measured were enjoyment of online shopping, product involvement, attitude toward the product, physical attractiveness of the spokesavatar, and information value of the advertisement. Interestingly, though, the authors administered a pretest of several of the variables.

A paired-samples *t*-test indicated that participants who were presented with an avatar reported significantly higher attitude toward the product in the posttest than their pretest scores, whereas the no-avatar control group showed no significant difference in pre- and posttest scores. In addition, Jin and Bolebruch (2009) found that in the two avatar groups, the perceived attractiveness of the avatar was a significant predictor of the perceived information value of the message. An interesting side note in the experiment was that a paired-sample *t*-test between the pretest and posttest involvement measure indicated that the presence of an avatar actually resulted in a significantly higher level of product involvement. This may help to explain some of the counterintuitive findings with regard to the ELM in Holzwarth et al.'s (2006) study. Alternate explanations were also offered in the study by Pentina and Taylor (2010).

The Effect of Buyer–Avatar Similarity

Pentina and Taylor (2010) investigated whether the effectiveness of virtual sales representatives can be improved by their similarity to buyers, which had been proven effective in human-to-human sales situations. Existing personal selling literature generally concurs on the positive role of buyer–seller similarity in sales outcomes (Lichtenthal & Tellefsen, 2001). Such characteristics as shared attitudes, morality, personality traits, music preferences, background, and perceptions about life have been found to positively affect a sales situation outcome (Byrne, 1962; Byrne, Griffitt, & Stefaniak, 1967; Dion, Easterling, & Miller, 1995; Stotland, Zander, & Natsoulas, 1961; Taylor & Woodside, 1982). However, mixed findings exist regarding the effects of observable (physical) similarity, most frequently operationalized as age, gender, and race (Churchill, Collins, & Strang, 1975; Crosby, Evans, & Cowles, 1990; Dwyer, Richard, & Shepherd, 1998). Some studies report a positive effect of observable similarity between buyer and seller on purchase intentions (Gadel, 1964; Smith, 1998), altruism (Harris & Baudin, 1973), and confederate assessment (Hendrick, Stikes, & Murry, 1972). Others find no significant relationships between physical similarity and sales outcomes (Jones, Moore, Stanaland, & Wyatt, 1998). Still others propose the reverse effects (e.g., gender dissimilarity) of observable characteristics to be instrumental in increasing sales performance (Dwyer et al., 1998).

In order to test the role of buyer–avatar similarity effect, two experiments were conducted using fictitious e-commerce Web sites. In Experiment 1, initial questions about participant demographics and physical appearance determined how specific avatars would be assigned: half of the participants were greeted by avatars similar to them in gender and race, and the other half were exposed to dissimilar avatars. In Experiment 2, need for cognition (NC) defined as an "individual's propensity to engage in and enjoy cognitive activities" (Wheeler, Petty, & Bizer, 2005) was used as an internal similarity variable. Participants' answers to the 18-item NC scale (Cacioppo, Petty, & Kao, 1984) determined how specific avatars would be assigned: half of the respondents received avatars that described themselves as similar in NC (high or low), and the other half were exposed to dissimilar avatars. For example, in the introductory paragraph, the following phrases were used to describe high versus low NC avatars, "I like my job because it lets me think and find new facts about [the product]," and, "I never really enjoy solving complex problems and try to avoid situations that require a lot of thinking." In addition to avatar (dis)similarity manipulation, respondents were randomly assigned to three conditions of purchase situation involvement: Web sites selling a children's game (low involvement), a foldable bed (moderate involvement), and a Web site advertising a student apartment complex (high involvement). Strength of arguments was manipulated following Wheeler et al. (2005) by using statements about level of product quality, rankings by experts, and number of desirable product attributes.

The results of Experiment 1 supported the elaboration likelihood model in the online context. Avatar physical dissimilarity was stronger related to purchase intentions under the conditions of low purchase involvement (F = 3.13; p = .082) than under the conditions of high purchase involvement (F = .175; ns). In Experiment 2, avatar internal similarity to the buyers did not affect their intentions to make a high-involvement purchase either independently (F = .121, p = .73), or by interacting with the argument strength (F = .047, p = .829). Under low involvement conditions, none of the variables of interest was significant: F-value for argument strength was .062 (p = .804), and for internal similarity match .902 (p =.345). Finally, under moderate involvement condition, avatar internal similarity produced a significant main effect (F = 4.321, p = .039) as did strength of arguments (F = 3.477, p = .064). That is, matching avatars and respondents in such internal characteristics as need for cognition, apparently did not activate their elaboration of message resulting in differential purchase intentions based on argument strength. Instead, under moderate involvement conditions, two separate message elaboration routes appear to be activated: a peripheral route wherein avatar internal similarity alone brings about positive response to persuasion, and a central route where argument strength alone affects online buyers' choices. This finding echoes the combined influence hypothesis (Lord, Lee, & Sauter, 1995) that posits simultaneous consumer response to both message arguments and peripheral cues, and has been widely supported in the advertising context (Mick, 1992; Miniard, Bhatla, Lord, Dikson, & Unnava, 1992).

Additional tests for the potential impact of the participants' self-reported cognition showed neither an interaction between NC-match and self-reported NC (F = 1.2, p = .275), nor an independent effect of self-reported NC on buying intentions (β = .052, p = .444). However, there was a significant interaction effect between the self-reported need for cognition and argument strength (F = 4.561, p =. 037) in determining buying intentions. Thus, a tentative explanation may be that under moderate involvement conditions, personal characteristics determine the choice of message-processing route, such that consumers high in need for cognition would pay more attention to argument strength (central route) while making purchase decisions. For individuals with a less salient need for the cognition trait (Markus, 1977) similarity to virtual representatives may be sufficient to elicit a positive purchase intent without evaluating the sales pitch arguments (peripheral route). This explanation is consistent with the earlier finding that the quality of arguments is a more important determinant for people high (versus low) in their need for cognition (Cacioppo, Petty, & Morris, 1983).

Prior investigations into the effects of avatars in online retail environments have produced results that appear to be inconsistent with ELM. Although ELM suggests that peripheral cues such as avatar similarity should affect only low-involvement customers, Holzwarth et al. (2006) found that moderately and highly involved customers are influenced by both attractive and expert avatars. Similarly, Wang et al. (2007) found that social avatars increase purchase intention only for involved consumers. Pentina and Taylor (2010) provide potential theoretical explanations of these findings by outlining the mechanisms of differential source similarity effects in different involvement conditions.

The Effect of Buyer–Avatar Ethnic Match

Although, as discussed previously, electronic agents have been anthropomorphized since the advent of the computer, the idea of ethnicity appears to be unique to avatars. Just as Pentina and Taylor (2010) supported the idea that avatars are more effective when the consumer perceives them as being similar in appearance or personality, a pair of studies also suggests that ethnic identity may be particularly salient as one dimension of similarity. Appiah and Elias (2009) found that Black consumers responded more positively to Black avatars than White avatars, and indeed simply a voice that they identified as being Black was enough to contribute to this effect.

For their experiment, Appiah and Elias (2009) recruited a sample of 121 participants who identified themselves as Black/African American. The experiment was a three (avatar: Black versus White versus ethnically ambiguous) × two (ethnic identity: weak versus strong) between-subjects design. The avatar was manipulated by randomly assigning each participant to one of the three conditions, and the ethnic identity groups were split using a measured variable. A version of the Acura automobile Web page was created, and a female avatar whose ethnicity varied with the condition served as a spokesperson. The experimenters then measured five dependent variables: perceived similarity to the avatar, identification with the avatar, attitude toward the avatar, attitude toward the brand, and recall of product information.

The participants, as expected, rated the Black avatar as being more similar to themselves than the White or ethnically ambiguous avatar; and they rated the ethnically ambiguous avatar as being more similar to themselves than the White avatar. The researchers also found a main effect for race of the avatar on attitude toward the avatar and recall, although no main effect was found for attitude toward the brand. Although Appiah and Elias don't attempt to explain this apparent disparity (i.e., the lack of transfer from attitude toward the avatar to attitude toward the brand), the result is not unexpected given that the experimenters used an existing brand, (i.e., Acura), so a laboratory experiment would be unlikely to have much impact on these pre-existing attitudes.

Appiah and Elias (2009) repeated the experimental procedure in a second study, but they replaced the ethnically ambiguous voice used in the first study with a voice specific to the race of each avatar. With the addition of the voice, the researchers found an interaction between the race of the avatar and the strength of the participants' ethnic identity. Blacks with weak ethnic identities actually perceived themselves as being more similar to the White avatar. This, of course, does not change the fact that, whatever the perceptions of race and ethnic identity, consumers appear to be more positively disposed toward avatars they perceive as being similar to themselves.

Managerial Implications: Outcomes of Avatar Salespeople

Each of the studies discussed in this chapter has led to the conclusion that avatars produce desirable outcomes for marketers. The mechanism by which these outcomes occur appears to be a social response process by which humans perceive and respond to cues that initiate relational schema that they use in interactions with other humans. The presence of an avatar is not necessary for this phenomenon to occur, as computer users have been shown to respond to computers themselves as they would to another person, despite knowing full well that they are interacting with a machine (Moon, 2000; Moon & Nass, 1996; Nass & Moon, 2000; Reeves & Nass, 1996). However, the multiple studies recounted in this chapter demonstrate unambiguously that the presence of an avatar—by providing the consumer with more social cues through voice, interactivity, and personality—magnifies the social response from the consumer. This leads, both directly and indirectly, to a number of outcomes that marketers should find desirable and beneficial.

First, the presence of an avatar has been linked to increased purchase intent. By increasing the levels of arousal, pleasure, and flow, an avatar provides more hedonic and utilitarian value to the consumer, which in turn increases purchase intent (Wang et al., 2007). The hedonic value of an avatar is derived from the increased enjoyment a consumer may experience in his or her online shopping, and the utilitarian value may be derived from the perceived information quality provided toward the completion of a task. Online consumers are motivated by both utilitarian needs, such as problem-solving, and hedonic needs, such as fantasies, feelings, and fun (Childers, Carr, Peck, & Carson, 2001). The hedonic value of the online transaction is derived from an experiential component that includes pursuing fantasies, feelings, and fun (Hirschman & Holbrook, 1982; Holbrook & Hirschman, 1982). The avatar appears to satisfy the need for pleasure by providing social interaction that simulates the presence of a shopping companion or guide. The utilitarian value of the online transaction lies in the functional aspect of the transaction, that is, how well the consumer is able to complete the task to his satisfaction. Consumers perceive information provided by avatars as being more credible (Holzwarth et al., 2006) and trustworthy (Bente, Rüggenberg, Krämer, & Eschenburg, 2008; Wang & Bodness, 2010) than online information without an avatar, and perceive the communication quality to be higher (Taylor, 2010). Thus, the avatar contributes to the fulfillment of both hedonic and utilitarian needs, resulting in increased purchase intent.

Second, the presence of an avatar is linked to enduring attitudes that may lead to enduring relationships and future purchases. Holzwarth et al. (2006) found not only a positive relationship between avatars and purchase intent, but also satisfaction with the retailer and attitude toward the product. Bente et al. (2008) found that the increased social presence from avatars improved interpersonal trust, and Wang and Bodness (2010) demonstrated that consumers' emotional responses and trust in online retailers are more positive when an avatar is present. Taylor (2008, 2010) suggested that the presence of avatars might improve the consumer's perception of the benefits she derives from a relationship with the retailer, which has positive implications for relationship marketing efforts. Moreover, Taylor (2010) found that, after a service failure, consumer loyalty remained higher when an avatar was present during the experience or service recovery.

Undoubtedly, marketing managers should explore the possibility of using avatars as virtual sales agents. The empirical evidence supporting the positive outcomes from avatars continues to mount, adding to the increasingly large store of anecdotal evidence. Using avatars appears to improve purchase intent, brand attitude, trust, and loyalty. Moreover, these studies suggest that online marketing managers who implement avatars on their Web sites should pay close attention to the physical characteristics and personalities of their avatar salespeople. Research into ethnic identity and salesperson/buyer similarity in avatars suggests that segmentation strategies should be considered when employing avatar agents on their sites. Finally, a well-designed and strategically integrated avatar salesforce may very well provide a retailer with a competitive advantage.

Theoretical Implications and Directions for Future Research

For marketing theoreticians, avatars provide an interesting context for expanding and building upon previous research in several areas. First, social response theory (Reeves & Nass, 1996) is a natural fit in this area, inasmuch as it argues that people apply social rules to respond to computers when they possess humanlike attributes. Because avatars possess humanlike attributes such as appearance, personality, voice, and interactivity, an avatar-enabled Web site provides the perfect context to explore the dimensions and boundaries of social response theory. A number of years ago, Moon and Nass (1996) posed the question, "How 'real' are computer personalities?" With advances in interactivity, speech recognition, animation, and voice simulation, the answer to that question will soon be, "Very real!" Indeed, as avatars' level of realness continues to improve, future researchers may ask not whether humans treat computer-generated avatars as social actors (they inarguably do), but whether there are any differences at all between interactions with a hyperrealistic avatar and an actual salesperson.

Avatars also provide a context for expanding the literature on customer/salesperson interactions and source effects. Consistent with the similarity-attraction hypothesis (Byrne, Clore, & Smeaton, 1986; Byrne & Nelson, 1965), consumers appear to prefer to interact with avatars who are similar to themselves in both appearance and personality. The studies cited in this chapter have focused on race and gender (Appiah & Elias, 2009; Pentina & Taylor, 2010), attractiveness and expertise (Holzwarth et al. 2006), and need for cognition (Pentina & Taylor, 2010). Future research should explore many of the other dimensions of personality from the Big Five to test the boundaries of this effect.

The advent of the walking, breathing, three-dimensional avatars that inhabited the world of the motion picture *Avatar* may be relegated to a distant future, if ever, but the present is home to an increasing assortment of avatar salespeople and spokespersons. As they become more sophisticated and realistic, marketing practitioners will certainly find innovative new roles for avatars in their marketing efforts. Avatar research, although

still in its nascent stages, holds much potential not only for guiding practitioners in the application and utilization of virtual representatives, but
also for exploring the relationship between human consumers and nonhuman salespeople.

References

Aaker, J. L. (1997). Dimensions of brand personality. *Journal of Marketing Research*,
34(3), 347–356.

Appiah, O. & Elias, T. (2009). Effects of ethnic identity and ethnic ambiguous
agents on consumer responses to websites. In N. T. Wood & M. R. Solomon
(Eds.). *Virtual social identity and consumer behavior* (pp. 159–180). Armonk,
NY: M.E. Sharpe.

Baker, J., Grewal, D., & Levy, M. (1992). An experimental approach to making
retail store environmental decisions. *Journal of Retailing*, *68*, 445–445.

Bargh, J. A. & Chartrand, T. (1999). The unbearable automaticity of being.
American Psychologist, *54*(7), 462–479.

Batra, R., Lehmann, D. R., & Singh, D. (1993). The brand personality compo-
nent of brand goodwill: Some antecedents and consequences. In D.A. Aaker
& A. Biel (Eds.), *Brand equity and advertising* (pp. 83–102). Hillsdale, NJ:
Lawrence Erlbaum.

Bente, G., Rüggenberg, S., Krämer, N. C., & Eschenburg, F. (2008). Avatar-
mediated networking: Increasing social presence and interpersonal trust
in net-based collaborations, *Human Communication Research*, *34*(2),
287–318.

Berry, L. L., Carbone, L. P., & Haeckel, S. H. (2002). Managing the total customer
experience, *MIT Sloan Management Review*, *43*(3), 85–89.

Berscheid, E. (1994). Interpersonal relationships. *Annual Review of Pscyhology*,
45, 79–130.

Byrne, D. (1962). Response to attitude similarity-dissimilarity as a function of
affiliation need. *Journal of Personality* (30), 659–663.

Byrne, D., Clore, G. L., & Smeaton, G. (1986).The attraction hypothesis: Do similar attitudes affect anything? *Journal of Personality and Social Psychology*,
51(6), 1167–1170.

Byrne, D., Griffitt, W., & Stefaniak, D. (1967). Attraction and similarity of personality characteristics. *Journal of Personality and Social Psychology*, *51*(1),
82–90.

Byrne, D. & Nelson, D. (1965). Attraction as a linear function of proportion of
positive reinforcements. *Journal of Personality and Social Psychology*, *1*(6),
659–663.

Cacioppo, J. T., Petty, R. E., & Kao, C. F. (1984). The efficient assessment of need for
cognition. *Journal of Personality and Social Psychology*, *45*, 306–307.

Cacioppo, J. T., Petty, R. E., & Morris, K. (1983). Effects of need for cognition on message evaluation, argument recall, and persuasion. *Journal of Personality and Social Psychology, 45*, 805–818.

Cerezo, E., Baldassarri, S., & Seron, F. (2007). Interactive agents for multimodal emotional user interaction. *IADIS Multi Conferences on Computer Science and Information Systems*, 35–42.

Childers, T. L., Carr, C. L., Peck, J., & Carson, S. (2001). Hedonic and utilitarian motivations for online retail shopping behavior. *Journal of Retailing, 77*(4), 511–535.

Churchill, G. A., Jr., Collins, R. H., & Strang, W. A. (1975). Should retail salespersons be similar to their customers? *Journal of Retailing, 51*(3), 29–42.

Colburn, R. A., Cohen, M. F., & Drucker, S. M. (2000). The role of eye gaze in avatar mediated conversational interfaces. *Microsoft Research, Microsoft Corporation.*

Connelly, M. (2007). Solstice transforms in summer flick. *Automotive news.* Detroit, MI: Crain.

Crosby, L. A., Evans, K. R., & Cowles, D. (1990). Relationship quality in services selling: An interpersonal influence perspective. *Journal of Marketing, 54*(3), 68–81.

Csikszentmihalyi, M. (1988). *Optimal experience: Psychological studies of flow in consciousness*, Cambridge, UK: Cambridge University Press.

DeMara, R. F., Gonzalez, A. J., Hung, V., Leon-Barth, C., Dookhoo, R. A., Jones, S., Johnson, A., Leigh, J., Renambot, L., & Lee, S. (2008). Towards interactive training with an avatar-based human-computer interface (Vol. 2008). NTSA.

Digman, J. M. (1990). Personality structure: Emergence of the five-factor model. *Annual Review of Psychology, 41*(1), 417–440.

Dion, P., Easterling, D., & Miller, S. J. (1995). What is really necessary in successful buyer/seller relationships? *Industrial Marketing Management, 24*(1), 1–9.

Dwyer, S., Richard, O., & Shepherd, C. D. (1998). An exploratory study of gender and age matching in the salesperson-prospective customer dyad: Testing similarity-performance predictions. *Journal of Personal Selling & Sales Management, 18*(4), 55–70.

Gadel, M. S. (1964). Concentration by salesmen on congenial prospects. *Journal of Marketing, 28*(2), 64–66.

Hampp, A. (2007). Second Life losing lock on virtual-site marketing. *Advertising Age, 78*(27), 10.

Harris, M. B. & Baudin, H. (1973). The language of altruism: The effects of language, dress and ethnic group. *Journal of Social Psychology, 91*, 37–41.

Hayes-Roth, B. Sincoff, E., Brownston, L., & Lent, B. (1995). Directed improvisation with animated puppets. In *CHI '95 Conference on Human-Computer Interaction*, Denver, May 7–11, pp. 79–80.

Heeter, C. (2000). Interactivity in the context of designed experiences. *Journal of Interactive Advertising, 1*(1). Retrieved December 29, 2011 from http://jiad.org/article2

Hemp, P. (2006). Avatar-based marketing. *Harvard Business Review, 84*(6), 48–56.

Hendrick, C. C., Stikes, S., & Murry, E. J. (1972). Race versus belief similarity as determinants of attraction in a live interaction setting. *Journal of Experimental Research in Personality, 6*(2–3), 162–168.

Hirschman, E. C. & Holbrook, M. B. (1982). Hedonic consumption: Emerging concepts, methods and propositions. *Journal of Marketing, 46*(3), 92–101.

Holbrook, M. B. & Hirschman, E. C. (1982). The experiential aspects of consumption: Consumer fantasies, feelings, and fun. *Journal of Consumer Research, 9*(2), 132–140.

Holzwarth, M., Janiszewski, C., & Neumann, M. M. (2006). The influence of avatars on online consumer shopping behavior. *Journal of Marketing, 70*(4), 1, 19–36.

Isbister, K. & Nass, C. (2000). Consistency of personality in interactive characters: Verbal cues, non-verbal cues, and user characteristics. *International Journal of Human-Computer Studies, 53*(2), 251–267.

Jin, S.-A. A. & Bolebruch, J. (2009). Avatar-based advertising in Second Life: The role of presence and attractiveness of virtual spokespersons. *Journal of Interactive Advertising, 10*(1), 51–60.

Jin, S.-A. A. & Sung, Y. (2010). The roles of spokes-avatars' personalities in brand communication in 3d virtual environments. *Journal of Brand Management, 17*(5), 317–327.

Jones, E., Moore, J. N., Stanaland, A. J. S., & Wyatt, R. A. J. (1998). Salesperson race and gender and the access and legitimacy paradigm: Does difference make a difference? *Journal of Personal Selling & Sales Management, 18*(4), 71–88.

Langer, E. (1989). *Mindfulness*. Reading, MA: Addison-Wesley.

Lichtenthal, J. D. & Tellefsen, T. (2001). Toward a theory of business buyer-seller similarity. *Journal of Personal Selling & Sales Management, 21*(1), 1–14.

Lord, K. R., Lee, M.-S., & Sauter, P. L. (1995). The combined influence hypothesis: Central and peripheral antecedents of attitude toward the ad. *Journal of Advertising, 24*(1), 73–85.

Markus, H. (1977). Self-schemata and processing information about the self. *Journal of Personality and Social Psychology, 35*(2), 63–78.

McCracken, G. (1988). *Culture and consumption*. Bloomington: Indiana University Press.

McGoldrick, P. J., Keeling, K. A., & Beatty, S. F. (2008). A typology of roles for avatars in online retailing. *Journal of Marketing Management, 24*(3–4), 433–461.

Mick, D. G. (1992). Levels of subjective comprehension in advertising processing and their relations to ad perceptions, attitudes, and memory. *Journal of Business Research, 56*, 247–255.

Miniard, P. W., Bhatla, S., Lord, K. R., Dikson, P. R., & Unnava, H. R. (1992). Picture-based persuasion processes and the moderating role of involvement. *Journal of Consumer Research, 18*(June), 92–107.

Moon, Y. (2000). Intimate exchanges: Using computers to elicit self-disclosure from consumers. *Journal of Consumer Research, 26*(4), 323–339.

Moon, Y. & Nass, C. (1996). How 'real' are computer personalities? *Communication Research, 23*(6), 651–674.

Nass, C. & Moon, Y. (2000). Machines and mindlessness: Social responses to computers. *Journal of Social Issues, 56*(1), 81–103.

Nass, C., Moon, Y., & Carney, P. (1996). Are people polite to computers? Responses to computer-based interviewing systems. *Journal of Applied Social Psychology, 29*(5), 1093–110.

Pentina, I. (2011). Exploring self–brand connection in the social media context: The case of Twitter. *Proceedings of Academy of Marketing Science Conference*, Coral Gables, FL.

Pentina, I. & Taylor, D. G. (2010). Exploring source effects for online sales outcomes: The role of avatar-buyer similarity. *Journal of Customer Behaviour, 9*(2), 135–150.

Petty, R. E. & Cacioppo, J. T. (1981). *Attitudes and persuasion: Classic and contemporary approaches*. Dubuque, IA: Wm. C. Brown.

Petty, R. E., Cacioppo, J. T., & Goldman, R. (1981). Personal involvement as a determinant of argument-based persuasion. *Journal of Personality and Social Psychology, 41*, 847.

Petty, R. E., Cacioppo, J. T., & Heesacker, M. (1981). Effects of rhetorical questions on persuasion: A cognitive response analysis. *Journal of Personality and Social Psychology, 40*(3), 432–440.

Reeves, B. & Nass, C. (1996). *The media equation: How people treat computers, television and new media like real people and places*, Cambridge, MA: CSLI.

Ryckman, R. (2004). *Theories of personality*. Belmont, CA: Thomson/Wadsworth.

Smith, J. B. (1998). Buyer-seller relationships: Similarity, relationship managements, and quality. *Psychology & Marketing, 15*(1), 3–21.

Steuer, J. (1992). Defining virtual reality: Dimensions determining telepresence. *Journal of Communication, 42*(4), 73–93.

Stotland, E., Zander, A., & Natsoulas, T. (1961). Generalization of interpersonal similarity. *Journal of Abnormal Social Psychology, 62*(2), 250–256.

Taylor, D. G. (2008). Virtual connections: The role of avatars in online relationship marketing. In *Academy of Marketing Science Annual Conference*, Vancouver, BC.

Taylor, D. G. (2010). Putting a face with a name: Avatars, relationship marketing and service recovery. *International Journal of Electronic Commerce & Retailing, 3*(4), 363–381.

Taylor, J. L. & Woodside, A. G. (1982). Effects on buying behavior of references to expert and referent power. *Journal of Social Psychology, 117*(1), 25–31.

Trevino, L. K. & Webster, J. (1992). Flow in computer-mediated communication. *Communication Research, 19*(5), 539.

Wang, L. & Bodness, D. (2010). Can avatars enhance consumer trust and emotion in online retail sales? *International Journal of Electronic Commerce & Retailing, 3*(4), 341–362.

Wang, L. C., Baker, J., Wagner, J. A., & Wakefield, K. (2007). Can a retail web site be social? *Journal of Marketing, 71*(3), 143–157.

Wheeler, S. C., Petty, R. E., & Bizer, G. Y. (2005). Self-schema matching and attitude change: Situational and dispositional determinants of message elaboration. *Journal of Consumer Research, 31*(4), 787–797.

Wood, N. T., Solomon, M. R., & Englis, B. G. (2005). Personalisation of online avatars: Is the messenger as important as the message? *International Journal of Internet Marketing and Advertising, 2*(1–2), 143–161.

Yadav, M. S. & Varadarajan, R. (2005). Interactivity in the electronic marketplace: An exposition of the concept and implications for research. *Journal of the Academy of Marketing Science, 33*(4), 585–603.

Zaichkowsky, J. L. (1985). Measuring the involvement construct. *Journal of Consumer Research, 12*(3), 341–352.

3

Overcoming Human Limits Through the Satisfaction of Desires on Virtual Worlds

Lilia Boujbel
ESG, Université du Québec à Montréal

Leila El Kamel
TELUQ, Université du Québec à Montréal

After video games, network games, and multiplayer online games, metaverses include thousands of residents distributed worldwide. The enthusiasm is due to an immersive and rewarding experience offered by virtual worlds during which residents play, interact, build, and express themselves. This offer generates a significant monthly income amounting to billions of dollars for the companies' editors and the various actors in the chain of production and distribution of these metaverses.

Consumption is an important activity within virtual worlds (Kaplan & Haenlein, 2009; Lin, 2007). These worlds are full of opportunities to live different kinds of experiences and to realize consumption desires and dreams that are sometimes unattainable in real life (RL); (Castronova, 2005; Markos & Labrecque, 2008). Several consumers as well as companies adopted these spaces where almost everything could be attainable and feasible. These universes are spaces of virtual consumption, where everything could be bought and sold (Castronova, 2005). There is almost no limit to what could be done within these worlds; perhaps, the only limits are the technical aspects of the game and the imagination of the resident (Castronova, 2005).

This research is the second exploratory step of a research project designed (1) to explore the extent to which virtual worlds could represent an opportunity to satisfy or to meet several types of desires unattainable in the real world, (2) to see whether the conceptualization of the virtual influences the way consumption desires are apprehended in the virtual and the real worlds, (3) to elaborate a typology of consumption desires that may be satisfied through virtual worlds, (4) and finally to verify the consumer's eternal dissatisfaction. Because it is a project in progress, in this chapter we focus mainly on addressing the third objective.

The first section presents the theoretical background in the areas of virtual worlds and consumption desires. Virtual worlds are presented in general as well as the different motivations that let consumers engage in these worlds. Additionally, a discussion of the importance of consumption as an activity in these worlds and the place of desires in virtual worlds is held. The second section describes the methodological approach selected to answer the research issues of this chapter. More specifically, it details the steps of a nonparticipant observation of a French-speaking forum. The third section discusses the results, and the last section highlights the main contributions and the limits of the research.

Literature Review

Virtual Worlds

Schroeder (2008) defines a virtual world as "a persistent virtual environment in which residents live and interact with others." It is a synchronized and persistent network where people are represented by avatars and which is facilitated by connected computers (Bell, 2008). Virtual worlds as a playful practice of a new age appeared with the enlargement of Internet bandwidth, the improving of the interface and computer capacities, but also with the development of software and real-time simulation programs. Unlike their precursors such as MUDs (multiuser domains), virtual worlds allow the meeting of several thousand residents simultaneously and give them the opportunity to evolve through avatars in persistent worlds. Virtual worlds are not limited in time and continue to occur even when residents are disconnected. In these universes, residents live individually or in groups, and discuss and create objects, scenery, and stories. By logging on for hours and hours, residents are creating virtual lives almost parallel to their real lives. The resident has the freedom to choose one or more individual or collective identities (avatars and groups) throughout the experience, implying consumption choices. The universe is defined by the edition company and inspired by fantasy, historical battles, science fiction, sports practices, real life, and so on. In addition to the theme, the world also differs according to the available attributes of avatars, items that residents can create and manipulate, and actions they can undertake. Thus, the resident could choose the virtual world, in part, according to his needs in terms of construction and expression of the individual and collective identity he wants.

From the beginning of the metaverses' appearance, noting that these virtual worlds combine technical, psychological, and social aspects, researchers in different disciplines such as science communication and information, social psychology, and sociology have been interested in studying them. Therefore, the phenomenon was studied according to different issues, different perspectives, and different approaches. El Kamel (2009) considers that the literature review of work in these disciplines has shown that in addition to technical aspects, examples of the main issues dealt with include:

- Economic issues: Direct revenues, virtual economy, parallel trade, copyright
- Sociodemographic issues: Gender, age, country of origin
- Motivational issues: Motivation and reasons for players to participate in virtual worlds
- Experiential issues: Immersion, player-actor concept, narratology versus ludology
- Identity issues: Multiavatars, avatar choice, player body versus avatar body
- Social issues: Sociality, group play, guilds, relations
- Subversive issues: Addiction, violence, confusion of real and virtual

Moreover, as the amount of research on virtual worlds has increased, some studies have also focused on virtual worlds as a research context and specifically studied the specificities of this research field and the adaptations of traditional methods with respect to these specificities (El Kamel & Rigaux-Bricmont, 2009). Several researchers have also focused on studying the residents' motivations in terms of the reasons that stimulate them to spend many hours in front of their console or their computers at the expense of other activities (Alix, 2005; Bartle, 1996; Iversen, 2005; Kellar, Watters, & Duffy, 2005; Lucas & Sherry, 2004; Taylor, 2003; Yee, 2002). Some studies have led to a typology of motivational profiles of the residents. The most famous and the oldest study on motivations is that of Richard Bartle (1996). The author builds a typology based on a participant observation of MUDs, which are the first generations of virtual worlds. According to the virtual world nature, a list can be easily drawn of the main motivations, such as accomplishment and challenge, exploration and immersion, manipulation and fighting, leadership, relationship and socialization, identity game, imagination and narrative, fun, excitement, and addiction. These motivations tend to sway the choice of activities that residents decide to undertake during their experiences in the metaverse.

Consumption in Virtual Worlds and the Place of Desires

As mentioned in the introduction to this chapter, consumption is an important aspect of virtual worlds. The residents of these worlds have the freedom to choose one or more avatars to evolve in the virtual world, and in doing so they find themselves faced with several consumption choices (El Kamel, 2009). Noticing the importance of consumption activities within these worlds, researchers on consumer behavior have begun to consider the phenomenon of virtual worlds as consumption experiences. Virtual worlds seem to offer a fun experience for the residents, allowing them to undergo strong emotions by consuming virtual objects and avatars. Several studies focus on the implications of virtual worlds in terms of consumption. El Kamel and Bricmont (2011) distinguished different types of research in the domain such as studies addressing the representation of identity through avatars (Parmentier & Rolland, 2009; Messinger et al., 2008; Vidcan & Ulusoy, 2008; Becerra & Stutts, 2008; Boostrom, 2008; Bryant & Akerman, 2009; Sundar & Kim, 2009; Belisle & Bodur, 2010), studies about the consumption of products and brands as well as possessions and attachment to virtual objects (Haenlein & Kaplan, 2009; Landay, 2008; Martin, 2008; Park, Nah, DeWester, Eschenbrenner, & Jeon, 2008), and studies about the implications of social interactions on consumption in virtual worlds (Hinsch & Bloch, 2009; Brown & Tracy, 2009; Crete, St.-Onge, Merle, Arsenault, & Nantel, 2009).

Kaplan and Haenlein (2009) focused on studying the motivations of the residents of virtual worlds from a consumption perspective. In their consumption experience, residents seem to seek the hedonic side of the experience, as well as interpersonal relationships, learning, and financial enrichment. The authors also conclude that these motivations are likely to influence the activities that residents undertake in the virtual world and therefore result in an important activity of shopping for improving the appearance of the avatar, for fun, and for the achievement of selected activities.

Although some researchers have sought to highlight the specificities of the consumer experience in virtual worlds, Denegri-Knott and

Molesworth (2010) present a detailed overview of the concepts and practices of digital virtual consumption (DVC) and conclude that practices of the online consumer are not at odds with those of material consumption but rather an extension of the use of imagination in the generation of pleasure and fun.

The corpus of studies about consumption in virtual worlds is more and more significant, however, some general questions remain unanswered. What is the place and importance of consumption desires within these worlds? What are the different kinds of desires that could be satisfied through virtual consumption? Before synthesizing the literature on consumption desires within virtual worlds, it is important to briefly define the concept of desire in general.

Consumption desires are an important aspect of human life because they represent what people want to obtain, as well as their aspirations (Diener & Seligman, 2002). The concept has been studied in consumer behavior to provide a more realistic comprehension of the daily experiences of consumers and their relationship to consumption (Belk, Ger, & Askegaard, 2003; Boujbel, 2010). The experience of desire is subjective, as each consumer experiences it with a different level of intensity (Boujbel, 2007, 2010). The desire is induced by the thought of, or the encounter with, a fit object not possessed when such possession seems to be called for (Frijda, 1986). Desire is defined as "a powerful cyclic emotion that is both discomforting and pleasurable" (Belk et al., 2003, p. 326), and as such it is an emotionally ambivalent experience (Belk et al., 2003; Ramanathan & Williams, 2007).

Through virtual worlds, new alternatives and opportunities are available to help consumers satisfy more eccentric consumption desires and fantasies. Indeed, the emergence of virtual worlds offers alternatives to consume virtually an unlimited set of objects that seem inaccessible in real life (Lin, 2007). Studies, specifically dedicated to explore the manifestations of consumption desires within a virtual world, are still scarce in the literature on consumer behavior. However, there is interest in the concept. Recent studies reveal that such a concept of desire is inherent to the existence of these worlds (El Kamel & Boujbel, 2011; Landay, 2008). While studying consumption experiences in this context, Markos and Labrecque (2008) noticed that residents are more likely to try to live different experiences without feeling the pressure of social norms that can sometimes be restrictive in real life. Residents are less inhibited and they feel free to explore their creativity. Results of the research support the idea that practically anything is possible in a virtual world. As the researchers mention, in the virtual world, Second Life (SL), desires and dreams become feasible, and they are of different natures such as to fly, go beyond the barriers of gender (male–female), and even to live a nonhuman life (e.g., an object or an animal).

In the same vein, the majority of participants in the individual interviews conducted for this research within Second Life associate their consumption activities to desires or cyber-needs rather than to real needs. The origin of consumption desires could be the real or the virtual world, however, the participants in the interviews point out that there are no real or vital needs in a virtual world. Cyber-needs are, for their part, functional in the sense that they are necessary to the evolution of the avatar in the game (El Kamel and Boujbel, 2011).

In recent research, Denegri-Knott and Molesworth (2010) elaborate a taxonomy that considers digital virtual consumption (DVC) as a stimulation of consumers' desires, an actualization of their daydreams and fantasies, and an experimentation of behaviors reprehensible in real life. The authors indicate that virtual worlds permit living strong emotions that constantly motivate the player to explore, imagine, discover, and experience new things. The emotions seem to be strong enough to reiterate the desire to consume new virtual objects and to live different kinds of experiences.

Looking more closely at the desires expressed by residents of Second Life, El Kamel and Boujbel (2011) find that they can be a priori related to three different types: desires of virtual material objects (e.g., cars, houses, clothes), fantasy desires (e.g., flying, teleporting, staying forever young), and shameful desires (e.g., socially reprehensible desires). Noting the importance of the concept of desire in the context of virtual consumption as well as the opportunity to deepen research in this field, the exploration of the concept is further extended in this chapter by suggesting a typology of desires that can be satisfied through virtual consumption.

Method

In order to explore consumption desires in virtual worlds and contrast them with desires in the real world, the authors opted for a qualitative approach to delve deeply into the lived experiences of the residents of the virtual world, Second Life. Wacheux (1996) considers that the implementation of a qualitative research process seeks to understand the why and the how of events in concrete situations. There are different ways of doing qualitative research. According to Creswell (2007), there are five types of qualitative research: (1) narrative research, (2) phenomenology, (3) grounded theory, (4) ethnography, and (5) case study. The choice of the approach adopted has been greatly colored by the synthetic comparison conducted by Creswell (2007) concerning these different methodological approaches in qualitative research and the case study was, finally, selected. Yin (1984) defines the case study as an empirical inquiry that examines a contemporary phenomenon in its real-life context where the boundaries between phenomenon and context are not clearly evident and in which multiple sources of information are used. Also, Gagnon (2005) considers that the case study method provides access to a deep understanding of phenomena, processes that compose them, and the actors who are implicated.

Case Study

In this research, the case study type is instrumental in the sense that the case is considered of secondary interest. It plays a supporting role, which facilitates the exploration of consumption desires. In addition, given the time and energy invested in this exercise, it was too ambitious to try to explore several virtual worlds simultaneously. However, this approach has limitations regarding external validity and thus the generalization of the results (Gagnon, 2005).

To conduct the empirical case study it was necessary to choose a virtual world, and it was the metaverse, Second Life, in the research at hand. In what follows, a brief presentation of the main features of Second Life is given and the rationale underlying it is presented. Second Life is a virtual world that is difficult to define. It is a mixture of MMOG (massively multiplayer online games) and simulations. It is a virtual world where consumers choose an avatar to live in a parallel persistent world. Unlike in MMOGs, in Second Life the user has no predetermined goal or quest. In 2009, users totalled over 481 million hours of attendance and the transactions were worth 567 million U.S. dollars (Hervet, El Kamel, & Rigaux-Bricmont, 2010). It derives its popularity from the almost absolute freedom it offers to consumers in terms of creation of avatars and objects. Its second advantage lies in the fact that access to the world is free. Beyond entertainment, SL is a true place of enrichment and a market where all creations can be sold, bought, traded, and rented. Second Life was created in 2003 by LindenLab and co-produced by the residents (Bonsu & Darmody,

2008). Companies such as Telus, IBM, Toyota, American Apparel, Wells Fargo Bank, BBC, and Harvard University among others used it to promote their products and services or provide a Web site for meeting and entertainment for their staff. Second Life is a phenomenon that has become increasingly popular worldwide and the number of residents has been growing exponentially. In their work on social media, Kaplan and Haenlein (2010) considered Second Life as a virtual social world (MSV) that they compared with virtual game worlds such as World of Warcraft. A main difference is that one of the main activities of the residents of SL is to communicate and meet people rather than play the role of an imaginary character.

In the first step of the project, individual interviews were held within the virtual world of Second Life (El Kamel & Boujbel, 2011). The two major advantages the first step of the project provides are the immersion of the researcher and the preliminary results of 10 in-depth interviews realized within the virtual world (El Kamel & Boujbel, 2011). In fact, to meet the objectives of the research project, the long experience and expertise of one of the researchers with Second Life was of great usefulness. One of the authors had already held different studies within this metaverse and had been immersed in this virtual world since 2006. The researcher had a perfect knowledge of the functioning of the game (technical aspects) and the culture of its residents. She was familiar with the specific vocabulary used and had an elaborated list of contacts that permitted us to recruit participants for the in-depth interviews.

The individual interviews were conducted via the interaction between the researcher's avatar and 10 participants recruited on a voluntary basis. The in-world data collection was done through avatars that moved in a 3-D graphical environment and interacted through chats and instant messages. The two main themes covered during the interviews were: (1) consumption desires in Second Life and the extent to which this virtual world is considered as an alternative to satiate real consumption desires, and (2) experiences of consumption desires in the real world, the nature of those desires, and their importance in everyday life.

In this chapter, the results of a nonparticipant observation of a French-speaking forum dedicated to the residents of Second Life are reported. As a second step of the whole project, the main objective of the nonparticipant observation is to elaborate a typology of consumption desires that may be satisfied through virtual worlds.

Nonparticipant Observation of a French-Speaking Forum

A nonparticipant observation of an online forum consists of the analysis of text-based talk on discussion boards posted by the members of a community (Hewer & Brownlie, 2007; Kozinets, 2010). To address the objectives of the research previously mentioned, we examined and analyzed the respondents spontaneously posted by the participants on a French-speaking forum dedicated to the residents of Second Life. We used the information publicly available in the forum as a source of data.

Criteria and Procedure to Select the Forum

In order to select the appropriate forum to be analyzed, the procedure and criteria established by Kozinets (2010, p. 89) were followed for the site choice and entrée. The author insists on looking for online communities that are: relevant (they relate to the research focus and questions), active (they have recent and regular communications), interactive (they have a flow of communications between participants), substantial (they have a critical mass of communicators and an energetic feel), heterogeneous (they have a number of different participants), and data-rich (offering more detailed or descriptively rich data).

To locate the online community that meets these criteria and that will provide us with the richer set of data, the procedure recommended by Kozinets (2010) was followed. The initial step was doing research with key words on Google, such as "French Second Life forum." Because French-speaking residents were interviewed at the first stage of the project, it was considered more coherent to analyze a forum where participants were also francophone. After a careful examination of the results using the search engine previously mentioned, the decision was made to choose the site JeuxOnLine (Online Games; e.g., http://www.jeuxonline.info/).

The selected Web site covers the most innovative and popular MMOGs. It has as its objective to offer to the francophone players a collaborative service platform, where they are the main actors. JeuxOnLine allows participants to follow the daily news of several virtual worlds, publish their impressions about their favorite virtual world, view different game guides written by other gamers, share information, and read several messages posted by the members of the community. JeuxOnLine has more than 50 fan sites involving more than 400 enthusiastic residents who participate actively in the community of players.

The site page devoted to Second Life integrates several types of forums: general, technical, role-play, creation, and announcements. Our choice was to analyze the "general forum" because it has the widest set of respondents. Residents post on the forum different reflections about their experiences in SL.

The authors examined the respondents posted between July 2006 (7-22-2006) and April 2011 (4-04-2011), resulting in more than 4,600 posts in the forum. From the initial set of posts, 121 respondents were selected for further examination because they seemed to be directly or indirectly representative of consumption desires in the virtual world. To identify these posts, the authors took into account the relevance of the topic—based on the title of the post and a quick overview of the content—and they also considered the number of interactions among the members over this issue. A minimum of 20 interactions was deemed necessary unless the subject of the post was directly related to the topic of interest. The next step was the re-examination of the relevance of each subject, assessed through a more systematic examination of the content of the 121 selected posts and an evaluation of the richness of the interaction among the participants. Before presenting the results, Figure 3.1 summarizes the methodological steps undertaken for data collection

Results

The data to be analyzed were publicly available on the general forum dedicated to Second Life, on the Web site JeuxOnLine. The texts of the selected posts were compiled into a single file in order to be analyzed.

Despite the significant amounts of relevant data, a manual on-paper coding was privileged. As recommended by Kozinets (2010, p. 127), researchers with impressive, hard-copy filing skills may opt for manual data analysis and interpretation methods. The closeness to the data (Kozinets, 2010) was also a major concern inasmuch as the concept of desire is subtle and sometimes difficult to grasp.

The data analysis was inspired by the approach outlined by Spiggle (1994) consisting of categorization, abstraction, comparison, dimensionalization, integration, and iteration. These operations allow the researcher to organize the data, extract meaning, arrive at conclusions, and generate or confirm conceptual schemes and theories that describe the data (Spiggle, 1994, p. 493). For the interpretation of the data, a process based on a hermeneutic circle was adopted. As explained by Thompson, Pollio, and Locander

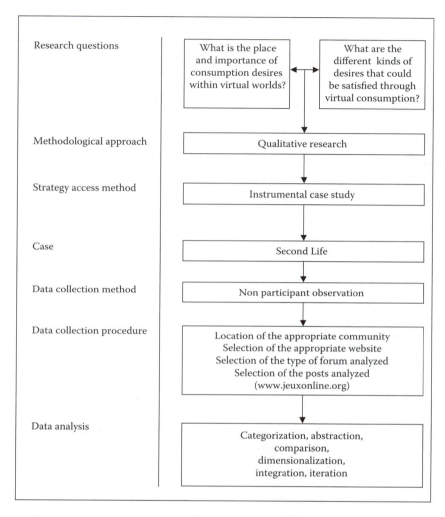

Figure 3.1 Methodological steps for the project.

(1994), the process is iterative and the parts of data are interpreted and reinterpreted in relation to the developing sense of the whole.

In the following sections, the findings of the nonparticipant observations are presented by including them verbatim to illustrate the main conclusions. Although the researchers didn't interact directly with the participants in the forum, no less than 121 posts were identified to be indicative of the nature and types of desires the residents may have or feel in the virtual world SL.

The respondents of the posts are also very suggestive about the ways residents feel their desires, think of them compared with the real world, and manage them.

Consumption and Desires in a Virtual World

As stated in the introduction to the chapter, consumption is an important activity in SL. On a post discussing "leisure and consumption," the consumption activities in SL are related by several participants as being at the heart of this virtual world.

> Second Life is for me the culmination of a world of consumption. We spend, there, without even having the notion of primary need. Everything has been created for this purpose and we find all the components necessary for a market economy: a currency, creation copyright and a cost of living. (Post "leisure and consumption")

> In my opinion, SL is one of the highest consumption spaces of any product whatsoever. The consumption of virtual unnecessary products in a capitalist societal mode of organization is truly a top, and that is true whatever the product consumed is; even to some extent the relationships between avatars. (Post "leisure and consumption")

Two posts discussing the average spending of residents in SL ("the average spending," "I spend a little, too much, to the madness") indicate a great variability. Some residents do not spend real money at all in SL and pay just for their Internet and electricity bills, expenses that are not limited or specific to SL. Other residents consider SL as a leisure pursuit or hobby, and as such they allocate a monthly budget to their SL activities.

Beyond the simple purchase of objects, the activity of shopping in SL is a very pleasant and hedonic experience. As in RL, in order to find the desired object or product the resident has to go around the shops. Whether individually or collectively, during the shopping activity the resident chooses places where to shop and, as in RL, has the opportunity to try the items before buying them.

> In SL , I love to shop and blow my inventory at least once a month.... (Post "And You, what are you doing in SL?")

> ... There is [sic] not one or two places (where to shop) but an astronomical quantity because we do not always find what we are looking for in one place

while it is in another; you need to do a "shopping promenade" in all what you can find as stores, until miraculously the Grail is carried out. (Post "shopping")

While analyzing the whole set of data, it has become evident that consumption activities in the virtual world Second Life reflect and turn around the satisfaction of desires, and for most cases they refer to consumption desires. As found through the individual interviews (El Kamel & Boujebl, 2011), the concept of "need" has little place in this world and is limited to "cyber-needs" useful for the functioning and evolution of the avatar. Nothing is really necessary or vital to an avatar; all of what is consumed reflects a desire of the resident for her avatar, or for herself (e.g., to live atypical experiences through the avatar).

In addition, in two interesting posts dealing with "the 1000 and one reasons to prefer SL to RL" and "SL = Dream," the majority of the participants state that they do not necessarily prefer their SL to their RL, but find that in the virtual world there are several advantages and attractions lacking in RL. Although the participants use the terms desire, dream, and fantasy interchangeably, SL is considered a space where a wide range of desires can be satisfied and where the limits of the RL can be overcome, as shown in the following quotation:

[SL is a . . .] Zone of escape, peaceful place. No irreversibility of certain decisions, no real drama, no destiny, no fate. Few tears, no blood, no foul zone. As a vain attempt to escape kitsch and the human condition. (Post "the 1000 and one reasons to prefer SL to RL")

SL is somehow an escape from RL. . . . We can access everything we want easily and without (or with little) constraints! (Post "the 1000 and one reasons to prefer SL to RL")

Real Life or Second Life: Where to Satiate the Desire?

Looking more closely at the types of desires expressed by the participants in the forum, we noticed that some desires expressed in SL mirrored RL desires of the residents whereas other desires were specific to the virtual world. A continuum of consumption desires going from what can be feasible in both worlds to what can be feasible only in SL can be drawn. It is worth noting that some desires can logically be satisfied in RL, but different kinds of constraints (time, money, competence) make them out of reach for the consumer (Boujbel, 2007), as can be seen through the comment of a resident:

> We often use the concept of "dream" for the "desires" or "illusions" of things that we know are almost on the borderline of what is possible. For example, I dream of having a sailboat of 20 meters long. . . . In such a case, SL comes into play because I can buy a yacht of 20 meters in SL and browse an open space. . . . So yes, these dreams I live them in SL; SL helps me to visualize them and to make them a little more "palpable.". . . (Post "SL = Dream")

The dynamics of virtual worlds offer many more alternatives to consumers because there is almost no limit to what they may desire. The object of desire does not even need to be realistic, giving free rein to the proliferation of the imagination. Video games are considered an imaginative escape from everyday routine (Molesworth, 2009).

> When you open the door of the world SL, it is the door of your imagination that you open. . . . Suddenly, you can, through a small avatar that you model at your image or at the image you would like to have, make a lot of things, things that you dreamed of; you can be whoever you want to be. . . . Forget the frustration, shyness, loneliness, illness. . . . (Post "SL = Dream")

The desires that can only be satisfied through SL represent fantastic desires and reveal the richness of imagination of the residents, as well as the wide range of possibilities offered in SL to satisfy these desires. As an example, for the appearance of the avatar, the resident may choose an imaginary shape. Such desires break completely with the real world, as they are feasible only in a virtual world.

> . . . My first avatar looks remarkably like me so that some residents recognized me. My second (avatar) breaks definitively with my humanity as it is one of those sublime Wyrms dragons. It is so nice to see that I spend my time looking at smoothing the color of my wings and extending my paw. . . . It is a way to leave anthropomorphism to get into fantasy. Now, I find humans so dull. Of course, I do not "dragonify" anywhere or at anytime, and especially not in crowded places. A dragon should remain a mythical character, shouldn't it? (Post "lets talk about your avatar")

The Typology of Consumption Desires in Virtual Worlds

Consumption in SL covers different aspects of the life of an avatar, so how can desires be distinguished from mere functional cyber-needs? A thorough reading and analysis of the data permit the researchers to distinguish and identify four types of desires expressed by the participants in the forums. These desires are related to the body and the appearance of the avatar, to its possessions, its relationships, and its environment.

Desires Related to the Body and the Appearance of the Avatar
The desires related to the body and appearance of the avatar translate on consumption of skins, shapes, hair, clothes, accessories, and animations. A resident can choose to evolve in the virtual world with a basic avatar, as it comes when he first registers. However, most residents in SL choose to improve the appearance of the avatar, trying for more sophisticated looks. Several posts attest to the presence of these desires. In fact, participants look for special clothes (e.g., posts "the best clothes shops," "looking for special clothes," "Japanese clothes," "oriental clothes," "the best place to shop for shoes"), special kinds of skin and shapes (e.g., post "skin and shape for black"), special accessories (e.g., post "pendant soul mate"), or particular animations (e.g., post "seeking a special dance"). Despite the existence of RL brands within SL (e.g., Adidas, American Apparel), the residents prefer SL designers for more originality and creativity.

Some desires related to the appearance of the avatar have their equivalent in RL and can be satisfied in both worlds (RL and SL). For instance, a consumer may choose from a variety of the available clothes and accessories in order to attain the look she desires. She may resort to plastic surgery to enhance her physical appearance. On the contrary, the satisfaction of some desires is only possible in SL. Through the manipulation of the avatar, the resident could change to different skin colors, she could try the transgender, or opt for a neutral gender avatar, and she can also choose a fantastic appearance.

> I am looking for a new skin, I don't like mine at all anymore. . . . I wish I could say the same thing in RL. (Post "Skin shops")

> There are costumes including shape, skin, objects, etc. . . . to turn into a cat, wolf, cow, snoopy or beep . . . whatever you want actually. Some are free; others are more sophisticated, available only in special shops, and paid. (Post "animals")

From several discussions between participants, it appears that desires related to the body and the appearance express the willingness of some residents to dissociate themselves from what is called a "noob" appearance (a "noob" is a new avatar; Boostrom, 2008). Investing and working on the appearance of the avatar is somehow an indicator of the evolution of the resident in the virtual world. This observation is coherent with the results of Boostrom (2008) related to the stigmatization of beginners in virtual worlds. The appearance of the avatar changes over time according to the desires of the resident. The changes result in the consumption of different kinds of objects to customize the avatar. They can also be a sign of the expertise and ability of the resident to create what he wants for the avatar. As expressed through the following quote, consuming and creating objects are done to reach the desired image the resident holds of his avatar.

> I think the conversation above mainly shows that each one has an idea of the avatar he wants; this idea may also vary or change over time. Similarly, willingness to pay or not (and how much) changes in relation to the capacities (or not) to create what we want. . . . (Post "a decent avatar")

Beyond the aesthetic aspect, the expression of concrete consumption desires related to the appearance of the avatar reveals a higher-order or more abstract desire. In fact, through an attractive avatar several residents are defying aging, death, handicaps, and several physical limits and constraints they face in RL. Exchanges between residents on the posts "Avatar, bold and beauty" and "skin for an old avatar", reveal that there aren't many old avatars and that the majority are young and beautiful. Some participants point to the fact that there is no need to have an older or an ugly avatar in a world where one can be forever young and attractive.

> This is Lisa (avatar's pseudo), my new avatar; I find her beautiful, very beautiful, touching, romantic, sad but dreamy. She is at my image. She is wandering into a world where everything is beautiful; she is wandering in a dream, in a utopia. I think we're all a little Lisa in SL; we dream; we are beautiful; we have a beautiful home and friends. This may not be the case in real life, so if a virtual platform can make us smile and make us dream, why not? (The avatar's pseudo has been changed. Post "avatar, bold and beauty")

Consumption desires related to the appearance of the avatar are also revealed through the search for uniqueness. Several residents invest time, money, and energy to distinguish their avatar from others in order to feel unique.

> I can say I am unique because I do everything including: the shape, skins, hair and clothing. What I'm wearing is not on the market and will never be. . . . Too many people have the same skins and clothes while I hate to be cloned, so I create some clothes and some skins that are only for me. (Post "To be unique in SL")

It's almost an everyday "work"; I try to choose a skin that is not well known or that is even customized. I make a mix-match of clothes and I choose a custom-ized AO (animation). . . . For those who are asking for shapes to sell: No way . . . I jealously or even religiously keep my shopping stores. . . ." (Post "To be unique in SL")

Desires Related to the Possession of Products and Objects

Within SL, a resident can have a huge elaborate inventory of products and objects. There is almost no limit to what he can possess. As shown through the quotation presented previously about the possession of a sailboat, some desires expressed by the participants mirror what they are eager to have in RL (e.g., luxurious houses, cars, furniture). Other desires are specific to the virtual world and could only be satisfied within this world; in SL a resident can own a sky-house or a spaceship.

Several posts in the forum reveal the diversity of possession desires felt and expressed by the residents. Several passionate discussions about the ownership of boats ("boats in SL," "boat on the water," "a small boat," "Ô my boat"), cars ("cars and Co."), airplanes ("I believe I can fly"), or spaceships ("to buy a spaceship") point not only to the diversity of these desires, but also to their intensity and the relative ease of their realization within the virtual world. On the post about the possession of an airplane, participants exchange all kinds of information about technical aspects of the models, locations for flights, and flying maneuvers. The discus-sion between participants is similar to that which can occur between real enthusiast pilots.

> . . . [N]o need to spend hours of reading to learn how to pilot a plane; this remains accessible to all people although not having any notion of aviation. (Post "I believe I can fly")

Another revealing example is the way the possession of a house takes place in SL. Residents who choose to have homes for their avatars are for the most part interested and invested in their decoration. Unlike real life where an individual needs a roof and a home, the avatar does not neces-sarily need one. Buying a home is in most cases a response to a desire and not a utility. This desire is even carried to the extreme when some residents express the willingness to go further in the decoration and customization of their homes, as expressed in the following:

> I love taking care of my 32.000 m² of heaven for that my few visitors like to spend a little time in it and feel like coming back . . . a little detail here, a new

little thing there. . . . I spend about 90% of my SL time there. (Post "and you, what are you doing in SL?")

The two types of desires related to the appearance and to the possessions of the avatar are somehow linked to the motivations of the residents within the virtual world. The resident who wants to have a job or business, to engage in an activity, a hobby, or a social event has to possess the appearance, the products, or objects that will allow her to do so.

Unlike in real life, working in SL is not necessary for the survival of the avatar. This is an activity that residents choose to undertake deliberately to earn RL money or simply to earn Lindens (SL money) to spend within SL and cover their fees. The work may represent a desire to exercise a particular profession such as a photographer or a manager, or just to establish a project that allows the resident to have a feeling of achievement and hold on the universe. The data collected show that, in general, working in Second Life leads to the emergence of several consumption desires related to the body, appearance, and possessions of the avatar. For example, to be a model, the resident must have a fairly provided inventory of clothing, hair, skins, shapes, poses, and animations. Just as in real life, to succeed in a career in modeling, the avatar must have the appropriate attitude, be professional, have a "book," and use the services of a professional photographer. However, unlike those in real life, all the effort and energy in SL are expended to satiate the desire to do this job and mostly for pleasure.

> In terms of inventory, you must have a wide range of high quality clothes that fit you well. (Post "to be a model")

> Being beautiful is easy; being a good model is difficult. You need a good knowledge of the rules of the game in general without being an expert, but you need to quickly learn how to use objects that could be given to you for example. . . . In terms of equipment, I met people who had more than 100 shapes and skins available. (Post "to be a model")

Desires Related to Relationships

Unlike virtual games, SL is considered as a social virtual world (Kaplan & Haenlein, 2010). It permits the residents to create a social network and to exchange with other people from different horizons. Because there is no real objective to the game, it gives the player the complete freedom to do whatever he wants and to evolve at his own pace.

The resident experiences a social life through the avatar. He can develop a sense of belonging to different groups and communities. Some relationships, such as friendship, marriage, and sexual ones can be enjoyed and lived similarly in both worlds (RL and SL) whereas others are more easily expressed in SL.

Each culture in RL frames what could be desired and the ways to satisfy those desires (Belk, Ger, & Askegaard, 2003), however, in the virtual world the resident can overcome the cultural and social limits. She has the opportunity to undergo different kinds of atypical experiences with others and can even have an asocial behavior that is illegal in RL. Within SL, many residents realize sexual fantasies (e.g., prostitution, BDSM, zoophilia) they do not have the opportunity or the courage to undertake in RL because of cultural or social pressures. Some exchanges between participants in the forum mention the existence of hard sexual experiences. Engaging in these activities is always synonymous with consumption of specific clothes and animations for the avatar.

> A friend of mine has the fantasy to sell her body, and this is what she loves the most in this "job" in SL. (Post "morality in SL")

> What I like about SL is this side which is not "clear" at all; a world of adults that is far away from any other MMO (massively multiplayer online game), and especially it is virtual! . . . And being adult is also having phantasms, and everyone does have his own, and SL, I think, is just a way to satisfy them." (Post "morality in SL")

> We are three (female avatars) living in our home for almost two full months now, and it's going well . . . very well. (Post "marriage and polygamy")

Similarly, some behaviors such as stealing or harming others are condemned in SL but without real moral or legal consequences, which makes it easier to undertake them through what is called grieving. Through data analysis, it is detected that several examples of relationship desires can only be satisfied in SL. For example, some residents experience polygamy, having a harem or being a member of a harem, extrahuman sexual relationships, and so on.

Desires Related to the Environment
The participants in the forum expressed several desires related to the environment in which their avatars evolve. These desires are mainly related to landscapes, weather, time, space, and the laws of physics. In SL, the resident can manipulate these elements and have control over them. Kozinets

and Kedzior (2009) talk about "god-like powers" that allow residents to shape the ambiance of the virtual surroundings.

> For me, SL brings me back to my childhood dreams, that's what I specified in my profile: As before, in my childhood dreams, As before, on a white cloud, As before, turning on the sun, Being a rainmaker And do wonders. That's what SL allows; it adds another dose of phantasms and dreams of adults and we have a delicious cocktail. (Post "SL = Dream")

Teleporting and flying are technical functions of SL and a common way to explore the sims (the different geographical places) or to go from one place to another in this virtual world. Many participants to the forum mention these functions as special experiences that permit the defiance of the laws of physics and the limits of time and space. On a post named "a genius" the residents mention the one thing they desire is to go from one world to another (from SL to RL, and vice versa). To fly and to teleport are two functions many participants want to import to their RL.

It is important to notice that some desires related to relationships and to the environment do not necessary imply a consumption activity inasmuch as they are expressed through behaviors such as living within a harem, grieving, teleportation, flying, and the like. Table 3.1 includes some examples summarizing the typology of desires that can be satisfied through both worlds or only in SL.

Overcoming Human Limits—The Ultimate Desire

Through the analysis and interpretation of the data, a higher-order desire emerges that encompasses the four types previously described: the desire to overcome the limitations of the human condition. In fact, the desires related to the body and the appearance of the avatar, to her possessions, her relationships, and her environment allow the resident to defy the physical, material, and sociocultural limitations she faces in RL and even the limitations related to nature. The satisfaction of some of these desires in SL gives to the resident the feeling or the illusion that he has almost the absolute control over himself (who and how he wants to be) and his environment (what he wants to possess, where he wants to evolve as an avatar).

On the post about the "1000 and one reasons to prefer SL to RL," many exchanges attest of this ultimate desire. In the following, the opinion of a participant to the post illustrates the point:

In SL everything is sometimes easier:
We fly, we teleport at leisure, (whereas in the RL to teleport from office to home, there is a lot of lag)
We can live with love and fresh water,
We can do tons of shopping without finishing in debts' commission,
One changes instantly head, body shape and hair cut at will (I love this)
Dancing divinely for hours while chatting or putting some order into ones' affairs, and one is not even out the breath!
One fears neither cold nor hot, or idiots :-)
We do things we will never do in real life. example: spend an afternoon with the teddy bears, jump from the Eiffel Tower, knock the zombies (and be bitten 50 times at the same time, and not even feel hurt!), dance the waltz in a long dress . . . and the list goes on. (Post "the 1000 and one reasons to prefer SL to RL")

TABLE 3.1 The Typology of Desires in the Virtual World SL

		Desires That Could Be Satisfied	
		In RL or in SL	Only in SL
Desires related to...	**Body and appearance** Skin, shape, hair, clothes, accessories (e.g., tattoo, jewelry, hat), animations for the movements of the avatar, etc.	A better physical appearance or look	Transgender; a fantastic appearance (e.g., a manga, a neko, a fury); neutral gender avatar (e.g., object avatar); gender-bending
	Possessions of products or objects House, land, furniture, transportation (e.g., car, boat, plane), animals, etc.	A luxurious house, car, or furniture	A fairy house; a spaceship; a sky-house
	Relationships Social and sexual desires; asocial behaviors, etc.	Marriage; friendship; sexual fantasies; BDSM; prostitution; grieving (e.g., to harm others, to steal)	Extrahuman sexual relationships; polygamy
	Environment Time, space, nature and weather, laws of physics, etc.	To challenge time and space by using transportation means (e.g., plane, car) and technology (e.g., Internet).	To fly; to teleport; to be in a fairy tale

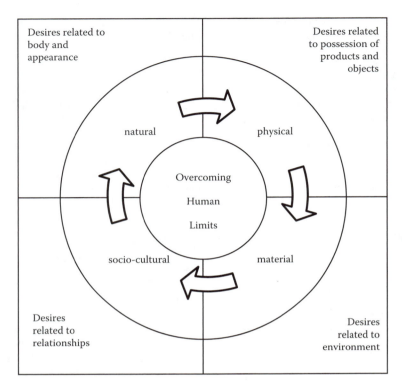

Figure 3.2   Overcoming human limits: the ultimate desire.

Conclusion

This study constitutes the second step of a research project exploring consumption desires in real and virtual worlds (see Figure 3.2). Through a nonparticipant observation of a French-speaking forum about SL, the authors establish a typology of the different kinds of desires a resident may hold in the virtual world SL. These desires are related to the body and appearance of the avatar, to his possessions, his relationships, and his environment. Some of these desires mirror what the resident wishes to have in RL whereas others are specific to SL.

Looking more closely at the nature of these desires, the researcher places them on a continuum going from desires that can be satisfied in both worlds to desires that can be satisfied only in SL because of their fantastic nature. The four types of desires reveal a willingness to overcome the human condition through defying physical, sociocultural, material, and environmental limits.

Future research questions are ripe in the rich topic of online identity. The authors encourage scholars to examine the role of avatars on consumer's social media (e.g., Facebook, Twitter) behavior. To what extent do consumers use brand-related avatars to create or reinforce their desired image? And, building on the theory of the extended self, to what extent can an avatar be a consumer's extended self? Over time, how does avatar consumption and use progress or change? These questions and others are topics for future scholarly inquiry.

References

Alix A. (2005). Beyond P-1: Who plays online? *Proceedings of DiGRA 2005 Conference: Changing Views—Worlds in Play*, Vancouver, BC, Canada.

Bartle R. (1996). Hearts, clubs, diamonds, spades: Players who suit MUDs. *Journal of Online Environments, 1*(1).

Becerra E. & Stutts, A. (2008). Ugly duckling by day, super model by night: The influence of body image on the use of virtual worlds. *Journal of Virtual Worlds Research, 1*(2), 1–19.

Belisle J. F. & Bodur, O. (2010). Avatars as information: Perception of consumers based on their avatars in virtual worlds. *Psychology & Marketing, 28*(7), 741–765.

Belk, R. W., Ger, G., & Askegaard, S. (2003). The fire of desire: A multisited inquiry into consumer passion. *Journal of Consumer Research, 30*(3), 326–351.

Bell, M. (2008). Toward a definition of "virtual worlds." *Journal of Virtual Worlds Research, 1*(1).

Bonsu, S. K. & Darmody, A. (2008). Co-creating Second Life: Market consumer cooperation in contemporary economy. *Journal of Macromarketing, 28*, 355–368.

Boostrom, R. (2008). The social construction of virtual reality and the stigmatized identity of the newbie. *Journal of Virtual Worlds Research, 1*(2), 1–19.

Boujbel, L. (2007). Never-ending desires: Assessing consumers' propensity to desire consumption objects. In S. Borghini, M. A. McGrath, & C. Otnes (Eds.), *European Advances in Consumer Research* (Vol. 8, pp. 319–324), Milan: Association for Consumer Research.

Boujbel, L. (2010). Uncovering the affective and cognitive dimensions of consumer desires: An exploration. In M. Meloy & A. Duhachek (Eds.), *Advances in consumer psychology* (Vol. 2, pp. 236–237). St. Petersburg, FL: Society for Consumer Psychology.

Brown, J. E. & Tracy, L. T. (2009). I don't know you, but I trust you: A comparative study of consumer perceptions in real-life and virtual worlds. In T. Wood & R. M. Solomon (Eds.), *Virtual social identity and consumer behavior*. New York: M.E. Sharpe, pp. 61–72.

Bryant, J. A. & Akerman, A. (2009). Finding mii: Virtual social identity and the young consumer. In T. Wood & R. M. Solomon (Eds.), *Virtual social identity and consumer behavior*. New York: M.E. Sharpe, pp. 127–140.

Castronova, E. (2005). *Synthetic worlds, the business and culture of online games*. Chicago: The University of Chicago Press.

Creswell, J. W. (2007). *Qualitative inquiry and research design: Choosing among five approaches*. Newbury Park, CA: SAGE.

Crete, D., St.-Onge, A., Merle, A., Arsenault, N., & Nantel, J. (2009). Personalized avatar: A new way to improve communication and e-service. In T. Wood & R. M. Solomon (Eds.), *Virtual social identity and consumer behavior*. New York: M.E. Sharpe, pp. 93–108.

Denegri-Knott, J. & Molesworth. M. (2010). Concepts and practices of digital virtual consumption. *Consumption, Markets & Culture, 13*(2), 109–132.

Diener, E. & Seligman, M. P. E. (2002). Very happy people. *Psychological Science, 13*, 81–84.

El Kamel, L. (2009). For a better exploration of metaverses as consumer experiences. In *Advertising and Virtual Social Identity and Consumer Behavior*, Consumer Psychology Book Series. New York: M.E. Sharp.

El Kamel, L. & Boujbel, L. (2011). Is it possible to satiate real consumption desires in virtual worlds? Second Life case study. *10th International Marketing Trends Conference*, January 20–22, Paris.

El Kamel, L. & Bricmont, B. (2011). Les apports du postmodernisme à l'analyse des univers virtuels comme expérience de consommation. Cas de Second Life, *Recherche et Applications en Marketing*, September.

El Kamel, L. & Rigaux-Bricmont, B. (2009). Online qualitative research and metaverses. *Online IV Congress of Cybersociety*.

Frijda, N. H. (1986). *The emotions*. Cambridge, UK: Cambridge University Press.

Gagnon, Y. (2005). *Étude de cas comme méthode de recherche*. Quebec, Canada: Presses Universitaires du Québec.

Haenlein, M. & Kaplan, A. M. (2009). Les magasins de marques phares dans les mondes virtuels: l'impact de l'exposition au magasin virtuel sur l'attitude envers la marque et l'intention d'achat dans la vie réelle. *Recherche et Applications en Marketing, 24*(3), 57–80.

Hervet, G., El Kamel, L., & Rigaux-Bricmont, B. (2010). Entretien de groupe dans Second Life, *Recherches Qualitatives, 29*(1), 69–98.

Hewer, P. & Brownlie, D. (2007). Cultures of consumption of car aficionados: Aestheticas and consumption communities. *International Journal of Sociology and Social Policy, 27*(3–4), 106–118.

Hinsch, C. & P. H. Bloch (2009). Interaction seeking in second life and implications for consumer behavior. In T. Wood & R. M. Solomon (Eds.), *Virtual social identity and consumer behavior*. New York: M. E. Sharpe, pp. 43–60.

Iversen, S. (2005). Challenge balance and diversity: Playing the sims and the sims 2. *Changing views—Worlds in play*. Proceedings of DiGRA 2005 Conference, Vancouver, BC, Canada.

Kaplan, A. & Haenlein, M. (2010). Users of the world, unite! The challenge and opportunities of social media. *Business Horizons, 53*, 59–68.

Kaplan, A. M. & Haenlein, M. (2009). The fairyland of Second Life: Virtual social worlds and how to use them. *Business Horizons, 52*, 563–572.

Kellar, M., Watters, C., & Duffy, J. (2005). Motivational factors in game play in two user groups. *Changing views—Worlds in play*, Proceedings of DiGRA 2005 Conference, Vancouver, BC, Canada.

Kozinets, R. V. (2010). *Netnography: Doing ethnographic research online*. Newbury Park, CA: SAGE.

Kozinets, R. V. & Kedzior, R. (2009). I, avatar: Auto-netnographic research in virtual worlds. In T. Wood and R. M. Solomon (Eds.), *Virtual social identity and consumer behavior*. New York: M.E. Sharpe, pp. 3–19.

Landay, L. (2008). Having but not holding: Consumerism and commodification in Second Life. *Journal of Virtual Worlds Research, 1*(2), 1–5.

Lin, A. (2007). Virtual consumption: A Second Life for Earth? Available at http://papers.ssrn.com/sol3/papers.cfm?abstract_id=1008539)

Lucas, K. & Sherry, J. (2004). Sex differences in video game play: A communication-based explanation. *Communication Research, 31*(5), 499–523.

Markos, E. & Labrecque, L. I. (2008). Blurring the boundaries between real and virtual: Consumption experiences and the self concept in the virtual world. *Association for Consumer Research North American Conference*, October 22–26, 2008, San Francisco.

Martin, J. (2008). Consuming code: Use-value, exchange-value, and the role of virtual goods in Second Life. *Journal of Virtual Worlds Research, 1*(2), 1–21.

Messinger, P. R., Ge, X., Stroulia, E., Lyons, K., Smirnov, K., & Bone, M. (2008). On the relationship between my avatar and myself. *Journal of Virtual Worlds Research, 1*(2), 1–17.

Molesworth, M. (2009). Adults' consumption of videogames as imaginative escape from routine. *Advances in Consumer Research, 36*, 378–383.

Park, S. R., Nah, F. F., DeWester, D., Eschenbrenner, B., & Jeon, S. (2008). Virtual world affordances: Enhancing brand value. *Journal of Virtual Worlds Research, 1*(2), 1–18.

Parmentier, G. & Rolland, S. (2009). Les consommateurs des mondes virtuels: Construction identitaire et expérience de consommation dans Second Life. *Recherche et Applications en Marketing, 24*(3), 43–56.

Ramanathan, S. & Williams, P. (2007). Immediate and delayed emotional consequences of indulgence: The moderating influence of personality type on mixed emotions. *Journal of Consumer Research, 34*, 212–223.

Schroeder, R. (2008). Defining virtual worlds and virtual environments. *Journal of Virtual Worlds Research, 1*(1). Retrieved January 24, 2012 from https://journals.tdl.org/jvwr/article/view/294/248

Spiggle, S. (1994). Analysis and interpretation of qualitative data in consumer research. *Journal of Consumer Research, 21*, 491–503.

Sundar, S. S. & Kim, Y. (2009). Me, myself, and my avatar: The effects of avatars on SNW (social networking) users' attitudes toward a website, an ad, and a PSA. In T. Wood & R.M. Solomon (Eds.), *Virtual social identity and consumer behavior* (pp. 141–156). New York: M.E. Sharpe.

Taylor, T. (2003). Multiple pleasures: Women and online gaming. *Convergence, 9*(1), 21–46.

Thompson, C. J., Pollio, H. R., & Locander, W. B. (1994). The spoken and the unspoken: A hermeneutic approach to understanding consumer's expressed meanings. *Journal of Consumer Research, 21*, 432–453.

Vidcan, H. & Ulusoy, E. (2008). Symbolic and experiential consumption of body in virtual worlds: From (dis)embodiment to symembodiment. *Journal of Virtual Worlds Research, 1*(2), 1–22.

Wacheux, F. (1996). *Méthodes qualitatives de recherches en gestion.* Paris: Economica.

Williams, M. (2007). Avatar watching: Participant observation in graphical online environments. *Qualitative Research, 7*(5), 5–24.

Yee, N. (2002). Facets: 5 motivation factors for why people play mmorpgs. Doctoral thesis extract available at http://www.nickyee.com

Yin, R. (1984). *Case study research: Design and method.* Beverly Hills, CA: SAGE.

Section II

Social Media, Blogs, and Privacy Issues

4

Managing New Media
Tools for Brand Management in Social Media

Elsamari Botha
University of Cape Town

Adam J. Mills
Simon Fraser University

The Rise of Social Media

Two important milestones for social media, the Internet, and the way that consumers communicate were reached in 2010 to set a precedent for today and the future. First, the video hosting site YouTube announced that every minute, 24 hours of video content were uploaded to its servers (cf. http://youtube-global.blogspot.com/). Second, not only was the social network platform Facebook larger in terms of population than most of the world's nations, but also by February 2010 it was the second most popular Web site on the Internet, outperformed only by Google in the number of daily hits. However, according to A.C. Nielsen research (Arington, 2010), whereas Google received 154 million unique visitors per month with an average of one hour of usage time, Facebook's 118 million unique visitors per month spent an average of 6.5 hours each on the site, making it a much stickier site than Google.

Social media sites are now as influential as, and perhaps more so than, conventional media. This has a massive impact on brands, as witnessed in recent times by Unilever's Dove "Real Beauty" campaign (Deighton, 2008) and the Greenpeace versus Nestlé Kit Kat Palm Oil debacle. Literature seeking to analyze and dissect social media phenomena—what social media are, why, and how—has seen exponential growth in recent years. However, although such understanding is important for brand scholars and brand managers, some key questions remain unanswered with respect to understanding what happens to brands once they are released into the consumer-controlled landscape of social media. These would include questions such as: How do we find out what is being said about a brand in social media? What is being said about competing brands, and how is that different from our brand? Is our brand more or less visible in some social media than others, and how does that differ from our competitors?

It does not take expertise or hours of study to ascertain that attempting to answer these types of questions is difficult enough on just one social medium; it requires a regular tracking of what is being said by consumers, reading and then interpreting a mountain of consumer-generated information, spending an inordinate amount of time scanning Facebook, and following Twitter tweets or reading comments on YouTube. Compound this with an ever-evolving social media landscape and content that may be generated faster than it can be read, and the task of managing a social media campaign can quickly become overwhelming, not to mention expensive.

These are the issues we address in this chapter. First, we provide a brief general overview of social media and distinguish between the primary types of social media. Second, we describe a tool for simultaneously collecting brand visibility information, called How Sociable. Then we briefly describe a study to demonstrate how user-generated content may be analyzed efficiently, in this case the positioning of a number of South African university brands based on data from How Sociable. Here, we build from the first author's initial research on the topic (Botha, Farshid, & Pitt, 2011) in order to broaden the context and develop some of the themes. We explain the use of correspondence analysis to simultaneously portray the various university brands in multidimensional space so that they can be contrasted with each other in terms of their visibility in social media. We also comment on the current state of the positioning of these brands in social media. The chapter concludes with an acknowledgment of the limitations of the approach followed here, an outlining of the implications for brand managers, and an identification of avenues for future research in this domain.

Social Media: A Brief Overview

Social media, for the purposes of this chapter, is defined as media designed to facilitate the dissemination of content through social interaction between individuals, groups, and organizations using Internet and

Web-based technologies to enable the transformation of broadcast mono-logues (one to many) into social dialogues (many to many). At the very core of social media lie the empowerment of individuals and the democ-ratization of knowledge by creating the opportunity to turn content con-sumers into content producers. Social media are both accessible, in that they are easy to find and use by a broad audience, and scalable, as network effects play a very significant role (Brogan, 2010; Zarella, 2010).

Kaplan and Haenlein (2010, p. 61) describe social media as "a group of Internet-based applications that build on the ideological and technological foundations of Web 2.0, and that allow the creation and exchange of user-generated content." Web 2.0 is a term used to distinguish the progression of the Internet to interactive online communication, participation, and engagement from the early years of the Internet (Web 1.0) where usage was primarily based on one-way messaging and online information retrieval. Web 2.0 describes what people are doing with technology and how they are using it, more so than the technology itself. Rather than merely con-sume information, users can now create it, adding value to the Web sites that permit them to do so. Such content is referred to as user-generated content (UGC) or consumer-generated media (CGM), or if explicitly gen-erated in the form of an advertisement for a brand, consumer-generated advertising or CGA (Berthon, Pitt, & Campbell, 2008).

Tapscott and Williams (2007) contend that the economy of "the new web" depends on mass collaboration, with economic democracy as an outcome, as individuals simultaneously create value for themselves and others, in this case with particular respect to brands and organizations through profound network effects. Similarly, organizations are now not only able to reach and interact with existing customers online; they are equally able, if managed effectively, to seek out new customers as well as become part of customer conversations.

Social media are relatively new media formats and few readily accepted classification or categorization schemes exist to distinguish them. In what follows, we briefly describe some of the major types of social media, but do not claim that this is in any sense a definitive or even complete classifica-tion. Simply, we wish to lay a foundation for the study to follow. We distin-guish briefly here among blogs, microblogs, social network sites, picture sharing, video sharing, and social news Web sites.

Blogs (short for "Web logs") are Web sites maintained and written by indi-viduals, but hosted and technically owned by an organization that provides access to Web space and a content management system, or CMS. *Bloggers* (blog users) generally maintain regular commentaries or posts that may include text, graphics, video, or links to other blogs and Web pages, usually posted in chronological order. Rudimentary blogs function simply as online personal diaries, but more sophisticated and popular blogs tend to comment on a range of focused phenomena with news and views on particular subjects, covering a wide range of industries, products, services, and special interests. Many blogs permit readers to leave their own comments below the original in an interactive format. Bloggers sometimes use their blogs to differentiate themselves from mainstream media; others are like more traditional journalists who see blogs as an alternative or additional communication channel (see Steyn, Van Heerden, Pitt, & Boshoff, 2008). Some of the most popular blog sites are Blogger, LiveJournal, and WordPress.

Microblogs are social networking services that enable users to post and read very short messages, restricted by the number of characters in the message and type of content that can be posted. Essentially, these are scaled- and stripped-down versions of traditional blogs. The best known is Twitter, through which users can send messages known as "tweets," text-based posts of up to 140 characters displayed on the author's profile page and delivered to the author's subscribers who are known as followers. Senders can restrict delivery to those in their circle of friends or, by default, allow open access to any site visitors. Users can send and receive tweets via the Twitter Web site but also through text messaging on cell phones and external applications that can access the site. Twitter has gained much prominence in the recent past. For example, during the 2009 Victoria bushfires, the prime minister of Australia, Kevin Rudd, used his Twitter account to send out information on the fires, how to donate money and blood, and where to seek emergency help. In June 2009, following allegations of fraud in the Iranian presidential election, protesters used Twitter as a rallying tool and as a method of communication with the outside world after the government blocked several other modes of communication.

Video sharing Web sites allow users to watch, upload, and share videos. Typically, unregistered users can watch videos already posted to the site, whereas registered users are permitted to upload videos and comment on other users' videos. The best known of the video sharing Web sites is YouTube. It was estimated that in 2007 YouTube consumed as much bandwidth as the entire Internet in 2000 (*Daily Telegraph*, 2008), and by March 2008, YouTube's bandwidth costs were estimated at approximately 1 million U.S. dollars a day (Yen, 2008).

Picture sharing Web sites operate in much the same way as video sharing Web sites but with content based on still images instead of video. The most popular picture sharing Web sites are Flickr, Picasa, Yahoo Images, and Google Images.

Social networking Web sites are services on which users can create an individual profile page, find and add friends and contacts, send messages, and update their personal profiles to notify friends, contacts, or colleagues about themselves. On some social networking Web sites, users can join networks organized by workplace, school, or college. Social networking Web sites often combine several other social media technologies into one platform; for example, Facebook gives users the opportunity to post status updates (i.e., microblogs), notes (i.e., blogs), pictures, and videos. Often, users are able to tag other users in their networks in such posts, creating additional links between users and content. The most popular social networking sites with a generally social orientation are Facebook and MySpace. Facebook currently has more than 400 million active users worldwide (Facebook, 2010). There are also social networking sites with more specific foci, such as LinkedIn and Plaxo that specifically target professional and business networking.

Lastly, *social news Web sites* are sites that allow people to discover and share content from anywhere on the Internet by submitting links and stories to a central service. Most often, social news services allow visitors to vote and comment on submitted links and stories. The best known of these social news Web sites are Digg and Reddit.

Some social media Web sites (Facebook, Twitter, and YouTube) allow not only individual users but also groups and organizations to create and maintain profile pages. This provides the opportunity and access for firms to participate in social interactions online. As we discussed already, this can be hugely beneficial for organizations that wish to engage with their customers on a more personal or social level, but can also create significant risks for these organizations as managers, in part, by ceding control of what is being said about their brands to these consumers.

Gathering Brand Visibility Data in Social Media: How Sociable

It is important for those who manage brands to understand what is being said about their brands in social media, how frequently it is being said, and in what particular media it is being said (Botha et al., 2011). This type of data would give the brand manager an indication of the visibility of the brand in social media. In most cases, we assume the brand manager would primarily be concerned with the social media visibility of her own brand, but might want to make comparisons with the performance of similar or competitive brands. So, as we posed earlier, how would a brand manager be able to collect data accurately and efficiently from hundreds of millions of possible sources, and then compile all of those data into meaningful and useful information? Such data could be gathered in one of two ways. First, an employee or group of employees could be given the responsibility of trawling through vast amounts of data in the vast numbers of posts on the various social media platforms and counting and documenting this information manually. Alternatively, the data could be obtained using software or a service that regularly trawls through social media electronically, and compiles and counts a brand's visibility. One of these types of service is a Web site called How Sociable (http://www.howsociable.com).

How Sociable is currently a free Web service that tracks the visibility of any brand across 32 different social media platforms and provides a score for the visibility on each platform, as well as calculates an overall visibility score. The software scours the Web for all mentions of the brand in question, assigns each mention to the particular social medium on which it occurred, and counts these mentions. Simply by entering a brand name into a search box on the Web site, the user can obtain an overall visibility score and as well as visibility scores across the 32 different social media sites.

The overall visibility score assigned to a brand provides a quick way to compare the visibility of one brand to another (Botha et al., 2011). According to the site (Markwell, 2010), a visibility score is calculated by taking a set of benchmark results using one globally recognized traditional brand and giving it a score of 1,000. To ensure that even small local brands will have a chance of scoring, they use a sliding scale. For example, a brand such as Coca-Cola may have thousands more photos mentioning it on the photo-sharing site Flickr compared with a smaller brand, but the other brand will still get a score of 10 for having some photos rather than getting 0. Of course, in a practical application, not all brand managers would choose to benchmark their own brand's visibility against global megabrands like Coca-Cola. Rather, when comparing one's brand with similar brands in the marketplace, differences in visibility score will be less extreme and perhaps therefore more meaningful.

In Figure 4.1, we show the How Sociable brand visibility scores of 10 different well-known brands, for purposes of illustration. We chose the five most valuable brands in the world according to the annual Interbrand report on brand values: Coca-Cola, IBM, Microsoft, GE, and Nokia (see http://www.interbrand.com), and also five well-known social media

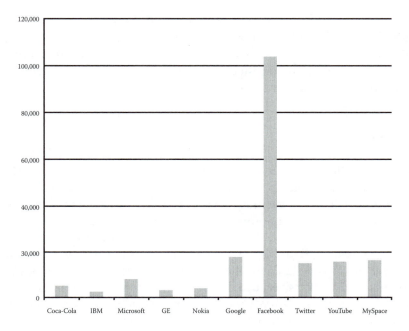

Figure 4.1   An illustration of brand visibility scores: most valuable brands and well-known social media brands.

brands, namely Google, Facebook, Twitter, YouTube, and MySpace. All these brands were chosen simply for purposes of illustration, rather than as an endorsement of the Interbrand brand valuation methods.

Key points from Figure 4.1 include that the most valuable brands in an economic sense are not always the most visible brands in social media (e.g., Coca-Cola is less visible than Microsoft). Social media brands, perhaps not unexpectedly, are far more visible than even the most valuable brands, and Facebook is many magnitudes more visible than all other brands.

Before proceeding to a description of our study and methodology, it is worth mentioning that How Sociable is just one of a number of tools available to assess brands in social media. For example, Google Analytics is a free service offered by Google that generates detailed statistics about the visitors to a Web site, which are useful to online marketers. Marketing research companies such as A.C. Nielsen provide a range of paid-for services to their clients that track various aspects of brand visibility in social media. Social Mention is an interesting (and also currently free) tool that allows users to assess a brand's real-time status in a wide range of social media in terms of the brand's strength, sentiment toward it, how passionate those who comment on it are, and the reach it enjoys across multiple platforms. However, as far as we are aware, How Sociable is the only free service that allows users to agglomerate a brand's social media awareness across a broad range of the most common social media in a relatively simple and easy to use manner.

Methods

In order to illustrate our approach to using data from How Sociable to portray similar brands in multidimensional space, we gathered data on five South African universities. We note that these are the same universities we examined in initial investigations (Botha et al., 2011). We entered their brand names into the How Sociable search engine, and had the Web site calculate overall visibility scores as well as visibility scores in each of the 32 social media platforms the site reports. These five universities were chosen as illustrations because they were the five South African universities with the highest visibility scores, after a previous exercise had entered all South African universities into the How Sociable visibility calculator. These universities were the University of Cape Town, the University of Pretoria, Rhodes University, the University of Stellenbosch, and the University of the Witwatersrand (Wits).

A contingency table was created with the five university brands as columns and the 32 social media as rows. The number of social media used was reduced for practical reasons: first, for further analysis using correspondence there was a danger that having 32 unique points on a map would make viewing and interpretation complex and difficult; second, there were scores of 0 for all five brands on several of the less-known platforms. The top 13 of the 32 social media sites were chosen for the final analysis: Google Page Score (Google PS), Twitter, MySpace, Ning, Digg, Ecademy, Yahoo Page Score (Yahoo PS), Facebook Groups (Facebook G), Facebook Pages (Facebook P), Google Images (Google I), Xing, LinkedIn, and YouTube Videos (YouTube V). The contingency table was then used as data input for correspondence analysis using Xlstat.

A summary of the scores for each university brand in each of the selected social media is shown in Table 4.1, and the overall brand visibility scores for each of the universities is shown in Figure 4.2.

Two points can be made from the table and graph. First, interpreting a reasonably complex table such as that in Table 4.1 can be difficult, as the observer wants not only to assess where a particular brand is performing

TABLE 4.1   Table of the University Brands by Visibility Score in Individual Social Media

	Cape Town	Pretoria	Rhodes	Stellenbosch	Wits
Google PS	74	190	127	113	161
Twitter	174	142	174	265	101
MySpace	40	27	22	24	21
Ning	209	166	101	109	335
Digg	53	32	23	29	43
Ecademy	203	176	51	144	125
Yahoo PS	134	111	85	71	42
Facebook G	837	693	575	394	381
Facebook P	1217	1189	1355	1415	1650
Google I	90	78	54	48	59
Xing	97	51	44	62	62
LinkedIn	895	830	475	685	865
YouTube V	45	41	19	32	21

Source: Botha, E., Farshid, M., & Pitt, L. *South African Journal of Business Management,* 42(2), 15-23, 2011. With permission.

well or poorly but also to determine how a brand stacks up to another brand on a particular social medium. Second, the graph in Figure 4.2 indicates that the most visible university brand in social media is that of Wits, followed by UCT, Pretoria, Rhodes, and Stellenbosch, although none of the five brands is markedly more visible than the others. However, what the simple bar graph based on the total visibility scores cannot indicate is

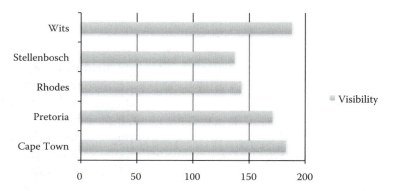

Figure 4.2   Overall visibility scores of the five university brands. (Reprinted from Botha, E., Farshid, M., & Pitt, L. *South African Journal of Business Management,* 42(2), 15–23, 2011. With permission.)

what specifically accounts for these scores. In other words, looking at the data from either the individual results or the cumulative visibility scores does not allow the user to interpret easily where particular brands might be performing well or poorly. In both cases, being able to construct a picture in which the brands and the social media were portrayed in two-dimensional space would make comprehension much easier and more meaningful.

Correspondence Analysis

To identify the associations between the university brands and the social media visibility indicators, we used correspondence analysis. This is a perceptual mapping technique based on cross-tabulation data that are converted into a joint space map by decomposing the X^2 statistic of the frequency matrix (Bendixen, 1995, 1996; Greenacre, 1993). The perceptual map created through correspondence analysis is useful in uncovering structural relationships between different variables (Opuku, Abratt, Bendixen, & Pitt, 2007a; Inman, Venkatesh, & Ferraro, 2004) and its graphical nature facilitates interpretation of data that would otherwise be difficult to comprehend (O'Brien, 1993). Moreover, Hair, Black, Babin, Anderson, and Tatham (2006) state that correspondence analysis is best suited for exploratory data analysis, and inasmuch as our study is exploratory in nature, its use in this type of study is appropriate.

Results

The results of the correspondence analysis are presented in Tables 4.2 and 4.3. Ideally, for correspondence analysis to proceed, the researcher would prefer to have interdependence between rows and columns. As can be seen from Table 4.2, the observed X^2 is 932, $p < .0001$, indicating a dependency between the rows and the columns of the contingency table (Bendixen, 1996). In order to determine the dimensionality of a solution, the eigenvalues and the cumulative proportion explained by the dimensions must be examined (Greenacre, 1993; Bendixen, 1995, 1996). Most researchers agree that a two-dimensional solution is also preferable due to its ease of display and interpretability (Bendixen, 1995, 1996; Hair et al., 2006; see also Opuku et al., 2007a, 2007b). We therefore chose a two-dimensional

TABLE 4.2 Test of Independence Between the Rows and the Columns

Chi-square (Observed value)	932.009
Chi-square (Critical value)	65.171
DF	48
p-value	< 0.0001
Alpha	0.05

Test interpretation:

H0: The rows and the columns of the table are independent.

Ha: There is a link between the rows and the columns of the table.

As the computed p-value is lower than the significance level (alpha = 0.05), the null hypothesis is rejected. The risk to reject the null hypothesis H0 although it is true is lower than 0.01%.

correspondence plot, which yields a retention of 79.67% across the first two dimensions.

An asymmetric plot, used to articulate the distance between row and column points of the university brands and the social media is shown in Figure 4.3. The plot reveals the underlying structure and positioning of the investigated university brands in relation to the various social media in which they appear. The graphical output also provides information about how the university brands and the social media are positioned vis-à-vis one another. Note that the horizontal and vertical axes themselves do not represent specific data, but rather the relative value of the brands' presence (i.e., there are no negative values).

It is apparent from an examination of the brands and their contributions to the dimensions in Table 4.3, as well as from their positioning in close proximity to each other on the correspondence analysis map in Figure 4.3, that these university brands do not appear to be overly distinctly positioned in social media. Although we are able to identify some minor differences—for example, Wits appears to be more visible on Facebook Pages, whereas Rhodes and Stellenbosch appear to be more visible on Twitter, and Pretoria more visible on YouTube—none of the brands stands out as being particularly more prominent than the others in any one or even a few social media. Table 4.3 does agree with the results in Table 4.2, as we see that both Wits and Cape Town are farther along the horizontal axis and therefore in proximity to a larger number of social media platforms. At the time of writing, these results were practically

TABLE 4.3   Correspondence Analysis: Eigenvalues and Inertia; Principal Coordinates of Rows and Columns

Eigenvalues and Percentages of Inertia

	F1	F2	F3	F4
Eigenvalue	0.025	0.016	0.007	0.004
Inertia (%)	48.499	31.178	13.109	7.215
Cumulative %	48.499	79.677	92.785	100.000

Principal Coordinates (Rows)

	F1	F2	F3	F4
Google PS	−0.124	0.012	0.147	0.244
Twitter	0.021	0.323	−0.184	0.002
MySpace	0.181	0.003	−0.043	−0.074
Ning	−0.198	−0.333	0.041	−0.075
Digg	0.050	−0.153	−0.059	−0.118
Ecademy	0.171	−0.141	−0.197	0.077
Yahoo PS	0.321	0.072	0.036	0.002
Facebook G	0.253	0.025	0.096	−0.024
Facebook P	−0.138	0.070	0.020	−0.019
Google I	0.158	−0.060	0.043	−0.001
Xing	0.098	−0.049	−0.121	−0.145
LinkedIn	0.011	−0.105	−0.056	0.031
YouTube V	0.235	−0.022	−0.123	0.081

Principal Coordinates (Columns)

	F1	F2	F3	F4
Cape Town	0.202	−0.075	−0.034	−0.070
Pretoria	0.114	−0.051	0.036	0.105
Rhodes	−0.019	0.185	0.126	−0.035
Stellenbosch	−0.080	0.143	−0.135	0.019
Wits	−0.236	−0.146	0.019	−0.017

Source: Botha, E., Farshid, M., & Pitt, L. *South African Journal of Business Management,* 42(2), 15–23, 2011. With permission.

confirmed by establishing (by means of a search on each of the major social media studies here) that none of the five institutions had established a formal or brand-directed social media presence. For example, there were fan pages on Facebook for the universities, however, these had been set up informally by current and former students; similarly, none of the five institutions was active on Twitter.

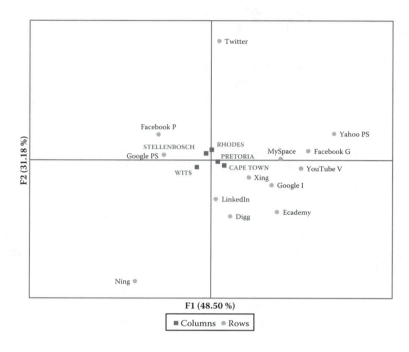

Figure 4.3 Asymmetric column plot (axes F1 and F2: 79.68%). (Reprinted from Botha, E., Farshid, M., & Pitt, L. *South African Journal of Business Management, 42*(2), 15–23, 2011. With permission.)

At first glance these results might seem lackluster, but they simply indicate that none of the five university brands is particularly visible in social media, and more important, that none of them currently seems to have a concerted strategy for engaging its stakeholders in a particular social medium. This means that there are both opportunities and threats to these institutions for taking a *laissez-faire* attitude to social media in these times when social media are coming to dominate the Internet, and in particular the communication and information-seeking process for Generation Y. As discussed already, these results show that the consumers, not the universities' brand managers, are responsible for what is being said about these brands in the social media sphere, for better or worse.

Limitations, Managerial Implications, and
Directions for Future Research

This chapter describes a methodology for simultaneously mapping a number of competing brands in multidimensional space based on their visibility in a number of social media. The chapter and the study within are not without limitations and do not claim to be a definitive study of the positioning of all South African university brands in social media, but merely a select few brands within a limited number of social media as a means of illustrating a technique. Second, data from a third-party source such as How Sociable has to be taken at face value; although there is little reason to distrust the motivations of the software's producers, any weaknesses in the collection or reporting methodologies will be reflected in the results of a study that relies on them. Finally, a study such as this provides a snapshot of facts at one particular point in time; the nature of social media is such that content evolves continuously, and therefore a very different picture may have emerged at another point in time. At the same time, this principle also highlights a great opportunity for researchers and brand managers using this technique: data collection and resultant visual maps would allow for a brand to be tracked over time relative to both social media platforms and competitors.

A number of managerial implications become apparent from this research. As with any media space, brand managers seeking to participate actively in the social media space must first define their online role and scope, then implement, maintain, and monitor these spaces to ensure consistent brand messaging. It is apparent that, at the time the data were gathered, none of the university brands had clearly defined social media strategies, however, there are similar opportunities for the brand managers of these universities in the future. Managers should first consider the kind of official presence they wish to establish in these media, for example, an official university fan page on Facebook, regular tweets on Twitter about newsworthy events, and frequent posting of videos concerning the university and its activities (e.g., sporting events, graduation ceremonies, interesting research) on a dedicated YouTube page. Managers may also regularly monitor unofficial content in social media by regular information scanning of social media sites, and creating contingency plans that will allow them to act and react appropriately to consumer-generated content in line with prescribed brand standards. They may monitor social media content and visibility of the other university brands they regard either as competitors or benchmarks, and track data over a period of time to measure the performance of their social media initiatives. Sources of data such as How Sociable and tools such as correspondence analysis that permit the simultaneous picturing of brands in multidimensional space might become invaluable tools for monitoring competition and benchmarking performance.

An exploratory study such as this opens up a stream of further opportunities for future research. First, it would be prudent to find ways of confirming or testing the reliability and validity of data gathered by third-party services such as How Sociable. As a possible solution to this issue, these service providers can be contacted directly in an effort to gain a better understanding of their methodologies and results, or by closely monitoring the performance results for a set of brands over a period of time and then establishing a test–retest pattern to determine reliability. Second, the results of secondary data research could be combined with primary data collection in the target markets of the brands concerned. For example, at a qualitative level, researchers might wish to hold online or face-to-face focus groups with users of the various social media sites in order to gather more rich, in-depth feedback on their involvement in these media. At a quantitative level, researchers could analyze the text of the interactions that users have concerning brands in social media (Reyneke, Pitt, & Berthon, 2011). For example, researchers such as Opoku et al. (2007a, 2007b) describe tools that can be used to analyze large amounts of text by means of computerized content analysis that could be employed in this regard. Third, researchers could employ a vast array of tools that are readily available online for social media analysis (some of which are listed earlier in this chapter; also see Barros, 2009) in conjunction with the data from How Sociable and then use tools such as correspondence analysis.

The advent of consumer-generated content and its rapid diffusion can take much of the control over messaging away from marketers, and empower consumers to create and disseminate messaging about their brands (Deighton & Kornfeld, 2007). This makes the management of brands in an era of social media not only more complex, but also more critical than it has ever been. Brand managers will need to use every tool at their disposal to take part in these conversations and try to direct the destinies of the brands for which they are responsible. We suggest that the approaches followed in the research presented in this chapter will be one tool in the brand managers' arsenal that will assist them in this endeavor.

References

Arington, M. (2010). Hitwise says Facebook most popular U.S. site. *Techcrunch*, Retrieved March 15, 2010 from http://techcrunch.com/2010/03/15/hitwise-says-facebook-most-popular-u-s-site/

Barros, S. (2009). *Know your numbers: 10 Free web analytics tools for your Web site.* Retrieved March 15, 2010 from http://www.penn-olson.com/2009/09/13/know-your-numbers-10-free-web-analytics-tools-for-your-website/

Bendixen, M. (1995). Composing perceptual mapping using chi-squared trees analysis and correspondence analysis. *Journal of Marketing Management, 11*(6), 571–581.

Bendixen, M. (1996). A practical guide to the use of correspondence analysis in marketing research. *Marketing Research On-Line, 1*, 16–38. Retrieved March 25, 2010 from http://marketing-bulletin.massey.ac.nz/V14/MB_V14_T2_Bendixen.pdf

Berthon, P., Pitt, L., & Campbell, C. (2008). Ad lib: When customers create the ad. *California Management Review, 50*(4), 6–30.

Botha, E., Farshid, M., & Pitt, L. (2011). How Sociable? An exploratory study of university brand visibility in social media. *South African Journal of Business Management, 42*(2), 15–23.

Brogan, C. (2010). *Social media 101: Tactics and tips to develop your business online.* Hoboken, NJ: John Wiley and Sons.

Daily Telegraph (2008). Web could collapse as video demand soars. Retrieved March 25, 2010 from http://www.telegraph.co.uk

Deighton, J. (2008). Dove: Evolution of a Brand. *Harvard Business School Case No. 9-508-047*. Boston: Harvard Business School Publishing.

Deighton, J. & Kornfeld, L. (2007). Digital interactivity: Unanticipated consequences for markets, marketing, and consumers. *Harvard Business School Working Paper, 8–17.*

Facebook. (2010). Facebook press room. Retrieved March 25, 2010 from http://www.facebook.com/press/info.php?statistics

Greenacre, M. (1993). *Correspondence analysis in practice.* New York: Academic Press.

Hair, J. F., Black, B., Babin, B., Anderson, R. E., & Tatham, R. L. (2006). *Multivariate data analysis* (6th ed.). Upper Saddle River, NJ: Prentice-Hall.

Inman, J. J., Venkatesh, S., & Ferraro, R. (2004). The roles of channel-category associations and geodemographics in channel patronage. *Journal of Marketing, 68*(2), 51–71.

Kaplan, A. M. & Haenlein, M. (2010). Users of the world, unite! The challenges and opportunities of social media. *Business Horizons, 53*(1), 59–68.

Markwell, J. (2010). Our visibility score. Retrieved March 15, 2010 from http://howsociable.wordpress.com/2008/08/08/our-visibility-score/

O'Brien, T. V. (1993). Correspondence analysis. *Marketing Research, 5*(4), 54–56.

Opoku, R. A., Abratt, R., Bendixen, M., & Pitt, L. (2007a). Communicating brand personality: Are the Websites doing the talking for food SME's? *Qualitative Market Research*, *10*(4), 362–374.

Opoku, R. A., Pitt, L., & Abratt, R. (2007b). Positioning in cyberspace: Evaluating bestselling authors' online communicated brand personalities using computer-aided content analysis. *South African Journal of Business Management*, *38*(4), 21–32.

Reyneke, M., Pitt, L., & Berthon, P. (2011). Luxury wine brand visibility in social media: An exploratory study. *International Journal of Wine Business Research*, *23*(1), 21–35.

Steyn, P., Van Heerden, G., Pitt, L., & Boshoff, C. (2008). Meet the bloggers: Some characteristics of serious bloggers in the Asia-Pacific region, and why PR professionals might care about them. *Public Relations Quarterly*, *52*(3), 39–44.

Tapscott, D. & Williams, A. D. (2007). *Wikinomics: How mass collaboration changes everything*. New York: Penguin.

Yen, Y.-W. (2008). YouTube looks for the money clip. *Fortune*. Retrieved March 25, 2010 from http://techland.blogs.fortune.cnn.com/2008/03/25/youtube-looks-for-the-money-clip/

Zarella, D. (2010). *The social media marketing book*. North Sebastopol, CA: O'Reilly Media.

5

Consumer Activism Through Social Media
Carrots Versus Sticks

Pia A. Albinsson
Appalachian State University

B. Yasanthi Perera
New Mexico State University

> The existence of united groups of online consumers implies that power
> is shifting away from marketers and flowing to consumers.

Kozinets (1999, p. 258)

Consumers in a Virtual World

Consumers increasingly refer to the Internet when making consumption choices. Due to the advent of the Internet and various forms of social media (e.g., Facebook, YouTube, and Twitter), consumers are more connected to each other and sources of information in the current marketplace than at any point in history. Seth Godin (2009), an entrepreneur, author, and public speaker, refers to this phenomenon when he speaks about the rise of "tribes" and silos of interest, where people with unique interests connect with each other on the Internet. This trend, coupled with the concept of value co-creation (Prahalad & Ramaswamy, 2004) between consumers and firms, has contributed to increased two-way engagement between consumers and providers. Although communication typically occurs through firm-sponsored activities such as online forums, focus groups, and test markets, firms also receive feedback from social or consumer movements.

Boycotts and "culture jamming" are the most familiar forms of consumer activism with material damage as the intended outcome (den Hond & de Bakker, 2007). Traditionally, boycotts connote action in the physical realm such as picketing or letter-writing campaigns, whereas culture jamming is often a rhetorical protest (Harold, 2004), utilizing ads and plays on words, logos, and taglines to either hurt corporations or to take a stand (e.g., Adbusters, Whirl-Mart, and Billionaires for Wealthcare). Adbusters, for instance, create "space for consumers to reconsider the role of consumption in their lives to build up capitalism anew from the grassroots level" (Micheletti & Stolle, 2007, p. 170).

The virtual world has undeniably revolutionized consumer activism. Not only is there a vast amount of information at the tip of one's fingers, there is also the capacity to send out mass e-mails, share videos, and sign petitions with the click of a button. Thus, with the advent of template e-mails and the "share" or "forward" buttons, consumer action has become much less costly in terms of resources, including time, money, and thought. As Norris (2002, p. 4) writes, Internet "users have nearly unlimited choices and minimal constraints about where to go and what to do. Commitment to any particular online group can often be shallow and transient when another group is but a mouse click away. Most purely online communities without any physical basis are usually low cost, 'easy-entry, easy-exit' groups."

Ease of online action may result in "convenience activists" or what Montgomery, Gottlieb-Robles, and Larson (2004) call "armchair activists," who care about certain issues enough to engage in online action but may not desire to participate in social movements beyond the online environment. Contrary to this point, we have witnessed the use of social media in organizing real-life activism in citizen-led campaigns in the Middle East (think of the role of social media in the recent Egyptian revolution). This space intersecting activism and social media is forming with respect to understanding how consumer movement organizers use social media to further engage online activists in their cause to facilitate seamless online and real-life action.

Recent research bridging consumer activism and the use of Internet, e-mail, social media, and so-called new media exist (Aaker & Smith, 2010; Albinsson & Perera, 2010; Bennett, 2003, 2004; Carty, 2011; Hollenbeck & Zinkhan, 2006; Kahn & Kellner, 2004; Kozinets & Belz, 2010; McCaughey & Ayers, 2003; Peretti (with Micheletti), 2004; Pickerill, 2003). However, additional research is warranted, particularly with respect to consumer movements' use of social networking sites such as Twitter, Facebook,

YouTube, and various blogs in furthering their causes. Therefore, we present a case study of Carrotmob, a consumer activist movement that integrates online and real-life action, to explore the use of social media in spreading a consumer movement and further engaging online consumer activists. As a secondary point, Carrotmob is a form of positive activism that brings material gain and focuses on cooperation with businesses (den Hond & de Bakker, 2007) and sustainable consumption. The movement highlights how pro-environmental organizers can co-operate with businesses to create win–win solutions that may initiate industrywide changes over time. By focusing on Carrotmob we aim to contribute to the discussion of how consumers and organizations co-operate to create win–win solutions in terms of social value in the marketplace. We study the evolution of Carrotmob's interaction with consumers from their start in 2008 to the present time through analysis of their blogs, and other social media output. The following broad questions guided our research: what influence do social media exert in consumers' decisions to participate in social change campaigns? What influences consumers and businesses to engage in "positive" campaigns?

Social Movements—A Matter of Approach

Throughout their history, Americans have engaged in almost continuous series of boycotts, demands for leisure and recreation, campaigns for access to the benefits of consumer society, and efforts to promote safe and ethical consumption. (Glickman, 2009, p. 1)

Social movements are collective efforts to transform the social order (Buechler, 2000) often with respect to consumption and marketing (Kozinets & Handleman, 2004) in terms of antibrands (Hollenbeck & Zinkhan, 2006) and other forms of resistance to consumption (Penaloza & Price, 1993). These movements typically comprise the goal, the activists, and their adversary (Melucci, 1989; Touraine, 1981). Traditionally such movements involved consumer boycotts, a term coined in the 1880s (Glickman, 2009), where organizers called for consumers to refrain from purchasing products or services generated by corporations that violated certain principles, for example, those using child labor, or those doing business in countries with human rights abuses. Examples of consumer boycotts from U.S. history involve British tea, slave-made goods, Japanese silk, Nestlé's chocolate, and Nike sneakers (Glickman, 2009). Boycotts create and spread negative messages about a particular target with the intent of raising consumers' awareness (O'Rourke, 2005) and persuading the target to change the undesirable practices. A current example is the Canadian Seafood Boycott organized by the U.S. Humane Society to stop commercial seal hunting which kills up to 200,000 seals annually in Canada. The organizers ask consumers to vote with the "power of our pocketbooks" and pressure restaurants and grocery stores to not buy or sell Canadian seafood until the seal hunting is stopped (The Humane Society, 2011). To date, more than 5,000 grocery store chains, including Trader Joe's and Harris Teeter, and restaurants such as Margaritaville Cafés are boycotting Canadian seafood until seal hunting is banned.

Although consumer boycotts may encourage some corporations such as Nike to re-examine and modify their value chain, they constitute "a collective effort to coerce corporate change" (Kozinets & Handelman, 1998, p. 475). Faced with coercive pressure, the possibility exists for corporations to pay lip service to newly adopted policies and practices that temporarily appease the boycotters without making lasting changes. However, consumers can also bring about desired changes through a positive cooperative approach instead of in an adversarial manner. This approach, referred to as "positive activism," entails organizing on behalf of what an activist is for, rather than against (Friedman, 1996). This idea is embodied in the environmental activist, Julia Butterfly Hill's quote, "Often activism is based on what we are against, what we don't like, what we don't want. And yet we manifest what we focus on. And so we are manifesting yet ever more of what we don't want, what we don't like, what we want to change . . . but [now] it is my feeling of 'connection' that drives me, instead of my anger and feelings of being disconnected" (as quoted in Brezsny, 2005, p. 76).

In keeping with this sentiment our case study is of a social-media-driven consumer movement that approaches activism with a positive focus; positive activism in the form of a *buycott* (or a reverse-boycott, a backward boycott) which we posit is part of Glickman's (2009) "new consumer activism." The extant literature also references both boycotting and buycotting activities as *political consumerism* (Stolle, Hooghe, & Micheletti, 2005) and *socially conscious consumption* (Anderson & Cunningham, 1972). According to an online blog, positive activism aims to promote action rather than argument and focuses on accountability and results, community involvement, and also aims to make a difference (It Is the Question, 2006).

Buycotting (not boycotting) rewards businesses that exhibit desirable behaviors. Buycotters make deliberate decisions to support desirable business practices through their consumption choices despite inconvenience, increased costs, and reduced choices (Neilsen, 2010). Several online communities and organizations promoting positive activism exist (e.g., Center for a New American Dream and Earth Aid Group Buys), with much of the activism oriented to political consumerism where consumers "vote" through their consumption choices in the form of purchasing dollars (Brinkman, 2004; Glickman, 2009; Shah et al., 2007; Shaw et al., 2005). There is evidence in recent social movement literature that practices by fringe actors, such as activists and volunteers, can provide for new industry and institutional praxis as with the U.S. recycling industry (Lounsbury, Ventresca, & Hirsch, 2003).

Social Media Driven Activism—A Mixed Bag?

> Activists have not only incorporated the Internet into their repertoire but also . . . changed what counts as activism, what counts as community, collective identity, democratic space, and political strategy. (McCaughey & Ayers, 2003, p. 2)

The goal with most forms of consumer activism is for "relatively powerless individual consumers and workers to redress the imbalance in the marketplace" (Hawkins, 2010, p. 123). This imbalance may lead to the emergence of consumer activism with positive outcomes. For instance, the development of public access features of the Internet stems from the work of community-based organizations and policy activists that built networks and developed online bulletin board systems to provide public access and share text-based information online. Although the World Wide Web was initially important in simply providing access to information, with today's more advanced technology, "Blogs make the idea of a dynamic network of ongoing debate, dialogue and commentary central and so emphasize the interpretation and dissemination of alternative information. . . ." (Kahn & Kellner, 2004, p. 91). Activism traditionally entailed activists gathering and engaging in protests, however, the Internet, and more recently, social media have given rise to online or cyber activism, with social media clearly revolutionizing the mobilizing efforts that are essential to all forms of activism (McAdam, McCarthy, & Zald, 1996). Today, social movement organizations (SMOs) and "wired activism," Carty's (2011) description of online consumer activism, is redefining political consumerism by using the Internet as an organizational tool for recruiting, mobilizing, and strategizing, fundraising, and campaigning.

Vegh (2003) classifies online/Web-based, or Web-enhanced, activism into three categories: awareness/advocacy, organization/mobilization, and action/reaction. Awareness/advocacy entail providing contrary information to raise awareness on a given issue, organizing the movement, and engaging in lobbying efforts. Organization/mobilization may comprise calling for offline action, where the offline mobilization efforts may be more effectively conducted through the Internet. Finally, action/reaction entail online attacks on various sites of interest by hackers or "hacktivists" (Vegh, 2003). Thus, social movement organizers have various options in terms of how they integrate online activism into their movements, and with the high accessibility to the Internet and social media, consumers also have the opportunity and the choice of the extent to which they participate in online activism.

Undoubtedly, the Internet offers individuals greater freedom of action in the absence of real-world constraints such as vast distances that may pose difficulties for individuals to participate in a given movement. The Internet connects people and provides them with unlimited possibilities in terms of what causes to engage in, and to what degree. Indeed, in the spirit of Godin's (2009) notion of "tribes" as masses of people congregating in cyberspace around common interests, the propagation of ideas over social media has resulted in individuals from far reaches of the globe joining forces on behalf of various causes. A recent example is an initiative by the Mining Zone People's Solidarity Group that is spearheading a petition by academics worldwide requesting the investment giant, TIAA-CREF, to reconsider its investments in POSCO, the South Korean steel company due to its abusive practices in India. However, despite the strong online activity such as signing petitions and spreading awareness of social causes, some writers allude to an inherent difference between online activism and real-life activism.

Malcolm Gladwell (2010), for example, argues that although social media may indeed increase participation in various causes, the level of commitment required for one to sign an online petition is distinctly different from the commitment that was necessary for four African American college students to sit at a segregated lunch counter in the American South in the 1960s. This point about increased cursory participation coupled with limited commitment references a new breed of activists who engage in social causes to a point. These individuals may sign online petitions and join Facebook activist pages but may not have the desire, or resources, to engage in traditional activism such as protests (Caplan, 2009). Hesse (2009) discusses the issues with Facebook activism whereby people click to join various causes but this online action does not translate into any worthwhile action. She quotes Mary Joyce of DigiActive, an organization that helps activists with the effective use of social media to advance their causes, as saying, "Commitment levels are opaque. Maybe a maximum of 5 percent are going to take action, and maybe it's closer to 1 percent. . . . In most cases of Facebook groups, members do nothing. I haven't yet seen a case where the Facebook group has led to a sustained movement." Although the media (Caplan, 2009; Kerwin, 2010) often refer to such online activists as "slactivists," based on our research and observations, we term them "convenience activists." However, Kerwin (2010) acknowledges that for some individuals, social media engagement with a particular cause may signify the beginning of more engaged activism later, especially if the social movement organizers use open-source platforms that enable digital sit-ins and allow for the sharing of user-generated content.

Despite the derisive attitude toward the slactivists they play a role in spreading the message about various issues, and, regardless of concerns about sustained action, they have delivered on event-based action. For example, consumers' online action halted the release of Lotus Marketplace in the early 1990s (Gurak & Logie, 2003). This product, created by Lotus Corporation (with information available through Equifax), would have provided easy access to data on millions of households; the ensuing activism revolving around privacy concerns halted the release of the product. More recently, overwhelming online consumer protests, particularly on Twitter and Facebook, in response to retail giant Gap changing their logo persuaded the company to revert to its original and beloved "blue box" within one week of the change (Richmond, 2010). Thus, despite concerns regarding sustained action and meaningful involvement, online activism has a record of producing results in terms of spreading a message and gaining attention of consumers, organizations, and mainstream media.

Past research on consumers using social media for social and environmental change has illustrated that social media foster a participatory culture, which builds awareness and encourages community building (Kozinets & Belz, 2010). The current work contributes to the literature because it studies the use of social media in the development of a consumer movement that integrates online and event-based, real-life action (i.e., one Carrotmob is a single activism event or a *single-target buycott*; Friedman, 1996). In essence, Carrotmob meets Rheingold's (2002) definition of a *smart mob,* as it comprises large masses of people using the Internet to mobilize online to accomplish common goals.

About the Site: Carrotmob.org

Carrotmob.org organized the first mob in San Francisco on March 29, 2008, and, between then and until the end of 2010, the movement has supported over 115 mobs in 70 cities/communities in over 20 countries (e.g., Figure 5.1; carrotmob.org). In addition to their primary Facebook site with over 11,390 members (as of May 2011), an increase of over 5,000 members since spring 2010, organizers create a new Facebook page for each city in which a mob is organized (Carrotmob NYC, Carrotmob Berlin, Carrotmob Melbourne). Through friendly competition, the various Carrotmob movements in different locales generate new ideas, urge new cities to participate, and challenge existing city-based movements to continue their efforts. As the company's Web site noted in the first year, Carrotmob's master plan and "model is not threatening, not expensive, not time-consuming, not uncomfortable, not 'radical,' not confusing, and not negative" (carrotmob.org).

The premise of the movement is simple: Carrotmob approaches several small businesses, for example, coffee shops, in a particular city about the possibility of greening their ventures by promising them "mobs" of customers during a specified date and time period. Local businesses then compete to do the most social good (e.g., increasing energy efficiency, reducing carbon footprints, or beginning recycling) and present their proposals on the Carrotmob Web site. For example, in Vancouver, Canada, Carrotmob approached 15 coffee shops and 5 submitted bids. Waves Coffee agreed to install energy-efficient lighting, water-efficient toilets/faucets, and refrigeration seals; Java-Licious would work on waste reduction; Gene Coffee Bar's suggestion was to upgrade to water-efficient toilets; Salt Spring Coffee promised to upgrade to energy-efficient lighting; and Re-Entry Espresso planned to establish a reusable cup exchange. Interested consumers registered on Carrotmob's Web site and voted on the various bids. In the case of our example, the Carrotmobber vote was: Waves Coffee–2%; Java-Licious–34%; Gene Coffee Bar–1%; Salt Spring Coffee–39%; and Re-Entry Espresso–24%. Once the vote was completed, the organizers announced the winner, Salt Spring Coffee, and the specific time and date of the mob via social media. On the day of the mob, local Carrotmobbers mobbed Salt Spring Coffee as a reward for their progressive action. These consumers performed a "buycott" and increased the business's sales during a specific time period; the buycott profits were allocated for helping the business implement the agreed-upon social value creating measure (e.g., energy-efficient lighting).

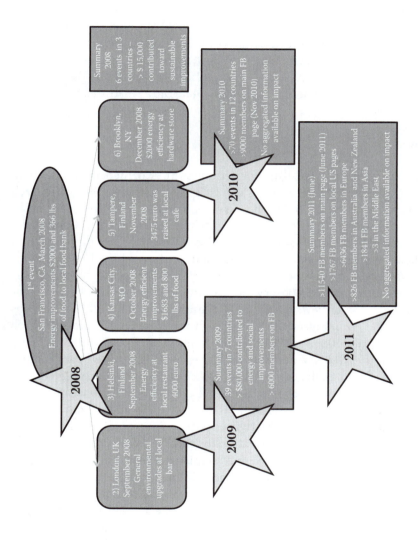

Figure 5.1 Growth of the Carrotmob movement.

Carrotmob presents a link between progressive business and motivated consumers, and the organization is a catalyst in the socially responsible business space with the potential for spawning long-term positive changes in business. Buycotters' actions directly benefit the chosen organization and, through the firm's adoption of sustainable practices, they indirectly benefit society. Since the first Carrotmob held in 2008, this grassroots social movement has spread virally through consumer traditional and electronic word of mouth (WOM, eWOM), YouTube, Facebook, Twitter, and the Carrotmob blog across the globe to countries as far-flung as Sweden, Germany, Malaysia, Sri Lanka, Qatar, and Australia.

Method

Data collection occurred through netnography (Kozinets & Handelman, 1998; Kozinets, 2002), otherwise known as online ethnographic research (Maclaran & Catterall, 2002) on Carrotmob.org, its blog, and select affiliated social media pages on YouTube, Twitter feeds, and Facebook pages of organized Carrotmobs (e.g., Carrotmob Toronto, Carrotmob Berlin). We became virtual members of these sites and established contact with other members of the virtual community. In addition to blog postings and field notes based on observations of the Web sites and blogs, we conducted online interviews via Skype (Ballantine & Creery, 2010) with various activists. We analyzed the blog posts from the official Carrotmob Web site from April 2008–May 2010 (in the latter part of 2010 Carrotmob.org redesigned the Web site and removed the previously posted data that we had archived and analyzed for a total of 127 pages of single-spaced text).

For triangulation purposes, and to explore the relationship among online activists, real-life mobs, and the use of social media, our research included hundreds of blog and twitter posts, 15 informal qualitative surveys of online activists in preparation for the 12 semistructured in-depth interviews we conducted via Skype. Semistructured, open-ended interview techniques were used with a range of informants (organizers, real-life participants, purely online activists) to uncover the role of social media in organizing Carrotmobs. In some cases, we interviewed the same informants multiple times to verify the data and expand their previous comments as the project progressed. Interviews were digitally recorded and transcribed. We maintained the privacy of our informants and the privacy of the virtual members who contributed to online posting by using pseudonyms instead of their names and online usernames.

Our analysis, conducted individually by each author through iterative readings of the data, yielded several themes pertaining to Carrotmob's development and mobilization efforts as its message spread through viral marketing and eWOM. Although the analysis of the blog posts provided evidence on how this specific consumer movement grew in its membership and mission, the interviews and online interaction with members gave us a more nuanced picture of the various issues the movement encountered. After coding, we collapsed the various themes into overarching categories that we anticipated played an important role in the use of social media in this consumer movement. Based on this analysis, we present a framework of the use of social media in consumer activism that offers an enhanced understanding of the intricacy in negotiating online/real-life action. We present our findings using Figure 5.2 as a guide.

Findings

> Activists often utilize the web to recruit, strategize, and create change, and some activism fixes on the politics of the Net itself. (McCaughey & Ayers, 2003, p. 15)

The posited framework of social media-driven consumer activism is comprised of five primary components: the draw of the cause, organizational strategy, consumer activists, influence of social media, and activism outcomes. These components interrelate at various times to engage consumers in the activism effort in terms of active individual participation and in spreading the movement's message to others and fueling their interest in the effort.

The Draw of the Cause: A "Normalized" Win–Win Grassroots Solution

> In a boycott everyone loses. In a carrotmob, everyone wins. (Carrotmob, Facebook)

The idea of positive activism (i.e., Carrotmob's focus on collaboration as opposed to coercion) proved to be a strong draw for many participants and organizers. For example, a blogger posted that she was attracted to Carrotmob for "the way that it brings members of a community together to effect real, grass-roots-level change . . . changing our [individual]

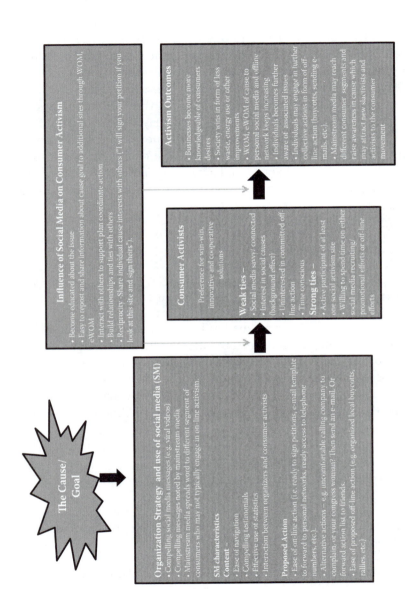

Figure 5.2 Framework of social-media-driven consumer activism.

lifestyles can only get us so far. Deeper changes are required, and we must come together to make them. Carrotmob seems to me like a really fun and positive way to do this" (Dietz, 2008). Another, a co-organizer of Canada's first Carrotmob, alluded to the movement's win–win proposition when noting, "Carrotmob is just a really cool way for businesses to engage with the community that they're in and also generate capital to be able to make changes, and that's something that's always a challenge for small businesses."

The uniqueness of the idea and the potential for generating meaningful social change, the sense of community and the energy associated with it in terms of mass mobs, and fun social media information (e.g., YouTube videos) led to many informants spreading Carrotmob's information readily within their personal networks. Our analysis indicates that the movement's positive message, eye-catching publicity, the mix of the serious (in terms of social change/social impact), the fun (shopping, mobbing en masse), and the event-specific engagement (one mob = one event) was instrumental in participants' decision to spread Carrotmob's message. For example, a Carrotmob supporter posted on the movement's blog, "Just learned about carrotmob . . . 15 minutes ago. Incredible idea. Got to the Web site, saw the animation, laughed and then read all the FAQs. I still think it's a cute animation . . . now I understand exactly how carrotmob works . . . This is really quite something and I am going to tell everyone I know!" (Carrotmob blog post, 2/27/09).

In addition to the positive activism approach, Carrotmob further played a role in individuals' decisions to participate in the movement through focusing on "normalized" event-based activism, which busy individuals could easily integrate into their lives. We use the term normalized to signify the fact that Carrotmob's brand of activism entailed a very typical activity, shopping, which is well within the comfort range of many of the participants. Thus, Carrotmob's positive, single-event approach (i.e., a manageable level of commitment) coupled with a low-risk means of expressing activism (as opposed to picketing in traditional boycotts) attracted many individuals to the movement who may not have participated in consumer activism. In addition, Carrotmob's use of social media to update its followers frequently (thereby maintaining the saliency of the movement in members' lives) in the initial years of the movement and direct encouragement to participate from Carrotmob founder Brent Shulkin, and other staff further fostered engagement. To illustrate, Carrotmob's Twitter feed contained several messages to the effect of, "We don't have a Carrotmob planned for [insert city name]. Do you want to organize one?" Shulkin also posted the following response to a supporter's blog posts.

> You want us to do more carrotmobs, but that is not our focus and you are won-
> dering why . . . you are emailing me constantly with ideas. . . You want to start
> chapters in Israel, Australia, Brazil, South Africa. . . What this demonstrates
> is NOT that the 4 of us here in San Francisco need to start flying around the
> world planning more campaigns. It demonstrates that we need to empower you
> all to run campaigns. You will be the strength and lifeblood of Carrotmob. . .
> we want to give you information resources, access to experts, and most impor-
> tantly, a vibrant social network of like-minded citizens in your location that
> you will be able to tap into to make your campaigns successful. . . So start
> thinking of what YOU might want to organize when the time is right. (Blog
> post, June 13, 2008)

Such direct exchanges, the availability of action guides on the Carrotmob site, and invitations to participate were important in helping people feel a desire to take action to the extent that they were able to in a movement that furthered their beliefs pertaining to pro-environmental action and responsible business. Thus, Carrotmob provided consumers a feasible way in which to enact their consumers' socially responsible ideas.

Reframing Sticks to Carrots: An Organization Strategy for Helping Business Help the World

The organization strategy and social media use component comprises whether the organizing group creates and distributes compelling mes-sages (e.g., viral videos), the various outlets (e.g., YouTube, Twitter) through which these messages are dispersed, and whether they are noted and further dispersed by mainstream media to consumers who may not necessarily frequent online venues. As indicated elsewhere in the chapter, the use of social media is a very prominent aspect of Carrotmob's strat-egy. Our analysis indicates that the effective use of statistics (e.g., amount of money raised, or number of mob participants), and personal stories that compel individuals to take action, ease of online action (e.g., access of video to forward), availability of alternative actions (e.g., template e-mails to forward to network, or planned mob events), and ease of proposed real-life action (e.g., local buycotts, rallies) are important in terms of social media content. In addition, we find that the interaction between organiz-ers and consumers, especially in the early stages of the movement, is also important. Shulkin, in an early blog post from April 5, 2008, posts that

Carrotmob has been mentioned on "Wired.com, Smart Mobs, *LA Times*, *GOOD Magazine's* blog, BoingBoing.net, Team Jaded, Treehugger, Civic Actions, Earthfirst.com and a little mention in the *SF Chronicle*." This indicates strong online presence and illustrates the importance of media imprints in spreading the word in the early stages of the movement with respect to raising awareness and recruiting supporters.

A Parisienne Carrotmobber, despite her somewhat derisive stance toward business, discussed the necessity of reframing the traditional boycott ideology to a more affirmative form of activism by "offering carrots instead of sticks" to enact social change. In her perspective, "Businesses have no soul and . . . their motive is growth and more earnings. By intervening [through Carrotmobs] you get the business back 'on track' on [addressing] the social issues it has to face as a major component of the motors of our society." In contrast, another informant argued that

> Rewarding business is fantastic . . . it gives power to the consumer; it promotes progressive and charitable efforts, and if the concept of rewarding ethical and responsible biz practices catches on, people will think of charity and social responsibility as a lifestyle rather than an infrequent contribution, and it makes business compete. Competition is healthy for small businesses to flourish.

In both selected examples, despite varied views on business, the informants understood the importance of incentive-based activism strategy for persuading businesses to adopt socially responsible behaviors. Additionally, we contend that the notion of rewarding or, in reality, helping small businesses adopt socially responsible practices is a form of value co-creation between the business and the consumers.

The cooperation between Carrotmob and the businesses being mobbed is evident in the various media imprints. For example, CarrotmobNYC organizers recognized Brooklyn's Tarzian Hardware in an advertisement in an online newspaper (www.BrooklynPaper.com). The publication noted that Tarzian pledged to spend 22% of the revenue generated from the three-hour mob on enhancing the store's energy efficiency. The business owner, John Ciferni, was quoted in the same article, "I had never heard of anything like this before . . . at first I didn't know what to expect, but now it really seems like a win-win kind of thing" (Gardner, 2008). According to the Carrotmob Web site, this specific event netted $12,200 yielding approximately $4,000 for energy improvements. Clearly, providing small businesses with incentives and, most important, a means of generating revenue with which to enact socially responsible behaviors is a distinctly different form of activism. It constitutes a partnership between business and society, a broad-based co-creation relationship, with the potential to create long-term value to society.

Are Online Activists Slactivists?

Carrotmob relies on its supporters to spread the movement. Our data indicate that the consumer activists who participate in Carrotmob are typically social media savvy, interested in social causes (stemming from past experiences, media exposure, and education), time conscious, participants in a minimum of one social activism Web site, and have a preference for win–win solutions instead of adversarial relationships. Indeed, Brent Shulkin notes that his movement is "unique . . . there are no enemies" (Caplan, 2009) in contrast to the adversarial component salient in traditional activism literature (Melucci, 1989; Touraine, 1981). This approach signifies a change in stance toward corporations as, historically, consumer activism efforts entailed a mistrust of business and the idea that a struggle was required to change the social order. Our data clearly indicate that Carrotmob focuses on fostering change through cooperation between consumer activists and small businesses. This is perhaps to be expected because, thanks to technology and social media, the world is more connected and transparent than before. Consumers reward corporations for transparency and engagement thereby further fueling such approaches and, in addition, the notion of business delivering social, as well as economic, value is now commonplace. Perhaps this mix, in conjunction with societal and systemwide factors such as the recent financial institution collapse, has resulted in conditions where it is feasible for consumers and businesses to collaborate in creating win–win solutions and changing existing social orders.

The notion of slactivism was prevalent in our conversations with various informants. There was little consensus regarding the meaning of this term, but it was clear that our consumers did not desire to self-identify as such, indicating that some sort of stigma was attached to the term. One Carrotmob organizer stated that the term implied "privilege" as "slactivists may indeed pay more for fair trade coffee or chocolate but they don't necessarily exhibit real commitment . . . paying an extra dollar for a product does not entail hardship and they do not have to do anything beyond their comfort zone to participate in the activism effort." Another organizer referred to slactivists' guilty conscience that drives them to take some form of minimal action. However, this informant noted that every consumer is in essence an activist because each individual "votes three times a day with whatever you buy and eat." As such, consumers have a responsibility to support good organizations and ethical brands that support "good systems," for instance, those eliminating or minimizing ecological devastation. This represented a contrast in the sense that although this particular organizer viewed consumer purchases as an opportunity to support ethical brands and business practices, the informant was somewhat derisive of slactivists, or low commitment activists. Thus, in this informant's categorization, all consumers are potential activists in terms of, "How you consume—what you buy"; however, a person who maintains her activism at the level of consumption is a slactivist, but those who participate in real-life action, such as rallies and other community-based events, represent a deeper level of commitment to activism efforts. Other informants who participated in Carrotmobs, but had more engaged activism experience in their backgrounds, also characterized these en masse mob events as a form of slactivism, due to what was seen as a one-time engagement and the fact that the activism centered upon purchasing. In a Skype interview from October 2010, Carina shared, "I believe Carrotmob is a form of slactivism for some people. I am currently working for a nonprofit saving endangered species full time for free, to me, that is activism."

Another organizer identified consumers' sense of self-efficacy and their belief that their actions (i.e., participating in a mob event or passing on information to their network) contribute to a systemwide positive impact as also influencing individuals' degree of participation. This informant identified self-efficacy as a differentiator between slactivists and serious activists. Although this needs further exploration, this organizer may have a point in that consumers who are interested in social causes but are unsure of their impact may yet engage in minimal online action but will not take concerted action. One must be careful to avoid painting all online activists as slactivists because we found several individuals who limited their activism effort to the online environment yet contributed significantly to the cause in terms of spreading messages and posting online content.

Online members' comments indicate that many see Carrotmob events as feasible opportunities to integrate activism into their busy lives. Many of our informants were comfortable with Carrotmob's convenient, and familiar (in terms of shopping activity), form of activism relative to participating in coercive movements. Moreover, some participated because they could be practically anonymous online yet support the cause by spreading its message. Some activists, for example, informant Brenda, "offset" her inability to participate in real-life events due to lack of opportunity in her local community by consistently disseminating Carrotmob messages through her blog and other social media sites.

Social Media as a Facilitator of a Global Community Through Real-Time Connections

Some of Carrotmob supporters' comments on the Internet clearly indicate how social media facilitate the spread of the movement's message around the world. For instance, Henri, a Carrotmob supporter who lives in Africa notes in an interview, "Social media has influenced me to become a member of their [Carrotmob] Facebook page and find out more about their ideas. I am willing to drop in and see what is going on, but without a tweet or a Facebook posting as a reminder, I would probably not dig enough to become fundamentally involved" (Skype interview, 10/14/10). The latter point about Carrotmob's frequent social media activity is important because our analysis indicates that the movement utilizes social media to create a sense of community and familiarity between the movement organizers and consumers. For example, in the case of Twitter, Carrotmob frequently informs their followers (3,480 individuals) of upcoming North American and global mobs (e.g., Indonesia, Germany, United Kingdom), and recognizes specific Twitterers and various organizations for spreading Carrotmob's message. In terms of locale-specific mobs, a Canada-based Carrotmob co-organizer shared that his mob used Facebook, Twitter, DigIt, and RSS feeds, which link all these sources, to raise awareness of the event. He noted, "It's great to be able to share links really quickly on iGoogle and other media . . . you ask members for help spreading the word and setting up accounts. Before an event, we spam as many people as we could and as many networks we can find . . . we constantly update [mob-related information] on Facebook and Twitter" (Skype interview, 11/3/10).

Carrotmob uses social media to announce major organizational shifts, for example the launch of the new Web site, and to solicit donations from supporters (e.g., "Hi mob. Very soon we will, for the first time ever, ask you for financial support. What clichés should we avoid when we do this?)" The latter point represents a significant change in the movement's operation, and Carrotmob posted the same message on its Web site (which changed from a .com address to a .org address), Facebook page, and blog presumably in order to garner the widest possible coverage. This, in addition to other data, indicates a heightened level of real-time engagement between

Carrotmob and its supporters, and a great willingness on the part of the movement to solicit feedback from its constituents, imparting to consumers that the organization values supporters' perspectives. For example, Carrotmob also used social media to solicit feedback on other items including their new Web page design and business-related matters (e.g., Tweet 4/29/11, "Going to Germany in June [2011] to meet with the world's top Carrotmob organizers! Who wants to meet? What should I do? My plan: http://is.gd/e4ouPN"). Such an approach also sends the message that supporters are shaping and developing this movement with the organizers.

Beyond encouraging online and event-based mob participation, Carrotmob fosters deeper engagement in the movement by asking their supporters to consider planning mobs in their home cities (e.g., Tweet 10/3/08, "@pollyannefaith thx! there's been 1 Cmob in PDX: http://portland.carrotmob.org but the organizer left for college so u can pick up torch!"). This direct, real-time encouragement from the movement's headquarters may persuade certain individuals to participate to a greater extent than they otherwise may. In keeping with close community feel, Carrotmob's Twitter feed asks potential organizers to contact the Carrotmob headquarters presumably for assistance in launching city-specific mobs. Carrotmob also encourages stronger engagement when it solicits volunteer participation beyond mob-related matters when the organization needs specific types of aid (e.g., Tweet 7/23/10, "We are hard at work on our new Web site! Any front-end designers willing to volunteer a bit during the next week or two? info@carrotmob.org").

Carrotmob uses social media outlets to impart a sense of transparency on factors such as ongoing development (e.g., the Web site), and founder Shulkin. In addition, Carrotmob educates its followers in general matters related to Carrotmob's aims (e.g., Tweet 3/18/11, "How Social Media Can Reinvigorate Consumer Advocacy - http://on.mash.to/fMAxFV") and informs them of media related to Carrotmob's efforts (e.g., FB Manchester post 12/22/10 "In case you missed it on 300 public radio stations, listen to Carrotmob's feature on Living On Earth: http://bit.ly/fi6Oql #AcidWashedDenim") through social media. The organization adds to the intimate feeling/closeness between itself and followers by introducing various staff to followers as they come on board (e.g., CM blog "It's Carrotmob's lucky day: Sarah has joined the team! http://carrotmob.org/blog/meet-sarah/"). We contend that familiarity with those at the movement's headquarters imparts supporters with the feeling of being knowledgeable and connected to the organization and its efforts. This sense of familiarity and transparency is enhanced through the Carrotmob Web site's new Q&A section where the organizers provide answers to questions via VYou, a conversational video software. Members are encouraged to post user-generated content (e.g., promotional videos for mobs, follow-up videos of successful mobs, interviews with participating business owners and supporters) on Carrotmob's official Web site, Facebook pages, and their YouTube account. We noted that members, proud of their efforts, indeed publicize their mob successes through the means offered by Carrotmob HQ. For instance, a Swedish female mob organizer posted the question, "I would like to registrate [sic] a carrotmob at your homepage we did in Sweden a couple of weeks ago. We were about 500 people! How to do?" (November 1, 2010) to which Carrotmob responded through VYou with instructions.

Thus, Carrotmob builds a sense of community with its followers over social media by providing information, recognizing individuals and other organizations for supporting Carrotmob, imparting a sense of transparency, and building a sense of familiarity with the organizations by introducing staff and providing updates on happenings within the movement. The fact that Carrotmob solicits feedback from supporters is indicative of a two-way communication stream between the movement and its members. This interaction, and the fact that followers have the option of sending tweets that come to the movement organizers' immediate attention and adding user-generated content to Carrotmob social media pages conveys the sense that these consumers have a hand in shaping the development of this movement beyond being the driving force behind the success of the city-specific Carrotmobs.

Influence of Social Media on Consumer Activism

This influence is very prominent in the current context. Many of our informants reported finding out about the movement through an online source (e.g., seeing the logo on blogs or a Facebook wall) and through local news TV/radio programs. Our data also revealed that members with high levels of online activity, and well-developed social media skills such as posting online videos and blogging were especially valued by the mob organizers. One organizer stated,

> No one really teaches you about the different Facebook groups or pages or how to tweet . . . a friend of mine across the country . . . she has her own blog and is constantly tweeting. . . . I let her be the main tweeter person/social media person so she slowly racked up 300 followers in about a month from her personal iPhone. She was never there during the organizing process but she was our main driver for our Twitter account. (Skype Interview, September 3, 2010)

This illustrates that sole online participation is not necessarily indicative of slactivism, and some activists contribute significantly to a cause without ever participating in a real-life mob.

In addition to utilizing social media sites, many local organizers spammed people in their networks to raise awareness and recruit members. They conducted searches on sites such as wiseearth.org for causes related to the mobs they were organizing (in order to identify more collaborative partners and new networks) and issued press releases to online and local print and other media. Neilson (2010, p. 216) writes, "Through networks of associations, and trusting, reciprocating relationships, people gain access to information and resources that motivate and facilitate political consumerism." In this regard, we note that Carrotmob collaborates with different partners, for example, with 350.org and Net Impact, to pursue endeavors that are reflective of both partners' interests. Shulkin, in a blog post on April 24, 2008, notes the importance of partnerships. He writes, "Team up with other groups to use their infrastructure [for instance, YouTube] and expertise. . . . we team up with them to do a campaign. They get the benefits of our network and we get the benefit of their infrastructure." For example, Carrotmob's partnership with 350.org resulted in a successful outcome on October 24, 2009 when eight Carrotmobs were organized worldwide (two in Germany, four in the United States, one in Australia, and one in Canada) in conjunction with International Day of Climate Action. In several instances, the mobs increased the participating businesses' revenues by as much as 100% relative to typical transactions resulting in over $8,400 being earmarked for implementing energy efficiency and other sustainability-related endeavors for small businesses. Such collaboration allows access to a wider range of resources and consumers' networks, thereby furthering the interests of all partner organizations.

Finally, in terms of Carrotmob's weaknesses, the movement modified its blog and Web site two years after the launch of operations (around the time they became a nonprofit organization) but did not update them on a regular basis. Some of the modifications were quite different from existing practices, for instance, asking visitors to log in to the Carrotmob Web site with a new login name or through Facebook, and we found that much of the earlier material posted on their Web site was removed. We found this to be a weakness in Carrotmob's strategy in terms of showing the impact of the mobs, and Carrotmob's history as this information may play a role in whether newcomers decide to participate.

Social Change—Outcomes of Positive Activism

Our analysis indicates that in the case of Carrotmob, social media assist geographically dispersed activists in working toward the common goals of helping small businesses adopt environmentally friendly measures and ultimately of eradicating the need for the organization itself. Carrotmobs began in San Francisco, and spread across the world in a matter of a few years. It is fair to say that the growth Carrotmob has seen in its first three years would not have been possible without their strategic use of social media (e.g., one of the most recent mobs was held in Kuala Lumpur (Tweet 4/22/11) and the two most popular countries (per capita) to organize carrotmobs are Finland and Germany. The collaborative efforts of business and consumers alike have generated excitement, hope, and small-scale changes in terms of businesses adopting energy-efficient measures, and starting recycling programs, for example. In addition, the mass mobbing garners attention, and local mainstream media, as well as global networks such as CNN, have covered these events thereby contributing to spreading Carrotmob's message and the idea that consumers can make a difference with their "regular" purchases. This indeed empowers the average consumer. Juhn (2010) writes about a local Carrotmob in a university newspaper:

> It's about substantiating the "power" of the people. When everyday citizens in a community can generate change that government or private corporations cannot or refuse to accommodate, it speaks to the will and character of those people. If we want to complain about the state of affairs that our community, state, or country or even world is in, we have an obligation and duty to participate in the efforts to make it better.

The Importance of Weak and Strong Ties in Building a Movement

Carrotmob event organizers emphasized the importance of recruiting members with both strong and weak ties in activism efforts. The strong ties pertain to individuals with some form of stronger commitment to the movement, for instance, those who have previously participated in Carrotmob efforts or who know Carrotmob organizers. In contrast, those with weak ties could be individuals who have come across Carrotmob's message on the Internet and identify with it, but may not participate in real life, or may be constituents of affiliated organizations. Weak and strong ties offer different benefits and provide access to different kinds of resources (Adler & Kwon, 2002; Burt, 1992; Coleman, 1988; Granovetter,

1973). Strong ties provide social and psychological support (Putnam, 2000), cultivate trust and obligation leading to shared norms (Coleman, 1988), and grant individuals legitimacy thereby allowing them access to network resources (Adler & Kwon, 2002). Weak ties, or bridging ties, that typically develop among people with diverse interests and backgrounds, allow individuals to access resources, such as information, available beyond his or her immediate network (Granovetter, 1973; Burt, 1992).

A Canadian carrotmob organizer noted that basing a movement solely on weak ties could be problematic because when inconveniences surface, such as poor weather, it is easy for the participants to forego attending the event. In contrast, those with strong ties are more apt to attend and support the action irrespective of inconveniences because they feel a sense of obligation, or are committed to the effort. However, we do find that compelling activism messages influence this relationship because there were instances where people without strong ties participated, despite inconveniences, because they believed in Carrotmob's message. Finally, it is important to recognize that though weak ties may be less reliable in terms of real-life action, they are yet very important to a movement because they have the potential to facilitate the spread of the movement's message online.

Discussion and Conclusion

The posited framework social-media-driven consumer action guides our discussion. Carrotmob's collective action highlights how consumers, empowered by new tools, have elevated their expectations (Meadows-Klue, 2008) through the availability of social media. Findings suggest that social media are strategically used to inform, organize, and coordinate consumers. As the movement noted on their Web site, mobs are "the perfect level of involvement for most people" (carrotmob. org). Movements such as Carrotmob focus upon fostering cooperation between consumers and corporations and, we argue, value co-creation. Consumers may not co-create an actual product or service, however, they contribute to co-creating the firm's overall value chain proposition through the firm's adopting greener practices that add value to products or services. In the bargain, these consumers change the industry as corporations compete to participate in the mob. These corporations realize that consumers are rewarding them for adopting greener practices. This insight may encourage more firms to become green, thus contributing

to changing industry practices, as they realize that socially responsible behavior can be profitable. However, similar to nonprofit activist recyclers who used their own communication networks to mobilize
protests and join forces on behalf of other community-building issues
(Lounsbury et al., 2003), Carrotmobbers utilize their social media networks to spread the Carrotmob message, organize real-life participation,
and share information about other social causes. Although these nonprofit recyclers lost out to for-profit waste recycling models (Lounsbury
et al., 2003), Carrotmobbers co-operate with for-profit businesses to help
them adopt socially responsible business practices.

Social-media-powered messages are spread through consumers'
social networks, and consumer networks play a role in the integration
of online and real life activism. In this regard, the notion of strong and
weak ties stemming from the social capital literature surfaced in our
findings. Adler and Kwon (2002, p. 23) defined social capital as "the
goodwill available to individuals and groups" that stems from the individual's social relationships with its effects arising from the "information, influence, and solidarity it makes available to the actor." Putnam
(2000), in turn, regarded social capital as comprising norms of reciprocity and trustworthiness arising from individuals' relationships.
In terms of ties, weak ties represent relationships with acquaintances,
whereas strong ties are those relationships with friends (Granovetter,
1973). Intuitively, trust is more likely to exist within tightly knit communities that have strong ties as opposed to those having weak ties.
Trust is an important factor in buycotts. Individuals who are more
trusting are more apt to participate in buycotts "with the expectation
that institutions will be responsive to the people they represent" than
less trusting individuals who may be more interested in boycotts as a
means of punishing organizations (Neilsen, 2010, p. 217). Indeed, we
found that many of our informants were drawn to Carrotmob due to
its focus on positive activism and that they relished the idea of helping
small businesses adopt socially responsible practices.

As our data suggest, consumers understand that businesses do not
always know what consumers want. As one Carrotmob organizer
expressed, "Businesses needs [sic] guidance and support. The mob is
about helping local businesses, supporting business, and guiding them
from community that is surrounding the business. You are teaching them
what you want from them and how they can do better." This illustrates
the desire for consumers to be part of the value-creation process in the
marketplace and portrays the need for "reassurance, transparency, and

most of all, honesty" in the dialogue between corporations and consumers (Tucker, 2007, p. 9).

Interestingly, with respect to this point, we found that Arnould's (2007, p. 97) discussion of "agency" as "the physical or mental ability, skill or capability that enables actors to do something" came into play as some of our reported feelings of empowerment and a sense of agency when they decided to participate in Carrotmob by spreading their message to others. Additionally, consistent with Klandermans's (2004) reasons for participating in social movements (instrumentality, identity, ideology), our informants' Carrotmob participation involved *instrumentality* as many participated with the intent to influence the social and political environment, *identity* as most consumers participated due to their identification with Carrotmob's message and its positive activism approach, and *ideology* as some participated to express their social views.

To conclude, studying social-media-powered consumer activism is important in understanding the power of this medium in motivating consumers to integrate activism into their lives in the form of their purchasing dollars. Carrotmob organizers use social media to engage with, and coordinate, consumers' behavior/action to reward companies that adopt environmentally friendly practices that benefit the wider society. Social media have increased connections, and enhanced communication among consumers, and between consumers and corporations, some of whom are separated by distance. Online consumer activists now have the means to reach a wide range of fellow consumers through list serve, online communities, and even spam e-mails. Although some contend that this ease of access has given rise to slactivists, based on our research, we think of them as "convenience" activists. We further contend that consumer movements that persuade such online convenience activists to bridge the gap between online and real-life action make their causes more salient in consumers' minds. These movements create comprehensive win–win situations by showing consumers how they can integrate activism efforts into their lives with ease. The consumers win in terms of garnering psychological well-being thorough their contributions toward societal welfare, the corporations win through being rewarded for adopting socially responsible practices, society benefits as a result of these practices, and the activists win through achieving their goals of encouraging corporations to adopt socially responsible practices, thereby planting seeds or industrywide changes.

Limitations, Future Research, and Managerial Implications

Our findings provide insight into consumer movements' use of social media, and posit a framework of social-media-driven consumer activism garnered from studying the positive activism efforts of one organization over a three-year period. However, as with most qualitative research that explores a unique case, or a specific context with respect to a phenomenon of interest, these findings are not generalizable. The online posts (blogs, and Carrotmob Facebook page) are the perspectives of select Carrotmobbers. As we sourced our data from limited social media outlets and select organizers and participants, we do not claim comprehensive data collection and analysis. This framework is not guaranteed to be applicable to every social movement or activist group utilizing social media, however, it serves as a starting point for further exploration of consumers' use of social media to drive social change.

During our research process, more questions surfaced about the use of social media in consumer movements. For example, this case study focuses on positive activism centered on the idea that consumers and corporations can co-operate to facilitate social change and, in essence, co-create value. This is a markedly different approach to traditional consumer activism and one may be tempted to assume those who participate in positive activism movements are of younger, and more technology-savvy generations. Future research questions could indeed explore these assumptions, and the use of social media with respect to other, more traditional activist contexts such as real-life protests and boycotts. In addition, many informants spoke of issues pertaining to slactivism in this particular movement, and it would be interesting to explore whether this phenomenon arises in other activism contexts. Due to the importance of networks in spreading online activism and integrating online/real-life action, the application of social capital theory with respect to the use of social media in propagating consumer movements is also a promising area of research. In this respect, future research could focus on how tie strength and centrality of individuals in a particular social network influence individuals' propensity to act on social media information received from those in their networks.

From a positive activism perspective, it would be interesting to explore other positive activism movements, particularly with respect to their use of social media. One aspect of this research could explore what sets positive activism movements apart from the traditional, more coercive forms of consumer activism, and whether they have differential outcomes in terms of relationships with the community and business world. One could also explore whether buycotts are the only influential form of positive activism, and explore other ways in which businesses and consumers can co-create social value. Finally, with respect to Carrotmob, an important area of future research could focus on accountability and whether businesses follow through on their promises and to what extent. Further research could also be conducted on business owners' perspectives by way of longer-term impact in terms of whether Carrotmob experience leads them to incorporate social value components in their business decisions, and challenges with mobs (e.g., too large mobs causing chaos, or too small mobs not providing sufficient revenue for promised improvements).

In terms of managerial implications, those involved in disseminating new ideas, recruiting members or customers, and calling for specific actions from their members and supporters in various organizational contexts (social movement organizations, nonprofits, and for-profits) may be able to use the framework in their strategizing and planning. Our findings suggest that encouraging more transparency and interaction among businesses and consumers can lead to social change and co-creation of value by focusing on rewards, instead of sanctions, to change firms' business practices. As a related point, with the wide access to the Internet and social media, firms must be cognizant of the fact that their online image matters and strive to maintain a positive, and active, online presence.

References

Aaker, J. & Smith, A. (2010). *The dragonfly effect: Quick, effective, and powerful ways to use social media to drive social change.* San Francisco: Jossey-Bass.

Adler, P. & Kwon, S.-W. (2002). Social capital: Prospects for a new concept. *Academy of Management Review, 27*(1), 17–40.

Albinsson, P. A. & Perera B. Y. (2010). *Putting the roots back in grassroots: Consumer activism through social media.* Working paper presentation at the Association of Consumer Research North American Conference, Jacksonville, FL, October.

Anderson, T. W. & Cunningham, W. H. (1972). The socially conscious consumer. *Journal of Marketing, 36*(3), 23–31.

Arnould, E. J. (2007). Should consumer citizens escape the market? *ANNALS of the American Academy of Political and Social Science, 611,* 96–111.

Ballantine, P. W. & Creery, S. (2010). The consumption and disposition behaviour of voluntary simplifiers. *Journal of Consumer Behaviour, 9*(1), 45–56.

Bennett, L. W. (2003). New media power: The Internet and global activism. In N. Couldry & J. Curran (Eds.), *Contesting media power: Alternative media in a networked world*. Lanham, MD: Rowman & Littlefield, pp. 17–38.

Bennett, L. W. (2004). Branded political communication: Lifestyle politics, logo campaigns, and the rise of global citizenship. In M. Micheletti, A. Follesdal, & D. Stolle (Eds.), *Politics, products and markets: Exploring political consumerism past and present*. New Brunswick, NJ: Transaction, pp. 101–126.

Brezsny, R. (2005). *Pronoia is the antidote for paranoia: How the whole world is conspiring to shower you with blessings*. Berkeley, CA: North Atlantic.

Brinkman, J. (2004). Looking at consumer behavior in a moral perspective. *Journal of Business Ethics, 51*(2), 129–141.

Buechler, S. M. (2000). *Social movements in advance capitalism*. New York: Oxford University Press.

Burt, R. S. (1992). *Structural holes*. Cambridge, MA: Harvard University Press.

Caplan, J. (2009). Shoppers, Unite! Carrotmobs are cooler than boycotts. *Time Magazine*, online article, May 15. Retrieved April 23, 2011 from http://www.time.com/time/business/article/0,8599,1898728,00.html

Carrotmob (2008). Retrieved April 23, 2011 from http://carrotmob.org

Carrotmob is coming to Brooklyn! (2008). *Brooklyn Paper*, December 13, http://www.BrooklynPaper.com

Carty, V. (2011). *Wired and mobilizing: Social movements, new technology, and electoral politics*. Boca Raton, FL: Routledge.

Coleman, J. (1988). Social capital in the creation of human capital. *American Journal of Sociology, 94*, S95–S120.

Contributor (2011). SUNY Oswego go green team hosts Carrotmob function and Bridie Manor. April 16, http://oswegocountrytoday.com/?=59970&print=1.

Den Hond, F. & De Bakker, F. G. A. (2007). Ideologically motivated activism: How activist gropus influence corporate social change activities. *Academy of Management Review, 32*(3), 901–924.

De Vreese, C. H. (2007). Digital renaissance: Young consumers and citizen? *ANNALS of the American Academy of Political and Social Science, 611*, 207–216.

Dietz, M. (2008). Activism challenge: Bringing Carrotmob to Brooklyn. The SunnyWay.com, December 2, http://www.thesunnyway.com/index.php/site/comments/activism_challenge_bringing_carrotmob_to_brooklyn

Friedman, M. (1996). A positive approach to organized consumer action: They "buycott" as an alternative to the boycott. *Journal of Consumer Policy, 19*, 439–451.

Gardner, E. (2008). This mob wants more green. *Brooklyn Paper, 31*(49), http://www.brooklynpaper.com/stories/31/49/31_49_eg_carrotmob.html?comm=1

Gladwell, M. (2010). Small change—Why the revolution will not be tweeted. *The New Yorker*, October 4. Retrieved October 10, 2010 from http://www.newyorker.com/reporting/2010/10/04/101004fa_fact_gladwell

Glickman, L. B. (2009). *Buying power: A history of consumer activism in America.* Chicago: University of Chicago Press.

Godin, S. (2009). *On the tribes we lead.* Retrieved March 2, 2010 from http://www. ted.com/talks/lang/eng/seth_godin_on_the_tribes_we_lead.html

Granovetter, M. S. (1973). The strength of weak ties. *American Journal of Sociology, 78*(6), 1360–1380.

Gurak, L. J. & Logie, J. (2003). Internet protests from text to Web. In M. McCaughey & M. D. Ayers (Eds.), *Cyberactivism: Online activism in theory and practice.* Boca Raton, FL: Routledge, pp. 25–46.

Harold, C. (2004). Pranking rhetoric: "Culture jamming" as media activism. *Critical Studies in Media Communication, 21*(3), 189–211.

Hawkins, R. A. (2010). Boycotts, buycotts and consumer activism in a global context: An overview. *Management and Organizational History, 5*(2), 123–143.

Hesse, M. (2009). Facebook's easy virtue "click through activism" broad but fleeting. *Washington Post,* July 2, http://www.washingtonpost.com/wp-dyn/content/ article/ 2009/07/01/ AR2009070103936.html

Hollenbeck, C. R. & Zinkhan, G. M. (2006). Consumer activism on the Internet: The role of anti-brand communities. *Advances in Consumer Research, 33,* 479–485.

Humane Society (The). (2011). *You can make the Canadian seafood boycott a success,* March 8. Retrieved June 15, 2011 from http://www.humanesociety.org/ issues/ seal_hunt/tips/ seafood_ boycott_success.html

It Is the Question (2006). http://itisthequestion.blogspot.com/2006/08/what-is-positive-activism.html

Juhn, J. (2010). Carrotmob's "buycotting" a remedy for apathy, complacency. *Badger Herald,* November 15, http:badgerherald.com/oped/ 2010/11/15/ carootmobs_buycottin.php

Kahn, R. & Kellner, D. (2004). New media and Internet activism: From "Battle of Seattle" to blogging. *New Media and Society, 6*(1), 87–95.

Kerwin, A. M. (2010). How to get the social-media generation behind your cause. *Advertising Age,* June 28, p. 8.

Klandermans, B. (2004). The demand and supply of participation: Social-psychological correlates of participation in social movements. In D. A. Snow, S. A. Soule, & H. Kriesi (Eds.), *The Blackwell companion to social movements.* Malden, MA: Wiley-Blackwell, pp. 360–379.

Kozinets, R. V. (1999). E-tribalized marketing? The strategic implications of virtual communities of consumption. *European Management Journal, 17*(June), 252–264.

Kozinets, R. V. (2002). The field behind the screen. Using netnography for market research in online communities. *Journal of Marketing Research, 39*(February), 61–72.

Kozinets, R. V. & Belz, F.-M. (2010). Social media for social change: Sustainability-based community in a sustainable world. In D. W. Dahl, G. V. Johar, & S. M. J. van Osselaer (Eds.), *Advances in consumer research* (Vol. 38). Duluth, MN: Association for Consumer Research.

Kozinets, R. V. & Handelman, J. M. (1998). Ensouling consumption: A netnographic exploration of boycotting behavior. In J. Alba & W. Hutchinson (Eds.), *Advances in consumer research* (Vol. 25). Provo, UT: Association for Consumer Research, pp. 475–480.

Kozinets, R.V. & Handelman, J.M. (2004). Adversaries of consumption: Consumer movements, activism and ideology. *Journal of Consumer Research, 31*(December), 691–704.

Lounsbury, M., Ventresca, M., & Hirsch, P. M. (2003). Social movements, field frames and industry emergence: A cultural-political perspective on US recycling. *Socio-Economic Review, 1*, 71–104.

Maclaran, P. & Catterall, M. (2002). Researching the social Web: Marketing information from virtual communities. *Marketing Intelligence & Planning, 20*(6), 319–326.

McAdam, D., McCarthy, J. D., & Zald, M. N. (1996). *Comparative perspectives on social movements: Political opportunities, mobilizing structures, and cultural framings.* New York: Cambridge University Press.

McCaughey, M. & Ayers, M. D. (2003). *Cyberactivism: Online activism in theory and practice.* Boca Raton, FL: Routledge.

Meadows-Klue, D. (2008). Falling in love 2.0: Relationship marketing for the Facebook generation. *Journal of Direct, Data and Digital Marketing Practice, 9*(3), 245–250.

Melucci, A. (1989). *Nomads of the present.* London: Macmillan.

Micheletti, M. & Stolle, D. (2007). Mobilizing consumer to take responsibility for global social justice. *ANNALS of the American Academy of Political and Social Science, 611*(May), 157–175.

Montgomery, K., Gottlieb-Robles, B., & Larson, G. O. (2004). Youth as e-citizens: Engaging the digital generation, a report by the Center for Social Media School of Communication American University, http://www.centerforsocialmedia. org/ecitizens/youthreport.pdf

Neilson, L. A. (2010). Boycott or buycott? Understanding political consumerism. *Journal of Consumer Behaviour, 9*(May–June), 214–227.

Norris, P. (2002). The bridging and bonding role of online communities [Editorial]. *International Journal of Press/Politics, 7*(3), 3–13.

O'Rourke, D. (2005). Market movements: Nongovernmental organization strategies to influence global production and consumption. *Journal of Industrial Ecology, 9*(1–2), 115–128.

Penaloza, L. & Price, L. L. (1993). Consumer resistance: A conceptual overview. *Advances in Consumer Research, 20*, 123–128.

Peretti, J. (with Micheletti, M.) (2004). The Nike sweatshop email: Political consumerism, internet and culture jamming. In M. Micheletti, A. Follesdal., & D. Stolle (Eds.), *Politics, products and markets: Exploring political consumerism past and present*. New Brunswick, NJ: Transaction, pp. 127–142.

Pickerill, J. (2003). *Cyberprotest: Environmental activism online*. New York: Manchester University Press.

Prahalad, C. K. & Ramaswamy, V. (2004). Co-creation experiences: The next practice in value creation. *Journal of Interactive Marketing, 18*(3), 5–14.

Putnam, R. (2000). *Bowling alone: The collapse and revival of American community*. New York: Simon & Schuster.

Rheingold, H. (2002). *Smart mobs: The next social revolution*. Cambridge, MA: Perseus.

Richmond, S. (2010). Take that Malcolm Gladwell. Twitter just got the Gap logo back. *Telegraph*, October 12. Retrieved April 23, 2011 from http://blogs.telegraph.co.uk/technology/shanerichmond/100005858/take-that-malcolm-gladwell-twitter-just-got-the-gap-logo-back/

Shah, D. V., McLeod, D. M., Kim, E.,Lee, S. Y., Gotlieb, M. R., Ho, S. S., & Breivik, H. (2007). Political consumerism: How communication and consumption orientations drive "lifestyle politics." *ANNALS of the American Academy of Political and Social Science, 611*(May), 217–235.

Shaw, D., Grehan, E., Shiu, E., Hassan, L., & Thomson, J. (2005). An exploration of values in ethical consumer decision making. *Journal of Consumer Behaviour, 4*(3), 185–200.

Stolle, D., Hooghe, M., & Micheletti, M. (2005). Politics in the supermarket: Political consumerism as a form of political participation. *International Political Science Review, 26*(3), 245–269.

Touraine, A. (1981). *The voice and the eye*. Cambridge, UK: Cambridge University Press.

Tucker, A. (2007). Big brands out to address consumer activism positively. *Sunday Times* (South Africa – Business Times Edition), March 18, 2007, p. 9.

Vegh, S. (2003). Classifying forms of online activism: The case of cyber protests against the World Bank. In M. McCaughey & M. D. Ayers (Eds.), *Cyber activism: Online activism in theory and practice*. Boca Raton, FL: Routledge.

6

Authenticity in Online Communications
Examining Antecedents and Consequences

*Lauren I. Labrecque**
Northern Illinois University

Shabnam H. A. Zanjani
Northeastern Illinois University

George R. Milne
University of Massachusetts

Web 2.0 has raised new concerns for consumers in their experiences with brands and marketing communications. An increase in constructed realities in the Web 2.0 environment makes it increasingly difficult to differentiate between real and unreal objects, and consequently, consumers are left searching for authenticity. Recently, authenticity has been discussed widely in the online consulting literature (Mitra, 2002) and is considered a fundamental building block of an online strategy. Within the marketing literature scholars are beginning to explore the importance of authenticity (Alexander, 2009; Grayson & Martinec, 2004; Leigh, Peters, & Shelton, 2006), yet it remains unclear what factors lead to or result from authenticity. Some studies have tried to capture the meaning of authenticity and its attributes (Grayson & Martinec, 2004), however, their focus was on an offline context (authenticity of items and experiences). To date, little is known about the impact of online authenticity on communication effectiveness from consumers' perspectives.

This study investigates the factors that make an online interactive communication authentic and the effect of authenticity and its antecedents (i.e., interaction quality) on consumers' trust. The focus is on the

---

* The first two authors contributed equally and are listed alphabetically.

meanings that are co-created by companies and consumers in the context of corporate blogs and the beliefs they maintain in terms of authenticity, interaction quality, and trustworthiness. The underlying argument is that these constructs are interrelated and the relationships between them can be described based on the basic communication model. After defining and reviewing the literature related to each of these constructs, we present the conceptual framework guiding the empirical study. We end with a discussion of our methods, findings, and implications.

Conceptual Framework

Social Media

Organizations today can choose a mixture of traditional and new communication methods to implement an integrated marketing communication (IMC) strategy. Although effective IMC helps firms address their target market and satisfy their marketing objectives (Peltier, Schibrowsky, & Schultz, 2003), this choice demands extensive planning and a close examination of the costs and benefits.

There have been many advances in how firms design their IMC plans, but the most effective phenomenon is the advent of the Internet. The Internet provides a tremendous capacity and many features, with lowered costs over traditional communication channels. One important feature of the Internet is the capacity for firms to create two-way communication with consumers. This can be achieved through a variety of social media channels including blogs, social networks (e.g., Facebook), microblogging sites (e.g., Twitter), and geolocation sites (e.g., Foursquare). Blogs were one of the earliest online tools adopted by firms and their use has exploded (Lu, Lin, Hsiao, & Cheng, 2010) within the current decade. As the Internet altered the relationship between marketer and consumer (Deighton & Kornfeld, 2009), companies took notice of the power of online word-of-mouth communication to provide a powerful avenue to listen to and connect with their customers. For this reason, we focus on social media and blog communications in particular.

Blogs

Jorn Barger is credited as launching the first blog in December 1997 and coining the term "Weblog" (Wortham, 2007), which was later shortened to "blog." By 2004 the term "blog" was the most searched-for definition on multiple online dictionaries and began appearing widely in the news (Perlmutter & McDaniel, 2005). Then in June 2008, an Internet search engine designed specifically for searching blogs, Technorati, was created to index the approximately 112.8 million blogs and over 250 million pieces of tagged social media (Batts, Anthis, & Smith, 2008).

Four kinds of blogs have been distinguished in the literature: *personal, topic* or *industry, publication based,* and *corporate* (Smudde, 2005). A *personal blog* is one that is created by an individual to express his or her viewpoints about a topic (e.g., Jason Kottke, an early blog adopter, has maintained kottke.org since 1998 where he posts links and stories of personal interest). A *topic or industry blog* functions as a white paper about the nature and history of a specific topic, or discusses industry trends (e.g., Boing Boing and Techcrunch blogs focus on technology news). A *publication-based blog* is often created by editors or reporters with interests in specific subjects (e.g., Anderson Cooper 360 blog). Last, a *corporate blog* is one that is generated by companies to post messages to their audience and listen to their feedback (e.g., Dell's corporate blog). Among these four types, this study focuses on corporate blogs because they provide a medium for firms to communicate with customers.

Every day more companies are using social networks to make announcements about products and services, to react to events, interact with their customers, and gain insights and ideas by listening to their feedback. The subject-focused nature of blogs groups people with similar interests and engages them in timely conversations (Hsu & Lin, 2008). Delta airlines, General Motors, Amazon Web services, and Seagate are just few examples of companies who are actively involved in corporate blogging.

Despite the proliferation of blogs for many organizations, they have not gained wide acceptance as an integral part of their integrated communication strategy and their use is still under investigation. This hesitation in adopting blogs is partly related to supplying the resources required to maintain an active ongoing communication and the complexity of integrating blogs in the whole marketing communication strategy (Mack, Blose, & Pan, 2008).

Model of Communication

The basic mode of communication proposed by Shannon and Weaver (1949) offers a simple model that still holds relevance in today's media environment. The model includes three basic elements: sender, channel, and receiver, and describes the communication process as beginning with a sender creating a message, which is sent to a receiver via a communication channel. The sender (source) transforms information, thoughts, or ideas to a symbolic form, which represents the message (encoding process). The created message then transmits through a channel of communication (medium) to a receiver who interprets the sender's message (decoding process). The decoding of the message depends on the receiver's frame of reference and prior experience. The match between encoding and decoding is important as it can affect how accurately the receiver understands and interprets the message the source intends to communicate (Dennis, Fuller, & Valacich, 2008).

In interactive communications such as on the Internet, the source and receiver interchange positions as they respond to each other's messages. In the case of corporate blogs, consumers' postings are valuable sources of information for firms because they reflect the manner in which the corporate message is received and decoded and also enable firms to monitor how their intended messages are being interpreted. Whereas in a traditional communication model, consumers' responses are primarily gathered through research, with interactive communications, firms acquire feedback in real time (McMillan & Hwang, 2002).

In many respects blogging is an act of sharing and a new form of socialization (Hsu & Lin, 2008). In accordance with social construction theory, the information sharing in a social context depends on group interpretation and meaning development (Miranda & Saunders, 2003) in which the meaning derives from interactive interpretation by multiple people and not solely by one individual. That is, understanding is co-created by the interaction of participants. The important role of any medium in this process is the facilitation of this interaction.

Authenticity

The presentation of a company's messages through a medium helps consumers form interpretations and notions about the company. One of the most important concepts in postmodern consumer culture is authenticity, which has been a challenge for marketers to convey (Holt, 2002). The demand for authenticity has always existed among consumers; however, the issue has become more sensitive as technological advances obscure the difference between authentic and inauthentic objects (Grayson & Martinec,

2004). The literature describes three conceptualizations of authenticity (Wang, 1999; Leigh et al., 2006): (a) *objective authenticity*, which refers to authenticity of the origin; (b) *constructive authenticity*, which refers to constructive or subjective perceived values in the origin; and (c) *existential authenticity*, which refers to authenticity of the experience (not the object).

Despite the importance of this topic for marketing and consumer behavior, there exists scant research in these disciplines that attempts to define the construct or investigates its position in a broader setting (Alexander, 2009; Leigh et al., 2006). In defining the term "authenticity," Grayson and Martinec (2004) distinguish between *indexical* and *iconic* authenticity. An object is indexical when it is believed to be "the original" or "the real thing" and has a factual link (e.g., a paintbrush used by Picasso), whereas iconic authenticity describes when an object physically resembles the authentic object (e.g., an accurate reproduction of a painting or a re-enactment of an historical event). The definition of iconic authenticity is similar to Leigh et al.'s (2006) constructive authenticity, which places value in the object's origin.

Unlike in the marketing literature, authenticity has been widely researched in the tourism literature. Authenticity has been viewed as a segmentation variable to differentiate existential, experimental, recreational, and diversionary tourists, finding differences between the groups (Cohen, 1988). Authenticity has also been discussed as the key influential factor in overall satisfaction of historical districts' visitors with their tourism experience (Naoi, 2004) and as a key determinant of seaside resort choice (Sedmak & Mihalic, 2008).

Authenticity is seen as an important factor for brands, and it has been posited that brands should induce nostalgia and heritage to be seen as authentic or unique (Brown, Sherry, & Kozinets, 2003). In a study of the luxury wine industry, six authenticity attributes were identified: heritage and pedigree, stylistic consistency, quality commitment, relationship to place, method of production, and downplaying commercial motives (Beverland, 2006). These attributes were also validated in a mass-market context and were shown to assert authenticity (Alexander, 2009). Despite the prevalence of this brand- and place-focused research, little research examines authenticity in terms of online communications.

One recent study in this area examines authentic communication within the context of government blogs (Gilpin, Palazzolo, & Brody, 2010). The authors conclude that people are not likely to engage with the blog if they perceive it as being inauthentic. Their conceptual model and content analysis suggest that the expertise and credibility expressed by the author (authority), clarity and consistency of the communicator's identity (identity), open and verifiable information (transparency), and the extent of interaction between social media participants (engagement) are determinants of the perception of authenticity.

Trust

As discussed previously, the primary purpose of a corporate blog is to engage with consumers and listen to their feedback. However, consumers' participation and sharing of information is dependent on their interpretations of the sender and their decoding of the message. A key factor that determines whether customers continue participating in corporate blogs and are willing to share their feedback is their level of trust with the firm.

Trust has been widely discussed as one of the critical constructs in the process of relationship development (Dwyer, Schurr, & Oh, 1987) and has been identified as mediator to a successful strong relationship (Morgan & Hunt, 1994). Trust has been described as a multidimensional construct and many researchers find competency, integrity, and benevolence as the most important dimensions (Frazier, Johnson, Gavin, Gooty, & Snow, 2010; Jarvenpaa, Knoll, & Leidner, 1998; Mayer & Davis, 1999; McKnight, Choudhury, & Kacmar, 2002). Competency refers to the amount of expertise and abilities that enable success within a particular domain of interest. Integrity refers to perceptions of loyalty to a set of principles. Lastly, benevolence refers to a belief of caring and keeping the other party's best interests in mind.

The literature suggests that consumers will respond more to companies whose blogs have relevant subject matter content and that engender trust (Dwyer, 2007). In their model of relationship marketing, Morgan and Hunt (1994) showed that a partner's perception of communication quality results in greater trust. In other words, communication must have certain qualities before it can inspire trust (Dwyer, 2007).

Interaction Quality

Consumers' interpretations of the communication process affect their perceptions about the company. Companies convey their goals and ideas through messages (encoding) and share them with their target market.

The quality of the encoding process can be understood in terms of the beliefs consumers maintain about the quality of the interaction, and these beliefs can influence consumers' trust in the company. This study conceptualizes responsiveness and transparency as two dimensions of interaction quality. Responsiveness and transparency have been recognized as the key drivers of communication effectiveness (Rhee, 2008) and customers' perception of authenticity and trust (Gilpin et al., 2010).

Perceived responsiveness has been discussed as one of the key dimensions of perceived interactivity (Ha & James, 1998; McMillan & Hwang, 2002). Interactivity theory provides the conceptual basis of the role of responsiveness in determining interactive communications and posits that perception of interactivity can result from the quality of the content of the message and reciprocity of communication (Rafaeli, 1988). In studying antecedents of Web site interactivity, Song and Zinkhan (2008) identified personalization of the message content as a key factor that can lead to interactivity perception, and this effect is paramount for postpurchase complaints. Similarly, service encounter research has shown that listening and responsiveness are two important dimensions of interaction quality (Chandon, Leo, & Philippe, 1997). Ramsey and Sohi (1997), however, viewed responsiveness as one of the dimensions of a broader construct: listening. They found that listening is a multidimensional construct consisting of sensing, evaluating, and responding and found that listening skills of a salesperson have a positive significant effect on building customers' trust in the salesperson and their ultimate satisfaction with their interaction (Ramsey & Sohi, 1997).

The second characteristic of interaction quality is transparency. Transparency is defined as how open and visible a company is when interacting with customers (Blackshaw, 2008; Gilpin et al., 2010). There is an extensive body of literature on transparency and its effect on communication and trust. Openness is an important factor for developing positive relationships with stakeholders (Rhee, 2008), and transparency (in the form of complete or incomplete information) has been experimentally shown to increase trusting behaviors significantly in business environments of organizational alliances (Kanagaretnam, Mestelman, Nainar, & Shehata, 2010). Grimmelikhuijsen (2009) investigated the role of transparency on people's trust in government agencies and found heterogeneous effects of transparency on the three dimensions of trust. That is, Internet transparency influenced perceptions of honesty and benevolence but had no effect on perceptions of competency. Therefore, a more detailed investigation of the effect of transparency on trust is needed (Grimmelikhuijsen, 2009).

Hypotheses

Our study extends the investigation of Gilpin et al. (2010) by empirically testing the antecedents and consequences of authenticity in interactive communications. For our study, we examine responsiveness and transparency as antecedents, and trustworthiness as a consequence of consumers' perceptions of authenticity. Gilpin et al.'s (2010) model includes four antecedents to authenticity, however, we focus on responsiveness and transparency. We chose to focus on these two elements because they are message characteristics and are applicable to a number of different online communication contexts, including blogs and other social media, whereas the other two antecedents identified by Gilpin et al. (2010) relate to sender characteristics (identity and authority). Given that our study stimuli include only one short interaction with an unknown brand, these two message characteristics are suitable signals of interaction quality.

Based on the preceding discussion, we hypothesize that the quality of interaction created from responsiveness and transparency affects evaluations of authenticity and trustworthiness. The hypothesized relationships can be best conceptualized in relation to the basic communication model (Shannon & Weaver, 1949). Explicitly, we hypothesize that the dimensions of interaction quality (responsiveness and transparency) positively affect consumers' perception of a company's authenticity. Moreover, interaction quality and authenticity positively affect consumers' perceptions of the three dimensions of trustworthiness (competency, integrity, and benevolence). This is depicted in Figure 6.1.

H_{1a}: Consumers' perception of responsiveness has a positive relationship with perceived authenticity.

H_{1b}: Consumers' perception of transparency has a positive relationship with perceived authenticity.

H_2: Consumers' perception of authenticity has a positive relationship with perceived competency, integrity, and benevolence.

H_{3a}: Consumers' perception of responsiveness has a positive relationship with perceived competency, integrity, and benevolence.

H_{3b}: Consumers' perception of transparency has a positive relationship with perceived competency, integrity, and benevolence.

H_4: The relationship between interaction quality (responsiveness and trustworthiness) on trustworthiness (competency, integrity, and benevolence) is mediated by perceived authenticity.

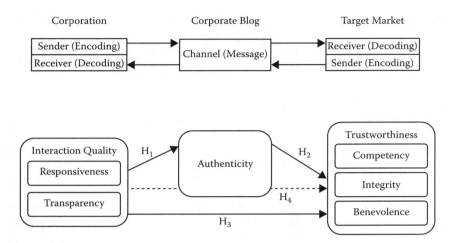

Figure 6.1   Conceptual model.

Method

Data Collection

Hypotheses were tested via an online survey with an undergraduate student population in exchange for extra credit in an introductory-level marketing course. Participants were provided with a link to the online survey and were randomly assigned to one of the four versions of a blog post. In order to create realistic stimuli, blog posts were taken from a real blog and all company information was removed. The posts included the original post by a company representative and responses from consumers. The four conditions allowed us to create variance in terms of interaction quality (responsiveness and transparency). For instance, one post showed high levels of responsiveness as a company representative addressed all consumer posts by responding quickly, whereas others exhibited low responsiveness by responding either not at all or with long response waiting times. A sample of the blog posts used in the study can be found in Figure 6.2.

Participants were instructed to review the post and comments carefully and then proceed to the questions about the company. The questionnaire included items related to the basic constructs, followed by demographic information. Based on a pretest, two minutes was set as a threshold for the minimum time necessary for respondents to read the blog and answer the questions; 252 met these requirements and were retained for the data

---

In-Flight Recycling Results

Posted March 10, 2009 by **Jennifer O** in Environment

AirlineA Flight Attendants, Cabin Service teams, and catering crews collected a total of 1,145,215 pounds (573 tons) of aluminum cans, plastics, newspapers and magazines in 2008.

On Earth Day 2008, AirlineA implemented an In-Flight Recycling Program on domestic flights into cities including: ANC, DTW, HNL, IND, LAS, LAX, MEM, MSP, SEA and SFO. During the program's first nine months, AirlineA collected 118,096 pounds (59 tons) of materials.

The combined In-Flight organization collected and diverted more than 1.2 million pounds (632 tons) of recyclable materials from landfills in 29 US cities.

And the best part is that AirlineA's In-Flight Recycling efforts raised $85,000 for AirlineA's Force for Global Good and Habitat for Humanity. The funds will be used to build one Habitat home in 2009, making this the second home we have fully funded through in-flight recycling efforts since 2007.

Jennifer O

5 Responses to "Sky High In-Flight Recycling Results"

LovelyJanet Says:
March 10th, 2009 at 12:59 pm
Thank you AirlineA for all your efforts.

Jim1031 Says:
March 10th, 2009 at 1:48 pm
WooHoo!!!!!

Lily007 Says:
March 10th, 2009 at 5:33 pm
This is an impressive amount of mateial COLLECTED. Would you be kind enough to let us know where it GOES? Within the world economy in the tank, the demand for waste to recycle is way, way down. I hope the stuff put in the Airline recycle bags does not go to the toxic landfill-cities in China that were showcased on 60 Minutes last year.

Deb_123 Says:
April 10th, 2009 at 9:05 pm
Another tremendous effort by AirlineA! Congratulations on your success with this! Do you have a breakdown of the 1,145,215 lbs of material collected separately by source product? I'm curious as to the amounts of each material collected. Congratulations again!

AirlineA Representative Jennifer O Says:
April 14th, 2009 at 5:18 pm
I have two updates to share:
On April 1st AirlineA implemented our In-Flight Recycling program for inbound domestic flights into Boston Logan International Airport.
The content of the 632 tons breaks down to include (from high to low) aluminum cans, newspapers/magazines then plastics.

Figure 6.2   Sample blog post.

analysis. The average amount of time participants spent on the task was eight minutes.

Measurement

To test the hypotheses, all the constructs in the study's framework were captured using reflective multi-item five-point Likert scales. Constructs were measured based on established scales in the literature with new items added when necessary. To assess the appropriateness and clarity of the questions, the items were reviewed by two marketing academics and pre-tested with an audience similar to the study participants. The final items are presented in the chapter Appendix.

Responsiveness was measured using five 5-point Likert-type scale questions adopted from Thompson, Ishii, and Klopf (1990). To assess the three dimensions of *trustworthiness*, we compiled and examined a set of items from the literature (Mayer & Davis, 1999; Dwyer, 2007) and chose those that applied to this online context. A total of six *authenticity* items relevant to the study context were adopted from the literature (Price, Arnould, & Deibler, 1995; Grayson & Martinec 2004), along with additional items obtained from a thesaurus that were found to be relevant to the context of this study. Finally, five items measuring *transparency* were developed by consulting the relevant literature and a thesaurus (Gilpin et al., 2010).

Validity and Reliability

Following the two-step procedure recommended by Anderson and Gerbing (1988), we estimated the measurement model prior to testing the relationships among constructs in the research model. A confirmatory factor analysis (CFA) was run with LISREL software for all the scales in the model to assess for measurement quality and all the indicators with factor loadings less than .5 were excluded from the measurement model. The refined measurement model (see Table 6.1) shows an acceptable fit (X^2 (260) = 544.82, p = .0; comparative fit index [CFI] = .98; and root mean square error of approximation [RMSEA] = .07) with all factor loadings except one (honest = .50) greater than .60.

Table 6.2 displays the psychometric properties of the measures; the covariance among the latent variables can be found in Table 6.3. Cronbach's alpha values and composite reliabilities for all constructs were greater

TABLE 6.1　Confirmatory Factor Analysis

	Factor Loading	*t*-Value
Responsiveness		
Is willing to listen	0.72	—
Responsive	0.71	11.24
Supportive	0.82	12.95
Understands properly what you want	0.72	11.33
Absorbs feedbacks from customers	0.70	11.07
Transparency		
Reveals its motives	0.61	—
Is open to share information	0.73	7.96
Is not one to hide facts	0.75	8.00
Authenticity		
Sincere	0.71	—
Speaks with genuine voice	0.70	10.39
Has motivations that are pure and not manipulative	0.68	10.22
Truly cares about me	0.71	10.66
Competency		
Competent	0.78	—
Able to perform consistently	0.68	11.18
Qualified	0.83	14.18
An expert	0.75	12.49
Accurate	0.72	11.95
Integrity		
Fair	0.79	—
Honest	0.50	7.96
Honorable	0.77	13.35
Not biased	0.60	9.89
Benevolence		
Good willed	0.75	—
Imposes positive feeling	0.85	13.50
Imposes affection	0.72	11.28
Imposes an expression of moral values	0.70	10.95

Notes: CFI = .979, RMSEA = .068, chi-square = 544.82 (p = .0), df = 260.

TABLE 6.2   Psychometric Properties of the Measures

Variables	M	SD	α	CR	AVE
1. Responsiveness	18.04	4.04	0.87	0.86	0.54
2. Transparency	10.15	2.22	0.74	0.74	0.49
3. Authenticity	13.33	3.10	0.80	0.79	0.49
4. Competency	17.10	3.96	0.87	0.87	0.57
5. Integrity	13.48	3.09	0.76	0.77	0.46
6. Benevolence	13.94	3.52	0.84	0.84	0.57

Notes: M = Mean; SD = Standard deviation; α = Cronbach's alpha; CR = Composite reliability; AVE = Average variance extracted.

TABLE 6.3   Covariance Matrix

Variables	1	2	3	4	5	6
1. Responsiveness	.54					
2. Transparency	.17	.34				
3. Authenticity	.44	.23	.46			
4. Competency	.52	.14	.38	.60		
5. Integrity	.60	.20	.50	.58	.71	
6. Benevolence	.51	.12	.48	.46	.58	.61

than .73, thus exceeding the recommended threshold (Bagozzi & Yi, 1988) for reliable scales. In addition, the average variance extracted (AVE) for all the scales was marginally close to or greater than .5, supporting convergent validity (Fornell & Larcker, 1981).

Discriminate validity was assessed with a pairwise restriction of models (Anderson & Gerbing, 1988). The correlation between each pair of factors was fixed to equal 1.0 and the significance of chi-square change was tested. All the chi-square changes were significant, showing better model fit for the model without these restrictions (please refer to Table 6.4). Additionally, randomization of questions and Harman's single-factor test were used to rule out common methods bias (Podsakoff, MacKenzie, Lee, & Podsakoff, 2003).

Analysis and Results

A bootstrap mediation test (Preacher & Hayes, 2004, 2008; Zhao, Lynch, & Chen, 2010) was used for testing the hypothesized relationships in the research model. The bootstrap mediation test offers a more powerful and

TABLE 6.4   Chi-Square Difference Test for Assessing Discriminant Validity

	χ^2 Value	$\Delta\chi^2$ ($df = 1$)	p-Value
Unconstrained Model ($df = 260$)	544.82	—	—
Constrained Model ($df = 261$)			
Responsiveness – Authenticity	573.14	28.32	< .001
Responsiveness – Transparency	635.14	90.32	< .001
Responsiveness – Competency	571.3	26.48	< .001
Responsiveness – Integrity	566.14	21.32	< .001
Responsiveness – Benevolence	570.11	25.29	< .001
Authenticity – Transparency	627.3	82.48	< .001
Authenticity – Competency	585.59	40.77	< .001
Authenticity – Integrity	569.92	25.10	< .001
Authenticity – Benevolence	569.91	25.09	< .001
Transparency – Competency	646.19	101.37	< .001
Transparency – Integrity	646.12	101.30	< .001
Transparency – Benevolence	667.25	122.43	< .001
Competency – Integrity	565.33	20.51	< .001
Competency – Benevolence	583.23	38.41	< .001
Integrity – Benevolence	554.81	9.99	< .001

rigorous approach to traditional mediation tests (Zhao et al., 2010). Prior to the mediation test, we performed a multivariate regression with the three dimensions of trustworthiness (competency, integrity, and benevolence) as dependent variables and responsiveness, transparency, and authenticity as independent variables. As shown in Table 6.5, the results demonstrate significant relationships between the independent and dependent variables. We proceeded with the mediation test using the Preacher and Hayes bootstrap script for SPSS (Preacher & Hayes, 2008; Zhao et al., 2010) and performed the analysis with each of the hypothesized relationships. The bootstrap analysis tests the direct effect of the independent variable on the mediating variable (path a), the direct effect of the mediating variable on the dependent variable (path b), the direct effect of the independent variable on the dependent variable (path c), the total effect of the independent variable on the dependent variable (c´), and the indirect effect of the independent variable on the dependent variable through the proposed mediator (path ab). The bootstrap method solves the problem of a nonnormal sampling distribution produced from the indirect effect being a product of two parameters a and b, (Preacher & Hayes, 2004; Zhao et al., 2010) by generating an empirical sampling distribution of a × b. Our estimates were based on 5,000 bootstrap samples.

TABLE 6.5   Results of Multivariate and Bootstrap Mediation Tests[a]

	Wilk's λ	Path	Authenticity (Mediator)	Competency	Integrity	Benevolence
Responsiveness →Authenticity →DV	.300**	c		.677***	.526***	.524***
Responsiveness →Authenticity		a	.687***			
Authenticity →DV	.801***	b		.116**	.285***	.431***
Responsiveness →DV		c'		.756***	.721***	.820***
Overall F				187.46***	194.03***	216.37***
Adj R²				.598	.606	.631
Mediation 95% Confidence Interval		ab		.080* (−.012, .173)	.196*** (.109, .294)	.296*** (.183, .414)
Mediation				None	Partial	Partial
Transparency →Authenticity →DV	.684***	c		−.007	.085	−.104
Transparency →Authenticity		a	.453***			
Authenticity →DV	.801***	b		.622***	.641***	.864***
Transparency →DV		c'		.275***	.375***	.267***
Overall F				72.51***	108.90***	139.38***
Adj R²				.363	.462	.524
Mediation 95% Confidence Interval		ab		.282*** (.177, .387)	.290*** (.195, .393)	.391*** (.271, .520)
Mediation				Full	Full	Full

***p<.001, **p<.01, *p<.05.

[a] Path a = the direct effect of the independent variable on the mediating variable;
Path b = the direct effect of the mediating variable on the dependent variable.;
Path c = the direct effect of the independent variable on the dependent variable;
Path c' = the total effect (ab + c);
Path ab = the indirect effect of the independent variable on the dependent variable through the proposed mediator.

Antecedents of Authenticity

As shown in Table 6.5, the results show that both responsiveness ($\beta = .687$, $t = 16.155$, $p < .001$) and transparency ($\beta = .453$, $t = 7.561$, $p < .001$) have a positive relationship with authenticity, providing support for H_{1a} and H_{1b}. That is, consumers' perception of responsiveness and transparency has a positive impact on authenticity perceptions.

Effects of Authenticity on Trust

In H_2 we predicted that authenticity would have a positive relationship with the three dimensions of trust and the results fully support this hypothesis. For the first model, with responsiveness included as an independent variable, we find a significant relationship between authenticity and integrity ($\beta = .285$, $t = 5.052$, $p > .001$), authenticity and benevolence ($\beta = .431$, $t = 6.929$, $p < .001$), and authenticity and competency ($\beta = .116$, $t = 1.985$, $p < .05$). For the second model, with transparency included as an independent variable, we find a significant relationship between authenticity and integrity ($\beta = .641$, $t = 12.555$, $p > .001$), authenticity and benevolence ($\beta = .864$, $t = 15.755$, $p < .001$), and authenticity and competency ($\beta = .622$ $t = 10.914$, $p < .001$). Taken together, these results indicate that authenticity leads to greater perceptions of integrity, benevolence, and competency.

Mediation Test

In order to determine mediation, we used the approach by Zhao et al. (2010) to assess the direct and indirect effects of the independent variables on the dependent variables. According to this approach, full mediation occurs when a nonsignificant direct path from the independent variable to the dependent variable (c path) is present with a significant indirect path (ab path); partial mediation is found when both the indirect (ab) and direct (c) paths are significant. The coefficient estimates for the direct and indirect effects are presented in Table 6.5.

Authenticity partially mediates the path from responsiveness to integrity as we find a significant indirect effect ($\beta = .196$, $z = 4.841$, $p < .001$) and a significant direct effect ($\beta = .526$, $t = 9.707$, $p < .001$). Likewise, authenticity partially mediates the path from responsiveness to benevolence as we find a significant indirect effect (β = .296, z = 6.39, p < .001) and a significant direct effect (β = .524, t = 8.768, p < .001). However, authenticity does not mediate the relationship between responsiveness and competency; whereas the direct path (β = .677, t = 12.054, p < .001) and the indirect path are significant (β = .080, z = 1.978, p = .048), zero is contained within the 95% confidence interval provided by the bootstrap analysis (–.012, .173). The bootstrap results are more robust, thus we conclude nonmediation.

Authenticity fully mediates the path from transparency to competency because of a significant indirect effect (β = .282, z = 6.23, p < .001) and a nonsignificant direct effect (β = –.007, t = –.116, p > .05). Likewise, authenticity fully mediates the relationship between transparency and integrity as we find a significant indirect effect (β = .290, z = 6.494, p < .001) and a nonsignificant direct effect (β = .085, t = 1.581, p > .05). Finally, authenticity fully mediates the relationship between transparency and benevolence, as we find a significant indirect effect (β = .391, z = 6.83, p < .001) and a nonsignificant direct effect (β = –.104, t = –1.809, p > .05).

Interpretation of the effects helps provide a deeper explanation of the role of authenticity. In all cases of mediation, the results show that authenticity strengthens the positive effect of responsiveness on the three dimensions of trust (competency, benevolence, and integrity) inasmuch as both direct and indirect effects are positive and significant. Partial mediation of responsiveness on integrity and benevolence conclude that authenticity strengthens the positive effect of responsiveness on these two dimensions of trust because both direct and indirect effects are positive and significant. These results support both H3a and H4.

In contrast to H3b, the nonsignificant direct effects provide evidence that transparency's effect on the three dimensions of trustworthiness is achieved through perceptions of authenticity. That is, authenticity fully mediates the relationship, which provides support for H4 and allows us to conclude that the positive effect of transparency on trustworthiness can be fully explained by the perceived authenticity of the online communication.

Discussion

This research investigates the impact of communication quality on consumer trust in corporate blogs and has direct implications for influencing opinions in events such as the BP Gulf oil spill, new product launches, and crowd-sourced mobilization. In a world where both everyday people and cable news networks source their information online, social networking channels such as Twitter and blogs provide a regular stream of information that influences public opinion in real time. In addition, new products are increasingly launched and researched online and the subsequent communication of information in an interactive online context is crucial in enhancing adoption of new products and receiving customer feedback.

This work is grounded on the belief that customers will continue to participate in a corporate blog and share feedback only if they maintain a belief in a corporation's trustworthiness. We find that the perception of trustworthiness can be generated through authenticity in its communications. Moreover, we find authenticity as a mediator of most of the expected outcomes of responsiveness and transparency on perception of trustworthiness.

The first purpose of this study is to examine the antecedents and consequences of authenticity in online communications. We find that transparency and responsiveness both have direct positive relationships with authenticity. We also find that authenticity increases perceptions of trustworthiness. Thus, companies can increase trustworthiness by building perceptions of authenticity with their audience through open communication and responding to consumer queries in a timely and thoughtful manner.

The second purpose of this research is to examine the direct effects of interaction quality (responsiveness and transparency) on trustworthiness, as well as the indirect effects through authenticity. Consistent with prior literature on the impact of listening and responsiveness on building trust (Ramsey & Sohi, 1997; Rhee, 2008), we find a positive relationship between responsiveness and all three dimensions of trust (competency, integrity, and benevolence). However, we also find a contrary result for the role of transparency, as it did not have a direct impact on perceptions of trustworthiness. Yet the results provide evidence supporting a positive indirect effect of transparency through authenticity. This finding provides support for prior research regarding the role of Internet transparency on trust (Grimmelikhuijsen, 2009), which uncovered heterogeneous effects of Internet transparency on the three dimensions of trust, and provided insights into these unclear mixed effects by examining authenticity as a mediator. Based on this finding, a company's candid disclosure of information about itself increases perceptions of authenticity; trustworthiness is created through authenticity and not directly from the disclosure.

Overall, the results show that authenticity can partially explain the mechanism underlying the effects of responsiveness on the three dimensions of trust and fully explain the mechanism underlying the effects of transparency on the three dimensions of trust.

Managerial Implications

This research provides insights about the roles that message characteristics play in generating consumers' perceptions of authenticity and trust of interactive communications. The results show that both perceived responsiveness of the message and transparency positively affect authenticity. Furthermore, the results show that authenticity has a positive relationship with all three dimensions of trustworthiness.

Although responsiveness had a direct positive impact on trustworthiness, transparency did not; however, transparency can have a positive impact on trust through the mediating role of authenticity. This finding identifies the important role that authenticity plays in open communication. Anecdotal evidence suggests that Millennials, a generation born in the digital age, are cynical in regard to marketing messages. Nick Shore, head of research for MTV, describes the importance of authenticity for this cohort:

> Millennials are digital natives and use the technology subconsciously. They are super-deconstructive of any kind of media messaging. They are entitled, but not stupid; and they know media exists to sell them things. They look for information that is real, honest, and transparent. (Pardee, 2010)

Thus, for this group in particular, it is pivotal that a message is perceived to be authentic in order to gain their trust.

Limitations and Direction for Future Research

This research has several limitations. Generalizability of the findings of this study is limited because the undergraduate students' reactions to authenticity may not be representative of the entire consumer population. Further work is needed to test the relationships for the various age groups and cultures.

The cross sectional nature of the current work did not allow for testing the long-term effects of authenticity. A longitudinal study can provide more understanding about the role of authenticity in online communication over time. A longitudinal study may also include other potential antecedents of authenticity relating to the identity and expertise of the communicator (Gilpin et al., 2010). The current work focused on the relationship between these variables and future work is needed to test the causal paths between constructs. Finally, the proposed communication model was only tested for the context of a corporate blog in this study. Therefore, it would be fruitful to test whether the same relationships hold for other types of interactive communications or whether it varies by channel (e.g., social networking Web sites such as Facebook, microblogging sites such as Twitter, and personal blogs).

Appendix

This company:
(1. strongly disagree, 2. disagree, 3. neutral, 4. agree, 5. strongly agree)

Transparency (5 Items)
- Reveals its motives
- Is open in sharing information
- *Is clear in its communication
- Is not one to hide facts
- *Is secretive (r)

Responsiveness (5 Items)
- Is responsive
- Is supportive
- Is willing to listen
- Understands properly what you want
- Absorbs feedbacks from customers

Authenticity (6 Items)
- Is sincere
- Speaks with genuine voice
- Has motivations that are pure and not manipulative
- Truly cares about me
- *Is classic
- *Has a rich history

Trustworthiness
Competency (5 Items)
- Is competent
- Is able to perform consistently
- Is qualified
- Is an expert
- Is accurate

Integrity (5 Items)
- Is fair
- Is honest
- Is honorable
- *Is committed to consumers
- Is not biased

Benevolence (5 Items)
- Is good willed
- Imposes positive feeling
- Imposes affection
- *Imposes an expression of gained enlightenment

* The items that were not retained in the final model.

References

Alexander, N. (2009). Brand authentication: Creating and maintaining brand auras. *European Journal of Marketing*, 43(3–4), 551–562.

Anderson, J. C. & Gerbing, D. W. (1988). Structural equation modeling in practice: A review and recommended two-step approach. *Psychological Bulletin,* *103*(3), 411–423.

Bagozzi, R. P. & Yi, Y. (1988). On the evaluation of structural equation models. *Journal of the Academy of Marketing Science, 16*(1), 74–95.

Batts, S. A., Anthis, N. J., & Smith, T. (2008). Advancing science through conversations: Bridging the gap between blogs and the academy. *PLoS Biology, 6*(9), e240.

Beverland, M. (2006). The "real thing": Branding authenticity in the luxury wine trade. *Journal of Business Research, 59*(2), 251–258.

Blackshaw, P. (2008).The six drivers of brand credibility. *Marketing Management,* *17*(3), 51–54.

Brown, S., Sherry. Jr., J. F. , & Kozinets, R.V. (2003).Teaching old brands new tricks: Retro branding and the revival of brand meaning. *Journal of Marketing,* *67*(3), 19–33.

Chandon, J.-L., Leo, P.-Y., & Philippe, J. (1997). Service encounter dimensions—A dyadic perspective: Measuring the dimensions of service encounters as perceived by customers and personnel. *International Journal of Service Industry Management, 8*(1), 65–86.

Cohen, E. (1988). Authenticity and commoditization in tourism. *Annals of Tourism Research, 15*(3), 371–386.

Deighton, J. & Kornfeld, L. (2009). Interactivity's unanticipated consequences for marketers and marketing. *Journal of Interactive Marketing, 23*(1), 4–10.

Dennis, A. R., Fuller, R. M., & Valacich, J. S. (2008). Media, tasks, and communication processes: A theory of media synchronicity. *MIS Quarterly, 32*(3), 575–600.

Dwyer, F. R., Schurr, P., & Oh, S. (1987). Developing buyer-seller relationships. *Journal of Marketing,* 51(2), 11–27.

Dwyer, P. (2007). Building trust with corporate blogs. *Proceedings of International Conference on Weblogs (ICWSM),* Boulder, CO.

Fornell, C. & Larcker, D. F. (1981). Evaluating structural equation models with unobservable variables and measurement error. *Journal of Marketing Research, 18*(1), 39–50.

Frazier, M. L., Johnson, P. D., Gavin, M., Gooty, J., & Snow, D. B. (2010). Organizational justice, trustworthiness, and trust: A multifoci examination. *Group & Organization Management, 35*(1), 39.

Gerbing, D. W. & Anderson, J. C. (1988). An updated paradigm for scale development incorporating unidimensionality and its assessment. *Journal of Marketing Research, 25*(2), 186–192.

Gilpin, D. R., Palazzolo, E. T., & Brody, N. (2010). Socially mediated authenticity. *Journal of Communication Management, 14*(3), 258–278.

Grayson, K. & Martinec, R. (2004). Consumer perceptions of iconicity and indexicality and their influence on assessments of authentic market offerings. *Journal of Consumer Research, 31*(2), 296–312.

Grimmelikhuijsen, S. (2009). Do transparent government agencies strengthen trust? *International Journal of Government and Democracy in the Information Age, 14*(3), 173–186.

Ha, L. & James, E. L. (1998). Interactivity reexamined: A baseline analysis of early business web sites. *Journal of Broadcasting & Electronic Media, 42*(4), 457–474.

Holt, D. B. (2002). Why do brands cause trouble? A dialectical theory of consumer culture and branding. *Journal of Consumer Research, 29*(1), 70–90.

Hsu, C.-L. & Lin, J. C.-C. (2008). Acceptance of blog usage: The roles of technology acceptance, social influence and knowledge sharing motivation. *Information & Management, 45*(1), 65–74.

Iacobucci, D., Saldanha, N., & Deng, X. (2007). A meditation on mediation: Evidence that structural equations models perform better than regressions. *Journal of Consumer Psychology, 17*(2), 139–153.

Jarvenpaa, S. L., Knoll, K., & Leidner, D. E. (1998). Is anybody out there? Antecedents of trust in global virtual teams. *Journal of Management Information Systems, 14*(4), 29–64.

Kanagaretnam, K., Mestelman, S., Nainar, K., & Shehata, M. (2010). Trust and reciprocity with transparency and repeated interactions. *Journal of Business Research, 63*(3), 241–247.

Kleinbaum, D. G., Kupper, L. L., Muller, K. E., & Nizam, A. (1998). *Applied regression analysis and other multivariate methods.* Pacific Grove, CA: Duxbury Press.

Leigh, T. W., Peters, C., & Shelton, J. (2006). The consumer quest for authenticity: The multiplicity of meanings within the mg subculture of consumption. *Academy of Marketing Science Journal, 34*(4), 481–493.

Lu, H.-P., Lin, J. C.-C., Hsiao, K.-L., & Cheng, L.-T. (2010). Information sharing behavior on blogs in Taiwan: Effects of interactivities and gender differences. *Journal of Information Science, 36*(3), 401–416.

Mack, R. W., Blose, J. E., & Pan, B. (2008). Believe it or not: Credibility of blogs in tourism. *Journal of Vacation Marketing, 14*(April), 133–144.

Mayer, R. C. & Davis, J. H. (1999). The effect of the performance appraisal system on trust for management: A field quasi-experiment. *Journal of Applied Psychology, 84*(1), 123–136.

McKnight, D. H., Choudhury, V., & Kacmar, C. (2002). Developing and validating trust measures for e-commerce, an integrative typology. *Information Systems Research, 13*(3), 334–359.

McMillan, S. J. & Hwang, J.-S. (2002). Measures of perceived interactivity: An exploration of the role of direction of communication, user control, and time in shaping perceptions of interactivity. *Journal of Advertising, 31*(3), 29–42.

Miranda, S. M. & Saunders, C. S. (2003). The social construction of meaning: An alternative perspective on information sharing. *Information Systems Research, 14*(1), 87–106.

Mitra, A. (2002). Trust, authenticity, and discursive power in cyberspace. *Communications of the ACM, 45*(3), 27–29.

Morgan, R. M. & Hunt, S. D. (1994). The commitment-trust theory of relationship marketing. *Journal of Marketing, 58*(3), 20–38.

Naoi, T. (2004). Visitors' evaluation of a historical district: The roles of authenticity and manipulation. *Tourism and Hospitality Research, 5*(1), 44–63.

Pardee, T. (2010). Media-savvy Gen Y finds smart and funny is "new rock 'n' roll". *Advertising Age, 81*(36), 17.

Peltier, J. W., Schibrowsky, J. A., & Schultz, D. E. (2003). Interactive integrated marketing communication: Combining the power of IMC, the new media and database marketing. *International Journal of Advertising, 22*(1), 93–115.

Perlmutter, D. D. & McDaniel, M. (2005).The ascent of blogging. *Nieman Reports, 59*(3), 60–64.

Podsakoff, P., MacKenzie, S. B., Lee, J.-Y., & Podsakoff, N. P. (2003). Common method biases in behavioral research: A critical review of the literature and recommended remedies. *Journal of Applied Psychology, 88*(5), 879–903.

Preacher, K. J. & Hayes, A. F. (2004). SPSS and SAS procedures for estimating indirect effects in simple mediation models. *Behavior Research Methods, Instruments, and Computers, 36*(4), 717–731.

Preacher, K. J. & Hayes, A. F. (2008). Asymptotic and resampling strategies for estimating indirect effects in simple mediation models. *Behavior Research Methods, 40*(3), 879–891.

Price, L. L., Arnould, E. J., & Deibler, S. L. (1995). Consumers' emotional responses to service encounters: The influence of the service provider. *International Journal of Service Industry Management, 6*(3), 34–63.

Rafaeli, S. (1988). Interactivity from new media to communication. In R. P. Hawkins, J. M. Wiemann, & S. Pingree (Eds.), *Advancing communication science: Merging mass and interpersonal processes*, Beverly Hills, CA: SAGE, pp. 110–134.

Ramsey, R. P. & Sohi, R. S. (1997). Listening to your customers: The impact of perceived salesperson listening behavior on relationship outcomes. *Academy of Marketing Science Journal, 25*(2), 127–137.

Rhee, Y. (2008). Risk communication management: A case study on Brookhaven National Laboratory. *Journal of Communication Management, 12*(3), 224–242.

Sedmak, G. & Mihalič, T. (2008). Authenticity in mature seaside resorts. *Annals of Tourism Research, 35*(4), 1007–1031.

Shannon, C. E. & Weaver, W. (1949). *The mathematical theory of communication*. Urbana: University of Illinois Press.

Smudde, P. M. (2005). Blogging, ethics and public relations: A proactive and dialogic approach. *Public Relations Quarterly, 50*(3), 34–38.

Song, J. H. & Zinkhan, G. M. (2008). Determinants of perceived Web site interactivity. *Journal of Marketing, 72*(2), 99–113.

Thompson, C. A., Ishii, S., & Klopf, D. (1990). Japanese and Americans compared on assertiveness/responsiveness. *Psychological Reports, 66*, 829–830.

Wang, N. (1999). Rethinking authenticity in tourism experience. *Annals of Tourism Research, 26*(2), 349–370.

Wortham, J. (2007). *After 10 years of blogs, the future's brighter than ever.* Retrieved January 3, 2012 from http://www.wired.com/entertainment/theweb/news/2007/12/blog_anniversary.

Zhao, X., Lynch. Jr., J. G., & Chen, Q. (2010). Reconsidering Baron and Kenny: Myths and truths about mediation analysis. *Journal of Consumer Research, 37*(2), 197–206.

7

Web 2.0 and Consumers' Digital Footprint
Managing Privacy and Disclosure
Choices in Social Media

*Ereni Markos**

Quinnipiac University

Lauren I. Labrecque
Northern Illinois University

George R. Milne
University of Massachusetts

In the modern marketplace, personal information is readily and widely available through the Internet, just as easily as stock prices are available in *The Wall Street Journal*. In a world of noisy self-confessions, evolving technology, and Web 2.0 tools (e.g., social networking, microblogging) that make it easy to divulge life stories, disclosure choices offer a means to keep personal information private, or not (Milne & Bahl, 2010; Poddar, Mosteller, & Scholder-Ellen, 2009). The aggregation of disclosed information creates a digital footprint or profile of personal information, accessible online to a wide spectrum of people (Madden, Fox, Smith, & Vitak, 2007). Such footprints are common; a recent study shows that 47% of adults use social networking sites (Pew Research Center, 2010). Accordingly, mounting participation in blogs and social networks creates new privacy issues related to digital profiles in the marketplace. Privacy settings may allow members to restrict others' access to their online profiles, yet unauthorized viewers, employers, and third-party applications clearly gain access to those profiles (Miyazaki, 2008). For example, U.S. employers actively

---
* All authors contributed equally.

trawl potential candidates' private Facebook profiles without their consent before making hiring decisions (Careerbuilder.com, 2009), and in Germany, a proposed law would prevent employers from becoming Facebook friends with prospective employees and make it illegal to check applicants' private online profiles (Roschmann-Schmitt, 2010).

In response, college graduates often attempt to conceal their social networking profiles during job searches to avoid potential misunderstandings (Goldberg, 2010). Contrary to popular beliefs (Palfrey & Gasser, 2008) young people express great concern about their privacy and are reluctant to disclose personal information in certain contexts. For example, a recent Gallup poll shows that young adults question the trade-off of personal information for tailored advertisements and view it as insufficient to prompt them to risk privacy invasions (Morales, 2010).

From a consumer perspective, participants in online communities thus must make disclosure decisions that enable them to control personal information dissemination. The ubiquitous technologies available on the Internet have widened the span of information available to friends, acquaintances, businesses, and strangers. Disclosure through these technologies can help consumers build relationships, communicate, and conduct business. It also conjures up images of privacy breaches. Therefore, for consumers faced with the dialectic between the benefits of information disclosure and the avoidance of harm through information restriction, the common decision of how much information to share and with whom is becoming increasingly complex.

This research examines how consumers navigate this dialectic tension between information disclosure and privacy online. Prior research notes several consumer motivations for posting personal information on the Internet (Miceli, Ricotta, & Costabile, 2007; Schau & Gilly, 2003), though the Web 2.0 environment offers new risks and privacy implications. The present research therefore provides an updated account of consumer privacy management and makes several key contributions. First, our research highlights new vulnerabilities introduced by the Web 2.0 environment, including consumers' loss of information control, privacy intrusions due to friends' behaviors, and the need for digital vigilance. Second, we underline different strategies that consumers use to control their information and discuss the difficulties involved with their implementation because of the complexities of this changing landscape. Third, we offer an updated perspective on privacy that reflects the notions of privacy boundary theory.

We begin by providing a theoretical and contextual background for this study, including discussions of privacy in the digital age, motivations for online self-disclosure, and the resultant privacy issues. After we outline our methodology, we organize our findings in terms of privacy boundary theory (Altman, 1975) and note the tensions that consumers face and the strategies they use to combat privacy concerns. We conclude with a discussion of the importance of consumer awareness and protection in this ever-changing context.

Background

Privacy in the Digital Age

Privacy entails a dynamic process, driven by changing internal and external circumstances that individuals respond to by regulating their privacy to achieve a desired state (Langenderfer & Myasaki, 2009; Milne & Bahl, 2010; Petronio, 2000). Early definitions of privacy focused on the right to be left alone (Warren & Brandeis, 1890); later scholars considered controlling access to and dissemination of information (Altman, 1975; Westin, 1967). From a marketing perspective, privacy involves the control of information disclosure and unwanted intrusions into a consumer's environment (Goodwin, 1991), although more recently this has expanded to include control over personal exchanges that use information technology to enhance autonomy or minimize vulnerability (Milne & Bahl, 2010).

In a digital era, the meaning of privacy also has evolved to focus on information (Langenderfer & Miyazaki, 2009) related directly to shared personal information that gets disseminated immediately through technology to family, friends, businesses, and strangers (Acquisti, 2004). People must actively participate in self-protection online, just as in the physical world, because technology can subject them to great vulnerability (Hoffman, Novak, & Peralta, 1999; Milne, Rohm, & Bahl, 2004; Milne, Labrecque, & Cromer, 2009).

Yet in many instances, an online setting mitigates self-motivated protection efforts even when consumers are aware of potential privacy harms, which may reflect their dialectic struggle. That is, the modern marketplace creates an atmosphere of casual information sharing, even as it fosters an air of uncertainty about transactions involving information. Most research also finds that consumers do not use the privacy tools available to them, such as clearing out needless cookies, reading privacy policies (Milne, Bahl, & Rohm, 2008), or paying attention to privacy seals on Web sites (Miyazaki & Krishnamurthy, 2002). Such consumer apathy toward privacy protection online can lead to unwanted intrusions and other inadvertent consequences, especially in rapidly changing environments.

Other causes for concern include consumer memory lapses, contrasted with the Internet's vast storage capacity and search functionality. First, few people can track and remember not only self-posted information but also details posted by others to their online profiles. Especially as online users gain multiple social networking accounts (Pew Research Center, 2010), the idea that users might forget comments, photographs, and other information they or friends have posted seems plausible. Second, the Internet stores information for an indefinite amount of time, such that it never forgets, even if users do (Schonberger, 2009). Third, the Internet can easily support the aggregation of consumer information through the use of self-reported disclosures. For example, Google maintains different data points for individual users, categorized by their Internet protocol (IP) addresses and other unique data points (Helft, 2009). If aggregated, these anonymous bits of data can identify a person (Solove, 2008). Although it may seem unlikely that a reputable business would use or sell private information that identifies customers, research repeatedly has shown that a minimal compilation of anonymous information (e.g., zip code, date of birth) can already distinguish members of the population (Golle, 2006; Sweeny, 1997).

Motivations for Online Disclosure and Privacy Implications

Computer-mediated environments offer a sense of freedom, primarily because the machine creates an aura of anonymity that encourages candid exchanges. Physical constraints, such as appearance or reputation that typically cause people to act more inhibited disappear in the online environment (Wynn & Katz, 1997; Turkle, 1995). As the Internet has flourished, people have embraced the idea of personal Web sites as spaces for self-expression and learning about others (Vazire & Gosling, 2004). Online pursuits also can help people satisfy their social goals (Zinkhan, Conchar, Gupta, & Geissler, 1999) and offer a means to communicate with friends and reach out to new groups (Schau & Gilly, 2003). Further research shows that consumers use disclosures to brand themselves (Kaputa, 2005; Labrecque, Markos, & Milne, 2011; Schwabel, 2009), and research on blogging reveals that motivations for online self-disclosure include impression management, relationship management, keeping up with trends, information sharing, and entertainment (Lee, Im, & Taylor, 2008).

However, Internet usage also has grown increasingly complex in the world of Web 2.0, compared with the Web 1.0 environment. Modern online applications (e.g., blogs, social networks) encourage interactivity but dilute individual control over personal information. For example, members of social Web sites such as Facebook may leave their profiles open for viewing by friends, acquaintances, or strangers. Others generally can add content to user profiles without the owner's explicit permission. Regardless of its source, content in an online forum is enduring and accessible by many audiences, which creates an ambiguous state of information ownership and control (Stelter, 2009). Shifting online norms and dynamic technology thus have intensified privacy concerns for consumers (Peltier, Milne, & Phelps 2009; Phelps, D'Souza, & Nowak, 2001) even as they simplify the processes for and encourage the creation of user-generated content. For example, with straightforward communication tools, virtually anyone can upload text, pictures, and video instantly to a Web site from a personal computer or mobile phone, which increases consumer-to-consumer information sharing and privacy concerns.

Establishing Privacy Boundaries

Privacy regulation theory (Altman, 1975) provides an explanation of why people seek social interaction at some times but not others. According to privacy regulation theory, privacy boundaries are not static but instead are subject to the "selective control of access to the self or to one's group" (Altman, 1975, p. 18). People thus can choose their level of openness or closedness toward someone at any given time, then change it if necessary. Each person moves along a continuum of openness and closedness, in response to different situations and environments, over time. To achieve an optimal level of privacy at a given moment for a specific situation, people might relax or tighten boundaries, using information dissemination and control mechanisms. Too much privacy may result in social isolation; too little may result in privacy violations.

Such dynamic disclosure behavior appears in communications literature, in the form of relational dialectics (Baxter & Montgomery, 1996), a theory that proposes contradiction always exists in managing relationships. Dialectic forces thus act on the relationship simultaneously, entering from and moving in opposite directions. As a result, a person must constantly manage the tensions between these forces by making changes and decisions that affect both forces. Similar to privacy regulation theory, relational dialectics assumes that an increase in openness results in a decrease in privacy.

Furthermore, relational dialectics identifies three fundamental relationship contradictions: integration–separation, expression–nonexpression, and stability–change (Werner & Baxter, 1994). Relationships occur at the junction of these opposing forces, so when they engage in a relationship people actively participate by offering information (integration) but also seek solitude at other moments in time (separation). Similarly, by modifying their behavior (change), they might enhance and excite relationships, but nurturing relationships generally require trust (stability). Finally, most relevant to this study, the expression–nonexpression dialectic refers to the conflict between revealing information and keeping it private, which exists at both internal and external levels. The internal level involves the tensions between a pair of people; the external level refers to the tensions between a person or couple and the rest of their social network. At the internal level, the openness–closedness dialectic refers to the simultaneous desire to disclose information and maintain privacy (Werner & Baxter, 1994). At the external level, revelation–concealment describes the tension between the desire to reveal and conceal information to others in a broader network (Werner & Baxter, 1994).

Method

To gain an understanding of the tensions and privacy implications in this environment from a consumer perspective, we use an interpretive orientation. First, with the consent of participants, we created digital dossiers of information about people through Internet searches. Second, we conducted in-depth interviews with participants to learn about their online behavior, privacy concerns, and strategies for managing and protecting their information.

Participants

We gathered a purposive sample of 12 men and women, equally representing two age groups, 18–25 years and 26–40 years (see Table 7.1). These participants appeared in our social networks; thus they are more likely to trust us to investigate their digital footprints. The sample of 12 was based on equal numbers across gender and age groups. Adding further

TABLE 7.1 Profile of Participants

Pseudonym/ Coding	Gender	Age	Marital status	Occupation	Number of Search Results	Number of Facebook Friends	Wall Post Status*	Number of Photos on Facebook	Number of Tagged Photos on Facebook
Ben	Male	18	Single	College Student	17	129	L	13	12
Aaron	Male	22	Single	Dental Student	189	487	M	88	125
Bart	Male	25	Single	Creative executive	125	912	H	2086	1076
Mark	Male	27	Single	Engineering Ph.D. Student	42	173	L	77	90
Mason	Male	27	Divorced	IT Manager	15	25	L	116	13
Clyde	Male	40	Married	Consultant	328	37	L	18	18
Grace	Female	22	Single	PR manager	11	649	WH	31	31
Paige	Female	25	Single	Fashion Designer	35	419	WH	190	0
Danielle	Female	25	Single	Model	807	497	M	69	86
Callie	Female	27	Single	Engineering Ph.D. Student	46	273	M	242	125
Cherie	Female	28	Divorced	Professional Organizer/ Artist	8	37	L	29	18
Clio	Female	37	Divorced	Artist	27	44	L	22	50

Note: *L = Light or less than 200; M = moderate or 201–49; H = heavy or more than 500; WH indicates wall hidden.

respondents did not provide significant new information. To improve the likelihood that the information we found would accurately reflect our participants, we also chose individuals with unique names, according to a search on whitepages.com, which reports the number of people in the United States with the same name. The average number of people who shared our participants' names was 1.67; none shared his or her name with more than 12 others.

Conducting Digital Searches and Dossier Creation

After obtaining permission from these participants, we conducted online searches using their name, physical address, and e-mail addresses. Two authors (with extensive online experience) used Google, Yahoo!, Microsoft Live, and Dogpile to conduct searches. Other searches relied on MySpace and Facebook. For closed social networking profiles, we obtained permission to access the pages, because well-documented methods exist that allow unauthorized or circuitous avenues to access such accounts (e.g., mutual friend tools, third-party applications, employer requests). We used any additional information discovered through our initial searches, such as affiliations and screen names, to refine our searches.

From this information, we compiled a digital footprint dossier for each of our 12 participants. The first summary page reported the number of search results, a summary of MySpace and Facebook activity (e.g., number of friends, posts, pictures), the number of blogs on which the person participated, and other Web site posting activity. Subsequent pages included screenshots from the Web and social networking site searches. The chosen screen shots reflected the various activities and content we found. The number of results varied for each participant, depending on his or her online activity, ranging from 8 to 16 pages.

Participant Interviews

After creating the digital footprint packets, we conducted semistructured, audio-recorded long interviews with each participant (McCracken, 1988). To begin, we asked participants to discuss their online experiences and motivations openly. This stage lasted 10–30 minutes. Next, we provided participants with a copy of their digital footprint dossier and gave them as much time as they desired to look over the material. We encouraged respondents to discuss the content as they leafed through the pages of the dossier and then explored the themes and experiences they mentioned pertaining to privacy issues related to their online activities.

After this initial examination and discussion, we provided respondents with feedback from others who had examined their profiles as well, as described elsewhere (Labrecque et al., 2011). In total, the interviews lasted 45 to 90 minutes. A follow-up interview (telephone, e-mail, or face-to-face) occurred approximately two months after the original interview to discuss changes the participants subsequently made to their profiles or online behavior. We also reviewed the accuracy of the data we gathered from the initial interviews and digital profile compilations.

Analysis Procedures

The authors transcribed the audio recordings of qualitative data from the interviews. All three researchers listened to the audio recordings and reviewed the transcripts multiple times. For each participant, we conducted an emic analysis; to compare across respondents, we also conducted an etic analysis. All three authors coded and analyzed the data using standard qualitative procedures (Siedman, 1991; Taylor & Bogdan, 1984); matrices served to compare the data across participants (Miles & Huberman, 1994). In an effort to gain new insights, we compared our results against prior literature in an iterative fashion (Belk, Wallendorf, & Sherry, 1989).

Findings

Consumers' Privacy Management

The summary of the participants' digital dossiers appears in Table 7.1. All respondents had Facebook accounts, two had MySpace accounts, and two maintained blogs. There was a wide range in the number of digital footprint search findings, spreading from 8 to 807. Moreover, participants' activity on their Facebook pages varied considerably in terms of the number of friends, posts, pictures, tagged photos from others, and blog posts.

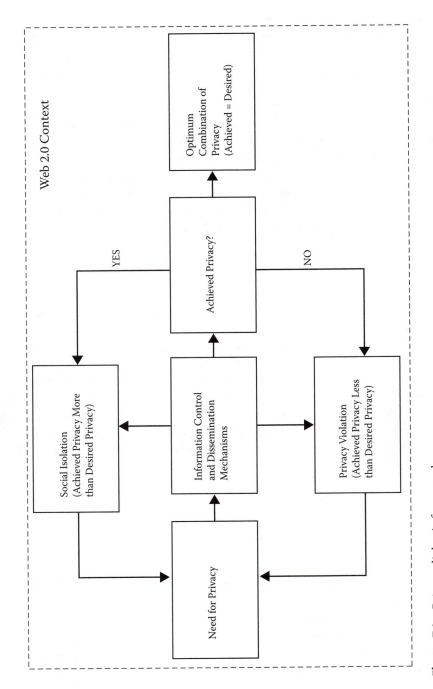

Figure 7.1 Privacy dialectic framework.

To organize our findings and gain a better understanding of the processes people undertake to balance their privacy against their self-disclosure, we adapt a Privacy Regulation Theory Model (Altman, 1975). In an updated framework (see Figure 7.1), we suggest that privacy boundaries, as embedded in a Web 2.0 context are fluid, such that each person decides how accessible his information should be to others. Shifts from open to closedness occur along a continuum, in response to both internal and external environments. This enables the person to attain a preferred or ideal level of privacy. By tightening or relaxing privacy boundaries, he controls openness and the degree of self-disclosure. These boundaries in turn depend on the amount of information dispersed and the extent of use of control mechanisms. For example, tight privacy boundaries may lead to social isolation; a relaxed position may result in privacy violations. As the person passes through different life stages, he or she moves along this continuum, likely adjusting boundaries to attain a dynamic desired state of privacy. The advantage of examining our data through this theoretical lens is that it provides a more systematic understanding of the strategies consumers use to resolve dialect challenges.

Information Control and Dissemination Mechanisms

A common theme among the participants was the implementation of some strategy to control the information found in their digital dossier. As part of their privacy regulation, participants used different tools, such as wall posts and photos, to disseminate personal information to a target audience. More than half our participants regularly engaged online, particularly through social networking sites. Most were forthcoming in admitting that they disclosed vast amounts of personal information on these platforms. Some, including Cherie (F, 28), expressed little concern for privacy and easily accepted that "It's the World Wide Web; you know anyone on the planet can find me." Others instead felt a need to implement some level of control, for various reasons.

The participants were not outwardly concerned about their data being collected by marketers; rather, they noted the potential consequences of their information being seen by the wrong people such that it would mar their reputations. One participant's privacy protection behavior was driven by a story about a violation that occurred to someone in her workplace; Clio (F, 37) thus noted that she monitored her digital footprint "to see that I'm not included somewhere. I also teach, so I want to make sure that no one has put anything . . . because it happened at school. Someone took a professor and made a fake Facebook page and went in and totally just destroyed him." Along with image protection, personal safety was a motivating factor for her to tighten privacy boundaries to control her private information.

Another participant, Grace (F, 22), echoed Clio's need for privacy control: "I think you need for your own, your own safety, you need to be a little more private . . . of course, I have privacy settings, because when people tag pictures of me, I'm not sure if I want everyone to know that I was out two nights ago." Grace went on to describe how she purposively managed and monitored information about herself online, as a privacy mechanism that could reduce her anxiety: "I'm not concerned with the things that are accessible because I've looked at them, and I'm well aware of what's out there. I would rather just be a little more limited to what I put on there." Grace withheld information she deemed too personal for public scrutiny and controlled the details she made available to her social network. This continual balancing act seems a common practice for members of online communities, as observed throughout our interviews.

Danielle (F, 25) noted that her naïve initial approach to Facebook left her vulnerable to others, before she limited her profile and established more privacy restrictions. However, she found it difficult to learn what mechanisms she could use to control her privacy and sustain the boundaries she desired: "I felt like with Facebook it's the only access someone has to me online. I didn't really know. I'm not a computer person so I didn't know how to make things private. It was more exposed, people could write on my wall, and people could search for me." During the interview, Danielle admitted that when she was a reigning pageant winner, she felt that any type of publicity was good regardless of any possible harm. She said, "Bad press is good press, any press is good press. I felt that it came with the territory. It was out of my control and I couldn't do anything about." Although she had been a very public figure during one stage of her life, when intrusiveness was a norm, she became more discreet after her pageant life ended, signaling a change in her privacy perceptions. As she phased out of the public arena, she thus faced the dialectic challenge of balancing her newfound private life with her previous celebrity-like status.

Many participants communicated similar shifting life phases that forced them to alter their privacy boundaries, whether by opening them to reveal more information or closing them for increased control. The primary mechanisms used to accomplish such shifts were the privacy settings available on social networking sites that allow users to restrict access to posted photos, remove photo tags, turn off the option that allows others to post on their page (e.g., Facebook wall), or enhance privacy settings. In particular, when young adults moved from college life to the workplace, they expressed a perceived need to ensure that any inappropriate images and content were not visible to professional colleagues. Grace (F, 22) stated that she deactivated her wall and changed her online image on Facebook over the years for just this reason: "I think my image, young, party, college, just having fun, going out a lot. That's all there really was. Now I try to be extremely conservative. I don't have a profile picture, it's gone. And now that I'm out of college, my image means a lot more because a potential employer could be looking at this and judging me and they could base that off if they wanted to take me. I could lose a job that way over bad pictures, so that's why." Aaron (M, 22), an aspiring dental student, noted similar concerns when describing his change from undergraduate to graduate school and later to professional life, "Yeah, this information, someone I'm interviewing for, someone at my school to see. I'm going to untag everything." Aaron also noted that he had not realized what a false impression his digital footprint conveyed and declared that later that night he would delete much of the inaccurate content from his profile.

For other respondents though, managing boundaries was not enough; they opted instead to use a segmentation strategy to gain control over the different parts of their lives. For example, several participants separated multiple selves and revealed different online personas to specific audiences. Mason (M, 27), who works as an information technology (IT) professional, tried to detach his professional identity from his DJ persona. He implemented this split because he did not want colleagues from his more conservative workplace to interact with or view the behavior of his friends from his DJ world. During the interview, he explained, "I am very well aware and I keep my DJ stuff, my personal and work stuff separate. . . . I have a lot of dumb friends and I would hate for some of their comments to bleed over to my work life or for someone to get the wrong impression about me in my work life."

Similarly, Bart (M, 25), a graphic design professional, maintained both a personal blog and commercial Web site, which supported his segregation strategy. He admitted that he kept the two Web sites completely separate so there could no confusion of his artist self and his business self. Therefore, "The [business site] was never meant to be more than just hey, if you're bored, there is a great site that has my work on it. [The business site] is something I am constantly trying to build." However, Bart was not particularly concerned about exposure on Facebook: "I'm not trying to hide anything I just filter. And it's like if you know me you probably are not much surprised by anything you read on my profile, it's the last thing I worry about." Despite managing multiple profiles and expressing little worry about information exposure, Bart continued to implement some level of privacy control.

Furthermore, Bart suggested that Facebook and other online profiles should be personal; he controlled his online content by excluding his family from his profiles and limiting content about himself and his friends. In his opinion, online profiles served a specific purpose: "The kind of music, books you know, it's a projection of life, a 5-minute version of yourself if someone was to meet you on the street. That's basically what the profiles are. They aren't too far from me but I filter. You will rarely see [pictures] of my family up on there. There are party photos, or a [picture] of me through spans of time, or when I do something obnoxious with my face for the sake of pure humor." That is, some people cautiously post information on personal profiles but express a sense of humor and a lax attitude toward those disclosures, which reinforces the duality and dialectic nature of the online world. Participants agreed that they disclosed a great deal of personal information but still desired and asserted some form of censorship.

Social Isolation

Isolation in several forms surfaced throughout our interviews, related to a failure to achieve a desired level of social interaction through disclosure. This failure occurred primarily because of tight privacy boundaries implemented through the use of privacy settings. Participants were outspoken about the realities of the Internet and the proliferation of social networks in their everyday lives.

In particular, multiple participants asserted that Facebook members often solicited friends online to compensate for real-world isolation. In so doing, they broadcast personal information to others with whom they might not have interacted in an offline context. Others chose to take specific measures to protect their privacy, which resulted in their reduced use of Facebook as a communication tool.

Because of her privacy concerns, Grace (F, 22) removed information from her profile and retained only a minimum level, such as her name and photo. She also explained how her decisions to protect her privacy made her appear and feel antisocial, in contrast with her offline personality: "I'm social, but on Facebook I seem kind of antisocial—no info, no wall, the pictures are limited, so those completely two opposite things."

Yet Cherie (F, 28) noted that people often share personal information by haphazardly adding friends, which might make them feel more social and popular: "Well, like I know there's like a lot of people on Facebook and MySpace like they really collect friends and they're really indiscriminant about it because they want to prove that they have a social life and that people like them." For others, their real-life interactions actually changed as a result of social networks, and some people become so heavily vested in their online persona that their physical contacts diminished.

For example, Paige (F, 25) pointed to how too much information on Facebook pages in effect could isolate people from real-life interactions:

> Like knowing a person should be something, like physically, actually knowing a person, sitting down talking to them should be valued a little more, my belief. Not looking up their Facebook profile and seeing everything they have done in the past year and all the [pictures], all the places, whatever you are doing and having all that knowledge about them. For me a little bit of that knowledge should be reserved for actually knowing someone.

In this context again, the challenge of determining how much information to offer versus what to keep private emerged in the narratives.

Danielle's (F, 25) view of privacy, both online and offline, changed drastically after she won a state beauty pageant. She began using Facebook as a tool to keep in touch with her friends from the pageant, but she quickly realized the potential privacy violations that could occur by leaving her profile open and searchable. She therefore chose to remove parts of her profile, yet kept her real name and other information to avoid becoming unreachable, noting, "There are good people out there and I do want the contact for work reasons, for real stuff and I want to participate in the real stuff. I really do." Danielle's struggle between self-isolation and opening herself to potential threats, offers a clear illustration of the dialectic tensions faced in this dynamic environment.

Privacy Violations

A privacy infringement occurs when a person's level of (achieved) privacy is lower than some desired state. Relaxed privacy boundaries, allowing for increased information disclosure, likely lead to this outcome, as well as other adverse consequences. Paige (F, 25) reinforced this idea with the notion of voyeurism, noting that she enjoys surveying other online profiles: "I look at other people's stuff, the more you put on, the more you are inviting me in. Even though I'm not a crazy person, it's a natural human psychology. I see something, I'm going to look at it, the more I look the more I wonder, the more I click on your page and then I wonder more. It's like you feed me, I'm going to keep eating." Although voyeurism can be an innocent act, it might easily create concerns if it evolved into threatening behaviors such as stalking.

Such unwanted intrusions by strangers represent a serious consequence of relaxed privacy boundaries, in that information disclosure makes people more susceptible or vulnerable to such forms of harm. Bart (M, 25) offered a story about his ex-girlfriend, who overexposed herself via pictures and other intimate posts on her Facebook and MySpace profiles and then suffered from the threat of multiple stalkers. He also expressed discomfort with the idea that his own information was exposed because of her relaxed privacy principles: "You kind of invite unnecessary things. She has 7,000 friends on MySpace and a good 100 of them are stalkers she has no idea of. And she does have a stalker and that's the thing."

Along similar lines, Clio (F, 37) noted the challenge between marketing herself as a freelance artist and the desire to preserve her safety. When making her boundary choices, she faced tensions with both professional and safety repercussions. Because she works from her residence she was forced to disclose her address so that her clients would not question her credibility; still she worries about her privacy. As she explained, "So, if I live in a home with a family, I don't think I want every Tom, Dick, and Harry to know where I live. So that becomes a bit of an issue to protect family."

Danielle (F, 25) enforced her privacy boundaries as a way to feel secure in light of her past stalking experiences. She shared: "If I'm not friends with you in person, there's no reason to be friends online. Can't accept it, I don't know, [there's] something [in] me that says no. Absolutely not, you know a lot of it is a safety issue. I don't know who is watching me. I had a lot of stalkers. . . . People don't realize that's a huge thing. Stalkers, I mean hundreds of weird of e-mails . . . a lot of stalkers, a lot of people."

An interesting point emerged in one interview in particular that highlighted the notion of memory lapses, a common concern in the digital era. Leaving personal details online for an extended time (often years) may pose a problem, because what was once appropriate for public display likely becomes less so as a person matures. Paige (F, 25) had forgotten what her Facebook profile entailed, apart from her latest postings and thus was surprised when reviewing her digital dossier. When asked initially about what information she shares, she responded, "Yeah, yeah I don't have anything really incriminating, I don't think. So anything that is public is just sort of based. . . . Um, like, a mediocre social life, nothing extravagant." After a pause, she realized her contradiction and recalled different layers of information posted over time. For example, she remembered that when she interned for a New York City-based fashion designer the year before, several racy pictures appeared on her profile. This recollection prompted a revision to her comments, "I just thought of what I have on there, ummmm . . . what I thought was on there. OK, my initial, what I just thought was like recent things which has been nothing too extravagant, now I'm traveling back a year, and all the designer craziness, that is the personification of extravagance, it's all crazy." This participant's experience underscored the vast amount of information accumulated online and the effort required by users to maintain their privacy while using an application (e.g., Facebook) for its intended purpose.

When they alter their adopted levels of openness and closedness, consumers also must take others' actions into consideration though, because of the interactive nature of the online environment. In particular, we note a heightened awareness of privacy and the need for regulation in our interviews, mainly because acquaintances and strangers had learned about the participants' pursuits without being part of their lives.

A younger participant, Ben (M, 18) recalled an incident in which a friend posted a picture after an afternoon of "secret" drinking and tagged him without his consent, sparking a sense of anxiety:

> I just didn't want to be in the picture. Actually I think something bad happened, something bad and I was like "delete." We were drinking outside of my neighbor's house and ah . . . they were away and we hid alcohol by the woods next to the house and the girls were taking pictures. So they tagged me and his father went to check up on the house and he saw a brown bag because it was not in the woods but on the border of the woods. . . . He told [friend's name] and my neighbors that he thought it was me . . . so I was friends with his son so I untagged them [the pictures] so he wouldn't be able to see them because you could see the side of the house and you knew it was me.

Paige (F, 25) instead restricted her photo access and removed her wall because she wanted more privacy: "I don't want someone going to my page and read conversations that I've had with other people. There is a point for having a conversation with someone. Or sharing a joke and I didn't like the thought of people that may not even like me, looking on my page and putting two and two together." She continued to discuss her rationale for removing her wall by noting, "It's just a window that I wanted to close, I think. There are certain layers of accessibility that you can open through the Internet and through Facebook and I wanted to close them." Like many of our participants, Paige faced a crossroads; she initially revealed many of her endeavors online, but she increasingly felt the need to close off and protect herself for the sake of privacy. In describing why she changed her privacy setting, Grace (F, 22) explained that she disliked when acquaintances would ask about life events that had been communicated through her friends' Facebook postings. For example, "What prompted me was that pictures were tagged of me and then someone would say, oh, I saw a picture of you from last night, and I was like, how the hell did you see that?"

Clio (F, 37) expressed a similar feeling about the popular Facebook feature of photo tagging, as well as the potential for others to influence her profile: "I'm more afraid of what other people post, pictures that other people put up of me. That's what I don't like, that tagging. . . . I just don't think that I need to have my name plastered all over everyone's board because I'm not friends with their friends and yet they get to see me."

Yet Callie (F, 27) had migrated from another social network to Facebook because the former did not give her the privacy control settings she preferred to manage her information disclosure choices. She considered her private information too exposed due to the absence of privacy features: "I didn't like it. [There is] no privacy because anyone can see your profile, not only your friends, at least when I was there. It felt like a meat market online. You had to register on Hi5 but you could go on to any profile you wanted and click on it and you could see everything. This is not what I wanted. That's why I'm on Facebook." However, in contrast with Callie's view, many participants mentioned that on sites including Facebook, opportunities to view strangers' profiles thrived because of the lax privacy settings implemented by users, as well as the social network itself.

Finally, many participants used self-monitoring as a mechanism for countering the effects of privacy invasions and loose privacy boundaries. By conducting vanity searches online, they could find floating information stored in unknown portals and take proactive action to avoid such exposure. Mark (M, 27) indicated that he has conducted self-searches occasionally but did not find it necessary to do so regularly:

> I've searched myself through like Google. . . . I think there are other things for instance besides just a Google search that your name could show up, looking a little more detailed. . . . Now, I've never clicked through the like 50 pages that show up, so I know my name will come up in that too, but I've only looked through a few pages and I haven't seen it. . . . But I know the first two pages that will show up. My name is fairly not common, so it's easy to find something. But

I imagine if I was someone with a common name you wouldn't bother . . . it's too time consuming to find yourself.

During a name search, Callie (F, 27) found that her new address was accessible to everyone without her permission, causing great concern: "And the second I saw my address online and I freaked out . . . and I changed addresses and I didn't tell them that I changed addresses because I don't want it online." A major consideration was how to weigh the degree of desired privacy. Consistently, a balancing act played out, depending on the point in time and how much control the participants desired. Most of them seemed to try to reach an optimum level of privacy, where she felt comfortable with a certain amount of information shared in an online forum.

Optimum Privacy

The respondents achieved optimum privacy when they could control their openness to others by effectively relaxing or tightening disclosure boundaries. In most cases, such control was achieved through a combination of information control and dissemination, along with vigilant online monitoring. As we mentioned previously, the participants used a plethora of strategies in an attempt to achieve this ultimate state. Tightening of boundaries included removal of a Facebook wall, untagging photos, and restricting their use of social networking sites.

For the participants who used a segmentation strategy by creating multiple accounts and aliases, there were difficulties in managing their multiple identities to maintain their ideal level of privacy. Mason (M, 27), explained how new tools offered by sites such as Facebook become problematic when he worked to control who had access to personal data. The purpose of such tools is to enable people to make new friend connections and facilitate seamless sharing, but they also make it easier for unwanted parties to find others and peer into private information.

Other participants spoke of the challenges surrounding life phases, such as graduating college, career changes, or parenthood. Mark (M, 27), as a new father, remained undecided about whether he should share his newborn's photographs online. His partner's parents and siblings lived outside the United States and regularly connected through Facebook and Skype. In a follow-up interview Mark discussed his conflicting feelings: "[the baby] is part of our daily life so it's hard not having her show up in pictures. We want to protect her but at the same time we want to introduce her to our family and friends." The ideal levels of privacy thus clearly shift with major life events. Changes that occurred just a couple of months after the initial interviews confirm that the optimization process is dynamic and reconsidered frequently.

Finally, even if they can achieve optimized privacy, the fluid nature of the online environment and permanency of digital information remains an ongoing concern for consumers. In particular, the long-term consequences are unclear, as Clio (F, 37) noted:

> We don't know what it's going to be like to have been a teenager and exposed your whole life and then be 30 looking for a job, looking for a partner, looking for anything and they have to see you at 18 and 15 doing these weird things because we all do things through our years. But we basically live them through our memory—here you have like tangible things—they're pictures, they're never going away and I don't think it's going to be good, it's going to be harmful.

Discussion

Although the popular press and other research might imply that consumers, especially younger ones (i.e., Generation Y), are not concerned with information privacy (Hoy & Milne, 2010), the evidence herein suggests otherwise. Our research reveals that heavy users of social media and other Web 2.0 applications desire control over their personal information and implement various strategies to exert this power. Online platforms such as Facebook encourage transparent information sharing and co-creation to foster a communal and apparently safe environment, yet privacy risks abound.

Themes related to the potential for cyberstalking, reputation damage, unwanted scrutiny, and misrepresentation surfaced in our research. Although the new Web seemingly allows for positive interactions, monitoring privacy and profiles remains a necessary task to ensure accurate and desired disclosure. Misinformation may cause unfavorable outcomes for consumers, ranging from physical harm, financial standing, or the prevention of employment opportunities (Eaton, 2009). Personal vigilance thus emerged as the main mechanism online users employed to protect their personal information from intrusion by multiple audiences (e.g., friends of friends, strangers). By using the privacy settings provided by Facebook, for example, participants gained a sense of control over their personal data, because they restricted and selected who could view their profile information.

This research has highlighted the dialectic challenges that consumers face in the marketplace when they try to protect their privacy (see Table 7.2). The rich accounts from the interviews suggest that one-time surveys, dominant in this literature, can convey only part of the picture. Even if they believe there is no or little privacy online, people still try to control what they can. According to our study narratives, dialectic pressures shift as people embark on different life phases and alter their privacy boundaries. For example, concern for privacy and a need for constrained disclosure differed for the college students compared with the professional and older adult participants in our study. A prevailing belief resonating throughout our interviews was that in college or high school, young people act frivolously, but once they enter the real (i.e., professional) world, they adopt an aura of seriousness that marks a change in their behavior. Adjusting to

TABLE 7.2 Adaptation of Altman's Privacy Model

Motivation: Need for Privacy Control
- Image management
- Life stages
- Reputation control
- Forgetting

Strategies: Information Control and Dissemination Mechanisms
- Controlling others' behaviors to ensure privacy
- Segmentation for controlling privacy
- Untagging photographs
- Removal of wall (Facebook)

Consequence: Privacy Violations
- Stalking
- Privacy invasions by others' behaviors
- Self-monitoring as a privacy tool

Consequence: Social Isolation
- Fewer real-life interactions
- Character misconceptions
- Inappropriate privacy settings

Optimization
- Updating and changing privacy settings
- Life changes prompt different privacy implementation

new life circumstances also creates a new set of dialectic challenges that involves another shift in desired privacy levels. Further research therefore should consider context-specific factors when measuring concern, while also noting the dialectic nature of privacy protection.

Furthermore, this updated analysis of Altman's (1975) privacy boundary model confirms that privacy boundary maintenance is a dynamic process. Our young respondents emphasized this dynamic nature in the transitory behaviors they described. Superficial claims (e.g., "No privacy exists online," "Youth don't care about their privacy," "Privacy will be a nonissue in the future because of young consumers' attitudes") are not supported by this study. Research that examines cohort-based and longitudinal approaches to privacy could shed more light on this observation (Gabisch & Milne, 2010); it seems likely that privacy boundaries will continue to shift as young adults' age and take on added responsibilities of family and careers. Consistent with this view is the finding that consumers adjust their privacy boundaries to minimize the potential harms and vulnerabilities they might face.

As technology continues to evolve, innovative online tools and new norms, including Web 3.0 and further (Markoff, 2006), will enter the marketplace and become integrated into daily transactions, all the while encouraging additional information sharing. These new technologies and standards create more privacy concerns for consumers. Because companies largely follow self-regulatory principles (FTC, 2000) and blurry guidelines for protecting consumer data prevail, an understanding and weighting of the impact of disclosure choices remains mainly the responsibility of the individual. Although this research highlights consumers' perceptions of Web 2.0 applications and techniques that can help them maintain a sense of control and privacy online, it focuses mainly on social networks, and future research should examine privacy management concerns beyond this context. For example, additional online applications embedded with sophisticated technologies in the marketplace will subject consumers to unfamiliar harms. Mobile marketing is a relatively new way to reach consumers but is projected to be a billion-dollar industry by 2012 (Patel, 2010). As with most new technologies, mobile applications create an ambiguous set of privacy issues that consumers must balance; they also thus offer ripe research opportunities.

In summary, our findings offer an updated perspective on privacy within the context of a privacy boundary model (Altman, 1975), by highlighting new vulnerabilities introduced by the dynamic Web 2.0 environment. This research illustrates the loss of information control that consumers perceive when their information becomes accessible and malleable by others. Our study further underscores the importance of digital vigilance and offers insight into different online strategies used to control consumer data as an onslaught of modern challenges surges in the marketplace.

References

Acquisti, A. (2004). Privacy in electronic commerce and the economics of immediate gratification. *Proceedings of the 5th ACM Conference on Electronic Commerce.* New York.

Altman, I. (1975). *The environment and social behavior.* Monterey, CA: Brooks Cole.

Baxter, L. A. & Montgomery, B. M. (1996). *Relating: Dialogues and dialectics.* New York: Guilford Press.

Belk, R. W., Wallendorf, M., & Sherry, Jr., J. F. (1989). The sacred and the profane in consumer behavior: Theodicy on the Odyssey. *Journal of Consumer Research, 15*(September), 139–167.

Careerbuilder.com (2009). Forty-five percent of employers use social networking sites to research job candidates, CareerBuilder survey finds. http://www.careerbuilder.com/share/aboutus/pressreleasesdetail.aspx?id=pr519&sd=8/19/2009&ed=12/31/2009&siteid=cbpr&sc_cmp1=cb_pr519

Eaton, K. (2009). If you're applying for a job, censor your Facebook page. http://www.fastcompany.com/blog/kit-eaton/technomix/if-youre-applying-job-censor-your-facebook-page

Federal Trade Commission (FTC) (2000). Privacy online: Fair information practices in the electronic marketplace: A report to congress. http://www.ftc.gov/reports/privacy2000 privacy2000.pdf

Gabisch, J. & Milne, G. R. (2010). Do digital natives have different online sharing and privacy concerns? *Proceedings of AMA and Public Policy Conference.* Denver, CO.

Goldberg, S. (2010). Young job-seekers hiding their Facebook pages. http://articles.cnn.com/2010-03-29/tech/facebook.job-seekers_1_facebookhiring-online-reputation?_s=PM:TECH

Golle, P. (2006). Revisiting the uniqueness of simple demographics in the US population. *WPES, Proceedings of the 5th ACM Workshop on Privacy in Electronic Society,* pp. 77–80.

Goodwin, C. (1991). Privacy: Recognition of a consumer right. *Journal of Public Policy & Marketing, 10*(1), 149–166.

Helft, M. (2009). Where Google is really big: India and Brazil. http://bits.blogs.nytimes.com/2009/09/14/where-google-is-really-big-india-andchina/

Hoffman, D. L., Novak, T. P., & Peralta, M. A. (1999). Information privacy in the marketspace: Implications for the commercial uses of anonymity on the Web. *Information Society, 15*(2), 129–140.

Hoy, M. G. & Milne, G. R. (2010). Gender differences in privacy-related measures for young adult Facebook users. *Journal of Interactive Advertising, 10*(2), 28–45.

Kaputa, C. (2005). *UR a brand! How smart people brand themselves for business success.* Mountain View, CA: Davies-Black.

Labrecque, L. I., Markos, E. C., & Milne, G. R. (2011). Online personal branding: Processes, challenges, and implications, *Journal of Interactive Marketing, 25*(1), 37-50.

Langenderfer, J. & Miyazaki, A. D. (2009). Privacy in the information economy. *Journal of Consumer Affairs, 43*(3), 380–388.

Lee, H.-D., Im, S., & Taylor, C. R. (2008).Voluntary self-disclosure of information on the Internet: A multimethod study of the motivations and consequences of disclosing information on blogs. *Psychology & Marketing, 25*(7), 692–710.

Madden, M., Fox, S., Smith, A., & Vitak, J. (2007). Digital footprints: Online identity management and search in the age of transparency. http://pewresearch.org/pubs/663/digital-footprints

Markoff, J. (2006). Entrepreneurs see a Web guided by common sense. http://www.nytimes.com/2006/11/12/business/12web.html

McCracken, G. (1988). *The long interview.* Thousand Oaks, CA: SAGE.

Miceli, G. N., Ricotta, F., & Costabile, M. (2007). Customizing customization: A conceptual framework for interactive personalization. *Journal of Interactive Marketing, 21*(2), 6–25.

Miles, M. B. & Huberman, A. M. (1994). *Qualitative data analysis.* Thousand Oaks, CA: SAGE.

Milne, G. R. & Bahl, S. (2010). Are there differences between consumers' and marketers' privacy expectations? A segment- and technology-level analysis. *Journal of Public Policy & Marketing, 29*(1), 138–149.

Milne, G. R., Bahl, S., & Rohm, A. (2008). Toward a framework for assessing covert marketing practices. *Journal of Public Policy & Marketing, 27*(1), 57–62.

Milne, G. R., Labrecque, L. I., & Cromer, C. (2009). Toward an understanding of the online consumer's risky behavior and protection practices. *Journal of Consumer Affairs, 43*(3), 449–473.

Milne, G. R., Rohm, A., & Bahl, S. (2004).Consumers' protection of online privacy and identity. *Journal of Consumer Affairs, 38*(2), 217–232.

Miyazaki, A. D. (2008). Online privacy and the disclosure of cookie use: Effects on consumer trust and anticipated patronage. *Journal of Public Policy and Marketing, 27*(Spring), 19–33.

Miyazaki, A. D. & Krishnamurthy, S. (2002), Internet seals of approval: Effects on online privacy policies and consumer perceptions. *Journal of Consumer Affairs, 36*(1), 28–49.

Morales, L. (2010). U.S Internet users ready to limit online tracking for ads. http://www.gallup.com/poll/145337/Internet-Users-Ready-Limit-OnlineTrackingAds.aspx?utm_source=alert&utm_medium=email&utm_campaign=synicationutm_content=morelink&utm_term=Americas

Palfrey, J. & Gasser, U. (2008). *Born digital: Understanding the first generation of digital natives.* New York: Basic.

Patel, K. (2010). Mobile to become a $1billion business in the U.S next year. http://adage.com/digital/article?article_id=146553

Peltier, J. W., Milne, G. R., & Phelps, J. E. (2009). Information privacy research: Framework for integrating multiple publics, information channels, and responses. *Journal of Interactive Marketing, 23*(2), 191–205.

Petronio, S. (2000). *Boundaries of privacy: The dialectics of disclosure.* New York: State University of New York Press.

Pew Research Center (2010). Millennials: Confident. Connected. Open to Change. http://pewsocialtrends.org/pubs/751/millennialsconfident connected-open-to-change

Phelps, J. E., D'Souza, G., & Nowak, G. J. (2001). Antecedents and consequences of consumer privacy concerns: An empirical investigation. *Journal of Interactive Marketing, 15*(4), 2–17.

Poddar, A., Mostellar, J., & Scholder-Ellen, P. (2009). Consumers' rules of engagement in online information exchanges. *Journal of Consumer Affairs, 43*(3), 419–448.

Roschmann-Schmitt, V. (2010). Germany to pass Facebook privacy law banning employers' Facebook checks. http://www.huffingtonpost.com/2010/08/25/germany-facebook-privacy_n_693938.html

Schau, H. J. & Gilly, M. C. (2003). We are what we post? Self-presentation in personal web space. *Journal of Consumer Research, 30*(3), 385–404.

Schonberger, V.-M. (2009). Delete: *The virtue of forgetting in the digital age.* Princeton, NJ: Princeton University Press.

Schwabel, D. (2009). *Me 2.0: A powerful way to achieve brand success.* New York: Kaplan.

Siedman, I. E. (1991). *Interviewing as qualitative research.* New York: Teachers College Press.

Solove, D. J. (2008). *Understanding privacy.* Cambridge, MA: Harvard University Press.

Stelter, B. (2009). Facebook's users ask who owns information. http://www.nytimes.com/2009/02/17/technology/internet/17facebook.html

Sweeney, L. (1997). Weaving technology and policy together to maintain confidentiality. *Journal of Law, Medicine & Ethics, 25*(2–3), 98–110.

Taylor, S. J. & Bogdan, R. (1984). *Introduction to qualitative research methods: The search for meanings* (2nd ed.). New York: John Wiley & Sons.

Turkle, S. (1995). *Life on the screen: Identity in the age of the Internet.* New York: Touchtone.

Vazire, S. & Gosling, S. D. (2004). e-perceptions: Personality impressions based on personal websites. *Journal of Personality and Social Psychology, 87*(1), 123–132.

Warren, S. D. & L. D. Brandeis (1890). The right to privacy. *Harvard Law Review, 4*(December), 193–200.

Werner, C. & Baxter, L. A. (1994). temporal qualities of relationships: Organismic transactional and dialectical views. In M. L. Knapp & G. R. Miller (Eds.), *Handbook of interpersonal communication* (pp. 323–379). Newbury Park, CA: SAGE.

Westin, A. F. (1967). *Privacy and freedom*. New York: Athenaeum.

Wynn, E. & Katz, J. E. (1997). Hyperbole over cyberspace: Self-presentation and social boundaries in internet home pages and discourse. *Information Society, 13*(4), 297–327.

Zinkhan, G. M., Conchar, M., Gupta, A., & Geissler, G. (1999). Motivations underlying the creation of personal web pages: An exploratory study. In E. J. Arnould & L. M. Scott (Eds.), *Advances in consumer research* (Vol. 26). Provo, UT: Association for Consumer Research, pp. 69–74.

Section III

Online Advertising and Online Search Behavior

8

Viewer Reactions to Online Political Spoof Videos and Advertisements

Anjali S. Bal
Simon Fraser University

Colin L. Campbell
Monash University

Leyland F. Pitt
Simon Fraser University

Traditional political campaigns use a variety of mass media tools, such as print and television, to influence voter perception of candidates. Since the rise of the Internet, the balance of power in the traditional communications continuum has shifted and the nature of politics and electioneering is undergoing massive change (Blumler & Kavanagh, 1999). The voter's ability to access information about candidates, share opinions, and discuss specific candidate's policies, image, and reputation has increased (Farrell & Webb, 2000). In addition, more people are creating and consuming online spoof content. Spoofs are an attempt by an individual to make light of, mimic, or mock a known entity (Bal, Pitt, Berthon, & DesAutels, 2009). Consumer-generated content is any "publically disseminated, consumer-generate[d] advertising message whose subject is a collectively recognized brand" (Berthon, Pitt, & Campbell, 2008, p. 8). Politicians have been the brunt of emotionally charged spoofs since the growth of democracy (Bal et al., 2009).

A critical task of campaign management is the measurement and validation of voter sentiment. Many individuals have come to rely on the Internet as their primary source of information and campaign managers have started using the Internet to interact directly with these voters on a personal level. This interaction serves multiple purposes, including persuasion and assessment (Vaccari, 2008). As the quality of interaction has increased, however, campaign managers have struggled with grouping, analyzing, and using online commentary in a meaningful way. Moreover, they continue to search for tools and processes that enable them to measure voter sentiment and ultimately predict voter behavior. Over the last 10 years, a number of market research techniques have been developed to help businesses analyze customer feedback on the Internet and predict future behavior. Unfortunately, only a small handful of those tools have been tested within the political environment. Within this chapter we examine whether analytical perceptual mapping software used to analyze online text commentary can be used within the political arena to help campaign and communication managers accurately measure and analyze voter sentiments. Furthermore, we test whether the resulting perceptual maps elicit themes that reliably predict potential voter behavior following exposure to political spoof videos, videos that have the potential to do significant damage to a candidate's electability, reputation, and brand.

Political Environment

Voter interaction with incumbent and potential candidates and policies and brands continues to evolve (Campbell & Dettrey, 2009) with increasing complexity of the global political environment, making it challenging for campaign managers to effectively prepare and execute large-scale electoral campaigns. One of the key focuses for campaign managers is to develop and manage a potential candidate's identity through a process known as identity manufacturing (O'Shaughnessy & Henneberg, 2007). This process has close parallels to brand management in which a potential candidate must embody personality characteristics that are perceived as conditions for success within the political climate (Shocker, Rajendra, & Ruekert, 1994). A key challenge within this process is the tracking and measurement of the voter's perceptions. These perceptions, when grouped collectively, provide the cognitive "cues" into the shortcuts and heuristics that voters use when assessing potential candidates and planning future actions (O'Shaughnessy & Henneberg, 2007). Within the business environment, research into customer perceptions, their attitudes toward brands, and their purchase intentions are fairly well developed (Goldsmith, Lafferty, & Newell, 2000). Due to the established link among advertising, positive consumer evaluations, and purchasing behavior, businesses use a variety of advertising media to communicate product and brand information to customers (Biehal & Sheinin, 1998; Biehal, 2007). The measurement of customer attitudes and response to these media provides organizations with critical stakeholder feedback that can be used to tweak and enhance corporate communications, increase receptiveness, and foster customer engagement.

Although many parallels can be drawn from customer perceptions of advertising, the political environment, especially that existing during electoral races, differs substantially from the traditional consumer environment. Within the political environment, the intensity of interaction (O'Shaughnessy & Henneberg, 2007) and costs associated with negative interaction are high. There is less predictability (Newman, 1999; O'Shaughnessy & Henneberg, 2007), greater pressures to align one's image to that desired by the electorate (Thomas, 2004), and increased manipulation of communication messages. Furthermore, the speed at which voters, critics, and media can respond to campaign communications is significantly faster than traditional consumer environments. This increased response time continues to challenge political campaign managers as the Internet begins to play a more predominant role in U.S. political campaign management. This shift has led to a significant decrease in the percentage of campaign funds allocated toward mass media promotions, and an increased focus in online media (Vaccari, 2008). It has been further underscored by the recognition that mass media communication has unmistakable limitations, including its inability to be targeted to specific segments, its perceived repetitive and biased nature, and the disconnect between mass media utilization and voter mobilization (Monson, 2004), as well as increases in cost (Warren, 2010). As a result, many political campaign managers now view the Internet as the primary medium through which political communications flow. The primary concern is selecting tools that enable attentive feedback to key stakeholders with a focus on tailored communication and messaging (Vaccari, 2008).

Politics Online

Historically, political communications were subject to far less manipulation due to the fragmentation and reduced interaction between members of an electorate. The general public lacked the technological literacy (Boler, 2008), empowerment, and marketing savvy necessary to manipulate mass media messages. As the percentage of Americans using the Internet for everyday tasks has risen (Vaccari, 2008), the ability of voters to participate in discussions of a candidate has increased. Online political communications no longer have a specific time and place and are instead subject to continuous informational processing (Baudrillard, 2001) and multiple feedback loops (Glynn, 2009). The lack of controls and decentralization means that commentary is uncensored and unrestricted (Tsfati & Weimann, 1999). As a result, even the most disengaged citizens can participate directly with the process of political branding (Weimann, 2008). This engagement frequently manifests itself through the posting of amateur videos on YouTube that create a portrait of the particular candidates (Berthon et al., 2008) and have the ability to damage a candidate's image and brand significantly. Thus, viewers' response to these portraits is of great interest to political campaign managers (Ormrod, Henneberg, Forward, Miller, & Tymms, 2007). Analysis of the portraits as well as viewers' commentary provides insights into voter perceptions, orientation, and intentions. Furthermore, a strong understanding of these insights provides campaign managers with quicker and more reliable feedback of voter perceptions and attitudes than is currently available using sample-based polling technologies.

Since the 2004 U.S. presidential election, a number of major U.S. political candidates have used the Internet to showcase spoofs of rival campaign footage or rival candidates. In addition, many consumers have used the Internet to create spoof content in response to candidate's communications campaigns. These spoofs directly challenge the perceived credibility of the candidate's image and brand within the political environment (Petrou, 2009). There is a variety of reasons individuals post content online, including information seeking (Papacharissi & Rubin, 2000), social utility (Kaye & Johnson, 2002), entertainment (Ebersole, 2000; Kaye & Johnson, 2002), interpersonal utility (Papacharissi & Rubin, 2000), and social or interpersonal interaction (Wolfradt & Doll, 2001). These diverse uses can be combined to create a consolidated list of three primary user motivations to post content online: intrinsic enjoyment, self-promotion, and perception change (Berthon et al., 2008). Intrinsic enjoyment occurs when a video creator is driven to production through her creative or technological love to create. Self-promoters are individuals who create and post ads for their own benefit such as a portfolio for a job interview (Berthon et al., 2008). Perception changers are individuals who create ads in order to change the beliefs, hearts, and minds of viewers. It is important to note that these are not exact groupings; video creators can have multiple sources of motivation. Within the political sphere, political advertisements and spoof videos posted online often have the goal of encouraging perception change.

This reality is an area of concern for campaign communication strategists, who would prefer to maintain control over the way voters perceive their candidate's image, personality, and political brand.

YouTube and Political Campaign Management

YouTube is one of the most significant online tools designed to enhance the sharing of media on the Internet. YouTube exemplifies the characteristics of the most effective online social environments, in which all users have the potential to be both a consumer and purveyor of content (Holtz, 2006). By the middle of 2006, YouTube was showing over 100 million videos per day globally and accounting for 60% of all videos watched online (Haridakis & Hanson, 2009). The quality of the videos posted is often low, but it is precisely this feature that has increased viewer interest in the platform due to the strong similarities with reality-generated television. After watching a video, viewers can share opinions about the content through online blogs, can rate videos, advertisements, and communications, and can easily share YouTube content by e-mailing the links to family and friends. Additionally, as video-editing software has been simplified, viewers of online videos have the ability to manipulate and repost online content into new formats and presentations that often carry significantly different meaning than originally intended. This ability to manipulate communication messages after receipt has significantly changed the traditional communications paradigm in political environments.

Although the increased interaction on YouTube has contributed to its rapid rise in popularity, it is precisely this openness of the Internet and the potential for message manipulation that make YouTube a dangerous political weapon. YouTube provides any stakeholder with the ability to actively influence the formation, improvement, or destruction of a candidate's political brand and identity. This reality is a matter of concern for political campaign managers, who would prefer to have singular control over their candidate's brand, image, and communications. This challenge is particularly true with political spoof advertisements. Frequently described as amateurish and sophomoric; nevertheless, these political spoof videos often satirize the image, policies, and personality of electoral candidates. These characterizations have the potential to destroy even the most well-crafted political images and campaigns. Unfortunately, despite these warnings, many politicians have chosen to ignore the impact of these videos or have attacked their creators, often causing significant damage to their political brand as well as the campaign. One challenge often associated with the analysis of online media is the lack of online assessment tools. Such tools would be useful in enabling political campaign managers to analyze and interpret viewer responses to political spoof videos effectively. If such tools existed, YouTube could potentially become a gold mine for popular opinion data that would give campaign managers real-time insights into voters' perceptions, sentiment, and future behavior (Cha, Kwak, Rodriguez, Ahn, & Moon, 2007).

Politics, the Internet, and Spoof Content

In fall 2007, Barack Obama, the Democratic presidential candidate, used the Internet to influence voter opinion positively, increase interaction with prospective voters, and use the efficiencies of the Internet to solve complex problems relating to fundraising and campaign organization (Stirland, 2008). Obama's campaign managers used YouTube to advertise and publicize their candidate's policy, develop a strong political brand, solicit donations, and mobilize supporters in a way that traditionally required an army of volunteers and paid organizers on the ground (Miller, 2008). The results of this action were substantial. In a recent review of President Obama's Internet campaign, it was noted that voters watched over 14.5 million hours of videos including speeches, campaign media, spoof videos, and caricatures posted exclusively on YouTube (Miller, 2008). The total cost of purchasing the same amount of viewership within traditional mass media was estimated at $47 million (Miller, 2008). After Obama's election victory, CBS News reported that throughout the 2008 presidential election, political videos and advertisements relating to the presidential campaign were viewed on YouTube more than 22 million times. This figure is significant, considering that only 24 million people voted in both the Democratic and Republican primaries combined (CBS, 2007).

Unfortunately, although the Internet has been shown to be a powerful tool to revolutionize voter engagement and mobilization (Nelson, 2005), many campaign managers struggle when incorporating online communications in their campaign communication plans. Furthermore, many candidates have found themselves portrayed negatively in political spoof videos that were widely posted and distributed on YouTube. These videos, as well as their resulting response, consistently challenged many candidates' brand, image, and personality. One politician who has experienced these challenges firsthand was the Republican presidential nominee

Senator John McCain. In October 2008, due to the consistent negative portrayal of McCain and his vice presidential running mate Sarah Palin on YouTube, McCain's campaign organizers wrote a letter to YouTube asking it to reconsider its policy on video takedowns, a policy that protects YouTube from infringing copyright laws. Although YouTube leadership rejected this request, it underscores how effectively the Internet, and YouTube in particular, can influence voters' beliefs regarding their candidates as well as their potential voting behavior.

Viewers' Perceptions of Online Content

Researchers and practitioners continue to search for novel ways to measure and analyze customer perceptions and attitudes toward online advertising. In a study on advertising perception and brand personality, van Rekom, Jacobs, and Verlegh (2006) used a 1,000-person study to evaluate customers' perception of brand personalities projected through advertising. After receiving and analyzing 146 completed questionnaires, they graphically built perceptual maps using Ahn's (1998) causal status hypothesis. Their research provided a useful departure point for brand communication modeling and encouraged the development of visual perceptual maps to understand customer responses to advertising more accurately. In a more recent study, Soh, Reid, and King (2009) used surveys of 265 college students along with expert interviews to develop a reliable and valid measure of the trust-in-advertising construct as well as a framework to analyze customer perceptions of advertising content. Although these methods are rigorous, their research methodology used surveys as well as focus groups and interviews to analyze customer perceptions of brand personality. These tools are practical academically but not efficient enough to provide political campaign managers with timely feedback on customer perceptions and attitudes. This critique is even more relevant in online settings, where the large amount of information and reduced feedback time requires the development and use of tools that precisely measure customer opinion.

Leximancer is a computer software tool that conducts conceptual (thematic) and relational (semantic) analysis on written words as well as visual text. It has been applied in a variety of settings and holds promise as an online perceptual measurement device. The software identifies the major concepts embedded within text as well as the relationship among the concepts that emerge. Leximancer's software uses Bayesian theory to analyze a piece of text; it determines the dominant themes and maps the relation-ship of these themes against each other. As output, Leximancer provides a conceptual map that identifies the dominant themes contained within a particular text sample. The relative importance of the concepts elicited by the software are determined based on where the words on the concept map appear; words representative of the consolidated themes appear closer to the center of a concept map whereas those less important are located nearer the periphery. Those concepts that are strongly semantically linked will appear near each other, and possibly overlap, and concepts that are not semantically linked will be farther away (Rooney, 2005, pp. 410–412). Concepts with larger concept dots indicate greater relatedness to other concepts on the map. The color of concepts also indicates their relative fre-quency in the text with more darkly colored concepts appearing more fre-quently. Clusters of concepts appear on the map when they tend to appear in similar semantic contexts.

Within the political environment, a tool such as Leximancer has a number of benefits that make it attractive for political campaign manag-ers. One key advantage is that automatic analysis begins with only a few seed words and can then go on to analyze vast sets of text that contain a large number of concepts, enabling the software to effectively analyze large blogs and user comments from videos posted on YouTube and other social media sites. Another advantage of Leximancer is that words form the unit of analysis. Thus, the software is able to incorporate all types of text, including comments often left by Internet users.

Researchers in a wide variety of domains have successfully used Leximancer analysis to extend public perceptions of advertising and com-munications media. For example, Smith and Humphreys (2006), research-ers in the field of behavioral research, validated the output of Leximancer, using a set of evaluation criteria taken from content analysis that were appropriate for knowledge discovery tasks. Scott and Smith (2005), in a tourism study, used the software to assess event images and determine how public representation of events changes over time. In corporate risk management, Martin and Rice (2007) employed Leximancer in examin-ing enterprise risks in large computer companies in order to identify risk themes, concepts, and ideas from the screening and contextual analy-sis of business reports and corporate data. These methods show prom-ise; however, little research has explored whether this software would be useful within the political environment to analyze voter perceptions and predicted behaviors. This is particularly relevant to political spoof advertisements posted on YouTube, where viewer feedback and comments to posted media can have a significant impact on the political candidate.

Methods

We used Leximancer to analyze three political spoof advertisements. Please refer to Table 8.1 for an overview of these three popular spoofs on YouTube. Despite focusing on different political candidates, the spoof videos were all posted on YouTube and contained representations that had a potentially negative impact. Furthermore, the spoof videos were chosen because of the large number of viewings and postings they each received relative to the constituency size and significance of political issues covered.

During the testing process, we developed a number of critical hypotheses that guided our analysis. The Leximancer software uses a Bayesian sampling methodology to analyze and consolidate textual data. Based on this ability, we hypothesized that the Leximancer software would effectively map a condensed list of themes after analyzing viewer's commentary posted in response to the three political spoof videos. Second, we hypothesized that the dominant themes elicited on the resulting perceptual maps would closely match the actual issues faced by the candidates within their electoral race. Finally, we hypothesized that an understanding of the themes elicited on the perceptual maps would help campaign managers predict future voter behavior. We did not establish projections regarding the predictive strength of the dominant themes elicited from our testing, but hypothesized that information gathered from our analysis would have high predictive value.

Video: *Jib Jab:* Time for Some Campaigning

The first video chosen for analysis was Jib Jab's *Time for Some Campaigning*. The creator of the advertisement, Jib Jab is an independent media company that creates online caricature videos for the public. It is clear that this spoof video was created with the intent to stir dialogue regarding the 2008 presidential election. In total, the *Time for Some Campaigning* video that our study analyzed had over 2.4 million viewings and was granted a five-star ranking on YouTube with over 12,000 votes and over 11,000 unique comments posted on the YouTube discussion board in response to the video. This video poked fun at the conservative nature of Republican

TABLE 8.1 Summary Information on Analyzed Ads

Ad	URL	Number of Views by 07-23-2009	Average Star Rating	Number of Ratings	Number of Comments by 07-23-2009	Total Words in Comments
JibJab.com – *Time for Some Campaigning*	http://www.youtube.com/watch?v=adc3MSS5Ydc (on YouTube > 1 year)	2,472,355	5	11,891	11,195	> 250,000
Robert Mugabe – Farmer Spoof	http://www.youtube.com/watch?v=0MFOXinbdFg (on YouTube >1 year)	18,532	5	20	34	> 1,100
Tony Blair – *Should I Stay or Should I Go?*	http://www.youtube.com/watch?v=a1vwKZiDsY4 (on YouTube > 2 years)	1,016,001	5	4,958	1,939	32,900

candidates, satirized the Democratic primary race between Obama and Hillary Clinton, and mocked the highly branded nature of Obama's "Change" campaign. Although the creators of *Time for Some Campaigning* used caricature to create a humorous and engaging video that included spoofs of both Republican and Democratic candidates, the overall video contained strong anti-Republican undertones. To be specific, although Clinton was mocked for her perceived ruthless ambition and Obama for his perceived naïveté, the Republican nominee, McCain, was mocked because of his age, medical conditions, and close relationship to then current president George W. Bush. Throughout the election, these three issues proved to be very damaging to his credibility, political image, and political brand, and were factors that swayed traditional Republican voters' perception of McCain. These factors, together with the engaging nature of Obama's presidential campaign, ultimately earned Obama a landslide victory in the 2008 presidential election. From an impact perspective, *Time for Some Campaigning* was hugely successful in terms of hits, response, and lasting viewership. The video was shown on all the major networks in the United States and replayed and shared thousands of times on social media tools and political blogs.

Video: Old Mugabe Had a Farm

The second video that this study analyzed was *Old Mugabe Had a Farm*, which is a political spoof video caricaturing Robert Mugabe, the president of Zimbabwe. Mugabe had implemented a land repossession program in his nation whereby land was appropriated from White farmers without compensation or notice and redistributed to Mugabe supporters. The cartoon was designed to modify known stereotypes of the president prior to the Zimbabwe elections (Bal et al., 2009), and was set to the theme of the *Old MacDonald* nursery rhyme. The creators of the video posted it primarily with the desire to change local and international perceptions of the president's policies, values, and character. The video attacked policy moves made by the president prior to the announcement of the election, which was important in this study because it focused on a controversial political incumbent. The video showed a cartoon version of Mugabe with a wheelbarrow farming barren land and satirized the president's lack of knowledge regarding contemporary farming principles and disregard for nonBlack citizens residing in Zimbabwe. It also highlighted accusations that members of the president's opposition party and his supporters were executed during the 2008 Zimbabwe presidential election. Despite the fact that Zimbabwe is a small country with poorly developed technological infrastructure, the importance of this video in this study cannot be understated. *Old Mugabe Had a Farm* was viewed over 18,000 times and received 34 comments. The video had an average star rating of five and was circulated and debated frequently on international television networks. The presence of this video on YouTube and intense commentary illustrate that political spoof videos can have an impact in both developing and developed nations. In fact, Mugabe often complained that the presence of similar videos left him unfairly victimized and resulted in the propagation of an image that was both malicious and false.

Video: Tony Blair: Should I Stay or Should I Go?

The final political spoof video that was analyzed in this study was entitled *Should I Stay or Should I Go?* The video spoofed Tony Blair, a longtime political incumbent who served as the British prime minister from May 2, 1997 to June 27, 2007. He is the only person to have led the British Labour Party to three consecutive general election victories and was the Labour Party's longest serving prime minister. During his last two years as prime minister, Blair received significant criticism for his support of the Iraq war, relationship with the United States, and decision to send British troops into war five times during his prime ministerial reign. He was also criticized for his interest in private sector leadership while still occupying public roles. Although not nearly as overtly damaging as the two other videos analyzed, this video's widespread appeal helped accelerate discussions within the popular press regarding Blair's political future. The resulting commentary had the potential to significantly affect the political brand and reputation of the prime minister and is representative of many videos posted on YouTube that satirize the policies or persona of electoral and incumbent political candidates. *Should I Stay or Should I Go?* received an average rating of five stars, and received over one million views and nearly 2,000 viewer comments. The video was discussed and debated on major news media platforms throughout Britain shortly after its release and was featured internationally on a number of major news networks.

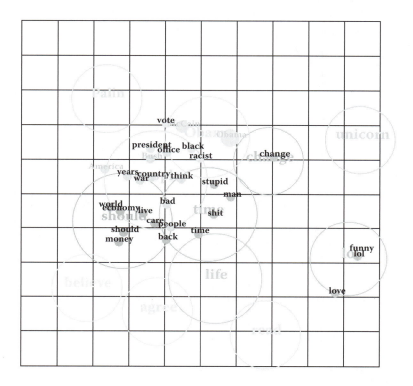

Figure 8.1   Leximancer analysis results of Jib Jab: *Time for Some Campaigning.*

Results

All viewer comments from the videos were input into the Leximancer software for interpretation. Leximancer analyzed the comments and used its Bayesian methodology to create three distinct visual maps (please refer to Figures 8.1 to 8.3) detailing the dominant themes existing within the discussion forums for each video. The resulting visual maps were then analyzed to determine whether the results matched the initial hypotheses.

Jib Jab: Time for Some Campaigning

Analysis of the Jib Jab map (see Figure 8.1) produced a dense conceptual map with a great deal of interrelation between the dominant themes.

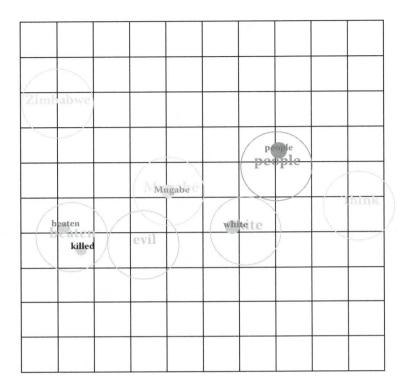

Figure 8.2 Leximancer analysis results of *Old Mugabe Had a Farm*.

Dominant themes and expressions that were discussed within the com-ments included: people, should, time, Obama, and change. Only two politicians—Obama and Palin—were discussed enough to be included as individual concept circles on the map. Analysis indicates that Obama's name was used more regularly and discussed within the same context as McCain's. In addition, Obama's name was located close to the concept "unicorn." The unicorn was used to depict Obama as a dreamer and was closely linked to the change theme that dominated most of Obama's presi-dential campaign. The concepts of change, time, and life were all domi-nant themes expressed within the video commentary. It is important to note that these dominant themes were also key elements of Obama's presidential campaign. The strong interrelationship of these themes on the competitive map indicates that the public understood and embraced these themes. A deeper analysis of this video helps to validate a number

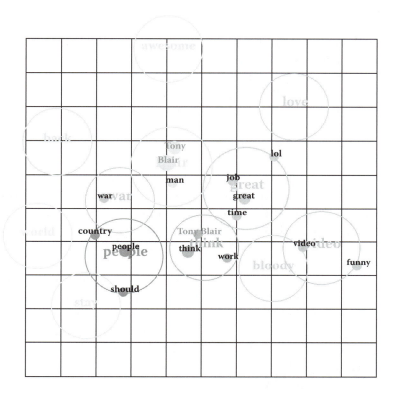

Figure 8.3   Leximancer analysis results of Tony Blair: *Should I Stay or Should I Go?*

of hypotheses regarding the effectiveness of the software in analyzing a large amount of information, producing dominant themes that were clear and interrelated, while producing themes that closely matched the themes, slogans, and key words used throughout the candidates' electoral campaigns. As expected, the Leximancer software quickly deciphered and analyzed the large amount of commentary and produced a number of critical themes.

Although the video heavily criticized the Republican electoral presidential and vice presidential candidates, a quick survey of mapped themes indicates that viewers did not focus their attention on these criticisms. Instead, we can conclude that the spoof videos' negative attacks on the Republican candidates were not strong enough to compel a significant viewer response and were trumped by the more polarizing themes emphasized by the Democratic nominees. Additionally, our analysis showed evidence that the themes elicited by the Leximancer software were in fact closely related to the themes that dominated the 2008 presidential election. It can be further argued that the resulting analysis provides evidence that the voter's strong affinity for these themes and the relationship these themes had to Obama's personal brand were a critical component of Obama's ultimate success in the election.

Old Mugabe Had a Farm

As the concept map shows (see Figure 8.2) fewer themes were identified from the analysis of this video. This result was in line with our expectations as significantly fewer individuals commented on the video. The dominant themes identified were: Zimbabwe, Mugabe, evil, people, White, and think. People, White, Mugabe, and Beaten were, in descending order, the most important concepts. Interestingly, the only interrelated themes were Mugabe and evil, although the concept beaten is adjacent to evil indicating a close interrelationship within the text. Also, it is important to note that the significance of race within the comments was a manifestation of the highly charged race debate that surfaced during the run-up to the election. A close analysis of the resulting concept map shows that Leximancer was able to produce dominant themes despite using a much smaller data sample. This result helps validate the use of Bayesian sampling methodology in smaller political races where a smaller sample of online users would be motivated to produce and respond to political spoof videos.

Our research also shows that, despite the smaller sample size, the themes elicited by the software were representative of the themes dominating discussions by members of the foreign media, opposition party members, and citizens of the general electorate living in Zimbabwe during the election. For example, Mugabe was highly criticized by opposition and international media for the bloody campaign of violence that ensued after his first round election loss. This loss saw thousands of opposition supporters and party members beaten in an effort to sway internal support and sentiment and preserve his election victory. Analysis of the spoof commentary and dominant themes showed that viewers of the video clearly resonated with these themes. These themes turned out to be the dominant themes characterizing the 2008 presidential elections in Zimbabwe.

Tony Blair: Should I Stay or Should I Go?

The final YouTube video that we analyzed was the *Tony Blair: Should I Stay or Should I Go?* political spoof. After analysis, the Leximancer software identified 12 dominant themes (see Figure 8.3) contained within viewer comments: world, stay, people, war, think, Blair, awesome, back, great, love, bloody, and video. Blair as a concept overlaps with the two concepts, war and great, indicating that these themes travel together within the comments. It was also interesting to note that the only word from the title of the song that was a significant part of the comments was stay. Although the context is not specified, this theme overlaps significantly with the concept of people. At the time the video was made, Blair was facing intense political pressure from members of his own party to resign. Popular sentiment was mixed over the attacks, and a significant portion of the electorate was supportive of his decision to stay in power despite negative characterizations in national and international media. After reviewing the resulting conceptual map it is clear that many of the critical themes elicited by the software closely matched the political issues Blair faced near the end of his tenure as prime minister. Words such as world, stay, people, think, great, and love closely mirrored the work that the prime minister did internationally. His contributions toward assisting the Northern Ireland peace process, for example, by helping negotiate the Good Friday Agreement after 30 years of conflict in Ireland, were widely recognized. On the other hand, the themes of war and bloody mirror the fact that his record on military policy was widely criticized, for example, in 2006 for his failure to immediately call for a ceasefire in the Israel–Lebanon conflict and for sending British troops into Iraq (*Washington Times*, 2003).

Discussion, Limitations, and Conclusion

There are a number of outcomes of this research that will be of critical interest to political campaign managers. The conceptual maps from all three videos show that Leximancer was effective in analyzing both small and large text samples and eliciting dominant themes from that analysis. Our results show that the perceptual maps provide users with a visual tool that was useful in accurately gauging public sentiment toward political spoof videos as well as the candidate's image, personality, and policies. Moreover, our research, combined with previous studies using Leximancer, helps demonstrate that the software is effective in analyzing viewer sentiment regarding online videos in general, irrespective of content. This validation helps encourage support for future research both within the political environment as well as other areas. In addition, our analysis provides evidence that the conceptual themes illustrated on the map closely mirrored the themes and issues facing the target politicians within their physical environment. This symmetry helps validate the effectiveness of the tool in producing thematic maps that may be correlated with viewer and voter behavior. This result is significant for campaign managers who are frequently faced with the task of consolidating and analyzing viewer feedback to online political videos and required to use this analysis to make policy and strategic positioning decisions.

However, the Leximancer approach to analyzing viewer comments is not without its limitations. A primary restriction, inherent to all qualitative research, is the subjectivity of interpretation. Different researchers may arrive at different understandings of the same map. Moreover, the presence of a dominant theme on a map does not specify public sentiment toward that theme. This can be challenging in cases where electoral populations have mixed opinions on either an electoral candidate's political brand or an incumbent's political brand or policy choices. As an example, consider the theme of war. This theme was dominant on the map analyzing the Tony Blair spoof video. Although a close positioning of the word "war" to other more positive themes on the conceptual map might indicate the existence of positive sentiment, the precise interpretation is open to discussion. Although a large portion of the British population was highly critical of his decision to support Bush in the Iraq war, a large portion of the electorate as well as his political opposition was supportive of his decision to send British troops into battle. Because the comments left on the video site do not indicate the writer's motivations and feelings, conclusions drawn from the resulting perceptual maps need to be validated using other quantitative or qualitative research analysis before firm decisions are made using the elicited themes.

A second key limitation to the Leximancer approach relates to the technique's newness, reliability, and validity. The software produced conceptual maps whose themes mirrored those facing the electoral candidates and politicians in real life, however, the significance of those themes was not quantitatively measured. Furthermore, as the analysis was only conducted on three videos, questions remain regarding the tool's ability to predict future voter behavior. Although the perceptual maps did provide insights into the cognition and attitudes of voters, a direct correlation between the conceptual maps and voter behavior cannot be assumed. Rather, more studies are needed that test the significance of correlation between the conceptual map themes, attitudes, voter's sentiments, and behavior. This will enable political campaign managers as well as public relations experts in all fields to use the Leximancer approach with confidence.

The final key limitation of the Leximancer approach is that the analyzed input and the resulting conceptual maps are time dependent and subject to change. Videos that are posted on YouTube exist essentially in perpetuity. Viewers continually comment on and discuss the videos. As a result, the conceptual maps that would be created through video analysis are usually out of date before the data analysis is complete. Moreover, one has to recognize that users possess varying motivations and can easily post multiple iterations of the same video on YouTube. To address this issue, researchers and practitioners could conduct staged analyses of comments to measure how the dominant themes on conceptual maps shift and evolve over time. This would ensure that conclusions drawn regarding viewer sentiment or behavior are validated over the entire life of the online video or advertisement.

Leximancer is a tool that enables politicians, political campaign managers, and public relations managers in general to measure and gauge consumer sentiment effectively and in a timely manner. The resulting data provide users with insights into voter sentiments toward a political brand, policy, or personality and produce thematic maps that are correlated with voter sentiment and, potentially, voter behavior. The insights gained from this study are significant. Like large corporations, politicians and political candidates exist almost entirely in the public eye. Presidential campaigns and political elections receive intense scrutiny and the political image of both electoral candidates and incumbents are attacked millions of times a day around the world. Yet public relations research has shown that image is the single most important factor influencing electability and voter sentiment (Davies & Newman, 2006). In the past, politicians had the ability to reduce the impact and incidence of image attacks because they controlled the modes of communication, the communication message, and the public's interpretation of those messages. Unfortunately, with the rise of the Internet, this control dynamic has shifted. Through the ability to post and comment without restriction, members of the general public can now play an active role in the image management of politicians. As this shift in power has become more pronounced, politicians have reluctantly moved to the responder position, and political campaign managers have been forced to look for tools that enable them to scan the external environment, gauge voter and electorate feedback, and respond quickly.

As the nature of Internet communication continues to evolve, viewer commentary is also expected to evolve. Today viewers of online videos respond using written posts, but one can already conceive of viewers of online videos responding with visual posts directly from their phones or computers. Therefore, future research should explore the development of a tool that could integrate both textual and video analysis. If such a tool were equipped with the ability to search and analyze multiple videos at the same time containing similar content, the software would be extremely powerful. In addition, further research is needed to validate the effectiveness of the Leximancer approach in predicting voter sentiment, mobilization, and behavior. Our analysis produced conceptual maps whose themes matched the issues being faced by the electoral candidates and incumbents, however, questions still remain regarding whether knowledge of these themes effectively predicts viewer behavior. Today, as viewers of content have taken a more active role, the nature of the traditional communication model, particularly within the online space, has changed. Money and advertising are no longer the sole controllers of message dissemination. Stakeholder interaction is now the key to brand and image development.

References

Ahn, W. (1998). Why are different features central for natural kinds and artifacts? The role of causal status in determining feature centrality. *Cognition*, 69, 135–178.

Bal, A., Pitt, L., Berthon, P., & DesAutels, P. (2009). Caricatures, cartoons, spoofs and satires: Political brands as butts. *Journal of Public Affairs, 8*, 1–9.

Balz, D. and Kornblut, A. E. (February 11, 2007). Obama joins race with goals set high, washingtonpost.com retrieved on December 13, 2008 from http://www.washingtonpost.com/wp-dyn/content/article/2007/02/10/AR2007021001544.html

Barclay, K. (November 4, 2008). United States 44th presidential election day. *MillionFace*, retrieved on December 13, 2008 from http://www.millionface.com/l/november-4th-2008-united-states-44th- presidential-election-day/

Baudrillard, J. (2001). *Selected writings* (2nd ed.). Stanford, CA: Stanford University Press.

Berthon, P., Pitt, L., & Campbell, C. (2008). Ad lib: When customers create the ad. *California Management Review, 50*(4), 6–30.

Bhattacharya, C. B. & Sen, S. (2003). Consumer–customer identification: A frame-work for understanding consumers relationships with companies, *Journal of Marketing, 67*(April), 76–88.

Biehal, G. & Sheinin, D. (1998). Managing the brand in a corporate advertising environment: A decision-making framework for brand managers. *Journal of Advertising, 27*(2), 99–110.

Biehal, G. S. (2007). The Influence of corporate messages on the product portfolio. *Journal of Marketing, 71*, 12–25.

Blumler, J. & Kavanagh, M. (1999). The third age of political communication: Influences and features. *Political Communication, 16*(3), 209–230.

Boler, M. (2008). *Digital media and democracy: Tactics in hard times.* (Edited collection). Boston, MA: MIT Press.

Brook, P. (1968). *The empty space.* New York: Simon & Schuster.

Butler, P. & Collins, N. (1999). A conceptual framework for political marketing. In B. Newman, *Handbook of political marketing.* Thousand Oaks, CA: SAGE, pp. 55–72.

Campbell, J. E. & Dettrey, B. J. (2009). Context and strategy in presidential campaigns: Incumbency and political climate. *Journal of Political Marketing, 8*(4), 292–314.

CBS (October 11, 2007). *YouTube emerging as campaign tool,* retrieved February 22, 2010 from http://www.cbsnews.com/stories/2007/10/11/earlyshow/main3356715.shtml

Cha, M., Kwak, H., Rodriguez, P., Ahn, Y., & Moon, S. (2007). I Tube, You Tube, Everybody Tubes: Analyzing the world's largest user generated content system. *IMC'07, October 24–26, 2007,* San Diego.

Davies, J. & Newman, B. (2006). *Winning elections with political marketing.* New York: Hawthorn Press.

Deighton, J. & Kornfeld, L. 2008. Obama versus Clinton: The YouTube primary. *Harvard Business School Case 9-509-032.* Boston: Harvard Business School.

Ebersole, S. (2000). Uses and gratifications of the web among students. *Journal of Computer-Mediated Communication, 6*(1), 1–17.

Farrell, D. & Webb, P. (2000). Political parties as campaign organizations. In R. Dalton & M. Wattenberg, *Parties without partisans: Political change in advanced industrial democracies.* Oxford: Oxford University Press, pp. 103–125.

Glynn, K. (2009). The 2004 election did not take place: Bush, spectacle, and the media nonevent. *Television and New Media, 10*(2), 216–245.

Goldsmith, R., Lafferty, B., & Newell, S. (2000). The impact of corporate credibility and celebrity credibility on consumer reaction to advertisements and brands. *Journal of Advertising, 29*(3), 43–54.

Haridakis, P. & Hanson, G. (2009). Social interaction and co-viewing with YouTube: Blending mass communication reception and social connection. *Journal of Broadcasting and Electronic Media, 53*(2), 317–335.

Hilton releases spoof of McCain celebrity ad. You Tube, retrieved on December 13, 2008, from http://www.youtube.com/watch?v=jBl42KO7JOoandfeature =related

Holtz, S. (2006). Communicating in the world of web 2.0. *Communication World, 23*(3), 24–27.

Hunt, S. (August 4, 2008). Eighteen-million cracks in the presidential glass ceiling. *Huffington Post*, retrieved December 13, 2008 from http://www.huffingtonpost.com/swanee-hunt/eighteen-million-cracks-i_b_116902.html

Huston, T. (January 18, 2008). Poll: Only 19% of Americans implicitly trust media. NewsBusters, retrieved on December 13, 2008 from http://newsbusters.org/blogs/warner-todd-huston/2008/01/09/poll-only-19- americans-implicitly-trust-media

Innis, H. A. (2008). The bias of communication, Toronto, CA: University of Toronto Press.

Jib Jab: *It's time for some campaiging* (July 16, 2008). *YouTube*, retrieved July 23, 2009 from http://www.youtube.com/watch?v=adc3MSS5Ydc

Kaye, B. K. & Johnson, T. J. (2002). Online and in the know: Uses and gratifications of the web for political information. *Journal of Broadcasting and Electronic Media, 46*, 54–71.

Klapper, J. (1963). Mass communication research: An old road resurveyed. *Public Opinion Quarterly, 27*(4), 515–527.

Martin, N. J. & Rice, J. L. (2007). Profiling enterprise risks in large computer companies using the Leximancer software tool. *Risk Management, 9*, 188–220.

Miller, C. (November 7, 2008). How Obama's internet campaign changed politics. Retrieved February 20, 2010 from http://bits.blogs.nytimes.com/2008/11/07/how-obamas-internet-campaign-changed-politics/

Monson, J. (2004). Get on television vs. get on the van: GOTV and the Ground War in 2002. In D. Magleby & J. Monson (Eds.), *The last hurrah? Soft money and issue advocacy in the 2002 congressional elections*. Washington, DC: Brookings Institution Press, pp. 90–116.

Moore, R. (2008, April 2). *Marketing of Barack Obama vs. Hillary Clinton in Democratic election campaign using YouTube*. Retrieved February 20, 2010 from http://www.profitminute.com/blog/marketing-case-studies/marketing-of-barack-obama-vs-hillary-clinton-in-democratic-election-campaign-using-you-tube/

Nelson, M. (2005). *The elections of 2004*. Washington, DC: Congressional Quarterly Press.

Newman, B. (1999). *The mass marketing of politics*. Thousand Oaks: SAGE.

Old Mugabe Had a Farm. (April 14, 2008). YouTube, retrieved July 23, 2009 from http://www.youtube.com/watch?v=4rd_V2PVZbA

Ormrod, R., Henneberg, S., Forward, N., Miller, J., & Tymms, L. (2007). Political marketing in untraditional campaigns: The case of David Cameron's Conservative Party leadership victory. *Journal of Pubiic Affairs, 7*, 235–248.

Ormrod, R. P., Henneberg, S. C., Forward, N., Miller, J., & Tymms, L. (2007). Political marketing in untraditional campaigns: The case of David Cameron's Conservative Party leadership victory. *Journal of Public Affairs, 7*(3), 235–248.

O'Shaughnessy, N. & Henneberg, S. (2007). The selling of the president 2004: A marketing perspective. *Journal of Public Affairs, 7*, 249–268.

Papacharissi, Z. & Rubin, A. (2000). Predictors of Internet use. *Journal of Broadcasting and Electronic Media, 44*, 175–196.

Petrou, D. M. (2009, Winter). Presidential politics and the power of public relations: How style and staying on message trumped substance and seniority during the election in 2008. *Strategist,* 24–25.

Poll: Clinton firmly positioned as Democratic front runner. (August 9, 2007). CNN.com retrieved December 13, 2008 from http://www.cnn.com/2007/POLITICS/08/09/2008.dems.poll/index.html

Poll: Congress and Bush share low approval. (May 11, 2007). msnbc.com, retrieved December 13, 2008 from http://www.msnbc.msn.com/id/18612770/

Rapoport, R., Metcalf, K., & Hartman, J. H. (1989). Candidate traits and voter inferences: An experimental study. *Journal of Politics, 51*(4), 917–932.

Reiser, M. & Zapp, A. (Eds.) (2002). *New screen media: Cinema/art/narrative.* London: British Film institute.

Rooney, D. (2005). Knowledge, economy, technology and society: The politics of discourse, *Telematics and Informatics, 22*(4), 405–422.

Scott, N. & Smith, A. E. (2005). Use of automated content analysis techniques for event image assessment. *Tourism Recreation Research, 30*(2), 87–91.

Schechner, R. (2003). *Performance theory.* Boca Raton, FL: Routledge.

Shocker, A., Rajendra, K. S., & Ruekert, R. (1994). Challenges and opportunities facing brand management: An introduction to the special issue. *Journal of Marketing Research, 31*(2), 149–159.

Smith, A. E. & Humphreys, M. S. (2006). Evaluation of unsupervised semantic mapping of natural language with Leximancer concept mapping. *Behavior Research Methods, 38*(2), 262–279.

Soh, H., Reid, L., & King, W. (2009). Measuring trust in advertising: Development and validation of the ADTRUST scale. *Journal of Advertising, 38*(2), 83–102.

Stirland, S. (October 29, 2008). *Obama's secret weapons: Internet, databases and psychology.* Retrieved February 20, 2010, from http://www.wired.com/threatlevel/2008/10/obamas-secret-w/

Stromer-Galley, J. (2000, Autumn). Online interaction and why candidates avoid it. *Journal of Communication,* 111–132.

Thomas, E. (2004). *Election 2004.* New York: Public Affairs.

Timberg, C. (2008, July 5). *Inside Mugabe's violent crackdown notes, witnesses detail how campaign was conceived and executed by leader, aides.* (Washington Post Foreign Service Saturday), retrieved February 20, 2010 from http://www.washingtonpost.com/wp-dyn/content/article/2008/07/04/AR2008070402771.html

Tony Blair: Should I stay or should I go? (October 12, 2006). YouTube, retrieved July 23, 2009 from http://www.youtube.com/watch?v=a1vwKZiDsY4

Tsfati, Y. & Weimann, G. (1999). Terror on the Internet. *Politika, 4,* 45–64.

Vaccari, C. (2008). From the air to the ground: The internet in the 2004 US presidential campaign. *New Media Society, 10*(4), 647–665.

Van Rekom, J., Jacobs, G., & Verlegh, P. (2006). Measuring and managing the essence of a brand personality. *Marketing Letters, 17,* 181–192.

Volosinov, V. N. (1973). *Marxism and the philosophy of language.* Cambridge, MA: Harvard University Press.

Warren, C. (January 4, 2010). *Pepsi to skip Super Bowl ads in favor of $20 m social media campaign,* retrieved February 20, 2010 from http://mashable.com/2009/12/23/pepsi-super-bowl/

Washington Times, The (November 8, 2003). Blair a casualty of U.K. support for Iraq war, retrieved February 20, 2010 from http://www.washingtontimes.com/news/2003/nov/08/20031108-111529-7094r/

Weimann, G. (2008). The psychology of mass-mediated terrorism. *American Behavioral Scientist, 52,* 69–86.

Wolfradt, U. & Doll, J. (2001). Motives of adolescents to use the Internet as a function of personality traits, personal and social factors. *Journal of Educational Computing Research, 24*(1), 13–27.

9

Advertising Versus Invertising
The Influence of Social Media B2C Efforts on Consumer Attitudes and Brand Relationships

Adriana M. Bóveda-Lambie
Rochester Institute of Technology

Neil Hair
Rochester Institute of Technology

The Internet became an advertising medium in 1994 with banner advertising; in the 17 years since, it has evolved to experiential campaigns and social media as the new trends in online advertising (Barnes & Hair, 2009; Winer, 2009). The Internet has vastly increased the set of marketing tools traditionally used by marketers (Winer, 2009); hence, marketers are now spending billions in online and new media categories such as Procter & Gamble's $1.4 billion investment in new media (Tedeschi, 2007).

More consumers are using the Internet to gather information related to their purchase (Adjei, Noble, & Noble, 2009; Rose, Hair, & Clark 2011), and at the same time the use of social media keeps growing with Facebook up 40% in a six-month period, 70% of bloggers organically talking about brands, and 38% of bloggers posting brand or product reviews (Hird, 2010). Social media such as blogs, Facebook, and Twitter provide an opportunity for brands to interact in a new way with current and new consumers thereby garnering a center stage in e-commerce (Bausch & Han, 2006).

This brings a shift in how marketing communications are seen and perceived by both sides of the aisle: marketers and consumers. New media provide more than just a new communication tool; they have also shifted marketers toward a strategy of creating experiences (Winer, 2009) and interacting with the consumer while simultaneously shifting control of the marketing communication over to the consumer (Acquisti & Spiekermann,

2011; Deighton & Kornfeld, 2009; Schlosser, Shavitt, & Kanfer, 1999; Winer, 2009). As consumers learn and become savvier, many of them find the technology to ignore online ads (Yoo, 2008). Still, new opportunities abound for consumers to perform their online purchases as the where and when are no longer spatially bound to a computer thanks to mobile technology (Rose et al., 2010; Coursaris & Hassanein, 2002). The same applies to online communications that can now reach customers anytime and anywhere.

According to Razorfish's third annual FEED Survey 40% of Facebook users "friend" or like a brand and 25% of Twitter users follow a brand (Razorfish, 2009). This may be good news for marketers, but companies must learn to strike the right balance in this new territory where the rules of the game have changed and traditional display advertising may not be the most effective way to reach consumers. As much as consumers will like or follow brands, they will be quick to "unlike" and "unfollow" if the content becomes boring, repetitive, posts too frequently, or crowds their "newsfeed" (ExactTarget, 2011).

The Interactive Advertising Bureau (IAB), in its report with PriceWaterhouse Cooper, states that for the past 10 years online advertising revenues have steadily increased, surpassing traditional advertising media such as newspapers and radio. In 2010 advertisers spent $26.04 billion dollars on online advertising, an increase of 15% over 2009 ($22.66 billion; PriceWaterhouseCooper, 2011). Currently, search advertising is the most popular effort garnering 46% of revenues in 2010, followed by display advertising with 38% (PriceWaterhouseCooper, 2011). Display advertising includes traditional display banner and button ads as well as rich media and digital video. Retail-oriented online advertisers account for 21% of these, which include stores and apparel. The IAB has not yet started keeping track of social media ad revenues, but according to eMarketer, advertisers spent $2.3 billion dollars worldwide ($1.4 billion in the United States) in social network advertising and this is projected to grow to almost $4 billion dollars by 2012 in the United States and $8 billion worldwide (eMarketer, 2011; Nielsen, 2011), mostly garnered by Facebook. Ad spending on Twitter is forecast to attract $150 million in 2011 and $250 million in 2012 (Williamson, 2011).

Social media and mobile use are growing at a fast rate and will garner more advertising dollars in the future. Demographics are becoming increasingly more relevant when looking at segments and traditional demographic segmentation for measuring online success is no longer relevant (Schlosser et al., 1999; Winer, 2009). The market with the highest use of social and mobile media are 12–17-year olds (Nielsen, 2011) who spent an average of seven hours watching mobile video in Q4 of 2010. At the same time they are the most receptive group to mobile advertising, outtext all other groups (doubling the text usage of 18–24-year-olds), and 78.7% of them visited social networks or blogs (Nielsen, 2011). Clearly, future markets will be reached more and more through social media and mobile messaging rather than only traditional or online media.

More specifically, Facebook boasts 600 million users (and growing), up from 150 million in 2009 (Phoster, 2010), and Twitter grew 752% from 2008 to 2009 with an average of about 200,000 active users per week and 3 million messages a day (Ostrow, 2009). However, the younger generations are not the only ones adopting social media, although they are adopting it at a faster rate. Forrester Research reports that 70% of adults read blogs, tweet, and watch user-generated video, and 60% of them have a Facebook profile with a third of them posting at least once a week to either Facebook or Twitter (Valentino-DeVries 2010).

Overall, the Internet allows "firms and customers to build and manage relationships with individual customers in a much more cost effective manner than is possible in other domains" (Machanda, Dubé, Goh, & Chintagunta, 2006, p. 100). Consumers are spending more and more of their time online (either at a computer or through a mobile device), increasing their time spent in social media sites by 82% (Nielsen, 2010). With consumers spending more and more of their time online and interacting with social media, the importance and relevance of advertising in these environments are clear. Yet research in both these areas of online and social media advertising as it relates to measurement of investment, building a customer–brand relationship, consumer perceptions, and purchasing behavior is still not as prevalent or timely.

This chapter aims to narrow that gap by providing a review of the most relevant literature in online advertising, providing future research directions, and presenting preliminary results of an exploratory study of social media invertising perceptions and its use as a tool to create and strengthen consumer–brand connections. The rest of this chapter is laid out as follows: a "where we are now" section that summarizes what the authors consider some of the most relevant online advertising and social media literature; a "future directions" section that provides relevant research propositions both for academics and for practitioners; and lastly an exploratory study into building businesss-to-consumer (B2C) consumer–brand connections through social media.

Literature Review

Online Advertising

The role and effectiveness of online advertising continues to be an issue of some debate (Machanda et al., 2006). Recent years show the investment of advertising dollars in online advertising continues to grow; however, its economic value remains questioned. A great deal of academic and practitioner skepticism exists on which online advertising actually works, or whether it works at all, making its economic value a somewhat controversial issue (Sherman & Deighton, 2001). A review of the most popular vehicles for online advertising follows.

Traditional Banner Ads

Prior research in online advertising has concentrated on banner advertising, showing that it is good for creating and maintaining brand and advertising awareness, building more favorable brand attitudes, and increasing purchase intention and visits to the Web site (Dreze & Hussherr, 2003; Ilfeld and Winer, 2002; Sherman & Deighton, 2001; Yoo, 2008), although only a small portion of the visits actually translate to purchases (Moe & Fader, 2003). At the same time Machanda et al. (2006) note that industry research on advertising response to banner ads—consistent with academic findings—has shown that banner ads have attitudinal effects and that CTRs (click-through rates) are an ineffective measure of banner ad effectiveness. More recently, banner advertising research moved away from traditional attitudinal effects and their focus on awareness, and looked at customer purchasing behavior as a result of banner advertising exposure (Machanda et al., 2006). In this research, ad exposure led to an increase of purchasing probability, finding that ad exposure can increase Internet purchases of current customers.

Although the Internet has changed much from its initial banner advertising days, for many this vehicle remains the preferred and most popular advertising method (Shankar & Hollinger, 2007). Shankar and Hollinger (2007) state that this popularity could be attributable to McLuhan's theory of the "rear view mirror" as explained by Barnes and Hair (2009). Customers increasingly ignore or avoid ads while online (Dreze & Hussherr, 2003; Yoo, 2008), leading to only a small fraction remembering the ad content or even interacting with the ad (Shankar & Hollinger, 2007). This is due to the fact that most consumers have their attention elsewhere while online (Yoo, 2008). The lack of active attention leads consumers to unconsciously process the ads they are exposed to while online, which still results in favorable brand attitudes through implicit memory priming (Yoo, 2008). However, the ability to follow the consumers' digital trail provides the opportunity of creating and delivering more targeted banner ads and messages that are relevant to the audience. Previous research has shown that contextually relevant ads can attract more attention, thereby influencing their effectiveness (Li & Bukovac, 1999).

Search Marketing
Search marketing is expected to become the largest segment of online advertising dollars, having already harnessed $11 billion in 2008 (eMarketer, 2009b). In addition Jupiter Research reports that 55% of e-commerce transactions originate from a paid search link. Although nonpaid links have a better response rate (70%), paid search links have a higher return of sales (Shankar & Hollinger, 2007). After all, 50% of consumers will search online before making a purchase (DoubleClick, 2005). The success of Google is proof of how knowing customer online behaviors can be beneficial for the advertiser (Deighton & Kornfeld, 2009). There are two main types of search marketing in use today: paid search where companies bid for placement among search results according to keywords, and search engine optimization which returns the target site as a natural result of the consumer's search increasing the chances of customer response (Shankar & Hollinger, 2007). Online advertising today presents several advantages: (1) each customer leaves a measurable digital trail of exposure and responses; (2) online advertising can be individually targeted to each visitor; and (3) we can seamlessly and quickly adapt the ad content on any page (Sherman & Deighton, 2001). These three advantages can be harnessed to design better campaigns that are better targeted and hence produce better results that are more measurable for companies. Because of its interactive nature, the Internet can record customers' behavior while online from searching, to clicking, to purchasing (Rodgers & Thorson, 2000). Behavioral targeting is on the rise as companies learn to use what consumers are doing online to deliver targeted messages (Winer, 2009).

Intrusive Versus Nonintrusive Marketing
Consumers are bombarded daily with ads through traditional, online, and new media, creating a cluttered advertising environment. This leaves ad messages competing for attention, and it has been argued that interrupting

consumer's activities is central in this effort (Acquisti & Spiekermann, 2011). As previously mentioned, control over messages is shifting from the advertiser to the consumer as new technology allows consumers to avoid commercial messages (Deighton & Kornfeld, 2009; Winer, 2009).

Shankar and Hollinger (2007) split Internet advertising into two categories: intrusive and nonintrusive. Intrusive advertising is when the consumer is presented with an ad when he is neither searching nor has an immediate need, a forced or involuntary exposure. The ad just appears in his online experience. Nonintrusive on the other hand, is initiated by the consumer because she has a need for which to search online, a voluntary exposure. The consumer is then presented with an ad targeted to her needs, increasing the likelihood of a positive response.

Under this model, for example, traditional untargeted Web banner and pop-up ads can be considered intrusive whereas search engine optimization, paid search marketing, or targeted banner ads can be considered nonintrusive as they are presented in response to a consumer action. This categorization can also be applied to permission-based marketing, which can be considered nonintrusive as a whole, inasmuch as the customer has agreed to receive the messages.

As some Internet ads are seen as disruptive (Rettie, 2001; Shankar & Hollinger, 2007), recent research looks at the effect these interruptions can have on consumer's online behavior. Acquisti and Spiekermann (2011) found that certain types of intrusive online ads may reduce the consumer's willingness to pay for the advertised item.

But traditional Internet browsing activity is not the only place where consumers can be interrupted. Although Shankar and Hollinger (2007) defined this model for Internet advertising, it can also be applied to mobile devices. Mobile phones and devices allow the consumer to have a ubiquitous connection—the anywhere anytime consumer—and marketers are eagerly looking for ways to tap this new channel. Demand for these devices is expected to keep growing and command $3.9 billion in advertising dollars by 2011 (eMarketer, 2007a). However, as there is an increasing trend toward spamming these devices, the success of mobile advertising rests solely on customer's opting in to receive marketing messages (Barwise & Strong, 2002). Allowing customers to opt-in to a mobile campaign resulted in better response overall or readership of the message, better brand attitude and awareness, and some members even forwarded the message to their contacts (Barwise & Strong, 2002). Therefore, as new media permeates the consumer's "private" space, being nonintrusive, allowing consumers to have control over how and where they receive marketing messages, becomes key to the success and acceptance of the advertising messages.

Social Media

Social networking sites are one of the fastest growing areas of the Internet (Trusov, Bucklin, & Pauwels, 2009) and social media in general are growing rapidly (Kozinets, De Valck, Wojnicki, & Wilner, 2010). Social media ad revenues are on the rise and are expected to garner 15% of U.S. online advertising dollars (eMarketer, 2009a). The rapid growth of social media among users caught advertisers' attention who are trying to figure out how to harness social media for advertising purposes (Hart, 2007). The most common social media being used today are Facebook and Twitter, blogs, and virtual worlds such as Second Life. However, marketers have been cautious about how they use social media as an advertising tool fearing that its members could be offended if the site becomes commercialized (Winer, 2009). Marketers are not unfounded in being cautious. Both the IDC (2008) and eMarketer (2009a) found that social network users tend to click less on online ads than nonusers; in fact, according to the IDC, 43% of social network users have never clicked on an online ad, and eMarketer reports that only 11% of social network users (versus 23% of nonusers) click on online ads (eMarketer, 2009a; Zeng, Huang, & Dou, 2009). Traditional banner/button advertising is apparently not the best option to acquire this market. Therefore marketers are left facing the challenge of how to engage customers and communicate with their target market while taking advantage of the interactivity and other benefits that traditional media cannot deliver (Winer, 2009).

New media carry two characteristics: they are interactive and also digital. Both characteristics are central themes as consumers can now interact with the company, the medium, and each other (Winer, 2009). Although marketers typically have had to interrupt customers to get their attention, the digital paradigm forces marketers to view the relationship more as a friend who the customers invite into their lives (Deighton & Kornfeld, 2009). As media change so does the marketing focus, which now is more about creating experiences, where one-way communication is replaced by two-way communication between customer and marketer (Winer, 2009).

Most of the attention that social media advertising is getting is due to social network services such as Facebook and LinkedIn, and microblogging sites such as Twitter. However, blogs also need to be considered not only as an advertising venue (in the traditional paid model) but also as a word-of-mouth (WOM) generator that can influence readers and generate attitudes toward a specific brand. According to eMarketer, blog advertising dollars were at $283 million in 2007, with 50% of all Internet users reading blogs; that number is expected to grow to 67% by 2012 (Kutchera, 2008). The success of blogs and why marketers are willing either to buy advertising or conduct seeding campaigns (Kozinets et al., 2010) is because their (the blogs') information is trusted, coming in second to newspapers (Brown, Broderick, & Lee 2007).

Blogs have become very popular among writers, readers, and marketers and have, together with other social media, been embraced by a number of businesses as part of their overall marketing initiative (Colliander & Dahlén, 2011). However, although blogs have contributed to the audience erosion of newspapers and magazines, clearly demonstrating they compete with print audiences, they have been called an "uncontrollable platform whose value is largely unproven" (Huang, Shen, Lin, & Chang, 2007, p. 472). Colliander and Dhalén (2001) found that blogs are seen by their readers as "fashionable friends" and exhibit superior publicity effectiveness to online magazines through a parasocial interaction effect, making the relationship between the blogger and the reader as powerful as a WOM relationship. Their research showed that readers of the blog exhibited higher brand attitudes and intentions toward the brand being presented (Colliander & Dahlén, 2011) versus the same effort in an online magazine.

Emerging Trends
Although mobile marketing initiatives are gaining importance, m-commerce is in its infancy in the United States and research in this area is scant (Shankar & Balasubramian, 2009; Winer, 2009). Mobile ad dollars are expected to rise to about $3.9 billion by 2011 (eMarketer, 2007a) and mobile messaging to $12 billion in 2011 (eMarketer, 2007b). The increasing market penetration of mobile devices is ushering in new ways to reach audiences including location-aware capabilities where the context can be matched to the user's location (Deighton & Kornfeld, 2009; eMarketer, 2008; Shankar & Balasubramanian, 2009) while at the same time presenting new challenges to marketers (Leek & Christodoulides, 2009). Mobile platforms give consumers ubiquitous connectivity, which means audiences are always on, not just when they are actively searching online (Deighton & Kornfeld, 2009; Leek & Christodoulides, 2009; Winer, 2009). Mobile marketing is defined as the "two-way or multiway communication and promotion of an offer between a firm and its customers using a mobile medium device or technology" (Shankar & Balasubramanian,

2009). According to Jupiter Research, 22% of companies who participate in online advertising have also participated in mobile marketing (Ask, 2006), with the younger demographic being more receptive as a consumer and to opt-in to mobile marketing (Ask, 2006; Barwise & Strong, 2002).

Two arenas in particular are attracting both consumer and marketer attention: mobile and Bluetooth marketing. Recently, mobile marketing has been garnering the most attention as more and more consumers purchase smartphones and other mobile devices and become ubiquitous, the anywhere anytime consumer (Deighton & Kornfeld, 2009; Leek & Christodoulides, 2009; Winer, 2009). Mobile marketing includes delivery of messages to a consumer's mobile device, be it via content, SMS messaging, or Bluetooth. As not everyone owns video capable devices and bandwidth can be limited (Shankar & Balasubramanian, 2009; Winer, 2009) SMS becomes more appealing for the marketer. However, this requires customers' permission or opt-in as charges can apply and the consumer's private space may be invaded. Barwise and Strong (2002) found that 24% of customers (over 50% of 14–17-year-olds) would agree to SMS marketing and they expected the delivered advertising to be relevant to them, allowing up to three texts a day. Consumers' attitudes toward mobile marketing will influence their response to mobile promotions; primarily the fear of spam and the intrusive nature of mobile marketing as it challenges their perceived control (Shankar & Balasubramanian, 2009).

A newer way to target consumers in location-specific spots is through Bluetooth marketing, which has no cost to either the consumer or the marketer, and again has the advantage of being location-specific or in-store which makes it of limited duration (Leek & Christodoulides, 2009). The only consumer action needed is to enable the device's Bluetooth capability. Bluetooth marketing is still in its infancy; however, both Coldplay in the United Kingdom and Lancôme in France used it to help promote new products (Leek & Christodoulides, 2009; Tsiantar, 2006). Recent research shows that consumers need to be educated on the safety of Bluetooth marketing in terms of privacy and that peer adoption plays a role in adoption of new Bluetooth technology (Leek & Christodoulides, 2009). As Bluetooth is limited only to the specific location, for marketers it would be a better option as the customers do not have to worry about receiving messages once they've left, and they have to participate actively by enabling the device. This is in contrast with SMS or mobile marketing where the consumers, once they opt in, are vulnerable to all the campaigns the marketer deems fit and may feel or experience content saturation.

Future Research Directions

Online advertising continues to grow significantly and is expected to be an integral part of companies' marketing plans. Through the change in technology and consumer's preferences, the online advertising model has shifted to become more about customer retention through information exchange than a revenue-based model (Shankar & Hollinger, 2007). As such this presents new challenges both to academics and practitioners.

Demographics
One not so new area of research that needs to be explored within the context of online advertising and social media is the impact of demographics. Previous research shows that demographics such as age and gender, education, and income can influence consumer's views of advertising and in turn of online advertising as a whole (Alwitt & Prabhakar, 1992; Shavitt, Lowrey, & Haefner, 1998). Markets today are becoming more and more fragmented, and previously defined demographic markets are becoming irrelevant or inaccurate to measure the effectiveness of different online advertising media efforts (Winer, 2009). For example, younger segments are believed to be more receptive to mobile or SMS marketing (Barwise & Strong, 2002), and it is a majority of college students who spend a significant portion of their day on social media sites such as Facebook (Raacke & Bonds-Raacke, 2008). Recent research by the DMA (2008) found that respondents to mobile marketing would most likely be males, teens, and young adults, individuals with higher incomes, and who engage in heavy use of phones and data features. Dreze and Hussherr (2003) found that different levels of Internet expertise, age, or gender can lead to differences in page processing behavior. As the usage demographics of the Internet and mobile devices become more specific, more research is needed in order to define the new groups and how the different media options available appeal (or not) to these groups. With the increase of behavioral targeting or behavioral advertising, demographics also take on a new light as it becomes essential to know which groups are more involved. For example, recent research found some evidence that women are more proactive about privacy protection behavior (Hoy & Milne, 2010), thereby affecting the behavioral targeting capabilities of the messages, in particular in online social network environments where the user can control the information that is known about her. Their research also found that there is

some extent of users either lying or not making all information available in their profiles in the hopes of avoiding behavioral ads.

Search Marketing

Search marketing continues to grow in popularity, yet more research is needed to better understand how consumers use search words and links, how it affects brand attitudes, and if search marketing does indeed lead to increased purchase probability or increased sales. In particular, looking at it from the intrusive versus nonintrusive lens: is paid search better than search engine optimization (SEO)? Do different products and different levels of involvement with these products yield different consumer responses from paid search versus SEO? Internet advertising can help a company achieve different goals, and has been found to help, from generating brand awareness and attitude to increasing purchasing probability and sales. Therefore, it would be of interest for academics and practitioners alike to better understand how paid search versus SEO affects the relationship between the consumer and the brand (awareness, familiarity, attitude) and under which situations is one better than the other at generating sales. In addition, as intrusive online advertising can lead to consumers purposely avoiding the ads (Dreze & Hussherr, 2003), another venue of research to consider is consumers' response to either type of search marketing depending on their stage in the decision-making process and their level of involvement with the product being presented or searched.

Social Media Advertising

Even though social media are commanding increasing advertising dollars, research in the social media area remains limited (Colliander & Dahlén, 2011). Recent social media research explored the user experiences and beliefs that contributed to the creation of attitudes toward social network advertising (Taylor, Lewin, & Strutton, 2011), compared the effectiveness of WOM to traditional marketing actions (Trusov et al., 2009), explored social media marketing narratives among bloggers who participated in a brand seeding campaign (Kozinets et al., 2010), and investigated blogger motivation and the WOM capabilities of blogs versus online magazines (Colliander & Dahlén, 2011; Thorson & Rodgers, 2006). Yet many areas remain underresearched. Social media are inherently social, yet it is this social feature that receives the least research attention: how brands can best use social media as a consumer relationship marketing and management tool.

Social games such as Farmville have become relevant as well in online social networks such as Facebook. These games attract followers and daily participation and involvement to the point of users purchasing items to help them advance in the game at a quicker pace. Social gaming presents a different marketing and revenue model that not only should be evaluated but that brands could possibly emulate with branded social games online.

Location-based applications such as checking in or Foursquare—which straddle the line between social media and nonintrusive mobile marketing—deserve attention as companies start including check-ins as a promotional tool. Currently, Foursquare and Showtime partnered to promote the reality baseball show, *The Franchise*. At a specific location in New York City called the MLB Fan Cave, users who check in with Foursquare will receive a free baseball from the promotional vending machine stationed at that location (Foursquare, 2011). Similarly, retail stores have started offering promotional discounts or coupons to customers who check in to Facebook at their location. It is clear that companies understand the power of social networks being used and that they believe the mere announcement to the consumer's friends of his location is promotional in nature.

Following this, another area that should receive research attention is the power of WOM, not only in blogs where product can be actively seeded and talked about but also in organic conversations among online friends, including the effect of actions as simple as liking, becoming a fan, or following a brand. This action by the user then gets published to her feed for all her friends and followers to see.

Although it is no secret that social media have not really affected the bottom line in terms of e-commerce, their use as a brand-building tool has been largely ignored. Building on the previous paragraph, more information is needed regarding the attitudes that social media users have toward behavioral advertising within the social media. Behavioral targeting in social media can take on a whole new meaning as brands can make their ads social including user friends who have clicked on the ad. In addition, exploring if there is a difference in attitudes to ads versus attitudes to invertising (profiles or accounts) becomes relevant for marketers to understand better the effectiveness of these campaigns as options to build a relationship with the consumer, and more important, understanding how these efforts influence consumers' attitudes toward brands and brand loyalty.

Summary

One of the most important areas for marketing today is building and maintaining customer relationships. Online advertising with its new technologies needs to focus on creating and maintaining these relationships in order to create robust consumer attitudes and in turn increase brand loyalty. It is clear consumers know how to avoid online advertising, yet their attitudes toward social media advertising and these brand "pages" are still unclear. As such we feel one of the bigger gaps in the research arena deals with nonintrusive advertising or "invertising" where companies using B2C social media communications try to become part of their customers' daily and social lives, increasing familiarity and access to the brand, as well as promotional activity, and what effect these actions have on the consumer. For this to work the customer has to invite the brand into his life through either "like/Fan" a page or following a brand account, hence the name "invertising". It is this gap that we address as we explore consumer attitudes toward invertising and how its use in B2C social media communications influences the consumer–brand relationship.

Social Media and Consumer–Brand Relationships: An Exploratory Study

Advertising Versus Invertising

Vargo and Lusch (2004) helped marketing scholarship evolve from transaction-oriented to a relationship-based discipline, in which creating an experience for the customer has become increasingly relevant (Winer, 2009), therefore heightening the value of consumer networks, groups, and communities (Cova & Cova, 2002; Hoffman & Novak, 1996; Muniz & O'Guinn, 2001). The Internet, and by definition its marketing tools such as social media, is considered a good medium for relationship marketing and can help create and maintain consumer loyalty (Armstrong & Hagel, 1996; Hagel, 1999; Peppers & Rogers, 1997; Schultz & Bailey, 2000; Thorbjornsen, Supphellen, Nysveen, & Pedersen, 2002). Interactivity is a crucial element of successful online marketing (Bezjian-Avery, Calder, & Iacobucci, 1998; Deighton, 1996; Hoffman & Novak, 1996; Peppers & Rogers 1997; Thorbjornsen et al., 2002), and it's this interactive nature that makes the Internet a promising tool for building relationships with consumers, further expanding marketers' CRM capabilities and assisting in building customer loyalty (Thorbjornsen et al., 2002). Yet the need to study how these various Internet applications, with their interactive nature, may develop or enhance consumer–brand relationships remains unmet (Thorbjornsen et al., 2002).

This section of the chapter addresses this gap by exploring attitudes and perceptions toward invertising, forms of nonintrusive marketing that consumers invite into their lives, versus advertising within social media and how invertising can influence the consumer–brand relationship, through the resulting self–brand connections.

Social media have been successfully used to attract users and revive old brands. Take, for example, the Old Spice Facebook campaign, which generated 120,000 fans, and Red Robin's brand ambassador effort, which resulted in 225,000 ad impressions through buzz marketing of their current fans (Morrisey, 2009; York, 2009). Social media such as blogs, Facebook, Twitter, YouTube, and MySpace provide an opportunity for companies and products to brand themselves and interact in a new way with current and possible consumers, thereby occupying a center stage in e-commerce efforts (Bausch & Han, 2006).

However, advertising in social media spaces has not been well received, and only 22% of consumers have reported a positive attitude toward social media ads (AdReaction, 2010). This can be due to the fact that although it is a public space, consumers imbue some privacy into these social spaces (Taylor, Lewin, & Strutton, 2011). Because consumer acceptance to social media ads is key for the site not to be viewed as commercialized and suffer an exodus (Taylor, 2011; Zeng et al., 2009), organizations have resorted to creating profiles such as fan sites and Twitter accounts that visually resemble a traditional user site and are nonintrusive in nature as the consumer must actively seek them out.

Advertising in social networks should be designed to invite advertising into people's lives (invertising) instead of the traditional broadcasting of messages method currently employed. A shift from broadcasting information to asking for information introduces a new approach to advertising that is facilitated by the social network environment because of the highly personalized nature of messages. Beniger (1986) describes how mass media gradually replaced interpersonal communication as a socializing force, and social media further this trend because the messages of advertisers and promoters are mixed in with the interpersonal messages exchanged by individuals.

Recent research has explored how member perceptions of advertising in social networks can influence its acceptance (Zeng et al., 2009). Consumers are exposed to a large number of ads a day including on the Internet as well as mobile handsets and computer games (Acquisti

& Spiekermann, 2011), leading many consumers to avoid ads actively, in particular on the Internet (Yoo, 2008). In general most ads serve to increase brand recall, brand recognition, and brand awareness (Acquisti & Spiekermann, 2011), and heightened recall and awareness are associated with a positive outcome on sales (Barry & Howard, 1990; Yoo, Kim, & Stout, 2004). Ads can also help foster positive attitudes toward brands (Acquisti & Spiekermann, 2011). Traditionally, intrusive or interruptive messages have been the norm for advertising because a consumer's attention can be a scarce resource. However, in the online setting, this can be a risky strategy resulting in a negative consumer reaction to the brand such as being willing to pay less for their purchases than when exposed to non-interruptive ads (Acquisti & Spiekermann, 2011).

The limited research that looks at social media advertising has focused on the general advertising term and not specifically looked at fan pages/brand accounts. As these pages are not intrusive and should not be perceived as invasive, they should be more readily accepted than traditional banner or button ads within the SNS. At the same time, Gao and Koufaris (2006) identified perceived informativeness and entertainment of a message as influencers of consumers' attitudes toward advertising. Fan pages as well as Twitter brand accounts can be both informative and entertaining while still respecting users' privacy concerns, therefore they should garner more favorable attitudes than social media advertising (SMA). When information shared on consumers' profiles is used for targeting purposes, this type of intrusiveness can be a source of irritation and foster negative attitudes toward the advertisement (Taylor et al., 2011).

H$_1$: Consumers will perceive social media invertising more favorably and
   less intrusive than social media advertising.

Consumer–Brand Relationships
Marketers are increasingly interested in how consumers use products and brands to build and maintain a social identity, and previous studies have emphasized that self–brand congruence alone can determine consumer choice (Malhotra, 1988). Brands, as social objects, are socially constructed and imbued with meaning, and customers actively engage in that creation using brands as bridges toward or fences against other people (Douglas & Isherwood, 1979; Escalas & Bettman, 2003, 2005; Muñiz & O'Guinn, 2001). Research on brand communities shows that customers can use commercial offerings (brands) and brand associations

as ways to create and further their self-image and shape their reality (Schau & Gilly, 2003).

Originally, advertisers had a rearview mirror attitude that looked at Internet advertising like older forms of advertising, such as billboards, commercials, and direct marketing, yet the Internet now allows for interactive rather than one-way flow of messages, with new types of advertising appearing in the form of blogs, viral marketing, experiential advertising, YouTube, and social networking (Barnes & Hair, 2009). Recent research found that e-commerce recommendation agents enhance the consumer experience (Aksoy, Bloom, Lurie, & Cooil, 2006; Holzwarth, Janiszewski, & Neumann, 2006), avatar-based advertising increases product and brand involvement (Jin & Bolebruch, 2009), and group identity plays a role in an online community's acceptance of advertising (Zeng et al., 2009).

The interactivity afforded by social media allows a continuous dialogue between the consumer and the brand, mostly on the consumer's terms, that allows both to share information and align interests (Bezjian-Avery et al., 1998). This daily contact allows brands in Facebook and Twitter to insert themselves, with the customer's permission, into the customer's daily life sharing product and brand information while creating a space for the consumer to respond to the brand and interact with it. As consumers become more experienced with the media, attitudes should improve. When their Internet experience increases, attitudes toward Web sites tend to be more favorable, indicating that these consumers could be more open to developing an online relationship with the brand (Thorbjornsen et al., 2002).

Self-connection with the brands is defined as the degree to which the brand delivers on important identity concerns, tasks, or themes, thereby expressing a significant aspect of the consumer's self (Escalas & Bettman, 2003, 2005; Thorbjornsen et al., 2002). As self–brand congruity increases and consumers perceive their self-identity is reflected in a brand presentation or positioning, the likelihood that they will reference themselves increases (Hennig-Thurau, Gwinner, Walsh, & Gremler, 2004).

Technology today allows for more targeted and personal messages to consumers and encourages consumers to interact with the brand and its messaging (Cappo, 2003; Jaffe, 2005). Just as brand community members use their membership to note a demarcation between them and users of other brands (Muñiz & O'Guinn, 2001), self–brand connections are used to highlight the meaning of the brand with the consumer's self-identity and reference group membership and to demarcate their nonassociation with brands used by out-groups (Escalas & Bettman, 2003, 2005). The meaning of a brand is its most important characteristic and can be negotiated by consumers (O'Guinn & Muñiz, 2005). Consumers have become more active in conversations around brands and products as the post-Internet market becomes more interactive (Moe & Schweidel, 2010). Today's consumer is more interested in how brands can afford them social ties and identities than in the brand itself (Cova & Cova, 2002). However, the meaning ascribed to—or elicited from—the brand is by no means static; it is a dynamic process maintained by the brand and its consumers (Cova & Cova, 2002; Escalas & Bettman, 2003, 2005; Muñiz & O'Guinn, 2001).

Brands are social objects, and consumers are active in their social meaning creation as well as their own meaning (Muñiz & O'Guinn, 2001; Muñiz & Schau, 2007). Brand communities are essentially a social network where the central tie, the one to which all members are connected, is the brand (Muñiz & O'Guinn, 2001). Although fan pages are not necessarily brand communities, having the users of a brand all in one place, and daily interaction with the brand, can certainly foster community building in which communication and interaction can expand to consumer-to-consumer contact as well. Therefore invertising in social media can foster community creation, leading to higher degrees of brand loyalty.

Consumers incorporate brands into their self-identity (Schau & Gilly, 2003). Through self–brand congruency, consumers actively use their brand choices to create their self-concept and present themselves to others, thereby forming connections to brands with the dual brand meaning (Escalas & Bettman, 2003; McCracken, 1989). When consumers use brand associations in this sense, a connection is then formed with the brand (Escalas & Bettman, 2005). Self–brand connections measure the extent to which consumers have incorporated the brand in question into their self-concept (Escalas & Bettman, 2003). Consumer–brand associations are an important component of brand equity and as such, self–brand connections can lead to enhanced brand loyalty, more robust brand attitudes, more forgiving of failures/blunders, and lessened price sensitivity allowing the brand to gain an enduring competitive advantage (Escalas & Bettman, 2003). Fan pages/brand accounts allow the brands to construct their own messages and meaning either as a standalone effort or complementing a larger marketing plan.

H_2: Social media invertising should result in higher consumer self–brand connections than brands with no social media invertising.

Methods

Survey

In order to learn more about social media advertising consumer perceptions and to test these hypotheses we conducted an exploratory survey. The survey contained a series of measures that asked participants to rate their attitudes toward social media advertising, social media invertising, and self–brand connections to brands they have "fanned" or "follow" as well as to brands with which they have no social media interaction at all. To ensure diversity of the sample, we distributed the survey via Facebook and Twitter. In exchange for their participation respondents would be entered in a raffle for a chance to win one Amazon $10 gift certificate. Respondents were told the research was about online advertising in general.

After agreeing to be part of the research, each participant proceeded to complete two attitude measures: attitudes to social media advertising (Att_{SMA}) as well as attitudes to social media invertising (Att_{SMI}), referring to brand pages in Facebook and brand accounts in Twitter. Next they were asked to report a brand they regularly purchase and use that they interact with in social media (both on Facebook and Twitter), and a brand they regularly purchase and use that they do not interact with on social media. All participants completed self–brand connection measures for the brand they reported as regularly used and purchased but not interacted with socially. Only participants who reported interacting with a brand on social media proceeded to complete the self–brand connection measure for that brand, and three open-ended questions about their motivation to interact socially with that brand. Before ending the survey, all participants completed demographic questions of sex, age, ethnicity, and employment status. At the end of the survey participants were debriefed and thanked for their participation.

Dependent Measures

Attitude to Social Media Marketing
In order to differentiate social media advertising from social media invertising, we measured two separate efforts: attitude to social media advertising and attitudes to social media invertising (brand presence in social media). We used the Haghirian, Madlberger, and Tanuskova (2005) 5-item scale (entertaining, informative, irritating, credible, useful) anchored by

TABLE 9.1 Descriptive Measures for Dependent Variables

Variable	Mean	SD	α
Att_{SMA}	2.88	.80	.82
Att_{SMI}	3.38	.64	.87
$Intrusive_{SMA}$	3.48	1.06	
$Intrusive_{SMI}$	2.83	.88	
SBC_{NF}	2.74	.91	.92
SBC_{FF}	2.42	.80	.93

a 5-point scale of "strongly agree" to "strongly disagree." All five items loaded in a single distinct factor and were averaged to create and index. In addition, we added one item to measure perceptions of intrusiveness of these efforts, anchored as well by a 5-point scale of "strongly agree" and "strongly disagree." Table 9.1 shows the descriptive measures and alpha coefficient for the scale and the extra item.

Self–Brand Connections
For both self–brand connection measures, Escalas and Bettman's (2003) 7-item brand connection scale was used. For each scale item participants reported their extent of agreement anchored by "not at all" and "very much" on a 7-point scale (1 to 7). All seven items loaded in a single distinct factor and were averaged to create an index. Table 9.1 shows the descriptive measures and alpha coefficient for both self–brand connection measures: for the brand without social media interaction (SBC_{NF}) and for the brand with social media interaction (SBC_{FF}).

Sample Demographics
Sixty-three adults voluntarily participated in the exploratory survey that was distributed via Facebook and Twitter ($n = 63$). After eliminating incomplete records, a final sample size of 51 participants was attained.

The age of survey respondents varied from 19 to 56 with an average age of 30.62. Participants' gender was evenly distributed with 51% males and 49% females. Fifty-seven percent are still in college, and 43% are not, with 30% of participants reporting having earned a bachelor's degree and 30% reporting having earned a master's degree. In regard to social media, 96% reported having a Facebook profile and 69% have a Twitter account.

Early Results and Analysis

Survey Measures

Social Media Advertising Versus Social Media Invertising

In order to test our hypotheses we conducted t-tests with Bonferroni corrections to control for Type I error. Social media advertising ($M = 2.85$, $SD = .80$) was viewed significantly more negatively ($t_{(50)} = -5.43$, $p < .01$) than social media invertising ($M = 3.76$, $SD = .64$) such as brand pages or brand accounts. To further explore consumer attitudes toward B2C social media efforts, we evaluated the perceived intrusiveness of social media advertising and invertising. Traditional social media advertising ($M = 3.51$, $SD = 1.05$) was perceived as significantly more intrusive ($t_{(50)} = 4.99$, $p < .01$) than social media invertising ($M = 2.83$, $SD = .88$). These results support H_1 that consumers perceive social media invertising more favorably and as less intrusive than traditional social media advertising.

Self–Brand Connections

Our second hypothesis proposes that consumers interacting with brands through brand pages or accounts (invertising) should develop stronger self–brand connections with these brands versus those brands with which the consumer has no social media interaction. We tested the hypothesis through a t-test. Surprisingly, self–brand connections with invertising brands – SBC_{FF} ($M = 2.42$, $SD = .80$) were not significantly different ($t_{(33)} = -1.90$, $p = .067$ than consumer self–brand connections with brands they did not interact with socially – SBC_{NFF} ($M = 2.70$, $SD = 1.01$). Actually SBC_{FF} was slightly lower than $SCBN_{FF}$.

Open-Ended Responses

To better understand this outcome we evaluated the open-ended responses regarding the extent of their interactions with the brand, their motivation to fan or follow the brand, and the value they obtained from belonging to the brand pages or accounts. We analyzed and coded the participants' responses ($n = 48$) to the three open-ended questions for common themes among them that would give insight as to how these brand pages/accounts are perceived and used by the customers. Both authors coded the responses and solved any differences through discussion (achieving an interreliability rating of 90).

Consumer Interaction with Invertising

Two main topics emerged: the "lurker" consumer who only reads and "likes" what the brand posts, and the more "active" consumer who not only reads, but also shares content, comments on posts (either from the brand or other consumers), or contacts the brand. However, the former heavily outnumbered the latter. One key quote, "Post on wall . . . liking of posts, videos, etc. *Sharing of posts if engaging enough*" (emphasis by authors), can point to an area of why interaction with the brand may not be as active as possible and that is that brands need to make sure that the content is interesting enough for the consumer not only to read it, but also to share it, effectively converting the consumer to a word-of-mouth (WOM)/buzz marketing campaign. Companies should take advantage of these voluntary "ambassadors" and try to use them effectively to spread their message and entice others to join the invertising effort (page/account).

Motivations to Join Invertising

Participants had different motivations, which we summarize in two main themes: they "consumed" the brand, or they were motivated by a brand "promotion" being offered to join the effort. Brand promotions played a big part in consumers joining the invertising effort. Brands shouldn't rely only on consumers' brand loyalty or brand use to entice them to join them in social media, but periodic promotions (e.g., deals, contests) will also help the brand gain more of a social media following. There were a few mentions of participants joining the effort because a friend did, which reinforces the argument of using these "members" to attract future users such as the previously mentioned Red Robin campaign, and that using the social factor of social media can be effective.

Value Obtained from Invertising

Participants reported only one dimension, "utilitarian benefits." Participants consider the value obtained from joining these invertising efforts as knowledge or information they receive from the brand. This knowledge allows them to stay updated on new products and upcoming promotions, and as they report, "The fact that I know all sales and latest clothing line, which is very beneficial for me," and "first to know about special deals they offer." So it also gives the customer the feeling of being part of a "special" group of customers or having an advantage over other customers. Although these efforts are typically used en masse, brands could convert some of these efforts to a loyalty/reward program where "special" promotions are available exclusively for the members of the page/account.

In addition, in all three open-ended responses some participants reported seeing the page/account as an extension of the brand Web site that was easier or more convenient to use and access lending credence to social media as a complementary vehicle to be used in the overall online marketing efforts of the brand and not as a standalone vehicle.

Discussion and Marketing Implications

Our early findings support H_1 that consumers view social media invertising more favorably and as less intrusive than social media advertising. We did not, however, find support for H_2 that consumer invertising interactions with brands develop stronger self–brand connections than when they don't interact with the brand in social media. We also offered some insight into the extent, motivation, and value that consumers obtain from belonging to brand pages/accounts.

This research found no support for stronger self–brand connections through invertising efforts, but it does support that consumers view invertising more favorably and less intrusive than social media advertising therefore letting brands know that invertising may lead to more positive brand attitudes. A possible explanation for not finding support for H_2 is that our exploratory survey in its limited scope did not account for other brand efforts the consumer may have been exposed to other than the invertising.

Brand invertising is a cost-effective way to keep consumers informed about new products and promotions, but the content of these pages/accounts should be more engaging so as to encourage the customers who have joined to share with others voluntarily, effectively conducting a WOM campaign. It has been shown that consumers will respond better and more positively to promotions delivered with some connection to a member of their social network (Hill, Provost, & Volinsky, 2006). It is easy to get consumers to join invertising efforts either because they already consume the brand or through a promotional effort; however, the challenge lies in getting the consumers to interact with the brand through these invertising efforts, increasing their brand involvement and strengthening the relationship with the brand. Consumers need to be moved from "lurkers" looking for information to more active "posters" that contact the company and interact with the other customers, as well as share its content with peers who may or may not consume the brand and may in turn entice them to join the effort.

It is clear that brands can benefit from favorable consumer attitudes by opting to have a presence in social media in the form of invertising (brand pages or accounts) that consumers can "fan" or "follow" versus implementing the traditional online advertising model of using button or banner advertising to attract the customer. However, although more favorably rated by consumers, its benefits to the brand are unclear versus not being present in social media, and more research is needed to better understand how effective they are as both standalone efforts and as complementary efforts (SMA versus SMI versus SMA+SMI).

Limitations and Future Directions

As we discussed avenues of future research in the review section of this chapter, we use this area to lay out our future research on this particular topic. This study is exploratory and as such, its explorative nature combined with the smaller sample size is our main limitation. It is also limited in scope in that we are only evaluating one type of effort in social media, invertising, and one type of social medium, and how it interacts with self–brand connections. However, this is only the first step in our continuing research which is now in its qualitative stage. We are moving forward with personal interviews and focus groups to understand further how consumers perceive B2C social media communications, how they respond to the B2C social media efforts and their effect on the consumer–brand relationship, brand attitudes, and purchase intentions. In addition, at the time of this writing we are conducting another more in-depth survey and exploring other social media efforts for brand relationship building as well as differences across groups by demographics and technology frequency use.

References

Acquisti, A. & Spiekermann, S. (2011). Do interruptions pay off? Effects of interruptive ads on consumers' willingness to pay. *Journal of Interactive Marketing*, 25(4), 226–240.

Adjei, M. T., Noble, S. M., & Noble, C. H. (2009). The influence of C2C communications in online brand communities on customer purchase behavior. *Journal of the Academy of Marketing Science*, 38(5), 634–653.

AdReaction (2010). Brands + consumer + social media: What marketers should know about who's getting social and why. Retrieved May 7, 2011 from http://www.dynamiclogic.com/na/research/industry_presentations/docs/DynamicLogic_AdReaction09_OMMASocial_26Jan2010.pdf

Aksoy, L., Bloom, P., Lurie, N. H., & Cooil, B. (2006). Should recommendation agents think like people? *Journal of Service Research, 8*(4), 297–315.

Alwitt, L. F. & Prabhakar, P. R. (1992). Functional and belief dimensions of attitudes to television advertising. *Journal of Advertising Research, 32*(5), 30–42.

Armstrong, A. & Hagel, J. (1996). The real value of on-line communities. *Harvard Business Review, 74*(3), 134–141.

Ask, J. (2006). *Mobile marketing forecast 2006-11.* JupiterResearch. (Company Report)

Barnes, S. B. & Hair, N. F. (2009). From banners to You-Tube: Using the rearview mirror to look at the future of internet advertising. *International Journal of Internet Marketing and Advertising, 5*(3), 223–239.

Barry, T. E. & Howard, D. J. (1990). A review and critique of the hierarchy of effects in advertising. *International Journal of Advertising, 9*(2), 121–135.

Barwise, P. & Strong, C. (2002). Permission-based mobile advertising. *Journal of Interactive Marketing, 16*(1), 14–24.

Bausch, S. & Han, L. (2006). Podcasting gains an important foothold among U.S. adult online population, according to Nielsen/Net ratings. Retrieved May 15, 2011 from http://www.nielsen-online.com/pr/pr_060712.pdf

Beniger, J. R. (1986). *The control revolution: Technological and economic origins of the information society.* Cambridge, MA: Harvard University Press.

Bezjian-Avery, A., Calder, B., & Iacobucci, D. (1998). New media interactive advertising versus traditional advertising. *Journal of Advertising Research,* July–August 23–32.

Brown, J., Broderick, A., & Lee, N. (2007). Extending social network theory to conceptualise on-line word-of-mouth communication. *Journal of Interactive Advertising, 21*(3), 2–19.

Cappo, J. (2003). *The future of advertising: New media, new clients, new customers in a post television age.* New York: McGraw-Hill.

Colliander, J. & Dahlén, M. (2011). Following the fashionable friend: The power of social media. *Journal of Advertising Research, 51*(1), 313–320.

Coursaris, C., & Hassanein, K. (2002). Understanding M-commerce: A consumer-centric model. *Quarterly Journal of Electronic Commerce, 3*(3), 247–271.

Cova, B. & Cova, V. (2002). Tribal marketing: The tribalisation of society and its impact on the conduct of marketing. *European Journal of Marketing, 36*(5–6), 595–620.

Deighton, J. (1996). The future of interactive marketing. *Harvard Business Review, 74*(6), 131–161.

Deighton, J. & Kornfeld, L. (2009). Interactivity's unanticipated consequences for marketers and marketing. *Journal of Interactive Marketing, 23*, 4–10.

Direct Marketing Association (DMA). (2008). *Mobile marketing: Consumer perspectives.* New York: Direct Marketing Association.

DoubleClick (2005). Search before the purchase: Understanding buyer search activity as it builds to online purchase. Retrieved May 31, 2011 from http://static.google-usercontent.com/external_content/untrusted_dlcp/www.google.com/en/us/doubleclick/pdfs/DoubleClick-02-2005-Search-Before-the-Purchase.pdf

Douglas, M. & Isherwood, B. C. (1979). *The world of goods.* New York: Basic.

Dreze, X. & Hussherr, F. (2003). Internet advertising: Is anybody watching? *Journal of Interactive Marketing, 17*(4), 8–23.

eMarketer (2007a). *Mobile brand advertising report.* New York: eMarketer

eMarketer (2007b). *Mobile mesage marketing report.* New York: eMarketer

eMarketer (2007a). *Mobile brand advertising report.* New York: eMarketer.

eMarketer (2008). *Mobile location-based services on the move report.* New York: eMarketer.

eMarketer (2009a). Online advertising pushes through. Retrieved April 15, 2010 from http://www.emarketer.com/article.aspx?r=1007024&ntt=online+ad&no=20&xsrc=article_head_sitesearchx&n=0&ntk=basic

eMarketer (2009b). *Will marketers get frugal with Google?* New York: eMarketer.

eMarketer (2011). *Social network ad revenues rising worldwide.* New York: eMarketer.

Escalas, J. E. & Bettman, J. R. (2003). You are what they eat: The influence of reference groups on consumers' connections to brands. *Journal of Consumer Psychology, 13*(3), 339–348.

Escalas, J. E. & Bettman, J. R. (2005). Self-construal, reference groups and brand meaning. *Journal of Consumer Research, 32*(3), 378–389.

ExactTarget (2011).The social breakup. Retrieved June 15, 2011 from http://www.exacttarget.com/resources/sfff8.pdf

Foursquare (2011). Showtime trades baseballs for checkins to promote the franchise. Retrieved July 18, 2011 from http://aboutfoursquare.com/the-franchise/

Gao, Y. & Koufaris, M. (2006). Perceptual antecedents of user attitude in electronic commerce. *ACM Signis, 37*(2–3), 43–50.

Hagel, J. (1999). Net gain: Expanding markets through virtual communities. *Journal of Interactive Marketing, 13,* 55–66.

Haghirian, P., Madlberger, M., & Tanuskova, A. (2005). Increasing advertising value of mobile marketing: An empirical study of antecedents. *Proceedings of the Thirty Eighth Hawaii International Conference of System Sciences,* (pp. 1–10). Hawaii.

Hart, K. (2007). Online networking goes small, and sponsors follow. *Washington Post,* December 29, 1.

Hennig-Thurau, F. T., Gwinner, K. P., Walsh, G., & Gremler, D. D. (2004). Electronic word-of-mouth via consumer-opinion platforms: What motivates consumers to articulate themseves on the Internet? *Journal of Interactive Marketing, 18*(1), 38–52.

Hill, S., Provost, F., & Volinsky, C. (2006). Network-based marketing: Identifying likely adopters via consumer networks. *Statistical Science, 21*(2), 256–276.

Hird, J. (2010). 20+ Mind-blowing social media statistics revisited. Retrieved February 3, 2011 from http://econsultancy.com/us/blog/5324-20+-mind-blowing-social-media-statistics-revisited

Hoffman, D. & Novak, T. P. (1996). Marketing in hypermedia computer-mediated environments: Conceptual foundations. *Journal of Marketing, 60*(July), 50–68.

Holzwarth, M., Janiszewski, C., & Neumann, M. M. (2006). The influence of avatars on online consumer shopping behavior. *Journal of Marketing, 70*, 19–36.

Hoy, M. G. & Milne, G. (2010). Gender differences in privacy-related measures for young adult Facebook users. *Journal of Interactive Advertising, 10*(2), 28–45.

Huang, C.-Y., Shen, Y.-Z., Lin, H.-X., & Chang, S.-S. (2007). Bloggers' motivations and behaviors: A model. *Journal of Advertising Research, 47*(4), 472–484.

Ilfeld, J. S. & Winer, R. S. (2002). Generating website traffic. *Journal of Advertising Research, 42*(5), 49–61.

Jaffe, J. (2005). *Life after the 30-second spot.* Hoboken, NJ: Wiley.

Jin, S.-A. A. & Bolebruch, J. (2009). Avatar-based advertising in Second Life: The role of presence and attractiveness of virtual spokespersons. *Journal of Interactive Advertising, 10*(1), 51–60.

Kozinets, R. V., De Valck, K., Wojnicki, A. C., & Wilner, S. J. S. (2010). Networked narratives: Understanding word-of-mouth marketing in online communities. *Journal of Marketing, 74*(2), 71–89.

Kutchera, J. (2008). Navigate the blogosphere's biggest ad networks. Retrieved December 11, 2010 from http://www.imediaconnection.com/content/20486.asp

Leek, S. & Christodoulides, G. (2009). Next-generation mobile marketing: How young consumers react to bluetooth-enabled advertising. *Journal of Advertising Research, 49*(1), 44–53.

Li, H. & Bukovac, J. L. (1999). Cognitive impact of banner ad characteristics: An experimental study. *Journalism and Mass Communication Quarterly, 76*(2), 341–353.

Machanda, P., Dubé, J.-P., Goh, K. Y., & Chintagunta, P. K. (2006).The effect of banner advertising on internet purchasing. *Journal of Marketing Research, 43*(February), 98–108.

Malhotra, N. K. (1988). Self concept and product choice: An integrated perspective. *Journal of Economic Psychology, 9*, 1–28.

McCracken, G. (1989). Who is the celebrity endorser? Cultural foundations of the endorsement process. *Journal of Consumer Research, 16*(December), 310–321.

Moe, W. W. & Fader, P. S. (2003). Dynamic conversion behavior at e-commerce sites. *Management Science, 50*(3), 326–335.

Moe, W. W. & Schweidel, D. A. (2010). Online product opinions: Incidence, evaluation and evolution. *Marketing Science Institute Special Report*, 10–204.

Morrisey, B. (2009). Brand seek fans on Facebook. Retrieved May 17, 2010 from http://www.adweek.com/news/advertising-branding/brands-seek-fans-facebook-104999

Muñiz, A. M. & O'Guinn, T. C. (2001). Brand community. *Journal of Consumer Research, 27*(4), 412–432.

Muñiz, A. M. & Schau, H. J. (2007). Vigilante marketing and consumer-created communications. *Journal of Advertising 36*(3), 187–202.

Nielsen. (2010). Led by Facebook, Twitter, global time spent on social media sites up 82% year over year. Retrieved May 17, 2011 from http://blog.nielsen.com/nielsenwire/global/led-by-facebook-twitter-global-time-spent-on-social-media-sites-up-82-year-over-year/

Nielsen. (2011). Kids today: How the class of 2011 engages with media. Retrieved July 1, 2011 from http://blog.nielsen.com/nielsenwire/consumer/kids-today-how-the-class-of-2011-engages-with-media/

O'Guinn, T. C. & Muñiz, A. M. (2005). Communal consumption and the brand. In D. G. Mick & S. Ratneshwar (Eds.), *Inside consumption: Frontiers of research on consumer motives, goals, and desires.* Boca Raton, FL: Routledge.

Ostrow, A. (2009). Twitter's massive 2008: 752 percent growth. Retrieved January 6, 2010 from http://mashable.com/2009/01/09/twitter-growth-2008/

Peppers, D. & Rogers, M. (1997). *Enterprise one to one: Tools for competing in the interactive age.* New York: Currency Doubleday.

Phoster, B. (2010). Facebook user growth chart. Retrieved February 5, 2011 from http://wwww.benphoster.com/wp-content/uploads/2010/07/Facebook-user-growth-chart.png

PriceWaterhouseCooper (2011). *IAB internet advertising revenue report: 2010 full year results,* Author.

Raacke, J. D. & Bonds-Raacke, J. M. (2008). MySpace and Facebook: Applying the uses and gratifications theory to exploring friend-networking sites. *CyberPsychology and Behavior, 11*(2).

Razorfish (2009). The data. Retrieved May 7, 2011 from http://feed.razorfish.com/feed09/the-data

Rettie, R. (2001). An exploration of flow during Internet use. *Internet Research: Electronic Networking Applications and Policy. 11*(2), 103–113.

Rodgers, S. & Thorson, E. (2000). The interactive advertising model: How users perceive and process online ads. *Journal of Interactive Advertising, 1*(1), 42–61.

Rose, S., Hair, N., & Clark, M. (2011). Online customer experience: A review of the business-to-consumer online purchase context. *International Journal of Management Review, 13,* 24–39.

Schau, H. J. & Gilly, M. C. (2003). We are what we post? Self-presentation in personal webspace. *Journal of Consumer Research, 30*(December), 385–404.

Schlosser, A. E., Shavitt, S., & Kanfer, A. (1999). Survey of internet users' attitudes toward internet advertising. *Journal of Interactive Marketing, 13*(3), 34–54.

Schultz, D. E. & Bailey, S. (2000). Customer/brand loyalty in an interactive marketplace. *Journal of Advertising Research, 40*(3), 41–53.

Shankar, V. & Balasubramanian, S. (2009). Mobile marketing: A synthesis and prognosis. *Journal of Interactive Marketing, 23,* 118–129.

Shankar, V. & Hollinger, M. (2007). Online and mobile advertising: Current scenario, emerging trends, and future directions. *Marketing Science Institute Special Report,* 07-206.

Shavitt, S., Lowrey, P. M., & Haefner, J. E. (1998). Public attitudes toward advertising: More favorable than you might think. *Journal of Advertising Research*, July–August, 7–22.

Sherman, L. & Deighton, J. (2001). Banner advertising: Measuring effectiveness and optimizing placement. *Journal of Interactive Marketing*, *15*(2), 60–64.

Taylor, D. G., Lewin, J. E., & Strutton, D. (2011). Friends, fans, and followers: Do ads work on social networks? *Journal of Advertising Research*, *51*(1), 258–275.

Tedeschi, B. (2007). P&G, the pioneer of mixing soap and drama, adds a web installment. *New York Times*, October 15.

Thorbjornsen, H., Supphellen, M., Nysveen, H., & Pedersen, P. E. (2002). Building brand relationships online: A comparison of two interactive applications. *Journal of Interactive Marketing*, *16*(3), 17–34.

Thorson, K. S. & Rodgers, S. (2006). Relationships between blogs as eWOM and interactivity, perceived interactivity, and parasocial interaction. *Journal of Interactive Advertising*, *6*(2), 34–44.

Trusov, M., Bucklin, R. E., & Pauwels, K. (2009). Effects of word-of-mouth versus traditional marketing: Findings from an internet social networking site. *Journal of Marketing*, *73*(September), 90–102.

Tsiantar, D. (2006).Getting on board. *Time*, April 16.

Valentino-DeVries, J. (2010). A third of adults now post to sites like Facebook, Twitter once a week. Retrieved April 7, 2011 from http://blogs.wsj.com/digits/2010/01/19/a-third-of-adults-now-post-to-sites-like-facebook-twitter-once-a-week/

Vargo, S. L. & Lusch, R. F. (2004). Evolving to a new dominant logic for marketing. *Journal of Marketing*, *68*(January), 1–17.

Williamson, D. A. (2011). *Worldwide social network ad spending: 2011 outlook*. New York: eMarketer.

Winer, R. S. (2009). New communications approaches in marketing: Issues and research directions. *Journal of Interactive Marketing*, *23*(2009), 108–117.

Yoo, C. Y. (2008). Unconscious processing of web advertising: Effects on implicit memory, attitude toward the brand and consideration set. *Journal of Interactive Marketing*, *22*(2), 2–18.

Yoo, C. Y., Kim, K., & Stout, P. A. (2004). Assessing the effects of animation in online banner advertising: Hierarchy of effects model. *Journal of Interactive Advertising*, *4*(2), 7–17.

York, E. B. (2009). Red Robin calls in a Facebook favor from 1,500 fans: Casual-dining chain uses recommendation app to turn passive customers into brand ambassadors. Retrieved June 13, 2010 from http://adage.com/article/digital/social-media-red-robin-facebook/139255/

Zeng, F., Huang, L., & Dou, W. (2009). Social factors in user perceptions and responses to advertising in online social networking communities. *Journal of Interactive Advertising*, *10*(1), 1–13.

10

Male Consumers' Motivations for Online Information Search and Shopping Behavior

Linda Tuncay Zayer
Loyola University Chicago

Peter Coleman
Loyola University Chicago

> *Alan leads a busy life, balancing his career and the demands of taking care of his family. Much like 84% of his male counterparts, he shares responsibility in household shopping decisions.[*] Healthcare for his young children is a big expense. As do 80% of Americans, he often seeks out health information online so he is knowledgeable and armed with information.[†] He is also a bargain hunter when shopping, even for low-priced items, so, as do 81% of Americans, he often researches a product online before he makes a purchase.[‡] Alan is also skeptical of advertising claims; instead, as do nearly half of Americans, he trusts the opinions of his peers.[§] Alan is an example of how online information search is increasingly becoming more salient in consumers' shopping patterns and in their daily lives.*

The opening vignette describes a common scenario occurring in many American households regarding the way consumers search for product information and how they shop. Consumers are increasingly engaging in extensive information searches not only for high ticket and important items (Dholakia, 1998; Dowling & Staelin, 1994; Schmidt & Spreng, 1996) such as health care but also for even the most mundane goods, such as cleaning products. For example, Penn (2007) finds consumers conduct a significant amount of research even on low-priced, relatively low-risk purchases, such as cold medicine and shampoo, 35% and 22% of all consumers,

---

[*] *Wall Street Journal*, April 23, 2011, http://online.wsj.com/article/SB10001424052748703521304576278964279316994.html

[†] Pew Internet & American Life Project, 2009, www.pewinternet.com

[‡] Pew Internet & American Life Project, 2009, www.pewinternet.com

[§] 2010 Edelman Trust Barometer, www.edelman.com/trust/2010/

respectively. Moreover, although some scholars (Grant, Clarke, & Kyria-zis, 2007; Ozanne, Brucks, & Grewal, 1992) have documented consumers' frustrations with the accuracy and credibility of online information, Penn (2007) finds 92% of consumers no longer trust the information they receive from traditional sources such as television and are increasingly turning to online sources, such as blogs and review sites, for product information.

Research has shown that consumers seek out external information about goods and services from personal sources, such as friends, inde-pendent outlets such as government agencies, and marketing entities such as salespeople and advertising. Bloch, Sherrell, and Ridgway (1986) refer to both a practical reason for information search, as well as a hedonic (emotional motivations) reason. That is, consumer information search is often attributed to the need to make better purchase decisions or because it is pleasurable for some individuals to engage in information-seeking behavior.

Moreover, Moore and Lehmann (1980) summarize the variables related to the amount of information search conducted, grouping them into (1) market environment, such as number of product alternatives; (2) situ-ational factors, such as urgency of purchase; (3) potential payoff/product importance, such as the financial risk of purchase; (4) experience and knowledge; and (5) individual differences, such as age and education.

However, little research has explored how these and other motivations interact with gender identity to influence consumers to engage in infor-mation search as they browse and shop for goods online. The purpose of the current research is to fill this gap in the literature and to explore how men engage in information search and shopping behavior online. Research has shown men to exhibit different consumer decision-making styles (Bakewell & Mitchell, 2004), display varied shopping motivations (Otnes & McGrath, 2001), and employ varying persuasion management strategies in some cases (Tuncay & Otnes, 2008). Thus, it is likely that men may display different motivations for information search and online shop-ping behavior as well. That is, what are male consumers' motivations for engaging in information search as they browse and shop for products and services online?

Literature Review

The Internet is the primary source for information search and has dras-tically affected the dynamics of the retail industry, both in terms of innovation and increased sales. In the U.S. Census Bureau e-stats Report released May 27, 2010, U.S. retail e-commerce sales were $142 billion in 2008, a gain of 3.3% from the previous year. For the first three quarters of 2011, U.S. retail e-commerce sales amounted to $135.901 billion (http://www.census.gov/retail/mrts/www/data/pdf/ec_current.pdf).

Marketers are becoming increasingly more engaged in learning how consumers conduct online information searches so they can be more targeted in their communication strategies. They are becoming more innovative in their approach and are tailoring Web sites to enhance the consumer's online experience. Throughout the years, researchers have examined the behavior of online consumers, in particular how demographics and psychographics play a part in prepurchase information search. Moreover, although women have long been studied as consumers, more recent research in consumer behavior has examined men's consumption patterns and shopping behavior (Otnes & McGrath, 2001; Holt & Thompson, 2004; Tuncay & Otnes, 2008; Zayer & Neier, 2011). In fact, some research suggests that men are just as important in household shopping decisions as women are. Men self-report they feel they influence 61% of all household spending (Bialik, 2011). The following is a comprehensive review broadly examining Internet usage, and more specifically, online information search and shopping behavior highlighting male consumers' motivations and behaviors.

Internet Usage, Information Search, and Shopping Motivations

Consumers are increasingly turning to the Internet as a main source for their information search process. A recent study by Pew Research Center (2011) concluded that 78% of all adults use the Internet. Ninety-two percent of these adults use it for broad information search and 78% percent use it specifically for product/service information search. Of the adult Internet users, 71% purchase a product or service from online retailers or sales channels. The vast amount of information available online as well as the low cost of engaging in search has been identified by several studies as the two leading motivations (Alba et al., 1997; Bakos, 1997; Hoque & Lohse, 1999; Peterson & Merino, 2003). However, a recent study identified that change in behavior is actually the driving factor, meaning, the more someone has used the Internet in the past, the more likely he will turn to it in the future (Jepsen, 2007). In addition, the fact that consumers turn to the Internet for prepurchase information in the first place is an indication they are more likely to purchase a product online versus a physical store (Shim, Eastlick, Lotz, & Warrington, 2001). Also, the more time they spend online, the greater the likelihood of their making a purchase decision (Bhatnagar & Ghose, 2004; McCloskey, 2003–2004; Zott, Amit, & Donlevy, 2000). Aside from gathering general product information, the Internet offers consumers a convenient and comfortable environment where they can socialize and entertain themselves. Web usage among consumers is predicted to increase significantly over the years (http://www.etforecasts.com/products/ES_intusersv2.htm) as technology advancements have literally put the Internet in consumers' pockets, making the Web accessible 24/7.

Initially, males dominated the Internet as they were early adopters (Asch, 2001), but recent research suggests the gender gap is closing (Zhang, 2005) with an equal 78% of male and female adults turning to the Internet for various online activities (Pew Research Center, 2011). Despite this equality, significant differences have been discovered between the sexes in terms of online search behavior. Access to the Internet is equal between both sexes; however, men use the Internet more for information search and even shop for products/services more than women (Davis, 2011; Li, Kuo, & Russell, 1999; Stafford, Turan, & Raisinghani, 2004). Men also spend more money per transaction (Nobbs & Ulrich, 2011; Susskind, 2004), have a greater inclination to buy online again in the future, and in general, have a more positive attitude toward online shopping (Alreck & Settle, 2002; Brown, Pope, & Voges, 2003; Donthu & Garcia, 1999; Hernandez et al., 2010; Korgaonkar & Wolin, 1999; Li et al., 1999; Lohse, Bellman, & Johnson, 2000; Rodgers & Harris, 2003; Van Slyke, Comunale, & Belanger, 2002; Stafford et al., 2004). However, another recent study concluded that women actually shop more than men at online retail stores, but men spend more time shopping on Web sites with a single sales channel, such as Amazon and Zappos (Abraham, Morn, & Vollman, 2010).

Jepsen (2007) states that heavy Internet users benefit the most from online information search because they are skilled in navigating the Web and therefore have a positive outlook on the available information. Assael (2005) finds heavy Internet users, defined as those who use the Internet 20 hours or more per week, are 40% more likely to be between the ages of 18 and 34 and males are slightly more likely to be heavy users than females. Davis (2011) also states 54% of males browse the Internet every couple days compared to 47% of females. According to Assael (2005), men are likely to fall under all six categories of heavy Internet users whereas women are not: *Web Generalists* (buy goods, obtain information about products, send and receive e-mails, and make travel plans), *Downloaders* (download music and software), *Self-Improvers* (hunt for jobs, read news, and gather information about education or for business), *Entertainment Seekers* (look to be entertained and seek out games), *Traders* (buy/sell stocks), and *Socializers* (chat in forums). A Pew Internet study also confirmed males tend to be heavier Internet users than females, but only slightly: 61% versus 57% (Fallows, 2005). Other research by Fallows (2005) finds males go online more often and spend a greater amount of time browsing. They are also more likely than females to use the Internet for the following activities: obtain weather, news, sports, political, financial information, and do-it-yourself information, as well as engage in job-related research, downloading of software and music, music listening, rating of products and services, using a webcam, and taking a class. Females are more likely to use the Internet for social interaction (Swaminathan, Lepkowska-White, & Rao, 1999; Weiser, 2000).

Website Design and Consumer Behavior

In terms of design, studies have determined that site design can affect consumers' decisions to purchase online (Cai & Xu, 2011; Lightner, Yenisey, Ozok, & Salvendy, 2002; Tilson et al., 1998) and the aesthetics of a site is one of the most crucial elements in the success of an e-commerce site (Tractinsky & Lowengart, 2007). The ones that offer useful content (Ahn, Ryu, & Han, 2004; Lin, 2007) and allow consumers to make the purchase in a reasonable amount of time (Bridges & Florsheim, 2007; Konradt, Wandke, Balazs, & Christophersen, 2003; Lin, 2007) will positively influence the consumer's purchase decision. In addition, the elements of a site that are enjoyable, engaging, and interactive (i.e., user participation) are more likely to lead to positive attitudes toward the online store brand (Childers, Carr, Peck, & Carson, 2001; Huang, Lurie, & Mitra, 2009; Mathwick, Malhotra, & Rigdon, 2002; Mathwick & Rigdon, 2004; Szymanski & Hise, 2000) and this could lead to an increased likelihood for purchases (Chen, Zhang, & Xu, 2009; Rosen & Purinton, 2004). The term stickiness is defined as the ability of a Web site to retain its visitors (Zott et al., 2000). The more stickiness a Web site has, the greater the likelihood of repeat visits and increased transactions (Zott et al., 2000). Bhatnagar and Ghose (2003) support this by finding that repeat visits can lead to customer loyalty, which in turn can lead to increased transaction rates. Lin (2007) discovered in her study that stickiness was indeed the most influential factor in repeat visits and increased the likelihood of transactions more so than Web site content and perception of trust.

Recent research sought to determine the effect expressive and classical aesthetics have on shoppers searching for hedonic goods (flowers, perfumes, and videos) versus utilitarian goods (cameras, watches, hardware items) (Cai & Xu, 2011). Lavie and Tractinsky (2004) refer to classical aesthetics as being clear and orderly in the design, whereas expressive aesthetics refer to the originality, creativity, use of imagery, and richness of the site design. One of the results of the study indicated that expressive aesthetics are more important to consumers when searching for hedonic goods, thus, it is important to avoid a uniform Web site design for different types of products being sold online (Cai & Xu, 2011).

In terms of sex differences, males have been found to prefer a much more functional online environment where product information is easy to find and the order process is quick and simple (Richard, Chebat, Yang, & Putrevu, 2009). They are able to absorb much more information from a site that is simply structured (Griffith, 2005) and tend to have more positive attitudes toward it as well (Richard et al., 2009). Additional research concludes that the need to register in order to make a purchase has a somewhat negative effect on the likelihood of a purchase. Filling out simple forms and creating user profiles also has a negative impact, but less than a full registration process (Fagerstrom, 2010).

Consistent with offline advertising, the use of imagery and descriptive wording supporting the products being advertised online is preferred by males (Putrevu, 2001). Men are also more prone than women to make compulsive purchases (quick purchase decisions) online if they feel the Web site challenges their skill level and enough product information is provided (Richard et al., 2009). On the other hand, women tend to use the Internet more for information search and then proceed to brick-and-mortar stores for their purchase (Richard et al., 2009; Wolin & Korgaonkar, 2003).

Importance of Trust in Online Environment

The Internet has replaced the face-to-face contact consumers experience when shopping in stores. Building and maintaining relationships online now depends on the Web site interface (Rayport & Jaworski, 2001). If it fails to connect with the consumer on a personal level, consumers are more likely to search for products on other Web sites. Without the personal contact, trust becomes an issue. Konradt et al. (2003) and McKnight, Choudhury, and Kacmar (2002) find that the trust a consumer perceives a Web site to have greatly influences his intention to purchase. In general, consumers who view a Web site as high quality are much more likely to trust the site—even if they have not heard of the vendor before. Consumers are more reluctant to trust Web sites that are of low quality (McKnight et al., 2002). In addition, the more transactions a consumer has with a particular Web site, the greater trust she develops (Gefen, Karahanna, & Straub 2003; McKnight, et al., 2002). That is, obtaining trust from online consumers is crucial in keeping them as repeat customers. With regard to trust in e-commerce, males indicate they have more trust in online retailers than females due to the fact that the emotional bond females require to establish trust is not present online (Rodgers & Harris, 2003).

Search Engine Use

Consumers rely heavily on the aid of search engines (e.g., Google, Yahoo, Bing) and advanced databases (e.g., Web Science, ProQuest) in their information searches. Maghferat and Stock (2010) found there to be significant differences between men and women when it comes to the use of both outlets. Men use scientific databases more often than women even when it isn't necessarily needed. For example, when posed with the simple task, "What is theory of relativity?" males more often than females use a scientific database over a simple search engine like Google or Yahoo, both of which can obtain information quicker. Men are also more likely than women to find results for searches by accident, whereas females are much more targeted in their approach and use operators (and, or, not) in their search queries more than males. Compared to women, men believe they are better searchers than they actually are and they are less satisfied with results than women (Maghferat & Stock, 2010). In a similar study, Lorigo et al. (2005) looked at behavior in terms of search engines and found that males enter shorter search queries than females, follow a linear path (i.e., did not click on the back button to see previous results as much as women), spend more time than females looking at result pages, and click on more results than females. In another study, men were determined to conduct more searches than women and Google was considered the favorite search engine (Abraham et al., 2010).

Moreover, Jansen and Solomon (2010) examined the search engine marketing log of a national retailer chain consisting of more than 7,000,000 records and 40,000 key phrases to determine if sex-specific wording had an influence on sales. To classify the key phrases as male- or female-oriented, the authors used the Microsoft adCenter Labs Demographics Prediction Tool, which takes a key phrase and gives the probability that it is male- or female-oriented. Advertisers use this tool to determine which key words/ phrases they should bid on for search engine marketing campaigns in order to enhance their demographic targeting. The data for this study spanned 33 months and the retailer has stores both offline and online. Results show that female-oriented key phrases (i.e., bed and bath devices, presents for Father's Day, or talking photo album) generated around 10–20% more impressions and 40–127% more clicks and led to more sales revenue than did male-oriented key phrases. The male-oriented key phrases had a higher cost per click (CPC) and were usually attributed to higher-priced goods than female-oriented key phrases. Despite these differences in sex-specific search phrases, the authors concluded that neutral key phrases actually performed best overall as they had the most impressions, clicks, items ordered, and highest sales revenue (Jansen & Solomon, 2010).

Shopping Motivations

In terms of attitudes toward online shopping, males tend to exude a more positive attitude than females and identify convenience, lack of social interaction, and price comparison as leading influencers (Hung & Chun, 2010; Rodgers & Harris, 2003). Men tend to appreciate the control and freedom they have over their online information search experience as well. Consistent with previous research, men prefer to gather information themselves (Meyers-Levy, 1989, 1994; Meyers-Levy & Maheswaran, 1991; Meyers-Levy & Sternthal, 1991; Putrevu, 2001; Xie, Bao, & Morais, 2006) versus relying on other people, and the Internet caters to this preference. Men also view the Internet as a more practical tool than women because it is convenient to purchase practical items such as books and music (Rodgers & Harris, 2003). Rodgers and Harris (2003) suggest women may not view the Internet as practical as men do because women tend to shop for more emotionally invested products, such as clothing, perfume, and makeup which can be more cumbersome online.

Some studies utilize uses and gratification theory, or the notion that consumers of media play an active role in choosing media to fulfill their needs, and are goal directed (Katz, Blumler, & Gurevitch, 1974) to explore motivations online (see Close & Kukar-Kinney, 2010) whereas other studies identify online shoppers as either utilitarian or hedonic in nature and look at the attributes of each (Childers et al., 2001; Hung & Chun, 2010; Wang, 2010). Utilitarian shoppers are more functional and go into the information search process with specific goals in mind (Batra & Ahtola, 1991; Babin, Darden, & Griffen 1994; Hoffman & Novak, 1996; Sherry, 1990; Wolfinbarger & Gilly, 2001) They typically value convenience, control, availability of information, price, selection, ease of use, and freedom, and have no need for commitment or socializing (Bridges & Florsheim, 2007; Wolfinbarger & Gilly, 2001). They prefer their online shopping experience to be more simplistic in nature and want easy-to-find, straightforward information about the products so they can get in and get out (Mathwick et al., 2002). Males also align more with utilitarian features online and think convenience is the primary motivation for shopping online, followed by the freedom from dealing with salespeople and ability to compare prices (Hung & Chun, 2010). Freedom from dealing with salespeople is a consistent finding for both men and women across several other studies over the years (Davis, 2011; Grimm, 1997; Hung et al., 2010; Jepsen, 2007; Maher, Marks, & Grimm, 1997; Wolfinbarger & Gilly, 2001). Moreover, shoppers who are goal-oriented perceive a higher return on the amount of time they invest, the effort put forth, and money spent during their online shopping experience (Mathwick et al., 2002). In addition, survey research conducted by the Conference Board and TNS finds that males are more likely to be bargain hunters online whereas women tend to be more last-minute shoppers online (http://blog.seattlepi.com/amazon/2008/11/14/women-versus-men-online-shopping-habits/).

On the other hand, hedonic or experiential shoppers are more concerned with the enjoyment aspect of shopping (Childers et al., 2001). They prefer to see pleasing aesthetics and features that appeal to their senses and give a sense of entertainment (Mathwick et al., 2002). Hedonic shoppers find that the enjoyment they perceive from using the Internet is more rewarding than any other factor (Mathwick et al., 2002) and they also have greater intentions to purchase online than simply engaging in information search (Wang, 2010). Typically, women are more likely to be hedonic shoppers both online and offline (Babin, Darden, & Griffin, 1994; Childers et al., 2001; Holbrook & Hirschman, 1982; Yang & Lee, 2010) and many indicate they use the Internet more for social interactions such as e-mail, social media, chat rooms, and the like (Abraham et al., 2010; Pew Research Center, 2011; Swaminathan et al., 1999; Weiser, 2000; Yang and Lee, 2010). However, men who are more hedonic in nature said adventure (i.e., seeking stimulation and excitement) is the number one motivation for online shopping (Hung & Chun, 2010).

Online Behavior Based on Level of Involvement

Penn (2009) finds that 24% of consumers engage in extensive information search for lower-priced goods such as toothpaste, shampoo, and beauty products. A recent study by a popular male grooming information site, apetogentlemen.com, explored the extent to which men research goods in the personal care industry. They find that 53.4% of males prefer to research and purchase grooming products from online stores, 18.7% favor purchasing grooming products from supermarkets, 9.3% favor beauty counters, and 8.4% prefer to research and purchase from male-based salons. The number one motivating factor for this is convenience, as most male grooming Web sites offering quality products use next-day delivery as their standard shipping for purchased items (Ankutse, 2010). Another reason suggesting that closet-groomers may prefer online shopping is they do not like to be seen at the beauty counter, which is typically dominated by female products (Mintel Group, 2008). A study by Mintel (2008, p. 51) finds, "The majority of men prefer to shop for toiletries in a self-selection environment. In many department stores, men's toiletries products are sold from the women's counter. However, men tend to find the idea of buying from a beauty consultant intimidating." In addition, Ankutse (2010) states that one in four men is more at ease using the Internet for information search and purchasing grooming products because he does not have to deal with sales associates.

In terms of high-involvement purchases, such as a car, consumers who are motivated by finding the lowest price often pay less than consumers who are more motivated for finding general product information (Viswanaathan, Kuruzovich, Gosain, & Agarwal, 2007). Consumers also turn to the Internet for high-cost goods to equip themselves with knowledge they can use in negotiations. In addition, the Internet substitutes the time that would be spent at a dealership (Ratchford, Talukdar, & Lee, 2007).

Influence of Online Recommendations

Online consumer recommendations also play an increasingly influential role in online purchase decisions (Riegner, 2007; Sénécal & Nantel, 2004). Riegner (2007) finds in her study that one-third of broadband Internet users rate or review products online and 50% of broadband users indicated that at least one online source influenced a recent purchase. People aged 24–44 are the most influential online as the Internet is seen as "a way of life" (Riegner, 2007, p. 447). This group, more than any other age group, tends to create online personas to express their feelings for products and services through ratings and reviews. They are avid online shoppers, tend to be the first to purchase the latest products, and look forward to adding their opinion to review forums (Riegner, 2007).

Sénécal and Nantel (2004) find online consumer recommendations to have a greater impact on purchase decisions than input from traditional offline experts. They find products that received recommendations are chosen twice as often as ones that do not have recommendations. Sénécal and Nantel (2004) also find that the nature of the Web site the recommendation is on, whether it is a popular retailer Web site (e.g., Amazon) or a noncommercial third-party Web site (e.g., consumerreports.org), does not make a difference in the perceived trustworthiness of the recommendations. Fagerstrom (2010) also confirms that customer reviews and ratings are the number one motivators for purchasing online, more so than any other variable (sale price, in-stock status, number of steps in order process, etc.). However, recommendations for experience products (i.e., wine) are significantly more influential than those for search products (i.e., calculator; Sénécal & Nantel, 2004). Search products are a class of products that have features a consumer can observe and investigate prior to purchase whereas experience products are a class of products where the features cannot be observed until consumed (Ford, Smith, & Swasy, 1988, p. 241). In a similar vein, Huang, Lurie, and Mitra (2009) provide evidence that Web sites offering feedback on purchases (e.g., comments, ratings) actually lead to the increased likelihood of a product purchase, regardless if the product is a search or experience good.

Use of Mobile in Information Search

Information search and online shopping is becoming increasingly popular on mobile devices. A Morgan Stanley Technology Research presentation (2009, p. 22) states that "the mobile Internet is ramping faster than desktop Internet did" and from the data gathered, it is believed "more users may connect to the Internet via mobile devices than desktop PC's within 5 years" (Morgan Stanley, 2009, p 22). Smith (2011) states that 83% of American adults own a cell phone and 35% of these owners possess a smart phone with a variety of capabilities. Consumers are using their mobile devices, such as iPhones, to aid in their shopping process more each year. Leo Burnett and Arc Worldwide (2011) states that 50% of adult mobile phone owners in the United States are mobile shopping and use their device to search for store hours, collect information, get coupons, download shopping applications, read reviews, and more. Of the 50%, 40% are considered light mobile shoppers and 10% are heavy mobile shoppers. Heavy mobile shoppers like to have the latest mobile phones, actively use their phone for tasks other than placing calls, and they tend to use a shopping-related app at least once a week versus once a month or less for light users. In terms of gender, males make up 57% of the heavy users and 42% of the light users. In addition, OgilvyOne and OgilvyAction conducted a study among thousands of participants across the United States, United Kingdom, and Singapore to identify how mobile devices are being used for information search and shopping. In the study, Lange (2011) identifies the mobile phone as a third point of sale where consumers are increasingly comparing product prices and collecting information. Mobile phone users were categorized in different segments based on their usage patterns, but across the board many were found to search Google for product information, compare prices, scan products with an app, and a small percentage even purchased products from their mobile phone while in a physical store (Lange, 2011). Mobile devices are providing consumers with the "21st century version of window shopping" (Leo Burnett & Arc Worldwide, 2011, p. 4) and consumers are demanding more from retailers in terms of mobile offerings and experiences. The retailers that are incorporating mobile offerings into their media mix are attracting the attention of consumers.

Influence of Sex and Gender

Whereas sex refers to biological maleness or femaleness, gender identity refers to a person's identification with masculinity or femininity (Palan, 2001). With respect to attitudinal differences, some research suggests that men exude higher self-confidence in certain achievement situations (Maccoby & Jacklin, 1974) and have higher levels of information processing confidence than women. This means that, on average, men feel much more confident about the research they are conducting prior to a purchase. The higher level of confidence allows them to make accurate price comparisons and reduce the risk of purchasing a product they won't be happy with in the future (Noble, Griffith, & Adjei, 2006; Maccoby & Jacklin,

1974). Men also tend to pay closer attention to messages that directly affect them (Putrevu, 2001) and give more weight to positive information over negative information (Dube & Morgan, 1996). This becomes an important factor online considering consumer reviews play such an influential role in purchase decisions (Fagerstrom, 2010; Huang et al., 2009; Riegner, 2007; Sénécal & Nantel, 2004).

Researchers who advocate the multifactorial gender identity theory (Spence, 1984) argue that gender identity is determined by measuring multiple factors such as personality traits, attitudes, and gender role behavioral differences as opposed to just looking at identifying differences (communal versus agentic orientation; Noble et al., 2006). On the other hand, gender schema theory states that males and females adopt differing behaviors by engaging in gender-based schematic processing (Bem, 1981). These schemas are said to guide consumers' perceptions and influence information attainment. That is, men's schemas are linked with achievement and success to a greater extent than women's schemas (Firat & Dholakia, 1998). With regard to shopping in general, Otnes and McGrath (2001, p. 129) find "men seem to view shopping as a competition, and try to defeat retailers who reap profits from high mark-ups." Furthermore, researchers believe that men view searching for the lowest price as "a sport to be won" and a "competitive game" (Herrmann, 2004, p. 69). They also have more positive attitudes toward comparative-themed advertising than females because this allows them to show their dominance (Prakash, 1992).

Putrevu (2001) also states gender is an influencing factor in information search. Males tend to be achievement- and agentic-oriented, meaning they are motivated to achieve external goals and seek out success by being assertive, autonomous, and self-centered (McClelland, 1975; Bakan, 1966). Advertising containing agentic-related messaging tends to persuade men more than communal-based messaging. They also are much more likely to favor information they gather themselves versus information provided to them by other sources and, as outlined by the selectivity model, tend to select single cues that are highly available rather than engage in detailed processing (Meyers-Levy, 1989). This suggests that males prefer to be in a dominant role when it comes to information search. Moreover, men are considered to be selective processors and do not take advantage of all the information available to them. Instead, they make an intuitive judgment based on a select portion of all available information (Meyers-Levy, 1989; Meyers-Levy & Maheswaran, 1991; Meyers-Levy & Sternthal, 1991; Putrevu, 2001).

Men show greater confidence in purchase situations and consider impersonal sources of information and published material to be most important in their information search process (Barber, Dodd, & Kolyesnikova, 2009). However, when it comes to purchasing gifts for other people, they tend to rely more heavily on friends/family and sales clerks. This behavior is also consistent with a past study by Laroche, Saad, Cleveland, and Browne (2000), which examines the differences in male and female strategies in shopping for Christmas gifts. Laroche et al. (2000) found that males rely more on sales clerks, start their shopping process much later, purchase fewer gifts, and make fewer trips to stores than females. They also refer to sales associates for assistance when facing an abundance of information. Similarly, when men feel vulnerable in their gender identities, such as shopping for fashion and grooming products in a brick-and-mortar setting, they oftentimes defer to women and salespeople (Tuncay & Otnes, 2008b). When considering price, men who consider purchasing higher-priced items spend more time engaging in information search (Laroche et al., 2000); on the other hand, men who are more concerned about brand labels spend less time gathering information. On the whole, Laroche et al. (2000) as well as a subsequent study by Cleveland, Babin, Laroche, Ward, and Bergeron (2003) find that women engaged in more comprehensive information search than men when shopping for gifts.

In summary, although much research has examined the differences between men and women with regard to Internet usage, information search, and shopping behavior, little research has detailed the influence of gender identity on male consumers' motivations online. One recent study by Ramkissoon and Nunkoo (2010) finds gender identity to be an important factor in predicting how much consumers search for travel information. That is, femininity related to more information search as compared to masculinity. Ramkissoon and Nunkoo (2010) utilized surveys to uncover these insights, however, the current research examines the influence of gender identity from a qualitative perspective in order to examine this process more holistically. This exploratory research takes a first step in bridging the gap in the literature by investigating male consumers' online motivations and the role that gender identity, or a person's identification with masculinity or femininity (Palan, 2001), plays in this phenomenon.

Method

In-depth interviews and observations were used in order to tap into men's motivations for engaging in online information search and shopping behavior. According to McCracken (1988), the in-depth interview offers researchers several distinct advantages, including providing a picture of the individual views and interpretations of the world. To recruit informants for the study, the authors used a snowballing technique from among a network of associates. Informants who stated they engaged in online information search and online shopping behavior were chosen for participation in this exploratory study. Thirteen men, ages 20–42, with various ethnic backgrounds, were selected for the study. Out of the 13 men, 3 men in particular were chosen because they self-reported that they engaged in extensive information search even for everyday goods. Thus, the authors purposefully selected a range of engagement in online search and shopping behavior in order to add diversity to the informant pool. In-depth interviews were conducted with these men, probing into their online information search behavior, how they browsed and shopped for goods online, and how their online activities influenced their brick-and-mortar shopping. Finally, informants were asked for their conceptualizations of their gender identity and if they believed it influenced their shopping behavior. All of the interviews were audiotaped and transcribed. In addition, 3 of the 13 interviews were also videotaped for the purpose of compiling an educational video for the Chicago Interactive Marketing Association, a professional organization of interactive marketing practitioners, who sponsored this research through a research grant. Please see the chapter Appendix for demographic information of the 13 informants, including age, marital status, education, and ethnic/racial backgrounds.

Moreover, to gather additional insights, the interviewers also observed informants as they engaged in information search and browsing behavior online. Although none of the informants purchased any goods during the observations, they did articulate favorite places to search for information, detailed what factors were important to them in their search, and what ultimately may influence them to purchase a good online. During these sessions, the interviewer taped or took detailed observation notes.

To analyze the data, the authors examined the text for emergent themes and engaged in dialectical tacking (Strauss & Corbin, 1998). That is, the authors immersed themselves in the research on online information search, shopping behavior, and gender to seek out parallels and differences in the text.

Findings

Based on our exploratory analysis we find that men do engage in online behaviors that resonate with previous research, particularly with regard to utilitarian, or goal-oriented, motives. The men in this study discussed online information search and shopping as a practical tool (Rodgers & Harris, 2003). For example, as found in past research (Wolfinbarger & Gilly, 2001; Bridges & Florsheim, 2007), some male informants in this study discuss their preference for online information search and shopping due to its convenience and the availability of information not attainable in a brick-and-mortar setting. Paul explains the convenience and advantages of online shopping, "I think [online] research is huge, especially if you're going to make a larger purchase—a television, anything you are going to spend some decent money—it is nice to go online." He further states, ". . . when you go online you typically see everything that is offered, so it expands your choices." Moreover, our informants stated readily available information about product specifications and the ability to engage in price comparisons (Noble et al., 2006) built up their confidence and reduced their risk in their purchase decisions. The ability to compare prices across sites ensured that they got the best deal, even better than what they might have obtained instore. For example, Jeff states a benefit of online shopping is, ". . . sometimes you get a better deal online. You get a cheaper price and many times you don't have to pay sales tax." Other informants, such as Jordan, cited the ability to find coupon codes and other discounts online as an advantage to online shopping. Another informant, Stewart, even has a bar code scanner application on his mobile phone which allows him to comparison shop between brick-and-mortar retailers and online sources.

In addition, some men stated that online reviews are vital in their information search and in their decision to shop online (see Riegner, 2007 for a survey on the importance of online reviews). The information obtained from online review sites boosted informants' confidence in the purchase. For example, Mark explains, ". . . online, you can see other people's reviews which is a really nice thing. In store, you don't get that." Scott states, "Reviews are really big to me also. I like to read reviews on quality. . . ."

In addition, as in previous research (Hung & Chun, 2010; Jepsen, 2007; Maher, Marks, & Grimm, 1997; Wolfinbarger & Gilly, 2001), some informants express that the added benefit of online shopping is being able to avoid salespeople either because it was a hassle to deal with them or because they felt they could obtain more useful information on their own. For instance, Mark feels more at ease online. He states, "I'm the type of person that usually doesn't want salesmen to follow me around, so online is very convenient. In stores, salesmen will follow me around and it makes me uncomfortable so I don't look at things as long." George finds salespeople are not useful to him in a retail setting and appreciates the fact he can seek out online reviews. He states, ". . . you aren't necessarily going to get someone who knows everything about the product you are buying. Online you can research a lot easier . . . you can go to another site and see reviews from other people, see what they thought about the product."

Although informants stated that there were many benefits online, some men also felt that they or others were prone to overspend online versus in store. For example, Edward states, ". . . people out there, give them credit and they'll max out without realizing it. So online is probably dangerous for a lot of people." Indeed, Richard and colleagues (2009) find men tend to engage in impulse purchases online more than women given certain contexts.

There were clear utilitarian motives for men's information search and shopping behavior online akin to previous research. However, unlike prior research, the informants in this study also reveal motivations that are intricately intertwined with their gender identities. That is, the Internet serves as an identity tool and their behaviors online reinforce their sense of masculinity. For instance, information search serves to minimize risk in purchase decisions, but it also reinforces the masculine discourse of men being knowledgeable. In other words, the quest for learning and being knowledgeable is also a key component of masculinity. For example, Harris (1995) developed a typology of male gender role norms based on a study of 500 American men. He uncovered 24 norms including the scholar, or the norm of pursuing knowledge. Similarly, Tuncay (2006) finds that the quest for learning and knowledge is a key component of masculinity for Gen X men. In this vein, Jordan explains his sense of masculinity and the link to his shopping behavior online. In addition to confidence and assurance, Jordan explains, ". . . in terms of masculinity, I have an ability to think clearly, cogently, and approach each and every engagement in life with a demeanor that is . . . very informed." To him, this translates to being a smart shopper and having ". . . well-conceived notions and methodologies of how to approach shopping . . . the ability to adjust when given different information. To me, that is what masculinity means." Another informant, Christopher, directly states that to him, masculinity means ". . . being aware, being knowledgeable." Moreover, Christopher discusses how being knowledgeable and winning go hand in hand with his notions of masculinity. He states, "I like to always be winning in whatever I apply myself to." Furthermore, when asked how his gender identity affects his information search and shopping behavior online, he explains, ". . . the characteristic of always being on top. Being a leader . . . being able to apply yourself which means I am willing to do research to be able to learn as much as I can about what I am doing and what I am buying."

In addition, other aspects of the online experience were linked with masculinity. One informant, Bill, even states that the practical nature of online shopping is itself more masculine. It allows him to avoid going shopping instore, which he dislikes, and what he associates more so with the feminine. Another informant, Andy, equates masculinity with control and engaging in information search and shopping online enables him to control his time. "When I am shopping online, or when I am browsing for things online, I am doing so I can control time, something I cannot do at the store. . . . I'm in control . . ." Indeed, Harris (1995) details the theme of control as one of the gender role norms for men in American society.

Furthermore, some of the male informants in this study discuss how competition, winning, bargain hunting, and achievement drive their behavior online. Scott discusses how he engages in extensive information search, even for everyday goods, in order to find bargains. "The motivation that drives me is getting the good deal; it's all about the good deal." He also explains, "The only time that I stop researching different sites is when I believe I have found the perfect deal." Scott attributes this behavior to his manhood, "If I walk away with a good deal, then I'm that much more of a man. I went into the battle and came out victorious." He further explains, "Going back to the battle, information is your weapon."

Keith also explains how finding a product at a good price is a competition to be won. "You want to find the best product at the best price. And then if somebody is telling you they got it a $100 less than Best Buy is selling it for then you . . . want to find it cheaper. And then if they got $100 off, OK, well can you get anymore off . . . in that sense . . . it's a game . . . men are competitive . . . if I come back and I tell somebody subtly that I paid less than they did, then I win." Keith's comments add credence to the finding by Herrmann (2004) and finding the lowest price at garage sales is a competitive game for some men. Moreover, these findings resonate with some of the research on the brick-and-mortar shopping behavior of men who display achievement motivations and who viewed it as a competition to overcome retailers (Otnes & McGrath, 2001).

Another interesting theme that emerged is that men view online shopping as a way to shop for items for which they perceive they might be ridiculed during a brick-and-mortar retail shopping experience. Interestingly, although Edward states that ". . . real men would shop in an actual store, get their hands dirty, check out the merchandise, the material, the tools or whatever they are buying . . . ," he suggests online shopping might be ideal "if there was something I was afraid to shop for in person. I could hide and shop for it online." In a similar vein, Mark gives a specific example of what a man might purchase online. He states, "I think men are more comfortable buying something for their wife or girlfriend that might be intimate . . . underwear . . . online rather than going into a store . . . they can do it privately, no one is watching them. . . ." George also discusses how online shopping allows him privacy. He explains, "Well shopping online there is no one there to judge you so you can look at a little something that might be considered more feminine without being scrutinized." Indeed, Tuncay and Otnes (2008a) find in their study of male shopping behavior of fashion and grooming products in a retail setting that men experienced apprehension and vulnerability in certain contexts. For instance, they were self-conscious when shopping for goods they felt might be taboo or that would appear to others to be outside the bounds of heterosexual masculine consumption. Future research should explore in more detail how men engage in masking, or hiding or de-emphasizing the consumption behavior they display to others (Tuncay, 2005; Tuncay & Otnes, 2008a) and how the Internet serves as a tool to accomplish this.

In summary, our exploratory findings indicate that men do hold utilitarian shopping and information search motives. However, men's motives extended beyond simply utilitarian drivers. That is, men reinforce their sense of masculinity in their online behaviors by using information search and online shopping as an identity tool. Men approach information search and shopping as a competition, a venue to find value and bargains, and a place to ensure that they are knowledgeable about their purchases. Moreover, they also use it as a tool to minimize possible ridicule or discomfort they might experience if they shopped in a brick-and-mortar retail setting. Future research should explore these findings more in order to refine these theoretical linkages.

Potential Contributions and Implications

Not only is this research important in taking a first step in building theory with regard to gender identity and online information search and shopping, but it also holds implications for business. There is an increased desire for information among consumers in a wide array of contexts and for the men in this study, their gender identity plays an important role in this search process. Much research has examined sex differences (i.e., comparing men vs. women); however, little research examines how gender identity influences men online. We find that much as gender identity plays a significant role in brick-and-mortar shopping, it drives some men's behavior online as well. This finding is particularly interesting given that gender is characterized as a performance (Goffman, 1971). That is, because much of online information search and shopping is done alone and even in a private setting at home, it begs the question of at whom the performance is directed.

This research also holds implications for online marketers as they develop online strategies that cater to the male consumer. By understanding how and why male consumers seek out information as they shop online, companies can present information about their goods and services in contexts that are meaningful for male consumers. For instance, the themes of competition, coming out on top, and winning hold value to some men and can be used effectively in developing messages that resonate with male consumers. However, online marketers should tread carefully as they should not use a cookie cutter approach in targeting men, as various motivations come into play in the purchase decision. In addition, men's conceptualizations of gender vary. Thus, marketers should avoid making broad generalizations. Lastly, due to the fact that consumers continue to struggle in a troubled economy and experience consumer skepticism about traditional media, the deep engagement in online information search and shopping is likely to continue, making this an important area for future research.

Acknowledgments

The authors would like to thank the Chicago Interactive Marketing Association (http://www.chicagoima.org) for the generous funding of this research. We would also like to thank Loyola University Chicago graduate students, Avro Deb and Aaron Torres, who provided assistance on this project, and graduate scholar, Kate Policht, who assisted in transcribing the in-depth interviews.

Appendix

Description of Informants

Andy: He is a 29-year-old Caucasian married man, has a graduate degree, works for the city.

Bill: He is a 36-year-old Caucasian married man with children, with some college education, working in law enforcement.

Christopher: He is a 29-year-old Caucasian single man, college graduate, self-employed.

Edward: He is a 34-year-old single man, college graduate, working in architecture. He characterizes his ethnicity as "other."

George: He is a 31-year-old Caucasian married man, with some college education, working as a manager.

Henry: He is a 28-year-old Caucasian single man, college graduate, working in banking.

Jeff: He is a 32-year-old African American single man, currently earning his graduate degree.

Jordan: He is a 30-year-old man, engaged to be married, graduate degree, working in real estate. He characterizes his ethnicity as "other."

Keith: He is a 30-year-old Caucasian man, engaged to be married, working in sales and is a part-time college student.

Mark: He is a 42-year-old Caucasian married man, with a graduate degree, working at a university.

Paul: He is a 32-year-old African American single man, college graduate, working in finance.

Scott: He is a 20-year-old Caucasian single man, currently earning his college degree.

Stewart: He is a 25-year-old Caucasian single man, college graduate, currently in graduate school.

References

Abraham, L., Morn, M., & Vollman, A. (2010). Women on the Web: How women are shaping the Internet. Retrieved January 2, 2012 from http://www.comscore.com/Press_Events/Presentations_Whitepapers/2010/Women_on_the_Web_How_Women_are_Shaping_the_Internet.

Ahn, T., Ryu, S., & Han, I. (2004). The impact of the online and offline features on the user acceptance of internet shopping malls. *Electronic Commerce Research and Applications, 3*(Winter), 405–420.

Alba, J., Lynch, J., Weitz, B., Janiszewski, C., Lutz, R., Sawyer, A., & Wood, S. (1997). Interactive home shopping: Consumer, retailer, and manufacturer incentives to participate in electronic marketplaces. *Journal of Marketing, 61*(July), 38–53.

Alreck, P. & Settle, R. B. (2002). Gender effects on Internet, catalogue and store shopping. *Journal of Database Marketing, 9*(January) 150–162.

Ankutse, E. (2010). Men prefer to buy male grooming products online. Retrieved April 25, 2011 from http://www.apetogentleman.com/apeish/men-prefer-to-buy-male-grooming-products-online/

Asch, D. (2001). Competing in the new economy. *Europe Business Journal, 13*(Spring), 119–126.

Assael, H. (2005). A demographic and psychographic profile of heavy internet users and users by type of internet usage. *Journal of Advertising Research, 45*(January) 93–123.

Babin, B. J., Darden, W. R., & Griffin, M. (1994). Work and/or fun: Measuring hedonic and utilitarian shopping value. *Journal of Consumer Research, 20*(March), 644–656.

Bakan, D. (1966). *The duality of human existence.* Chicago: Rand McNally.

Bakewell, C. & Mitchell, V.-W. (2004). Male consumer decision making styles, *International Review of Retail, Distribution, and Consumer Research, 14*(April), 223–240.

Bakos, Y. J. (1997). Reducing buyer search costs: Implications for electronic marketplaces. *Management Science, 43*(December), 1–27.

Barber, N., Dodd, T. H., & Kolyesnikova, N. (2009). Gender differences in information search: Implications for retailing. *Journal of Consumer Marketing, 26*(September), 415–426.

Batra, R. & Ahtola, O. T. (1991). Measuring the hedonic and utilitarian sources of consumer attitudes. *Marketing Letters, 2*(June), 159–168.

Bem, S. L. (1981). Gender schema theory. *Psychological Review, 88*(July), 354–364.

Bhatnagar, A. & Ghose, S. (2004). An analysis of frequency and duration of search on the Internet. *Journal of Business, 77*(April), 311–330.

Bialik, C. (2011). Who makes the call at the mall, men or women? *Wall Street Journal,* April 23, Retrieved May 23 2011, http://online.wsj.com/article/SB10001424052748703521304576278964279316994.html

Bloch, P. H., Sherrell, D. L., & Ridgway, N. M. (1986). Consumer search: An extended framework. *Journal of Consumer Research, 13*(June), 119–126.

Bridges, E. & Florsheim, R. (2007). Hedonic and utilitarian shopping goals: The online experience. *Journal of Business Research, 61*(April), 309–314.

Brown, M., Pope, N. K., & Voges, K. (2003). Buying or browsing? An exploration of shopping orientations and online purchase intention. *European Journal of Marketing, 37*(November–December), 1666–1685.

Cai, S., & Xu, Y. (2011) Designing not just for pleasure: Effects of Web site aesthetics on consumer shopping value. *International Journal of Electronic Commerce, 15*(4), 2011, 159–88.

Chen, J., Zhang, C., & Xu, Y. (2009). The role of mutual trust in building members' loyalty to a C2C platform provider. *International Journal of Electronic Commerce, 14*(1), 147–171.

Childers, T. L., Carr, C. L., Peck, J., & Carson, S. (2001). Hedonic and utilitarian motivations for online retail shopping behavior. *Journal of Retailing, 77*(April) 511–535.

Cleveland, M., Babin, B. J., Laroche, M., Ward, P., & Bergeron, J. (2003). Information search patterns for gift purchases: A cross-national examination of gender differences. *Journal of Consumer Behavior, 3*(September), 20–47.

Close, A. G. & Kukar-Kinney, M. (2010). Beyond buying: Motivations behind consumers' online shopping cart use. *Journal of Business Research, 63*(10), 986–992.

Cyr, D., Head, J., & Larios, H. (2010). Colour appeal in Website design within and across cultures: A multi-method evaluation. *International Journal of Human–Computer Studies, 68,* (1–2), 1–24.

Davis, K. (2011). Men are the "guided missiles" of the shopping world. *Windows On,* 12(October), 4–5. Retrieved January 3, 2012. from http://www.shopper-centric.com/download?type=report&id=49.

Dholakia, U. M. (1998). Involvement-response models of joint effects. *Advances in Consumer Research, 25*(January), 499–506.

Donthu, N. & Garcia, A. (1999). The Internet shopper. *Journal of Advertising Research, 39*(May–June), 52–58.

Dowling, G. R. & Staelin, R. (1994). A model of perceived risk and intended risk-handling activity. *Journal of Consumer Research, 21*(June), 119–134.

Dube, L. & Morgan, M. S. (1996). Trend effects and gender differences in retrospective judgments of consumption emotions. *Journal of Consumer Research, 23*(September), 156–162.

Fagerstrom, A. (2010). The motivating effect of antecedent stimuli on the web shop: A cojoint analysis of the impact of antecedent stimuli at the point of online purchase. *Journal of Organizational Behavior Management, 30*(June), 199–220.

Fallows, D. (2005). *How women and men use the Internet.* Washington, DC: Pew Internet and American Life Project.

Firat, A. F. & Dholakia, N. (1998). The making of the consumer. In F. A. Firat & N. Dholakia (Eds.), *Consuming people: From political economy to theaters of consumption* (pp. 13–20). London: Routledge.

Ford, G., Smith, D., & Swasy, J. (1988). An empirical test of the search, experience and credence attribute framework. In Michael J. Houston (ed.), *Advances in Consumer Research*, (vol. 15), Provo, UT: Association for Consumer Research, 239-243.

Gefen, D., Karahanna, E., & Straub, D. W. (2003). Inexperience and experience with online stores: The importance of TAM and trust. *IEEE Transactions on Engineering Management, 50*(August), 307–321.

Goffman, E. (1971). *The presentation of the self in everyday life.* Garden City, NY: Doubleday Anchor.

Grant, R., Clarke, R. J., & Kyriazis, E. (2007). A review of factors affecting online consumer search behavior from a utility perspective. *Journal of Marketing Management, 23*(July), 519–533.

Griffith, D. A. (2005). An examination of the influences of store layout in online retailing. *Journal of Business Research, 58*(October), 1391–1396.

Harris, I. M. (1995). *Messages men hear: Constructing masculinities.* London: Taylor & Francis.

Hernández, B., Jiménez, J., & Martín, M. J. (2011). Age, gender and income: Do they really moderate online shopping behaviour? *Online Information Review, 35*(May), 113–133.

Hernández, B., Jiménez, J., & Martín, M. J. (2010). Customer behavior in electronic commerce: The moderating effect of e-purchasing experience. *Journal of Business Research, 63*, 964–971.

Herrmann, G. M. (2004). Haggling spoken here: Gender, class, and style in US garage sale bargaining. *Journal of Pop Culture, 38*(August), 55–81.

Hoffman, D. L. & Novak, T. P. (1996). Marketing in hypermedia computer-mediated environments: Conceptual foundations. *Journal of Marketing Research, 60*(July), 50–68.

Holbrook, M. B. & Hirschman, E. C. (1982). The experiential aspects of consumption: Consumer fantasies, feelings, and fun. *Journal of Consumer Research, 9*(September), 132–140.

Holt, D. B. & Thompson, C. J. (2004). Man-of-action heroes: The pursuit of heroic masculinity in everyday consumption. *Journal of Consumer Research, 31*(September), 425–440.

Hoque, A. Y. & Lohse, G. L. (1999). An information search cost perspective for designing interfaces for electronic commerce. *Journal of Market Research, 36*(August), 387–394.

Huang, P., Lurie, N. H., & Mitra, S. (2009). Searching for experience on the web: An empirical examination of consumer behavior for search and experience goods. *Journal of Marketing, 73*(March), 55–69.

Hung, H. J. & Chun, Y. Y. (2010). Gender differences in adolescents' online shopping motivations. *African Journal of Business Management, 4*(June), 849–857.

James, A. & Eaton, N. (2008). Women versus men online. Retrieved April 25, 2011 from http://blog.seattlepi.com/amazon/2008/11/14/women-versus-men-online-shopping-habits/

Jansen, B. J. & Solomon, L. (2010). Gender demographic targeting in sponsored search. *Proceedings of the 28th International Conference on Human Factors in Computing Systems* (CHI). New York: ACM, pp. 831–840.

Jepsen, A. L. (2007). Factors affecting consumer use of the Internet for information search. *Journal of Interactive Marketing, 21*(Summer), 21–34.

Juliussen, F.-E. (2010). Internet user forecast. *eTForecast.* Retrieved April 25, 2011 from http://www.etforecasts.com/products/ES_intusersv2.htm

Katz, E., Blumler, J., & Gurevitch, M. (1974). Utilization of mass communication by the individual. In J. G. Blumler & E. Katz (Eds.), *The uses of mass communications: Current perspectives on gratifications research.* Beverly Hills, CA: SAGE, pp. 19–32.

Konradt, U., Wandke, H., Balazs, B., & Christophersen, T. (2003). Usability in online shops: Scale construction, validation and the influence on the buyers' intention and decision. *Behaviour & Information Technology, 22*(May–June), 165–174.

Korgaonkar, P. K. & Wolin, L. D. (1999). A multivariate analysis of web usage. *Journal of Advertising Research, 39*(March–April), 53–68.

Lange, M. & Ellen, G. (2011). From armed to charmed: Preparing for and profiting from the new mobile-enabled point of sale. OgilvyAction Presentation. Retrieved January 3, 2012 from http://www.slideshare.net/OgilvyWW/from-armed-to-charmed-whitepaper.

Laroche, M., Saad, G., Cleveland, M., & Browne, E. (2000). Gender differences in information search strategies for a Christmas gift. *Journal of Consumer Marketing, 17*(Winter), 500–524.

Lavie, T., & Tractinsky, N. (2004). Assessing dimensions of perceived visual aesthetics of Web sites. *International Journal of Human–Computer Studies, 60*(3), 269–298.

Leo Burnett & Arc Worldwide Agency (2011). Marketing to the mobile shopper. Retrieved January 2, 2012 from http://www.slideshare.net/LeoBurnettWorldwide/marketing-to-the-mobile-shopper.

Li, H., Kuo, C., & Russell, M. G. (1999). The impact of perceived channel utilities, shopping orientations, and demographics on the consumer's online buying behavior. *Journal of Computer-Mediated Communication, 5*(June), 41–62.

Lightner, N. J., Yenisey, M. M., Ozok, A. A., & Salvendy, G. (2002). Shopping behaviour and preferences in e-commerce of Turkish and American university students: Implications from cross-cultural design. *Behaviour and Information Technology, 21*(November–December), 373–385.

Lin, J. (2007). Online stickiness: Its antecedents and effect on purchasing intention. *Behaviour and Information Technology, 26*(November–December), 507–516.

Lohse, G. L., Bellman, S., & Johnson, E. J. (2000). Consumer buying behavior on the Internet: Findings from panel data. *Journal of Interactive Marketing,* *14*(Winter), 15–29.

Lorigo, L., Pan, B., Hembrooke, H., Joachims, T., Granka, L., & Gay, G. (2006). The influence of task and gender on search and evaluation behavior using Google. *Information Processing & Management, 42*, 1123–1131.

Maccoby, E. E. & Jacklin, C. N. (1974). *The psychology of sex differences.* Stanford, CA: Stanford University Press.

Maghferat, P. & Stock, W. G. (2010). Gender-specific information search behavior. *Webology 7*(2). Retrieved May 7, 2010 from http://www.webology.org/2010/v7n2/a80.html#5

Maher, J. K., Marks, L. J., & Grimm, P. E. (1997). Overload, pressure, and convenience: Testing a conceptual model of factors influencing women's attitudes toward, and use of, shopping channels. *Advances in Consumer Research, 24*(January), 490–498.

Mathwick C., Malhotra, N., & Rigdon, E. (2001). Experiential value: Conceptualization, measurement and application in the catalog and Internet shopping environment. *Journal of Retailing, 77*(Spring), 39–56.

Mathwick, C., Malhotra, N., & Rigdon, E. (2002). The effect of dynamic retail experiences on experiential perceptions of value: An Internet and catalog comparison. *Journal of Retailing, 78*(Spring), 51–60.

Mathwick, C. & Rigdon, E. (2004). Play, flow, and the online search experience. *Journal of Consumer Research, 31*(September), 324–332.

McClelland, D. C. (1975). *Power the inner experience.* New York: Irving.

McCloskey, D. (2003–2004). Evaluating electronic commerce acceptance with the technology acceptance model. *Journal of Computer Information Systems, 44*(Winter), 49–57.

McCracken, G. (1988). *The long interview.* Newbury Park, CA: SAGE.

McKnight, D. H., Choudhury, V., & Kacmar, C. (2002) Developing and validating trust measures for e-commerce: An integrative typology. *Information Systems Research, 13*(3), 334–359.

McKnight, D., Harrison, L., Cummings, L., & Chervany, N. L. (1998). Initial trust formation in new organizational relationships. *Academy of Management Review, 23*(July), 472–490.

Meyers-Levy, J. (1989). Gender differences in information processing: A selectivity interpretation. In P. Cafferata & A. M. Tybout (Eds.), *Cognitive and affective responses to advertising,* Lexington, MA: Lexington, pp. 219–260.

Meyers-Levy, J. (1994). Gender differences in cortical organization: Social and biochemical antecedents and advertising consequences. In E. M. Clark, T. C. Brock, & D. W. Stewart (Eds.), *Attention, attitude, and affect in response to advertising.* Hillsdale, NJ: Lawrence Erlbaum, pp. 107–122.

Meyers-Levy, J. & Maheswaran, D. (1991). Exploring differences in males' and females' processing strategy. *Journal of Consumer Research, 18*(June), 63–70.

Meyers-Levy, J. & Sternthal, B. (1991). Gender differences in the use of message cues and judgments. *Journal of Marketing Research, 28*(February), 84–96.

Mintel Group, Ltd. (2008). Men's toiletries. Retrieved April 27, 2010 from http://www.scribd.com/word/removal/21566182?query=mintel+mens+toiletries

Moore, W. L. & Lehmann, D. R. (1980). Individual differences in search behavior for a nondurable, *Journal of Consumer Research, 7*(December), 296–307.

Morgan Stanley. (2011). The mobile Internet report. Retrieved January 2, 2012 from http://www.morganstanley.com/institutional/techresearch/pdfs/2SETUP_12142009_RI.pdf

Nobbs, J. & Ulrich, E. (2011). Why do men and women shop online differently? Retrieved January 2, 2012 from http://www.extrabux.com/blog/2011/07/why-do-men-and-women-shop-online-differently/.

Noble, S. M., Griffith, D. A., & Adjei, M. T. (2006). Drivers of local merchant loyalty: Understanding the influence of gender and shopping motives. *Journal of Retailing, 82*(September), 177–188.

Otnes, C. C. & McGrath, M. A. (2001). Perceptions and realities of male shopping behavior. *Journal of Retailing, 77*(Spring), 111–137.

Ozanne, J. L., Brucks, M., & Grewal, D. (1992). A study of information search behavior during the categorization of new products. *Journal of Consumer Research, 18*(March), 452–463.

Palan, K. (2001). Gender identity in consumer behavior research: A literature review and research agenda. *Academy of Marketing Science Review, 1.* Retrieved April 27, 2011 from http://www.amsreview.org/articles/palan10-2001.pdf

Penn, M. (2009). New info shoppers. Retrieved August 1, 2011 from http://online.wsj.com/article/SB123144483005365353.html

Penn, M. J. & Zalesne, E. K. (2007). *Microtrends.* New York: Twelve.

Peterson, R. A. & Merino, M. C. (2003). Consumer information search behavior and the Internet. *Psychology & Marketing, 20*(February), 99–121.

Pew Research Center (2005). New data on blogs and blogging. Press release from the Pew Internet & American Life Project.

Pew Research Center: Pew Internet & American Life Project Tracking Surveys. (2011). Who's online: Internet user demographics. Retrieved January 2, 2012 from http://www.pewinternet.org/Trend-Data/Online-Activites-Total.aspx.

Prakash, V. (1992). Sex roles and advertising preferences. *Journal of Advertising Research, 32*(May–June), 43–52.

Putrevu, S. (2001). Exploring the origins and information processing differences between men and women: Implications for advertisers. *Academic Marketing Science Review.* Retrieved April 27, 2011 from http://www.amsreview.org/articles/putrevu10-2001.pdf

Ramkissoon H. & Nunkoo, R. (2010). More than just biological sex differences: Examining the structural relationship between gender identity and information search behavior. *Journal of Hospitality and Tourism Research.* Retrieved April 25, 2011 from November 19, DOI: 10.1177/1096348010388662

Ratchford, T., Talukdar, D., & Lee, M.-S. (2001). A model of consumer choice of the Internet as an information source. *International Journal of Electronic Commerce, 5*(Spring), 7–22.

Rayport, J. F. & Jaworski, B. J. (2001). *Cases in e-commerce*, Boston: McGraw-Hill.

Richard, M.-O., Chebat, J.-C., Yang, Z., & Putrevu, S. (2009). A proposed model of online consumer behavior: Assessing the role of gender. *Journal of Business Research, 63*(September–October), 926–934.

Riegner, C. (2007). Word of mouth on the web: The impact of Web 2.0 on consumer purchase decisions, *Journal of Advertising Research, 47*(December), 436–447.

Rodgers, S. & Harris, M. A. (2003). Gender and e-commerce: An exploratory study. *Journal of Advertising Research, 43*(September), 322–330.

Rosen, D. E. & Purinton, E. (2004). Website design: Viewing the Web as a cognitive landscape. *Journal of Business Research, 57*(7), 787–794.

Schmidt, J. B. & Spreng, R. A. (1996). A proposed model of external consumer search. *Academy of Marketing Science Journal, 24*(Summer), 246–256.

Sénécal S., Gharbi, J.-E., & Nantel, J. (2002). The influence of flow on hedonic and utilitarian shopping values. *Advances in Consumer Research, 29*(January), 483–484.

Sénécal, S. & Nantel, J. (2004). The influence of online product recommendations on consumers' online choices. *Journal of Retailing, 80*, 159–169.

Sherry, J. (1990). A sociocultural analysis of a midwestern flea market. *Journal of Consumer Research, 17*(June), 13–30.

Shim, S., Eastlick, M. A., Lotz, S. L., & Warrington, P. (2001). An online prepurchase intentions model: The role of intention to search. *Journal of Retailing, 77*(September), 397–416.

Smith, A., (2011). Americans and their cell phones. *Pew Research Center*. Retrieved January 3, 2012 from http://pewinternet.org/Reports/2011/Cell-Phones.aspx.

Spence, J. T. (1984). Masculinity, femininity, and gender-related traits: A conceptual analysis and critique of current research. *Progress in Experimental Personality Research, 13*, 1–97.

Stafford, T. F., Turan, A., & Raisinghani, M. S. (2004). International and cross-cultural influences on online shopping behavior. *Journal of Global Information Management, 7*(Fall), 70–87.

Strauss, A. L. & Corbin, J. M. (1998). *Basics of qualitative research: Techniques and procedures for developing grounded theory.* Thousand Oaks, CA: SAGE.

Susskind, A. M. (2004). Electronic commerce and World Wide Web apprehensiveness: An examination of consumers' perceptions of the World Wide Web. *Journal of Computer-Mediated Communication, 9*(April).

Swaminathan, V., Lepkowska-White, E., & Rao, B. P. (1999). Browsers or buyers in cyberspace? An investigation of factors influencing electronic exchange. *Journal of Computer-Mediated Communication, 5*(December). Retrieved April 27, 2011 from http://onlinelibrary.wiley.com/doi/10.1111/j.1083-6101.1999. tb00335.x/full

Szymanski, D. M. & Hise, R. T. (2000). e-Satisfaction: An initial examination. *Journal of Retailing, 76*(Fall), 309–322.

Tilson, R., Dong, J., Martin, S., & Kieche, E. (1998). Factors and principles affecting the usability of four e-commerce sites. In *Proceedings of Human Factors and the Web.* Retrieved May 5, 2011 from http://research.microsoft.com/ en-us/um/people/marycz/hfweb98/tilson/index.htm

Tractinsky, N. & Lowengart, O. (2007). Web-store aesthetics in e-retailing: A conceptual framework and some theoretical implications. *Academy of Marketing Science Review, 11*(1), 1–18.

Tuncay, L. (2005). *How male consumers construct and negotiate their identities in the marketplace: Three essays.* Dissertation, University of Illinois Urbana-Champaign, June.

Tuncay, L. (2006). Conceptualizations of masculinity among a 'new' breed of male consumers. In L. Stevens & J. Borgerson (Eds.), *Gender and consumer behavior* (Vol. 8). Edinburgh: Association for Consumer Research, pp. 312–327.

Tuncay, L. & Otnes, C. C. (2008a). Exploring the link between masculinity and consumption. In Tina M. Lowrey (Ed.), *Brick and mortar shopping in the 21st century.* New York: Lawrence Erlbaum, pp. 153–168.

Tuncay, L. & Otnes, C. C. (2008b). The use of persuasion management strategies by identity-vulnerable consumers. *Journal of Retailing, 84*(December), 487–499.

United States Census Bureau (2010). U.S. Census Bureau e-Stats. Retrieved August 1, 2011 from http://www.census.gov/estats

Van Slyke, C., Comunale, C. L., & Belanger, F. (2002). Gender differences in perceptions of web-based shopping. *Communications of the ACM, 45*(August), 82–86.

Viswanathan, S., Kuruzovich, J., Gosain, S., & Agarwal, R. (2007). Online infomediaries and price discrimination: Evidence from the automotive retailing sector. *Journal of Marketing, 71*(July), 89–107.

Wang, E. (2010). Internet usage purposes and gender differences in the effects of perceived utilitarian and hedonic value. *CyberPsychology, Behavior & Social Networking, 13*(April), 179–183.

Weiser, E. B. (2000). Gender differences in Internet use patterns and Internet application preferences: A two-sample comparison. *CyberPsychology & Behavior, 3*(April), 167–178.

Wolfinbarger, M. & Gilly, M. C. (2001). Shopping online for freedom, control, and fun. *California Management Review, 43*(Winter), 34–56.

Wolin, L. D. & Korgaonkar, P. (2003). Web advertising: Gender differences in beliefs, attitudes and behavior. *Internet Research: Electronic Networking Applications and Policy, 13*(5), 375–385.

Xie, H., Bao, J., & Morais, D. (2006). Exploring gender differences in information search among domestic visitors to Yellow Mountain and Guilin. Retrieved April 25, 2011 from http://www.nrs.fs.fed.us/pubs/gtr/gtr_nrs-p-14/16-xie-p-14.pdf

Yang, K. & Lee, H.-J. (2010). Gender differences in using mobile data services: Utilitarian and hedonic value approaches. *Journal of Research in Interactive Marketing, 4*(2), 142–156.

Zayer, L. T. & Neier, S. (2011). An exploration of men's brand relationships. *Qualitative Market Research: An International Journal, 14*(1), 83–104.

Zhang, Y. (2005). Age, gender and Internet attitudes among employees in the business world. *Computers in Human Behavior, 21*(March), 1–10.

Zott, C., Amit, R., & Donlevy, J. (2000). Strategies for value creation in e-commerce: Best practice in Europe. *European Management Journal, 18*(October), 463–475.

Section IV

e-Tail Consumer Behavior and Online Channels

11

Exploring Hybrid Channels from the Customer Perspective
Offering Channels That Meet Customers' Changing Needs

Angela Hausman
Howard University

Marketing channels increasingly take the main stage as organizations realize the impact of channel strategy on meeting customer expectations (Gundlach, Bolumole, Eltantawy, & Frankel, 2006). In addition to managing supply chains for optimal efficiency, this involves creating a desirable mixture of delivery strategies resulting in the ultimate exchange of goods and services at the right price, in the right place, and at the right time. Evidence suggests this mixture must increasingly include both physical and virtual channels (Coelho, Easingwood, & Coelho, 2003) and requires integration between them to meet customer needs (Bendoly, Blocher, Bretthauer, Krishnan, & Vankatraramanan, 2005). Integration forms hybrid channels whereby customers interact seamlessly between virtual and physical supply chains, such as when they purchase products online but pick them up or return them to the physical store.

Providing integration between channels can be an important source of value to both organizations and their customers. Evidence of organizational value comes from studies demonstrating that consumers who use multiple channels are a larger group and consume more than single-channel customers (DoubleClick, 2004; Kumar & Venkatesan, 2005; Pastore, 2001). Studies also show integration is critical for retaining customers and creating customer loyalty (Bendoly et al., 2005; Kumar & Venkatesan, 2005; Reda, 2002). The greater satisfaction reported by customers using hybrid channels also suggests that consumers value them (Kumar &

Venkatesan, 2005). However, satisfying these customers may come at a very high price (Jupiter Research, 2002) or lead to cannibalization across channels rather than incremental sales (Fitzpatrick, 2007).

Seamlessly blending channel options into hybrid offerings is difficult and costly because of the many obstacles encountered (Rosenbloom, 2007). For instance, implementing a hybrid channel strategy requires that firms: (1) create a coordinated system that transfers information, goods, and services in the customer's preferred channel; (2) create a single brand image of the firm across channels; and (3) provide channel flexibility both before and after the sale if they wish to create value for both the customer and the firm (Neslin et al., 2006). Moreover, developing a channel integration strategy is complicated by the paucity of research that otherwise might provide guidance as to what consumers' desire from channel integration (Bolton, 2003; Gundlach, et al., 2006; Neslin et al., 2006). It is this gap that is addressed in this study.

Existing research on hybrid channels primarily considers issues of cooperation and conflict generated by integrating channels. No study considers how customers use hybrid channels or the benefits they perceive in these channels, which deprives organizations of vital information in considering whether to offer hybrid channels or how to structure these offerings. Extant research is not only limited, but definitional issues obfuscate understanding. Some studies consider only interorganizational channel integration as forming hybrid channels, for instance, a customer who visits a manufacturer's Web site to gather information informing choice and then visits a retailer to make the purchase. Hybrid channels certainly include this situation, but also include intraorganizational channels such as those between a retailer's Web site and physical store. Moreover, hybrid channels are sometimes confused with dual or multiple channels, although these are vastly different. With dual or multiple channels, a customer chooses either a virtual or physical channel for a particular transaction. And, even though the customer may choose one channel for one transaction and a different channel for another transaction, she does not have the option of combining channels in a single transaction. The relative simplicity of these channels requires no integration across them, so these are not included in our definition of hybrid channels.

Despite these difficulties and dubious profitability, firms including Circuit City (now defunct), Victoria's Secret, and Sears have spent an enormous amount of time, money, and other resources to create innovative delivery systems that coordinate their physical and online operations (Jandial, 2006; Reda, 2002). Have these outlays been a waste of precious resources as Jupiter Research (2002) concludes in their study, or are these firms ahead of the curve in developing hybrid channels, thereby pushing the envelope by creating greater customer satisfaction and obtaining a competitive advantage over firms slower to adopt a hybrid channel strategy? Part of the answer revolves around understanding whether consumers perceive value in hybrid channels and under what conditions they prefer a hybrid channel. The answer also involves understanding how consumers utilize hybrid channels, the drawbacks they see in these channels, and contextual issues influencing channel choice. These insights help firms determine whether an integration strategy is appropriate for their firm or whether to optimize their existing hybrid offerings.

This study addresses this issue through depth interviews and a grounded theory approach. The following sections review existing literature on multiple channel strategies, especially as they relate to channel integration. Following a description of the research activity undertaken, findings emanating from informants show value they perceive from hybrid channels and situations where they might use them. Finally, insights from these findings show how firms can build better hybrid channels and the potential for future studies to flesh out issues of customer value from hybrid channels. This addresses calls for understanding of consumer attitudes and contextual issues that have been raised by others researching channel strategy (Gundlach et al., 2006; Jupiter Research, 2002).

Hybrid Channels

What Is a Hybrid Channel?

The use of multiple channels of distribution is not a new phenomenon and abundant research substantiates problems that arise when firms employ multiple outlets, such as channel conflict. However, what happens when we take this further, when consumers not only have the choice of different channels, but can also combine channels across stages in the purchase process? A hybrid channel generates structural problems, however, it potentially creates value for both consumers and distributors (Payne & Frow, 2005). For instance, studies suggest that providing customers with hybrid channel options is a critical factor in customer choice between retailers, especially for young affluent shoppers (Coelho, Easingwood, & Coelho, 2003; Murphy, 2001). Not only are multichannel users a larger group of consumers than those who prefer single channel options; they also spend more, making them an important target market for online firms (Pastore, 2001; Reda, 2002).

Few multichannel firms offer hybrid channels and, although consumers may choose from multiple physical or online retailers across purchases, the customer must complete each transaction in its original channel. For instance, Toys R Us gift certificates purchased online were not valid for purchases in their physical store until Amazon.com took over their online enterprise. Other online stores do not allow product returns to their physical store. Still others are unable to coordinate marketing efforts so that it may be nearly impossible for consumers to compare offerings across channels, forcing consumers to choose one channel rather than combine them. Even worse, customers may find one offer online and a different offer in the physical store or products only available in one channel.

Integration challenges grow with social media marketing efforts that put a global spin on marketing. Use of QR (quick response) codes and location-based social media, such as Foursquare, mandate changes to existing e-commerce sites to provide a suitable user experience to customers shopping in physical stores while accessing the Web site through their smartphones. Maintaining multiple offers or pricing has similar drawbacks in a world where consumers share information about brands on Facebook and Twitter. Integration requirements will likely increase as more firms open Facebook shops offering customers the convenience of shopping from within their Facebook platform because integration between three channels is now necessary: physical, online, and Facebook stores.

Hybrid channels offer richer information than single channels and information is integrated better than multiple channels because the information is invariant between virtual and physical worlds (a situation that rarely exists in multiple channels). Hybrid channels offer other advantages. For example, allowing purchases made online to be returned to a physical store (Victoria's Secret and Sears) and allowing items purchased online to be picked up in the physical store (Circuit City and Sears; Jandial, 2006). In addition, physical stores might offer Internet kiosks to enhance search and comparison of instore options with richer online information, allowing consumers to purchase products in the store or online from these kiosks (Infosys, 2007). Hybrid channels also give consumers the ability to use information from the online store to inform purchases made in a physical store, a strategy employed by over half of all multichannel users (DoubleClick, 2004).

Service firms may also offer hybrid channels. For instance, Pizza Hut allows customers to order food online for delivery or pickup from a local store and banking firms use information obtained about customers across branches and online to present more targeted offers to customers through all channels (Buchner, 2005). In effect, consumers are able to mix channel options across the decision-making process to optimize the process for their needs, conducting search and evaluation where it is more efficient, making the purchase where it provides the most value, and engaging in postpurchase behaviors, such as returns, to limit inconvenience.

Why Use a Hybrid Channel Strategy?

Corporate value hinges on both the costs incurred in implementing integration and the value customers perceive in making purchases using hybrid options. Costs accrue in hybrid channels through information and product-sharing across organizational units and channels (Montoya-Weiss, Voss, & Grewal, 2003). Additional costs accrue because information systems must be totally hybridized, product inventories must be managed to provide sufficient inventory for both virtual and instore customers, and supply chains must be redesigned to handle the increased demands on reverse logistics efficiently (Jandial, 2006). Also, accounting systems must be able to handle the complex flow of products and monetary instruments across organizational units and channels. More important from a consumer standpoint, the structure and flow of activity in the different channels must be hybridized so that all channels consistently deliver value and provide a seamless experience (Payne & Frow, 2004). This results in large capital outlays and increased fixed costs (Neslin et al., 2006).

Achieving integration at the organizational level also involves intangible costs. Organizational structures are often rigid, separating product lines, business units, channels, and information technologies into discrete units that thwart efforts aimed at information and product sharing (Sawhney, 2002). Attempts to reduce this rigidity may be destructive for the organization as it can take the focus from the organization's emphasis on excellence and result in lower performance of organizational units (Achrol & Kotler, 1999; Sawhney, 2002). Integration can also result in loss of organizational flexibility, decreased incentives for independent intermediaries, increased requirement for expertise, and loss of quick response within the organization (Neslin et al., 2006).

As mentioned, these costs must be offset by incremental sales to consumers who see channel integration as valuable, thus increasing market share for firms offering hybrid channels and increasing customer loyalty to these firms (Reda, 2002). Emerging evidence as to whether this happens is conflicting. Some evidence supports incremental sales through channel integration. For instance, Kumar and Venkatesan (2005) contend that hybrid channels enable firms to reach customers more easily and improve customer service, which generates higher levels of consumer satisfaction and loyalty. Bendoly and his colleagues (2005) also find support for the contribution of these channels to customer satisfaction and detect a link with retention, as well. It is important to note that sales increases are the result of incremental sales rather than simply substituting sales in one channel for sales in another. For example, a study by CyberAtlas (2002) reports that channel integration increases sales in physical stores by 64%, online sales by 26%, and catalogue sales by 10%. Integration may also eliminate sales lost to a competitor when an informational site sends shoppers to an authorized dealer. By using channels in a hybrid fashion, these firms could make the sale online and distribute through the local authorized dealer, thus both ensuring the sale and compensating the local dealer, which avoids conflict.

Consumers might also funnel more of their purchases to retailers offering hybrid channels. First, they might see these channels as less risky than making purchases within a single channel (Bendoly et al., 2005). Second, they might make additional purchases when they enter the store to pick up ordered merchandise or make returns. Supporting this potentiality, Sears executives estimate that 30% of their online sales are distributed in the store, which drives a 27% increase in additional online sales and additional sales when customers come to the store to pick up their online purchases (Reda, 2002). They also believe consumers who use hybrid channels tend to interact with the company more, spend more, and come into the physical store more frequently (Reda, 2002). As consumers become more comfortable with novel channel structures and more firms offer hybrid channels, sales increases will likely climb.

Conflicting evidence questions the utility of a hybrid channel strategy. Specifically, a large-scale study suggests the percentage of the U.S. online population engaging in nonhybrid transactions across multiple channels is much larger (52%) than the percentage using a hybrid channel to make purchases (10%; Jupiter Research, 2002). This study further argues that the 10% who use hybrid channels, although they might spend more, are more deal-dependent, more price-sensitive, and consume more expensive Web site features, which squeezes online profits. This led Jupiter analysts to question the viability of channel integration strategies and to suggest caution as firms contemplate implementation. A number of retailers have also voiced doubts regarding evidence of incremental sales achieved through hybrid channels, instead believing that the channels cannibalize sales from each other, generating substantially increased costs for the same sales volume (Fitzpatrick, 2007).

Consumer Attitudes

Studies of consumer attitudes toward multiple channels are relatively sparse and those available often do not address the issue of channel integration. They do offer a starting point by suggesting factors that influence channel choice. In their review, Neslin and his colleagues (2006) found that incentives, search convenience, risk, information quality, assortment, and speed of purchase affect channel selection, as well as social and situational factors and individual differences. They also propose that physical settings, urgency, task, and mood affect channel choice. Unfortunately, none of these factors have empirical support. Other authors suggest that the shopping task affects channel choice with some shopping tasks being more utilitarian, whereas others are more experiential (Mathwick, Malhotra, & Rigdon, 2001). Search goods, according to this argument, are more appropriately purchased online, where ease of search is maximized, whereas experience goods are more appropriate for physical store purchase, as it provides more sensory input to aid product selection (Gupta, Su, & Walter, 2004).

In an organizational buying context, we find some additional insights into channel choice across multiple channels. Among consumer attitudes uncovered by these studies are frequency of purchase, frequency of returns, and cross-buying (Kumar & Venkatesan, 2005). Sharma and Mehrotra (2007) take a more experiential approach to understanding channel choice decisions, finding that firms use symbolic meaning, economic goals, need for social interaction, and schemas to inform choice. However, in addition to dealing exclusively with business customers, these studies similarly address issues of channel choice, rather than the issue addressed in this chapter, specifically using channels that are hybrid. Also, whether and how well these translate into a consumer context is unknown.

Summarizing the literature review we find two problems: (1) too many variables are hypothesized as affecting channel choice and deciding which variables to include in an emerging model is unsubstantiated; and (2) determining how consumers make decisions in a hybrid channel context is basically unstudied with the exception of a recent work by Bendoly and his colleagues (2005), which deals exclusively with channel integration in the case where individual channels experience stockouts. Whether consumers would choose a hybrid channel without this pressure is not explicated by their study.

Description of Research Activity

Despite theory and research that might illuminate the issue of channel integration, there is a lack of research on the dynamic of this purchase activity able to determine when, how, and why consumers choose this option. This questions the ability of traditional deductive studies to address the issues raised here and suggests a more exploratory, inductive study might be more appropriate. Thus, an in-depth qualitative procedure was used as it provides an opportunity to develop theory from customer perspectives, rather than imposing predetermined models on the data (Huberman & Miles, 1994).

Depth interviews are particularly good at getting at these complex evaluations, as well as developing an understanding of factors affecting channel choice across various contexts. By selecting informants across multiple sites, the study provides both greater generalizability and explanatory ability by highlighting commonalities and particular factors affecting channel utilization providing both an emic and etic perspective (Huberman & Miles, 1994). This methodology is particularly useful when the underlying theoretical framework is not well understood, as was the case here (Babbie, 1998).

Interviews used a standard question guide that broadly outlined the topics of interest to ensure adequate coverage of the topic (see chapter Appendix). Because hybrid channels cover a wide range of behaviors, the question guide focused on the situation of purchasing online then using physical stores to either deliver order items or facilitate exchange of unwanted online orders. Not only does this simplify data collection; it also reflects the hybrid channel situation that is most troublesome and expensive for retailers. Issues of information gathering online prior to purchase in a physical store were also explored. However, newer integration tools, such as QR codes and location-based social networks, were not covered, as these tools were not pervasive at the time of data collection.

Following a phenomenological focus, interviews proceeded based on the topics introduced by informants, as recommended by Thompson (1997). Thus, the interviewer allowed the informant to determine the course of the interview while still making sure to cover the broad topic areas of interest to the researchers. Questions progressed from the more general questions outlined earlier to more focused questions. Interviews were designed to draw out stories about users' experiences with channel transactions within a single channel and those utilizing multiple channels by suggesting situations where they might have used hybrid channels. Not only do these stories reflect the underlying memories of past transactions, they may influence behavioral intentions inasmuch as individuals make decisions based on these memories rather than true representations of them (Flint, Woodruff, & Gardial, 2002).

Informants were prescreened to ensure they had experience shopping at online retailers. As is customary with qualitative data collection, informants were not representative of the population from which they were drawn in the statistical sense. Instead, a purposive sampling technique was used whereby informants were selected for their variability to provide a broad range of perspectives regarding the topic of interest (Lincoln & Guba, 1985). Interviews were conducted with 30 consumers with each interview lasting between 20 and 45 minutes. Some informants were late middle age, some in their twenties, and some were in between these ages; some were homemakers, some employed in managerial or professional jobs, some were married, some single, and both men and women were represented, as well as members of major U.S. ethnic groups (please see Table 11.1). All informants were assured confidentiality. Interviews took place in informants' offices or homes and were discovery oriented.

Interviews were recorded and transferred to the computer as .wav or MP3 files for analysis by HyperRESEARCH software. This software allows analysis of actual conversations, which, unlike transcribed interviews, provides researchers with nonverbal elements to facilitate accurate interpretation and categorization. Because analysis was built on a relatively small number of online consumers, questions regarding the likelihood of reaching saturation existed. However, the highly repetitive nature of later interviews argues strongly in favor of saturation (Glaser & Straus, 1967). Trustworthiness was assessed through member checks, triangulation across researchers, and conversations with other researchers familiar with the area (Wallendorf & Belk, 1989).

Analyses of the interviews were completed using the hermeneutic procedure outlined by Thompson (1997). Analysis proceeded through a series of part-to-whole iterations: first comparing within the text, followed by comparisons across texts to identify patterns and differences across utterances (Thompson, 1997). Earlier readings of the text informed

TABLE 11.1   Informant Description

First Name	Age	Occupation	Ethnicity	Marital Status
Adam	28	Engineer	Caucasian	Married
Patti	45	Teacher	Caucasian	Married
Julie	36	Engineer	African American	Married
Matt	23	Graduate Student	Caucasian	Single
Patty	42	Clerical	Caucasian	Divorced
Jen	29	Homemaker	African American	Married
Charlene	61	Retired	Caucasian	Married
Chuck	59	Manager	Caucasian	Married
Mike	23	Graduate Student	Caucasian	Single
Josh	26	Manager	Caucasian	Single
Aaron	30	Manager	African American	Married
Cecilia	23	Engineer	Caucasian	Single
Terry	42	Laborer	Caucasian	Divorced
Dave	37	Manager	Caucasian	Married
Soliel	25	Engineer	Hispanic	Single
Sherry	36	Manager	Caucasian	Married
Kathy	42	Clerical	Caucasian	Married
Fred	52	Laborer	African American	Divorced
George	20	Student	Caucasian	Single
Karen	51	Homemaker	Asian	Widowed
Drew	37	Manager	Caucasian	Divorced
Matt	19	Student	Caucasian	Single
Ruchira	63	Homemaker	Asian	Married
Ritesh	67	Retired	Asian	Married
Aika	29	Manager	Asian	Single
Susan	29	Communications	Caucasian	Married
Jules	28	Clerical	Caucasian	Married
Deborah	52	Professional	Caucasian	Divorced
John	22	Graduate Student	Caucasian	Single
Paul	26	Manager	Caucasian	Married

later readings, and reciprocally, later readings allowed the researcher to recognize and explore patterns not noted in the initial analysis. As the analysis proceeded through iterative listening to the interviews, textual interpretations broadened, with the resultant thematic structure reflecting an understanding of the broadest text. HyperRESEARCH software is particularly useful with this type of analysis as codes were assigned to individual utterances, which were later sequenced hierarchically, as understanding developed.

Findings

Informants purchase online products frequently across a relatively small number of categories: mainly clothing, electronics, travel, and books. Many of them used multiple channel Web sites (those with both an online and a physical store), rather than pure play Web sites (ones with only an online store), except when purchasing travel. Frequently mentioned sites included Best Buy, Overstock.com, Amazon.com, Nordstrom's, and Target.

Surprisingly, informants reported few incidences of integration despite using retailers that offered hybrid channels. In fact, some appeared surprised when interviewers brought up the topic of channel integration, as if they had never considered hybrid channels an option before. Several reported using multiple channels, sometimes shopping in the store and sometimes online, but few used hybrid channels. Several did, however, use hybrid channels to inform purchases. Most commonly this took the form of using either a manufacturer's or retailer's Web site to conduct research and compare products, then making the purchase in a physical store, which is called research shopping (Verhoef, Neslin, & Vroomen, 2007). This situation is so common, informants failed to identify it as a form of hybrid channel despite the definition provided.

Similarly, Adam reported using more complex combinations of physical and virtual stores that have not been studied in extant literature. For instance, he uses the physical store for its rich experiential character. After interacting with the product in the physical environment, he makes additional purchases online to enjoy the convenience offered by this channel. This is especially evident with respect to clothing items or other experiential goods. Informants also use this hybridization to acquire colors unavailable in the physical store or additional quantities required beyond the stock available in the physical store. Thus, the consumer strategy of researching in one channel and buying in another works in both directions.

What Factors Affect Preference for Hybrid Channels?

Despite having used hybrid channels relatively infrequently, informants express attitudes related to the value they perceive from the use of hybrid channels. Based on the analysis, individual traits appear to affect the choice to use a hybrid channel, especially the need for security. Context is another factor influencing choice of hybrid channels, with product features and immediacy being especially important.

Individual Traits

Individuals differ in their preferred channels. Some like to shop in physical stores and some prefer shopping online. In each case, they stick to purchases in their preferred channel rather than integrate purchases across channels, utilizing each in a synergistic manner to optimize their transaction. For instance, some see no value in integration because they hate shopping in physical stores. For them, virtual shopping is preferred whenever possible. Consider the following:

> I would hate life if I had to go shopping at the mall. I hate driving there, the traffic, the parking. I like shopping online to avoid the mall. Purchasing online, then picking up in a store has no value, since I still have to go to the mall to pick up my orders. (Patti)

Julie says it is the same with her husband, who hates to shop in physical stores. He makes all his purchases online. Matt says this well by comparing hybrid channels with physical shopping, saying that it was "just like shopping," hence it has no value. He states that, if he were going to pick up merchandise in the store, he would just make the purchase in the store.

Others prefer online shopping, not because they hate shopping in physical stores, but because they like shopping online. It provides an element of the unexpected they find enjoyable. For instance, consider Julie:

> I like shopping online because it is like Christmas to have all the packages delivered. You never really know what's in the boxes, so it's a surprise. I usually love the surprise inside the box. (Julie)

Shopping online, visitors see representations of the items offered. Using one's imagination, one can conceive of fantastic products able to solve one's problems or offering outstanding bargains. Rather than facing a reality of tangible products with their limitations, online shopping offers a nirvana where products are imbued with spectacular attributes. The potentiality for disappointment is very real, but, as Julie states, her online purchases usually provide satisfaction by meeting her expectations. Other buyers might not make the same assessment, but Julie is satisfied.

Other informants, such as Lori, love shopping in physical stores because of the atmosphere and camaraderie involved. They avoid online shopping as it fails to enrich their lives. Shopping for them is much like big game hunting; it is a matter of pitting one's wits against a formidable foe and outwitting competitors to bring home a trophy. To the victor go the spoils. Lori sees little value in hybrid channels because they deprive her of the challenge involved in hunting for bargains in the store. Online shopping is too sterile and does not provide the sense of fulfillment she gets from trolling the stores for bargains.

Others do not express a particular preference for either physical stores or online stores instead seeing a value in hybridization. For instance, Jen, who hates to shop in physical stores because of the demands of her toddler, likes being able to order online then return or exchange online orders in the store. Patty and Charlene also mention they like the idea of picking items up in the store, because they can combine picking up an online order with other errands and eliminate the need to wait for the delivery. Waiting for delivery, in this case, is framed in terms of being tied down to meet the delivery person, rather than waiting for the item to be transported.

Hence, some people will continue to make purchases in their preferred channel versus integrating their purchases across channels. Other people, not committed to either physical or online stores, will find value in hybrid channels. This seems to be a consumer trait, inasmuch as it is not qualified by examples of when they would prefer hybrid channels. This corresponds to findings from studies of multichannel shoppers that seemed to indicate a trait aspect of the behavior (Coelho, Easingwood, & Coelho, 2003; Murphy, 2001).

H_1: Individual preference for shopping in a particular channel has a negative impact on use of hybrid channels.

Security
Probably the biggest problem solved by hybrid channels is security, according to informants. Security is framed in two ways, with informants reflecting the salience of one or the other form of security, but commonly not both. The first type of security is concern for the delivery of products ordered. For instance, Chuck discusses his fears that products ordered online may not be delivered, requiring what Mike calls a leap of faith to buy products online. He fears unscrupulous companies might accept payment and never ship the purchased merchandise. Meanwhile, Charlene discusses that products may not be safe even if shipped, as they might be

stolen if in transit or if left unattended outside the home when no one is available to accept the delivery.

But by far the biggest concern discussed by informants is the security (or lack of security) involved in making payments over the Internet. Not only might credit card information be stolen online and used fraudulently, but informants fear identify theft might result because they provide not only the credit card number, but other information that makes it easier to steal a user's identity. In reality, security problems are not limited to online purchases, however, informants state they feel safer providing payment information to a physical store.

By using hybrid channels, consumers can choose to pick up their own merchandise at the store, thus avoiding a theft that might occur in transit or after delivery. Hybrid channels also offer some deterrent for unscrupulous practices, such as not delivering purchases, by giving consumers a means of face-to-face conflict resolution and providing law enforcement the ability to enforce statutes designed to protect the consumer from fraud. Conflict resolution and statute enforcement are more difficult in pure play contexts, where it is difficult to trace the site owner to obtain satisfaction, according to informants. Chuck feels this aspect makes physical purchases more comfortable from a security standpoint. Of course, firms can easily negate all security concerns when they implement hybrid channels by allowing customers to pay for purchased items in the store rather than online when picking an item up in the physical store.

H_2: Security concerns have a positive impact on use of hybrid channels.

Product Features
The type of product purchased does have an impact on whether informants would use hybrid channels. However, the difference between utilitarian and experiential products identified by Mathwick and colleagues (2001) did not emerge. Instead, a major factor affecting channel choice is the cost of procuring products, which leads consumers to prefer the least costly option. Two channel factors affect these costs: shipping/handling charges and taxes. For instance, Josh reported he would be more likely to use hybrid channels for heavy bulky items. Although seemingly surprising given the difficulties consumers might experience when transporting these items themselves, it reflects his reluctance to pay the shipping charges incurred with home delivery, charges that often vary by weight or size. By ordering online, Josh says he is assured his purchase is available, thus negating the possibility of having to return for the item or obtaining

it from a different location, and picking up in a physical stores obviates any shipping and handling charges. Aaron concurs, stating he is willing to use hybrid channels if it helps him avoid shipping or tax charges.

Small inexpensive products also make hybrid channels more attractive. Cecilia mentions shipping costs make it prohibitive to purchase these items online because the shipping charges make up such a large proportion of the final costs. Cecilia refrains from purchasing these small items online to avoid shipping charges or waits until she has a larger order composed of several small items to make the shipping cost less onerous. She likes the idea of hybrid channels for these small items.

Other informants did not report a similar pattern of hybrid channel use, possibly because, as reported by Julie, most of the companies she buys from offer free shipping. All that has been accomplished by offering free shipping is to shift cost from the consumer to the organization, not creating value, and likely companies compensate for free shipping by offering slightly higher prices on all products. This may be one explanation for the price differential between a company's virtual and physical stores.

Other product features similarly contribute to the use of hybrid channels. For instance, Chuck mentions he uses hybrid channels to ensure fragile products are delivered intact. He feels instore pickup of online purchases is preferable because it is less likely to result in damage to the product. Without this option, he contends he faces the hassle of returning damaged products and waiting for a replacement. Similarly, Jane likes to use hybrid channels to ensure availability of her desired products, especially during the holidays when popular toys sell out quickly. By purchasing the item online and picking it up in the store she reduces the costs associated with repeatedly shopping for the desired item in the physical store only to find a stockout situation when she arrives.

The same situation happens in reverse when consumers need to return goods to the retailer, which is nearly 40 times more common for online purchases (Rhee & Bell, 2002). In most cases, consumers pay for return shipping and may also pay a restocking fee to the online retailer. Informants report two issues related to returns: the cost of shipping and risks associated with handling credit for returns. Again, informants feel hybrid channels alleviate these problems, because returns are accomplished in the physical store regardless of the channel used for initial purchase.

Patti reports she prefers to take unwanted products back to the store for an exchange or refund rather than incur high shipping costs to return them to the online retailer. Jen uses this factor to inform retail choice, inasmuch as she will purchase only from online retailers who allow returns in the store or offer free return shipping. For Charlene, the shipping costs are not the primary concern, but the intangible costs associated with packing the return and going to the post office make exchanging in the store more attractive. Terry says he still has an item he ordered online six months ago that he needs to return. He is reluctant to shop online now because he knows how difficult it is to return items purchased online and feels that he needs to take care of this return before he orders more items that will potentially require return.

Dave discusses the hassle involved in making returns also deters him from shopping online. Here he refers to issues of receiving credit for his returns or replacement products, rather than actual shipping issues. He stated he believes that problems sometimes encountered in making returns are better resolved through face-to-face interactions than online, so he prefers to buy in physical stores where he can make returns to the store. Other informants report similar problems with returns to online retailers, including return policies that are not clear or are not honored, which adds to the risk assessment associated with online purchases.

In summary, our informants' comments suggest they see value in purchasing certain types of products using hybrid channels. Specifically, bulky or fragile items, low-cost items, or items likely to require return are seen as good candidates for purchase through hybrid channels. Informants also report they do, in fact, use this to inform store choice, suggesting that organizations who offer hybrid channel options to their customers gain a competitive advantage. Returns appear especially onerous, as the consumer has to search for boxes, make shipping labels, and make a trip to the post office. Therefore, allowing returns to physical stores has the potential to increase customer perceived value in online purchase. If firms can implement only some aspects of channel integration, accepting returns in the store appeared to be informants' preferred element.

> H_3: Products that are (1) bulky, (2) fragile, or (3) low cost have a positive impact on choice of hybrid channels.

Hybrid Channel Efficiencies

Immediacy
The ability of hybrid channels to meet consumers' needs for immediacy is important according to informants. Sometimes consumers need the product immediately, psychologically, for immediate gratification, or

functionally, to meet scheduled gift exchanges or impending use. This is especially true during the holidays, where evidence suggests consumers are waiting later to place holiday gift orders (Jupiter Research, 2004). Hybrid channels maximize efficiency by providing for last-minute needs without waiting for delivery through slow direct channels and without the discomforts associated with indirect channels, such as waiting in long lines. For instance:

> If I need an item now, I might order it online then go to the store to pick it up. I do that at Circuit City because they guarantee it will be ready within 24 minutes. If I order online and drive to the store, it takes me at least 24 minutes to get there. That way I just walk in and pick up the item without having to search the shelves or stand in line to pay for it. I get it in the same amount of time, but it's less hassle. (Soliel)

Increasingly consumers use hybrid channels when ordering food or other perishable items, again without registering this as a hybrid channel because it is so common and familiar to them. With food items, not only is the item needed immediately, but informants perceive the food is fresher when they pick it up from the store rather than having it delivered. Even having food delivered uses a hybrid channel if the product is ordered online. Ordering pizza online is becoming especially common to avoid the hassle involved in phone ordering. It is also more precise because it reduces miscommunication and allows for increased customization. Hybrid food channels have the additional advantage of security inasmuch as consumers can pay the driver for purchased items or pay for them when picking up, thus obviating the need to provide credit card information online.

For instance, Sherry uses online ordering from local restaurants extensively, especially at popular restaurants where long wait times are common or to maximize utilization of her lunch hour.

> It helps avoid crowds. You go straight to the front of the line, which is a wonderful advantage, especially if you're not in their delivery zone or if it's a large order that takes a while to put together. I'd love to see more restaurants offering pick-up and grocery shopping would be so much easier if you could order online and pick up the order at a specific time, like on you[r] way home from work, rather than having to stop, pick out what you need, then wait in long lines at the checkout when you just want to go home after a long day.

H_4: Time efficiency has a positive impact on choice of hybrid channels.

Search Efficiency

Using the Internet as a research tool is ubiquitous (Infosys, 2007). Our informants are no exception, stating they use the Internet extensively for product search and comparison prior to making purchases either online or in the store. The electronic environment is particularly well suited for these tasks and bots, or other online search tools, make this task particularly efficient. Online search reduces the amount of time spent in the physical venue, according to Kathy. It also helps ensure the consumer gets the most suitable product at the most advantageous price, according to several of our informants. Online search may also uncover unknown options for satisfying consumers' needs.

The online environment alone is excellent for aiding in product search, but "things are not always what I expect in terms of size, color, etc.," according to Charlene; hence, physical stores have their place. It is also hard to get more information about the product online according to Jane, and the thumbnails do not afford a sufficient view of the product to ensure acceptability; thus, hybrid channels are perceived as a valuable tool combining ease of search with the ability to view the tangible product in the store.

Fred agrees, saying he has a particularly difficult time distinguishing the fabric from online images. George sums up how hybrid channels solve these problems when he says they afford him "the best of both worlds." He can easily search and compare products online and he could get the item quickly by going to the store, that way he could "buy what I need and get out."

Although hybrid channels are not a requisite for this type of shopping, they do solve some problems, especially when the product will be purchased in the physical store subsequent to online search. Hybrid channels, if deployed properly, link search and purchase, provide store locations and directions, and make it easy for consumers to find the same item in both the physical store and online. Standardized pricing, a common element of hybrid channels, also ensures consumers will get the product at the same price. Another advantage of hybrid channels is the ability to touch, feel, and otherwise experience goods prior to purchase. Similarly, hybrid channels link customer information so that messages and offers are coordinated seamlessly as consumers move from virtual to physical environments, which reduces customer dissatisfaction likely to result if they encounter different prices or messages across channels.

H_5: Online search efficiency has a positive impact on choice of hybrid channels.

Geographical Dispersion

Product availability is one aspect informing channel choice and informants use online channels when products are not available locally. For instance, Josh shops at Patagonia online for hard-to-find items. Similarly, eBay and other online auctions are very popular because they sell unique items. Online shopping is also common when purchasing products unavailable at local retail stores in the sizes, colors, or quantities desired. Using hybrid channels with these sites would be cumbersome because creating a convenient physical presence would be prohibitively expensive due to the geographic dispersion of these niche consumers.

Similarly, for consumers living in remote areas, the appeal of channel integration is limited. For instance, Patty finds picking up or returning merchandise in a store unappealing because she lives in a rural area and the nearest store is distant. She prefers a single channel and would not choose hybrid transactions, even if available. In congested areas, hybrid channels are unappealing, because picking up or returning to the store involves difficulties with traffic, parking, and other headaches that are common in densely populated areas.

A final example of geographic dispersion occurs in gift giving when recipients are not collocated with givers. In the context of these purchases, informants report that integration was neither desirable nor did it provide any benefit for consumer. For instance,

> I sometimes order gift items online, then have them shipped directly to my nieces or parents. It saves me a lot of time because I don't have to pick the gifts up at the store and it gets there quickly. If I haven't started buying gifts in time for Christmas and such, shipping directly means I don't have to hassle with wrapping or going to the Post Office and standing in line to mail it. (Karen)

H_6: Geographic dispersion has a negative impact on choice of hybrid channels.

Summary and Concluding Remarks

In sum, the findings suggest that channel integration might not be right for every retailer. Some factors affecting the suitability of channel integration are types of consumers, product, and shopping task, and suggest an empirical model containing consumer traits, product, shopping task, geographic considerations, and security issues. Thus, as suggested by analysts at Jupiter Research (2002), firms need a careful analysis of the integration opportunity prior to making the commitment to this strategy. This study should aid in that evaluation.

Based on in-depth interviews with online shoppers, the study finds consumers rather lukewarm to the idea of channel integration. However, once probed for specific aspects of integration, consumers are able to identify situational factors delineating when integration contributes value from when it does not. These factors are much more nuanced than those uncovered by researchers investigating multiple channel strategies, suggesting a value to this study over existing ones. Some factors mentioned are relatively unsurprising, conforming to existing theories of multichannel shopping. Specifically, few would be surprised that immediacy or variety affects the perceived value of hybrid shopping channels.

Other findings are more surprising and are thus more valuable for developing theory. For instance, the depth of feeling (negative) for shopping in physical stores is surprising, especially among female shoppers, who are often portrayed in the popular media as shopping enthusiasts. Findings show that some consumers view this type of shopping as anathema, which negatively affects the value they perceive in channel integration because integration still requires visits to physical stores. Another surprising aspect, at least on the surface, is that consumers prefer to pick up large, fragile, or inexpensive items in the physical store, the former to save shipping costs and the latter to ensure merchandise is received intact. These product factors suggest that consumers not only seek to reduce tangible costs, but the psychic costs associated with product acquisition, which informs channel choice. A subtle reading of their conversations shows informants attach a high value to the utility of shopping online, such as convenience and product comparisons, but still like the option of interfacing with a human being. Channel integration offers this combination, which appears to maximize the utility of each channel for greatest customer satisfaction.

The potential of security concerns to affect perceived value from hybrid channels is also unexpected, although not totally surprising given that the U.S. Secretary of Commerce states that this fear is the largest single factor discouraging consumers from making purchases online (Mineta, 2000). Although one could argue that physical channels represent the same security dangers as online channels, the fact remains that consumers do not appear to view the dangers as analogous. Hence, informants reinforce previously reported notions that physical retailers offer a more secure purchase option, and the ability to shift more of the buying process to physical stores as part of the hybrid channel is seen as appealing.

The shopping task also has implications for channel integration. When shopping for gifts for geographically remote friends and relatives, channel integration is not seen as valuable. However, when looking at other ways that hybrid channels might provide value to the gift giver or the recipient, value emerges. Although the giver might not see value in hybrid channels the receiver might gain value through an ability to return unappealing gifts to the physical store and acquire something more desirable.

Managerial Implications

Firms obtain value from hybrid channels, at least in part, when these channels function to increase sales either through motivating incremental sales with each purchase (as reflected in Sears reports that consumers make additional purchases when they come to the physical store to pick up online items) or through informing retail choice. Our study only suggests that the former functions in hybrid channels; however, we find consumers use the availability of hybrid channels in their choice of retailers even though they may not use this consciously. Consumers use factors influenced by channel integration, such as ease of returns, security, and flexibility, indirectly to choose retailers, especially because the absolute differences in product offerings and prices are often seen as inconsequential (Jandial, 2006). However, some consumers and some situations do not seem appropriate targets for channel integration, a factor that must be considered when determining channel strategy.

The study also suggests types of products and situations where having a hybrid channel integration strategy would likely provide the most benefit to the firm, such as for large or fragile products, for product returns, or around the holidays. Not only do these products and situations benefit the retailer by informing retail choice; they also may provide an additional benefit by reducing operating costs for the firm. A number of firms feel obligated to offer free shipping to compete in today's online marketplace where such offers are common, thus using hybrid channels has the organizational advantage of providing a more efficient way to get products to consumers than providing free shipping: by having them pick them up from their local retail store. This greatly reduces the shipping costs incurred by the firm, which replaces shipping directly to the consumer at a higher cost, with the cost of shipping in bulk to the retailer at a much lower cost. The same argument works in reverse when talking about returns, where customers expect firms to pay reverse shipping costs, as well as provide return labels, boxes, and other associated items. When returns are made to the local retail store, undamaged items can be resold to physical customers and unsaleable returns from the store can be accumulated to return at a lower cost than when shipped individually.

Channel integration also offers benefits for companies who currently do not directly provide purchase options for their products, instead operating informational Web sites that facilitate product search. Currently, these Web sites send prospects to an authorized dealer rather than make the sale online in efforts to avoid channel conflict. Once at the dealer, however, the salesperson may convince the prospect to purchase a competitor's product. By integrating the channel, these firms could sell the product online then send the customer to the authorized dealer for fulfillment. Channel conflict would be avoided by sharing profits from the sale with the fulfilling retailer.

These processes highlight the importance of information sharing across organizational units in order to provide value to customers successfully. Customers also expect information sharing to ensure proper credit for returns and ensure products purchased online are ready for pickup when expected. They expect that pricing and other information will be identical across all sources. This requires organizations to reflect inventory levels accurately at each physical store in their online database so that customers can be confidently directed to a local store with sufficient inventory to fulfill the purchase. The organization has to share information regarding promotions and discounts offered through all media such that, regardless of which channel the consumer chooses, he sees the same products and the same prices. Firms have to make coordinated product, pricing, and inventory information available to customers in a variety of ways: online, through direct media, and through instore kiosks. They have to expand and secure options for enabling gift exchanges. Firms also have to expand electronic recordkeeping to allow easy returns of items purchased online, especially those received as gifts. This requires not only a strong information technology (IT) commitment, but also a management and culture that breaks down functional silos and rewards collaboration. Increasingly, competitive advantage will be a function of not only having integration capabilities, but the speed at which information can move across channels to satisfy customer needs. Ineffectively or inefficiently implementing channel integration might represent less profitability than not offering hybrid channels at all. Thus, not all firms might be ideal candidates for channel integration.

The study suggests additional ways that firms might manage their hybrid channels to increase sales. For instance, consumers may strain to see value in hybrid channels when they still face traffic, parking, and other hassles in obtaining purchases made online from the local store. Firms might optimize their hybrid channels by allowing pickup before or after store hours without incurring a major expense inasmuch as only one department has to remain functional, not the entire store. Furthermore, future construction and remodeling might incorporate drive-through options for pickup and return of online purchases. This has worked effectively for restaurants who offer curbside service where waitstaff bring orders to your vehicle without the hassle of parking (as spaces are reserved) or getting out of your car.

Similarly, firms might allow customers to place orders online, but suspend payment until the customer picks up the item inasmuch as security concerns severely hamper online sales. Unfortunately, few firms offer this option fearing this might result in inefficiencies when customers fail to pick up the item (Jandial, 2006). Allowing customers to pay for items in the store might open up entirely new segments of shoppers who currently avoid online shopping due to these security fears.

Finally, firms need to advertise their channel options more broadly. As noted in the presentation of findings, informants required probing to see situations involving hybrid channels despite seeing great value in them when instances were pointed out. They also do not appear to appreciate the availability of hybrid options for satisfying their various needs. Firms who offer hybrid channels incurred substantial costs in making them available to consumers. They need to capitalize on this investment through better advertising to position their hybrid channels as solving some of the consumer problems mentioned by our informants. Based on the comments of our informants, it appears that using channels interchangeably requires some degree of behavioral change and some learning. This suggests a more intense advertising campaign with subtly different messages than firms might currently use to support any of their multiple channels independently.

Limitations and Future Research

The data are qualitative, which has the advantages mentioned earlier, but also has some disadvantages. Specifically, the data reflect how a group of online consumers construct experiences surrounding shopping to reflect their personalized meanings and abstract relationships, which may not be generalizable in the traditional sense (Thompson, 1997). Certainly, future research will be necessary to test these understandings among a wider population. Hypotheses offer a starting point in discovering more about how consumers view hybrid channels and testing the generalizability of these findings.

In addition, to ease comparisons across informants, we investigated a relatively limited number of hybrid channel options. For instance, we really did not delve into issues of how catalogues fit within the hybrid channel or how retailers with strongly established catalogue businesses have fared against newer hybrid channel options. We also did not investigate contentions made by firms employing hybrid channels that consumers make additional purchases when they visit the physical store to make returns of online purchases or pick up items purchased online. Because this may greatly increase the value of channel integration for firms, these aspects warrant future study. Similarly, because most hybrid channels are currently owned by a single firm (e.g., Sears), we have not really explored the opportunity that might be available through blending the hybrid channel across independent firms.

Logically, a next step in elaborating our understanding might involve a quantitative assessment of various factors potentially affecting consumer value, elaborating on hypotheses from this study. An experiment creating scenarios that builds on our informants' comments might be just such a study. This type of study might generate further support for our findings, but additionally provide a more nuanced understanding of how pervasive the associations between perceived value and individual or situational aspects of channel integration. With this type of data, a calculation of the expected return from channel integration across various contexts to enable a cost/benefit analysis may help firms determine the level to which they want to commit to channel integration.

Appendix

Question Guide

1. What kinds of things do you buy online, and where do you shop online?
2. What are some things you like and dislike about these online shopping experiences?
3. How often do you return things purchased online, and do you find returning items purchased online to be a hassle?

4. What advantages do you see in being able to pick up an item bought online in a store versus having to wait for it to be delivered?

5. Have you ever done this, and what was that experience like?

6. Are there certain occasions when you would be more likely to pick up an online purchase in the store, for example, for a gift, for personal use, at holiday time, or others?

7. Are there other ways you use Web sites to help make purchases in the store?

8. Do you ever shop in the store and then purchase products online?

References

Achrol, R. S. & Kotler, P. (1999). Marketing in the network economy. *Journal of Marketing, 63,* 146–163.

Babbie, E. R. (1998). *The practice of social research* (8th edition). Belmont, CA: Wadsworth.

Bendoly, E., Blocher, J. D., Bretthauer, K. M., Krishnan, S., & Vankatraramanan, M. A. (2005). Online/ in-store integration and customer retention. *Journal of Services Research, 7*(4), 313–327.

Bolton, R. N. (2003). From the editor. *Journal of Marketing, 67,* 1–3.

Buchner, A. (2005). Observations from the Net.Finance conference. Retrieved July 2007 from http://weblogs.jupiterresearch.com/analysts/schatsky/archives/008059.html

Coelho, F., Easingwood, C. J., & Coelho, A. (2003). Exploratory evidence of channel performance in single vs multiple channel strategies. *International Journal of Retail and Distribution Management, 31,* 561–573.

CyberAtlas (2002). Consumers make use of multiple retail channels. *CyberAtlas.* Retrieved April 25, 2007 from http://cyberaltals, internet.com/ markets/retailing/

DoubleClick (2004). Multi-channel shopping study - Holiday 2003. *DoubleClick, Inc.* Retrieved March, 2007 from http://www.doubleclick.com/us/knowledge_central/research/email_solutions

Fitzpatrick, M. (2007). The seven myths of channel integration. *Chief Marketer.* Retrieved July 2007 from http://chiefmarketer.com/multi_channel/myths_integration_1001/index.html

Flint, D. J., Woodruff, R. B., & Gardial, S. F. (2002). Exploring the phenomenon of customers' desired value change in a business-to-business context. *Journal of Marketing, 66*(4), 102–117.

Glaser, B. & Strauss, A. (1967). *The discovery of grounded theory: Strategies for qualitative research.* Chicago: Aldine.

Gundlach, G. T., Bolumole, Y. A., Eltantawy, R. A., & Frankel, R. (2006). The changing landscape of supply chain management, marketing channels of distribution, logistics, and purchasing. *Journal of Business & Industrial Marketing, 21*(7), 428–438.

Gupta, A., Su, B.-c., & Walter, Z. (2004). An empirical study of consumer switching from traditional to electronic channels: A purchase decision perspective. *International Journal of Electronic Commerce, 8*, 131–161.

Huberman, M. A. & Miles, M. B. (1994). Data management and analysis methods. In N. K. Denzin & Y. S. Lincoln (Eds.), *Handbook of qualitative research.* Thousand Oaks, CA: SAGE, pp. 428–444.

Infosys (2007). Retail multi-channel integration: Delivering a seamless customer experience. Retrieved July 2007 from http://www.infosys.com/industries/retail-distribution/white-papers/InfosysMCIWhitePaperfinal.pdf

Jandial, A. (2006). Click and mortar: Achieving multi-channel integration. *Infosys,* Retrieved July 2007 from http://www.infosys.com/industries/retail-distribution/white-papers/achieving-multi-channel-integration.pdf

Jupiter Research (2002). Redefining the online retail consumer. Retrieved July 2007 from http://www.jupiterresearch.com/bin/item.pl/research:vision/107/id=89107

Jupiter Research (2004). Online channel pushes limits of last-minute shopping. Retrieved July 2007 from http://www.jupiterresearch.com/bin/item.pl/research:concept/107/id=94717

Kumar, V. & Venkatesan, R. (2005). Who are the multichannel shoppers and how do they perform? Correlates of multichannel shopping behavior. *Journal of Interactive Marketing, 19*(2), 44–62.

Lincoln, Y. S. & Guba, E. G. (1985). *Naturalistic inquiry.* Beverly Hills, CA: SAGE.

Mathwick, C., Malhotra, N., & Ridgon, E. (2001). Experiential value: Conceptualization, measurement, and application in the catalog and internet shopping environment. *Journal of Retailing, 77*, 39–56.

Mineta, N. Y. (2000). *Opening statement at online privacy technologies workshop and technology fair,* Washington, DC: U.S. Department of Commerce. Retrieved May 2006 from http://www.ntia.doc.gov/ntiahome/privacy/900workshop/mineta91900.htm

Montoya-Weiss, M. M., Voss, G. B., & Grewal. D. (2003). Determinants of online channel use and overall satisfaction with a relational, multichannel service provider. *Journal of the Academy of Marketing Science, 31*(4), 448–458.

Moriarty, R. T. & Moran, U. (1990). Managing hybrid marketing systems. *Harvard Business Review,* November–December, 146–155.

Murphy, D. (2001). How to exploit all forms of contact: companies need to increase their multi-channel CRM capacity. *Marketing* (May 17), 31.

Neslin, S. A., Grewal, D., Leghorn, R., Shankar, V., Teerling, M. L., Thomas, J. S., & Verhoef, P. C. (2006). Challenges and opportunities in multichannel customer management. *Journal of Service Research, 9*(2), 95–112.

Pastore, M. (2001). Multichannel shoppers key to retail success. *CyberAtlas*. Retrieved April 25, 2007 from http://cyberatlas, internet.com/markets/retailing/

Payne, A. & Frow, P. (2005). A strategic framework for customer relationship management. *Journal of Marketing, 69*(October), 167–176.

Reda, S. (2002). Active multi-channel shoppers may be a liability, less loyal than other on-line shoppers. *Store* (September), 78–80.

Rhee, H. & Bell, D. R. (2002). The inter-store mobility of supermarket shoppers. *Journal of Retailing, 78*(4), 225–237.

Rosenbloom, B. (2007). Multi-channel strategy in business-to-business markets. *Industrial Marketing Management, 36*, 4–9.

Sawhney, M. (2002). Don't harmonize, synchronize. *Harvard Business Review, 79*, 101–108.

Sharma, A. & Mehrotra, A. (2007). Choosing an optimal channel mix in multi-channel environments. *Industrial Marketing Management, 36*, 21–28.

Thompson, C. J. (1997). Interpreting consumers: A hermeneutical framework for deriving marketing insights from the texts of consumers' consumption stories. *Journal of Marketing Research, 34*(November), 438–455.

Van Birgelen, M., de Jong, A., & de Ruyter, K. (2006). Multi-channel service retailing: The effects of channel performance satisfaction on behavioral intentions. *Journal of Retailing, 82*(4), 367–377.

Verhoef, P. C., Neslin, S. A., & Vroomen, B. (2007). Multichannel customer management: Understanding the research-shopper phenomenon. *International Journal of Research in Marketing, 24*, 129–148.

Wallendorf, M. & Belk, R. W. (1989). Assessing trustworthiness in naturalistic consumer research. In E. C. Hirschman (Ed.), *Interpretive consumer research, proceedings from the 1989 conference*, Valdosta, GA: Association for Consumer Research, pp. 69–84.

12

Consumer Trust and Loyalty in e-Tail

Cuiping Chen
University of Ontario Institute of Technology

Matthew O'Brien
Bradley University

Lin Guo
University of New Hampshire

Trust is regarded as salient in the consumer and e-tailer exchange relationship because there are high risks involved in transactions with e-tailers and online consumers and e-tailers depend on each other to realize their respective interests (Chen & O'Brien, 2005). Literature review of current online business-to-consumer (B2C) trust studies indicates that they still reflect the early mentality of doing business online, which, in essence, is driven by discrete transactions (Urban, Amyx, & Lorenzon, 2009). Guided by the old mentality, online retailers were fighting for hits, click-throughs, eyeballs, number of visitors, number of shoppers, and pure purchase volume (Bain & Company and Mainspring, 2000; Reichheld, Markey, & Hopton, 2000). With marketing strategies for e-tailers switching to retaining customers, studies are needed to investigate how trust in an e-tailer influences a consumer's decision to remain with or be loyal to the e-tailer.

In addition, the trust literature in marketing has been focusing on identifying the factors that engender trust in interorganizational or consumer relational exchanges (Atuahene-Gima & Li, 2002) and emphasizing the influence of trust on constructs central to building long-term relationships with customers, such as commitment (Dwyer, Schurr, & Oh, 1987; Garbarino & Johnson, 1999; Morgan & Hunt, 1994) and loyalty (Berry, 1993; Sirdeshmukh, Singh, & Sabol, 2002; Sirdeshmukh, Brei, & Singh, 2003). To our knowledge, few studies have examined the factors that moderate the effect of trust on its outcome variables. Moderating factors play an important role in understanding how trust actually affects a person's risk-taking action (Mayer, Davis, & Schoorman, 1995). Even though the level of trust may be constant, the specific outcomes of trust will be determined by moderating factors. Therefore, it is very important to determine the moderating factors and how they affect the relationships between trust and its outcomes. Mayer et al. (1995) conceptually proposed perceived risk in the situation as the moderating variable between trust of one individual for another and risk-taking behaviors in two individuals' relationship in the organizational behavior settings. No study has yet empirically tested the moderators of the effect of trust on its outcomes, particularly in the online retail context. To fill this gap, this study aims to examine theoretically and test empirically the moderators of trust on its outcome variables.

To achieve the objectives outlined, this study proposed a conceptual framework and empirically tested it using a large-scale sample randomly selected from U.S. national online consumers. As a result, this study contributes to trust literature by identifying the moderators of the effect of trust on its outcomes. It also adds to online B2C trust studies by providing a deeper understanding of trust mechanisms in consumer–e-tailer exchanges.

Conceptual Development and Research Hypotheses

This study draws mainly upon trust literature and develops a conceptual model of consumer trust in an e-tailer that identifies future intentions and consumer loyalty as the consequences of trust and environmental uncertainty and competitive alternatives as the key moderators of the relationships between trust and its consequences. The model is presented in Figure 12.1. Conceptualization of consumer trust in an e-tailer and the research hypotheses underlying the relationships in the model are described in the following sections.

Conceptualization of Consumer Trust in an e-Tailer

The study of trust has been rooted in economics, social psychology, and sociology (Rousseau, Sitkin, Burt, & Camerer, 1998). It has been extended to other disciplines such as marketing, management, accounting, information systems, e-business, and so on (Shankar, Urban, & Sultan, 2002).

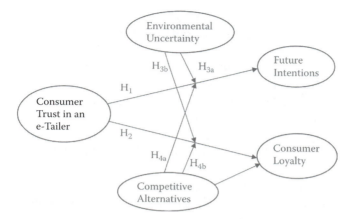

Figure 12.1   Moderators of consumer trust in an e-tailer.

In marketing, trust has been studied primarily in the context of relational exchanges (i.e., relationship marketing) either between a buyer and a seller (Doney & Cannon, 1997; Ganesan, 1994; Ganesan & Hess, 1997; Lusch, O'Brien, & Sindhav, 2004; Moorman, Deshpande, & Zaltman, 1993; Moorman, Zaltman, & Deshpande, 1992; Morgan & Hunt, 1994) or between a consumer and a firm (Garbarino & Johnson, 1999; Singh & Sirdeshmukh, 2000; Sirdeshmukh, Singh, & Sabol, 2002). This research stream emphasizes the influence of trust on constructs central to building long-term relationships with customers, such as commitment (Dwyer, Schurr, & Oh, 1987; Garbarino & Johnson, 1999; Lusch et al., 2004; Morgan & Hunt, 1994), long-term orientation (Ganesan, 1994), propensity to stay in a relationship (Anderson & Weitz, 1989), and loyalty (Berry, 1993; Sirdeshmukh et al., 2002; Sirdeshmukh et al., 2003), and focuses on identifying the factors that engender trust in interorganizational relational exchanges or consumer relational exchanges (Atuahene-Gima & Li, 2002) using either the psychological approach, the economic approach, or the two combined (Singh & Sirdeshmukh, 2000).

Definition of Trust
Trust has been defined in various ways across disciplines. For example, it has been defined as the belief by one party that another party will act in a predictable way (Luhmann, 1979), "the willingness to be vulnerable to the actions of another party" (Mayer et al., 1995), and a willingness to depend on another party in whom one has confidence (Garbarino & Johnson, 1999; Morgan & Hunt, 1994; Moorman et al., 1992, 1993; Sirdeshmukh

et al., 2002) regarding credibility and benevolence (Doney & Cannon, 1997; Ganesan, 1994; Ganesan & Hess, 1997; Singh & Sirdeshmukh, 2000). However, when examining trust from a cross-disciplinary perspective, Rousseau et al. (1998) found that scholars from different disciplines actually agree fundamentally on the definition of trust. "Confident expectations" and "a willingness to be vulnerable" are identified as the fundamental elements of definitions of trust, regardless of the underlying discipline. By integrating common dimensions from various disciplines, Rousseau et al. (1998) developed a widely held definition of trust: "Trust is a psychological state comprising the intention to accept vulnerability based on positive expectations of the intentions or behavior of another" (Rousseau et al., 1998, p. 395). In essence, trust is psychological, which is the root assumption about trust across disciplines. Trust is not a choice or a behavior (Mayer et al., 1995; Rousseau et al., 1998), but a psychological state that can cause, or result from, particular human choices or behaviors. Trust implies a willingness to be vulnerable, but with an expectation or a feeling of confidence that one can depend on the other party (Rousseau et al., 1998). There is an expectation that the other party will act not opportunistically but with goodwill.

By applying this definition of trust to the consumer–e-tailer relationship in the current study, the researchers define trust as a consumer's psychological state comprising the consumer's intention to accept vulnerability based upon his or her positive expectations of the intentions or behavior of an e-tailer. A consumer's trust in an e-tailer is specified as the unit of analysis for this study and it is termed "consumer trust in an e-tailer."

Relevance of Consumer Trust

Trust does not always exist in a relationship. There are two necessary conditions for trust to emerge: risk and interdependence (Rousseau et al., 1998, p. 395). Risk, defined as "the perceived probability of loss," is one condition regarded as essential for trust to arise. Risk is requisite to trust (Mayer et al., 1995). Trust only emerges in a risky situation, and would not exist in a situation where actions could be undertaken with complete certainty and no risk. Interdependence, the second condition needed for trust to arise, means that "the interests of one party cannot be achieved without reliance upon another" (Rousseau et al., 1998).

In the consumer–e-tailer exchange relationship, trust is relevant because it is risky for a consumer to conduct transactions with an e-tailer and online consumers and e-tailers need to depend on each other to realize their respective interests (Chen & O'Brien, 2005). The high risks involved in transactions with an e-tailer come from two sources: the uncertainty involved in the general online transacting environment (i.e., environmental uncertainty) and the uncertainty regarding whether an e-tailer intends to and will be able to perform appropriately (i.e., behavioral uncertainty).

The online transaction environment is highly uncertain because it carries the following characteristics: (1) it uses an open technological infrastructure (i.e., the Internet) for transactions (Pavlou, 2002); (2) the technological structures it relies on are unstable because the Internet and Internet-related technologies are still new (McKnight, Choudhury, & Kacmar, 2002); (3) the protective institutional (i.e., legal, governmental, contractual, and regulatory) structures supporting it are still slowly arriving; and (4) it is impersonal in nature, as opposed to the face-to-face transactions with which consumers are familiar (Pavlou, 2002). For example, when information is transmitted on the Internet, it could be intercepted by unintended parties or lost due to the instability of the technological structures. When those problems occur for a consumer, there are no strong institutional systems in place to protect her interests. In addition, the impersonal nature of the online environment creates many other disadvantages for online shopping, such as the fact that consumers cannot try the merchandise prior to purchase, and there are delays in delivery for physical products. These disadvantages create more risks for consumers to shop and purchase online. For the above reasons, it is perceived as risky for a consumer to conduct personal business in an online environment.

Behavioral uncertainty also creates risks for a consumer to do business online. Behavioral uncertainty comes from two sources: an e-tailer's opportunistic behavior and its inconsistent ability. Given an opportunity, an e-tailer may unscrupulously seek to serve its self-interests by taking advantage of its customers (Williamson, 1981). For example, an e-tailer may misuse a customer's personal information for its own interests (e.g., it may sell customer information for a profit); it may purposely manipulate information on the Web (in order to attract customers) so that the information inaccurately reflects reality, and it may bill a customer for items that are out of stock. An e-tailer's potential opportunistic behavior adds even more risks to the consumer in an online transaction.

The potential of an e-tailer's inability to manage its business online consistently comprises the other source of an e-tailer's behavioral uncertainty. An e-tailer may not be capable of consistently managing its business online well, despite its intentions. For example, an e-tailer may lack the technological ability to the extent that the system may "crash" when a consumer is doing business using it; an e-tailer may not have the management ability to fulfill all promises made to customers, such as the promise of on-time delivery of physical products. Like the potential for opportunistic behavior, the potential of an e-tailer's inconsistent ability makes a consumer's transacting with it even more risky.

Although there are risks involved in transacting with an e-tailer, consumer trust will not arise if online consumers do not rely on e-tailers to secure the goods or services they need in the ways they want. Online consumers could avoid transacting with e-tailers by resorting to non-Internet retailers, but they do not. In fact, online consumers rely upon e-tailers to get what they want. Why? The answer is that e-tailers offer many unique advantages that are not provided by other types of retailers, including lower prices, unique products, easy access to rich information, and, particularly, no location barriers or time limits for transacting (Silverhart, 2002; Wind & Mahajan, 2002). In fact, online consumers can reach e-tailers 24 hours a day, seven days a week. They can transact with e-tailers wherever and whenever they want without confronting salespeople. By eliminating the barriers of time and distance for transactions, e-tailers greatly reduce transaction costs for consumers.

Online consumers' dependence on e-tailers, together with the risks involved in the consumer–e-tailer relationship, creates the need for trust for consumers to engage in transactions with e-tailers. Accordingly, consumer trust is significant in the consumer–e-tailer relationship.

Consequences of Consumer Trust in an e-Tailer

As discussed above, risk creates an opportunity for trust to arise, which in turn will lead to risk-taking behaviors (Mayer et al., 1995; Rousseau et al., 1998), which "can occur only in the context of a specific, identifiable relationship with another party" (Mayer et al., 1995, p. 725). In other words, the level of trust will influence the amount of risk that a party is willing to take in its relationship with another party. Additionally, the specific form of the risk-taking depends upon the situation in which the two parties are involved (Mayer et al., 1995). For example, in consumer–firm relational exchanges, a consumer's trust in a firm affects the consumer's commitment to his relationship with the firm (Garbarino & Johnson, 1999), loyalty toward the firm (Berry, 1993; Singh & Sirdeshmukh, 2000; Sirdeshmukh et al., 2002; Sirdeshmukh,

Brei, & Singh, 2003), and future intentions toward the firm (Garbarino & Johnson, 1999). In buyer–seller interorganizational relational exchanges, a buyer firm's trust of a supplier firm influences the buyer's commitment to its relationship with the supplier (Dwyer et al., 1987; Morgan & Hunt, 1994; Lusch et al., 2004), the buyer's choice of supplier for a purchase (Doney & Cannon, 1997), the buyer's anticipated future interaction with the supplier, and the buyer's long-term orientation toward the supplier (Ganesan, 1994). Even though the form of risk-taking depends upon the situation, the amount of trust for the other party will affect how much risk a party will venture in the relationship. In the consumer and e-tailer exchange relationship, after a consumer has some transactional experience with an e-tailer, from the consumer's perspective, the risk-taking behavior in the relationship concerns continuing doing business with the e-tailer. In this study, two variables are used to capture a consumer's relational continuance with an e-tailer: future intentions and loyalty, with loyalty involving a deeper relationship and more risks.

Role of Trust in Future Intentions

In this study, future intentions are defined as a consumer's willingness to engage in future interactions with an e-tailer. The proposed link between trust and consumers' future intentions is also supported by global evaluations theory. According to this theory, global evaluations (e.g., customer satisfaction with a firm, perceptions of service quality of a firm, trust of a firm, commitment toward a firm, and perceived value of a firm, etc.) guide consumer decision making with respect to a marketing organization (Garbarino & Johnson, 1999). As a global evaluation, consumer trust in an e-tailer guides a consumer's decision making with respect to an e-tailer. In terms of consumer decision making, the most frequently studied construct in the research of global evaluations is a consumer's future behavioral intentions (Cronin & Taylor, 1992; Garbarino & Johnson, 1999; Ostron & Iacobucci, 1995; Parasuraman, Zeithaml, & Berry, 1994). Zeithaml, Berry, and Parasuraman (1996) emphasize the importance of measuring future intentions of customers to evaluate their potential to remain with, or defect from, an organization. Therefore, it is posited that consumer trust in an e-tailer positively influences a consumer's future intentions toward the e-tailer.

Prior online trust studies also suggest that online trust has a positive effect on consumer behavioral intentions (Shankar et al., 2002; Yoon, 2002; Bart, Shankar, Sultan, & Urban, 2005). Behavioral intentions may include willingness to visit a Web site, browse (or shop around), register at a Web site, buy in an electronic store, abandon a Web site, and return to a Web site (Bart et al., 2005). Empirical evidences from Shankar et al. (2002) and Bart et al. (2005) support that trust of a Web site positively affects consumer's behavioral intentions. Pan, Shankar, and Ratchford (2002) find that online trust had a positive impact on Web site traffic and visits to such Web site categories as gifts, flowers, and computer hardware. Jarvenpaa, Tractinsky, and Vitale (2000) and Yoon (2002) demonstrate that trust in a Web site positively influenced the willingness to buy in an electronic store. Therefore, the researchers propose the following:

> H₁: Consumer trust in an e-tailer positively influences a consumer's future intentions toward the e-tailer.

Role of Trust in Loyalty

Consumer loyalty toward an e-tailer is defined as a consumer's favorable attitude toward an e-tailer that results in repeat purchase intentions toward the e-tailer (Assael, 1992; Keller, 1993; Jacoby & Chestnut, 1978; Oliver, 1997; Srinivasan, Anderson, & Ponnavolu, 2002). The proposed relationship between consumer trust and loyalty is also supported by social exchange theory. According to this theory, both parties to the exchange are motivated to provide value to the other party commensurate with the value gained (Sirdeshmukh et al., 2002). Therefore, consumers are likely to reciprocate an e-tailer delivering social relational benefits: trust (intrinsic value) with friendship (noninstrumental value) or repeat purchase (instrumental value). Increments in consumer trust increase the social embeddedness of the consumer–e-tailer relationship, thereby enhancing a consumer's loyalty to the relationship (Singh & Sirdeshmukh, 2000).

Corroborating this relationship, Sirdeshmukh and colleagues (2002) find consumer trust had a significant effect on consumer loyalty in the contexts of both retail clothing and nonbusiness airline travel. Support for this relationship also comes from online trust research. For example, Sirdeshmukh et al. (2003) demonstrate online trust significantly influenced consumer loyalty toward the service provider in the context of consumer banking. Bart et al. (2005) find that trust of a Web site had a positive impact on the willingness of a visitor to recommend the site to a friend. Ratchford, Pan, and Shankar (2003) suggest that trust may significantly affect prices that consumers are willing to pay. On the basis of the above arguments and findings, the following hypothesis is posited:

H₂: Consumer trust in an e-tailer positively influences a consumer's loyalty toward the e-tailer.

Moderators of the Effect of Trust on Its Outcomes

Mayer and colleagues (1995) argue that, in order to understand how trust actually affects a person's risk-taking action, one must separate trust from other contextual factors that necessitate trust. The context in which risk is to be taken is very important. Even though the level of trust may be constant, "[T]he specific consequences of trust will be determined by contextual factors such as the stakes involved, the balance of power in the relationship, the perception of the level of risk, and the alternatives available to the trustee" (Mayer et al., 1995, pp. 726–727). Environmental uncertainty and competitive alternatives are proposed as two important contextual factors that will influence a consumer's future intentions and loyalty toward an e-tailer along with trust. The role of each in the relationship between consumer trust and its outcomes is detailed below.

Environmental Uncertainty as a Moderator

As discussed above, consumer trust is salient in the consumer–e-tailer exchange relationship because there are risks involved in doing personal business with an e-tailer. The risks come from two sources: an e-tailer's behavioral uncertainty and the uncertainty regarding the general online transaction environment (Mayer et al., 1995). Behavioral uncertainty is under the control of an e-tailer. It is within the relationship between a consumer and an e-tailer. Level of trust is a result of a consumer's assessment of an e-tailer's behavioral uncertainty (e.g., potential opportunistic behavior). Accordingly, the effect of behavioral uncertainty is accounted for by trust, which directly influences risk-taking behavior (i.e., future intentions and loyalty) in the relationship. On the other hand, environmental uncertainty is caused by contextual and situational factors outside the relationship between a consumer and an e-tailer. It is beyond the control of an e-tailer. Like behavioral uncertainty (i.e., trust), it affects risk-taking behavior in the relationship but acts as a moderator between trust and its outcomes.

Specifically, when a consumer perceives higher uncertainty surrounding the general online transaction environments, to avoid loss or at least reduce the probability of loss in an online personal transaction, she would be more likely to patronize the e-tailer in which she has built trust if she prefers to secure a product or service online. For a trusted e-tailer, if things go wrong in a transaction, a consumer would expect the e-tailer to be honest, have the intention and ability to solve the problems, and act in her best interests. A consumer feels vulnerable when doing personal business online if she perceives high uncertainty in the online transaction environment. It is reasonable that such a consumer would be more likely to put her vulnerability in a more trusted e-tailer's hands.

In contrast, under conditions where a consumer perceives lower uncertainty in general online business environments, he would perceive lower risks involved in online personal transactions. Such a consumer would not worry much about things going wrong and thus would feel less vulnerable in online personal transactions. For such a consumer, it is not as necessary to select a trusted e-tailer for an online purchase if there are competitive ones that he may not trust as much but that offer better deals. Therefore, consumers who perceive lower environmental uncertainty may not patronize a trusted online retailer as much as those who perceive higher environmental uncertainty. Accordingly, the following hypotheses are advanced:

> H_{3a}: Environmental uncertainty strengthens the relationship between consumer trust and a consumer's future intentions toward the e-tailer.
> H_{3b}: Environmental uncertainty strengthens the relationship between consumer trust and a consumer's loyalty toward the e-tailer.

Competitive Alternatives as a Moderator

Competitive alternatives are defined as the availability of unique retailers (both online and offline) in a consumer's mind for the consumer to secure the product or service she wants. Mayer and colleagues (1995) argue that "the alternatives available to the trustee" will determine the specific outcomes of trust along with trust. The proposition is applicable to the trust–risk-taking relationship between a consumer and an e-tailer. Specifically, if a consumer has many alternative online or offline retail outlets to secure a product or service, even if the consumer highly trusts an e-tailer, she may not intend to stay with or be loyal to the e-tailer. In contrast, if a consumer has no or few competitive alternatives available to secure what he needs in the way he wants, high levels of trust will more likely make the consumer stay with or even be loyal to the e-tailer. Hence,

> H_{4a}: Competitive alternatives weaken the relationship between consumer trust and a consumer's future intentions toward the e-tailer.

H_{4b}: Competitive alternatives weaken the relationship between consumer trust and a consumer's loyalty toward the e-tailer.

Direct Effect of Competitive Alternatives

Competitive alternatives also have a direct effect on both future intentions and loyalty (as shown in Figure 12.1), although the relationships are not the focus of this research. When there are fewer competitive options, customers are more likely to seek out and enter into relational exchange with a single e-tailer because they are more dependent on the e-tailer (Voss & Voss, 2008). When there are more competitive suppliers available, customers would seek variety and innovation and thus should be reluctant to enter into relational exchange with a single e-tailer.

Research Design

We collected data via survey to test the hypotheses presented in Figure 12.1. The design was cross-sectional in nature and was conducted online, which was appropriate given the context of the study (i.e., online shopping).

Sample

An online survey was conducted using Zoomerang's Zoom Panel, under MarketTools, Inc. A national sample of 4,156 members age 18 and older was randomly drawn from its panel, which is close to 3 million people. An embedded URL link to the Web site hosting the questionnaire was sent to each of the 4,156 potential respondents. An incentive of entrance into a monthly sweepstakes (via the Zoom Panel monthly sweepstakes) was provided to compensate for their participation. Two reminder invitations were e-mailed to those respondents who had not yet participated in the survey at one day and five days after the initial invitation. This e-mail campaign produced 937 responses, representing an overall response rate of 23%. The entire data set was subjected to listwise deletion to account for missing data, resulting in 908 usable responses.

To evaluate the nonresponse bias of this study, a wave analysis was conducted to examine the profile difference of early and late respondents in the entire sample ($n = 908$), which is widely used in examining nonresponse bias (Armstrong & Overton, 1977). Results indicated no significant demographic differences ($a = .05$) between the two waves except that the education level of early respondents was significantly higher than that of late respondents. Hence, we find nonresponse bias to be negligible.

Measures

Five constructs were measured by using a structured questionnaire. To answer the five questions related to the construct of environmental uncertainty in the questionnaire, participants were asked to recall the general online shopping security. To answer the questions related to the other four constructs (i.e., trust, future intentions, loyalty, and competitive alternatives), participants were asked to recall the online store from which they made their most recent purchase of tangible goods. Reverse coded variables were recoded to maintain directional consistency. The LISREL 8.20 (Joreskog & Sorbom, 1998) software package was used to produce the results presented in Table 12.1. Please refer to Table 12.2 for the descriptive statistics and correlations. All indicators of the constructs were included in an overall confirmatory factor analysis model to determine the psychometric properties of the measures.

Trust

Consumer trust in an e-tailer is operationalized as the amount that a consumer has in the reliability and integrity of an e-tailer (Morgan & Hunt, 1994). Respondents were asked to rate the amount that they have in the reliability and integrity of the online store from which they made their most recent purchase of a physical product by responding to seven Likert-type statements. The items were adapted from Morgan and Hunt (1994) and produced a Cronbach's alpha of 0.93. The confirmatory factor analysis conducted indicated the scale fits the data acceptably. Six of the seven factor loadings are above the recommended criterion of 0.70 (Nunnally, 1978), all are significant at the 0.01 level, and six of the seven squared multiple correlations are above the 0.5 level. The variance explained by the factor was 76%, exceeding the recommended criterion of 60% (Hair, Black, Babin, Anderson, & Tatham, 2006).

Future Intentions

The future intentions construct measures a consumer's willingness to engage in future interactions with an e-tailer. The items for measuring future intentions were adapted from Sultan, Urban, Shankar, and

TABLE 12.1   Across-Construct Measurement Validity Assessment

Indicator	Standardized Loading	Std. Error	t	Composite Reliability[a]	Average Variance Extracted[b]
Trust in e-Tailer				0.96	.76
T1	0.92	0.03	36.15*		
T2	0.92	0.03	36.38*		
T3	0.94	0.03	37.80*		
T4	0.95	0.02	38.76*		
T5	0.95	0.03	38.42*		
T6	0.90	0.03	34.85*		
T7 (Rev. coded)	0.38	0.05	11.79*		
Future Intentions				0.90	.75
FI1	0.95	0.02	38.08*		
FI2	0.98	0.03	39.94*		
FI3	0.62	0.04	20.49*		
Consumer Loyalty				0.90	.65
CL1	0.85	0.04	31.24*		
CL2	0.90	0.04	34.11*		
CL3	0.80	0.05	28.15*		
CL4	0.81	0.05	28.92*		
CL5	0.63	0.03	20.68*		
Competitive Alternatives				0.82	.54
CA1 (Rev. coded)	0.79	0.05	26.46*		
CA2 (Rev. coded)	0.89	0.05	31.29*		
CA3 (Rev. coded)	0.66	0.07	21.01*		
CA4	0.56	0.06	17.38*		
Environmental Uncertainty				0.94	.76
EU1 (Rev. coded)	0.87	0.03	33.06*		
EU2 (Rev. coded)	0.72	0.04	24.78*		
EU3 (Rev. coded)	0.89	0.04	34.72*		
EU4 (Rev. coded)	0.94	0.03	37.77*		
EU5 (Rev. coded)	0.92	0.03	36.11*		

* $p < 0.001$.

[a] $(\Sigma = \text{Std. Loadings})^2/(\Sigma = \text{Std. Loadings})^2 + \Sigma e_j$.

[b] $\Sigma = (\text{Std. Loadings})^2/\Sigma = (\text{Std. Loadings})^2 + \Sigma e_j$.

TABLE 12.2　Model Variables Descriptive Statistics and Correlations

Model Variables	Mean[a]	Standard Deviation	Corr.[b] 1	2	3	4	5
1. Trust in E-Retailer	5.83	0.94	—				
2. Future Intentions	6.02	0.99	0.634	—			
3. Consumer Loyalty	5.07	1.33	0.441	0.555	—		
4. Competitive Alternatives	3.97	1.55	−0.049*	−0.091	−0.347	—	
5. Environmental Uncertainty	3.03	1.21	−0.302	−0.235	−0.145	0.049*	—

　[a] Variable summated and averaged.
　[b] All correlations are statistically significant ($p < 0.01$) except those marked with an asterisk.

Bart (2002) and from Zeithaml et al. (1996). Respondents were asked to indicate their level of agreement using a 7-point Likert scale. Two of the three factor loadings exceeded the preferable criterion of 0.70 (Nunnally, 1978). Internal reliability for the factor, based on Cronbach's coefficient alpha, was 0.86, exceeding the threshold value of 0.70 (Nunnally, 1978). Furthermore, the average variance extracted was deemed adequate.

Consumer Loyalty
Consumer loyalty toward an e-tailer is defined as a consumer's favorable attitude toward an e-tailer that results in repeat purchase intentions toward the e-tailer (Assael, 1992; Keller, 1993; Jacoby & Chestnut, 1978; Oliver, 1997; Srinivasan et al., 2002). The items for measuring loyalty, using a seven-point Likert scale, were adapted from a scale used by Srinivasan et al. (2002), which was adapted from Gremler (1995) and Zeithaml et al. (1996). All factor loadings were significant at the 0.01 level. Internal reliability for the factor, based on Cronbach's coefficient alpha, was 0.89, exceeding the threshold value of 0.70 (Nunnally, 1978). The variance explained by the factor was 65%, exceeding the recommended criterion of 60% (Hair et al., 2006).

Environmental Uncertainty
Environmental uncertainty is operationalized as a consumer's perception of the level of security of shopping online. These items were adapted from a scale developed by McKnight and colleagues (2002). Factor loadings of

these five items ranged from 0.72 to 0.94, all exceeding the preferable criterion of 0.70 (Nunnally, 1978). Internal reliability for the factor, based on Cronbach's coefficient alpha, was 0.94, exceeding the threshold value of 0.70. The variance explained by the factor was 76%.

Competitive Alternatives

Competitive alternatives are operationalized as the availability of competitive alternative retailers (both online and offline) for a respondent to purchase the same physical product the next time he purchases it. This scale utilized four items and was adapted from Ganesan (1994). Factor loadings of these four items ranged from 0.56 to 0.89 with two of them exceeding the preferable criterion of 0.70 and one just below the 0.70. Internal reliability for the factor, based on Cronbach's coefficient alpha, was 0.81, exceeding the threshold value of 0.70 (Nunnally, 1978). The variance explained by the factor was 54%. Although the variance explained fell slightly below the recommended criterion of 60%, this factor is considered acceptable and retained based on its adequate factor loading and reliability.

The overall confirmatory factor analysis, including all constructs, produced an acceptable model fit ($\chi2$ = 1644.97, df = 242, p = 0.000; RMSEA (root mean square error of approximation) = 0.080, GFI (goodness-of-fit index) = 0.87; CFI (comparative fit index) = 0.93; IFI (incremental fit index) = 0.93; NFI (normed fit index) = 0.92; RFI (relative fit index) = 0.91). In addition, the composite reliability coefficients for each multi-item construct measure exceeded Bagozzi and Yi's (1988) acceptability criterion of 0.60. These results suggest that our measures are sufficiently reliable and valid.

Data Analysis

The hypotheses were tested using moderated regression analysis. As Jaccard, Turrisi, and Wan (1990) note, multicollinearity between the interaction terms and their components is a concern. As such, each scale comprising the interaction term was mean-centered in order to mitigate the effects (Aiken & West, 1991) and, accordingly, the interaction terms were created by multiplying the relevant mean-centered scales. The largest variance inflation factor (VIF), an indicator of the extent of multicollinearity in regression analysis, was 1.122, which is substantially lower than the 10.0 benchmark for multicollinearity (Mason & Perreault, 1991). Accordingly, multicollinearity appears not to be a major concern.

TABLE 12.3   Moderated Regression Parameter Estimates

	Dependent Variable					
	Future Intentions			Consumer Loyalty		
	Estimate			Estimate		
Parameter	Unstd.	Std.	t-Value	Unstd.	Std.	t-Value
Focal Relationship						
Intercept	2.039	0.000	11.440[a]	0.642	0.000	2.452[b]
Trust	0.631	0.600	22.381[a]	0.574	0.407	13.850[a]
Moderator Constructs						
Competitive Alternatives	−0.037	−0.058	−2.195[b]	−0.278	−0.323	−11.179[a]
Environmental Uncertainty	−0.043	−0.052	−1.940	−0.040	−0.036	−1.230
Trust × Comp. Alter.	0.005	0.008	0.292	−0.008	−0.009	−0.314
Trust × Enviro. Unc.	0.106	0.125	4.907[a]	0.062	0.057	2.056[b]
R-Square		0.423			0.305	
F		132.198[a]			79.177[a]	
df		5, 902			5, 902	
Largest VIF		1.122			1.122	

[a] $p < 0.001$.
[b] $p < 0.05$.

Results and Discussion

Table 12.3 includes the results of the moderated regression analysis. The parameter estimates are used to test the hypotheses. Discussion and implications of this research are also provided in this section.

Direct Effects of Trust

For H_1, we predict that consumer trust in an e-tailer will positively influence a consumer's future intentions toward the e-tailer. The results presented in Table 12.3 support this hypothesis ($\beta = 0.600$, $p < 0.001$). Consumer trust in an e-tailer is also central to our second hypothesis where we predict that such trust will engender a consumer's loyalty toward the e-tailer. The results shown ($\beta = 0.407$, $p < 0.001$) indicate support for H_2.

The results suggest that trust increases the amount of risk consumers are willing to take in their relationship with an e-tailer. If consumers trust an e-tailer, it is very likely that they will continue to patronize the e-tailer. Furthermore, consumers are likely to reciprocate an e-tailer delivering trust benefits with positive attitude and repeat purchases. Increments in consumer trust increase the social embeddedness of the consumer–e-tailer relationship, thereby enhancing the consumer's loyalty to the relationship.

Moderating Effect of Environmental Uncertainty

We hypothesized that these two focal relationships would be moderated by both environmental uncertainty and competitive alternatives. The results presented in Table 12.3 are mixed in support of the developed hypotheses. Specifically, H_{3a} and H_{3b} predicted the relationship between trust and both future intentions and consumer loyalty, respectively, would be strengthened by environmental uncertainty. The data support both H_{3a} ($\beta = 0.125$, $p < 0.001$) and H_{3b} ($\beta = 0.057$, $p < 0.05$). The results indicate that consumers who perceive high uncertainty surrounding the online transaction environment are more likely to repatronize or stay loyal to an e-tailer if they trust it. In contrast, consumers who perceive low environmental uncertainty are less likely to come back or remain loyal even if they trust the e-tailer. They easily switch to competitive alternatives who offer better deals or a superior shopping experience. The findings are consistent with Mayer, Davis, and Schoorman (1995) who argue that the consequences of trust will be determined by contextual factors such as the perception of the level of risk even though the level of trust may be constant.

In addition, the results in Table 12.3 indicate that environmental uncertainty had no main effect on both future intentions ($\beta = -0.052$, $p > 0.10$) and loyalty ($\beta = -0.036$, $p > 0.10$). The findings imply that perceived uncertainty involved in the general online transaction environments do not prevent consumers from repatronizing or staying loyal to a specific e-tailer directly. However, it does interact with trust in influencing both future intentions and loyalty in a positive direction as discussed already.

Moderating Effect of Competitive Alternatives

Our last set of hypotheses, H_{4a} and H_{4b}, predicted competitive alternatives would weaken the relationships between trust and both future intentions and consumer loyalty, respectively. The results in Table 12.3 indicate neither H_{4a} ($\beta = 0.008$, $p > 0.10$) nor H_{4b} ($\beta = -0.009$, $p > 0.10$) is supported. This finding indicates that regardless of the amount of competitive alternative retail outlets available for a consumer to secure the product or service he needs in the way he wants, trust in an e-tailer alone will make the consumer repatronize or stay loyal to it.

Although competitive alternatives did not interact with trust in influencing the outcome variables, it had a main effect on both future intentions ($\beta = -0.058$, $p < 0.05$) and loyalty ($\beta = -0.323$, $p < 0.001$), as were shown in Table 12.3. Of the two direct effects, the one of competitive alternatives on loyalty was stronger. The findings imply that no or few competitive alternatives available for a consumer to secure what she needs in the way she wants will make her repatronize an e-tailer, and what is more important, stay loyal to it.

The empirical test failed to support the moderating role of competitive alternatives in the relationships between trust and its outcomes. This finding is contradictory to Mayer, Davis, and Schoorman (1995), who argue that the consequences of trust will be determined by contextual factors such as the alternatives available to the trustee even though the level of trust may be constant. However, the developed model suggests that competitive alternatives are an antecedent of both future intentions and loyalty. This finding is consistent with Reinartz and Kumar (2003) and Voss and Voss (2008), who propose that customers with no or fewer competitive alternatives are more likely to enter into a relational exchange relationship with a single seller.

Contributions

This study attempts to answer questions surrounding consumer trust in an e-tailer such as the following. Does trust matter in the consumer–e-tailer exchange relationship? What is consumer trust in an e-tailer? What does it affect? And what are the key moderator(s) between trust and its outcomes? By developing a conceptual framework of consumer trust in an e-tailer that is grounded in strong theories and empirically testing it using a large-scale sample randomly selected from U.S. national online consumers, this study directly addresses some questions that have remained largely unanswered by previous research. Specifically, this study provides a solid analysis of why trust is relevant in the consumer–e-tailer exchange relationship.

Second, this study identifies future intentions and consumer loyalty (constructs closely related to customer retention) as the direct consequences of consumer trust in an e-tailer. By drawing upon the framework of trust, global evaluations theory, and social exchange theory, this study provides strong arguments for the direct impact of consumer trust on a consumer's decision to remain with, or be loyal to, an e-tailer. The empirical results also indicate that consumer trust is intrinsically beneficial to an e-tailer because it helps retain customers.

Last, this study examines the factors that moderate the impact of trust. This consideration has been largely ignored in past research. Specifically, this study identifies both a consumer's environmental uncertainty perceptions and competitive alternatives perceptions as the key moderators of the effect of trust on a consumer's decision to repatronize, or be loyal to, an e-tailer. Although the empirical results failed to support the moderating role of competitive alternatives, they do indicate that environmental uncertainty is a moderator between trust and its outcome variables. What is more, the empirical results revealed a direct effect of competitive alternatives on both future intentions and loyalty.

This study also has some implications for e-tailing practices. First of all, because trust was confirmed to affect a customer's decision to repatronize and be loyal to an e-tailer, e-tail managers are advised to position trust as an important marketing tool that can help retain customers.

Second, inasmuch as environmental uncertainty was confirmed to moderate the effect of trust on both future intentions and loyalty, e-tailers are advised to assess the uncertainty factor carefully before utilizing the trust marketing tool. If the general online transaction environments are perceived as highly uncertain by consumers, e-tailers are advised to invest heavily in building consumers' trust. If consumers perceive low uncertainty involved in online shopping environments, e-tail managers should realize that trust alone would not prevent their customers from switching to their competitors. Accordingly, to retain their customers, in addition to trust, e-tail managers have to improve their relative (compared with their competitors) performance in other areas such as merchandise selection, prices offered, or shopping experience.

Third, a direct effect of competitive alternatives on both future intentions and loyalty revealed by the study implies that staying competitive in the market and in consumers' minds will help retain customers. Hence, e-tail managers are advised to always keep an eye on both current and potential competitors and craft sound business strategy and tactics to compete with them effectively.

Limitations and Future Research

This study possesses two main limitations. First, because this study was cross sectional in nature, the findings may be biased by spurious cause/effect inferences. Therefore, it is difficult to infer causality between research variables. Longitudinal studies can and should be designed to build the hypothesized sequence of the effects. Moreover, the cross sectional survey research methodology employed by this study may introduce another bias, a bias caused by common method variance. Common method variance is known to inflate structural relationships, resulting in overestimations of the effect of hypothesized predictors. Future attempts are needed to examine the impact of common method variance on this study's results, or to control over common variance when replicating this study.

Second, the sampling method employed by this study will introduce frame error and sampling error, which will limit the generalizability of this study. Although a national sample of 4,156 members age 18+ was randomly drawn from a three-million online shoppers panel and the overall response rate of 23% was relatively high, there remains the question of the representativeness and generalizability of the sample. Therefore, replication studies with varying sampling procedures are needed to provide more confidence in these findings.

For future research, in addition to the opportunities suggested by the limitations set forth above, three avenues are worth exploring. First, the empirical test failed to support the moderating role of competitive alternatives. Future research is needed to further examine its role in trust mechanisms.

Second, although the proposed model was to understand trust mechanisms in the consumer–e-tailer exchange relationship, it is not limited to consumer–e-tailer relationships only. It can be applied to other relationship contexts such as interorganizational relationships, interpersonal relationships (e.g., consumer–consumer relationships), or other B2C relationships.

Lastly, this study shows that consumer trust was intrinsically beneficial. Then the next questions are: how to build consumer trust and what are the key mediators between consumer trust and its outcomes. Future research into these areas is warranted.

Appendix

Measurement Items for Study Constructs

Trust

This online store:
- T1. Operates with integrity.
- T2. Is always faithful.
- T3. Can be counted on to do what is right.
- T4. Can be trusted.
- T5. Is honest and truthful.
- T6. Is an organization in which I have great confidence.
- T7. Cannot be trusted at times. (reverse coded)

Future Intentions

- FI1. I will shop at this on-line store in the future.
- FI2. I will purchase from this on-line store in the future.
- FI3. I will do more business with this on-line store in the next few years.

Consumer Loyalty

- CL1. I try to use this online store whenever I need to buy this kind of product.
- CL2. When I need to buy this kind of product, this online store is my first choice.
- CL3. I seldom consider switching to another online store in terms of buying this kind of product.
- CL4. I doubt that I would switch online stores in terms of buying this kind of product.
- CL5. To me, this online store is the best one to do business with.

Environmental Uncertainty

- EU1. The Internet is secure enough to make me feel comfortable when I shop online. (Reverse coded)
- EU2. I feel assured that the laws adequately protect me from problems on the Internet. (Reverse coded)

EU3. I feel assured that technologies adequately protect me from problems on the Internet. (Reverse coded)

EU4. I feel confident that security technology on the Internet makes it safe for me to do business online. (Reverse coded)

EU5. In general, the Internet is now a secure form of doing business. (Reverse coded)

Competitive Alternatives

CA1. I do not have a good alternative to this ONLINE store for buying this kind of products. (Reverse coded)

CA2. It would be difficult for me to find a competitive ONLINE store alternative to this one to buy this kind of product. (Reverse coded)

CA3. It would be difficult for me to find a competitive OFFLINE retailer alternative (e.g., retail store or catalogue) to this online store to buy this kind of product. (Reverse coded)

CA4. It would be easy for me to find a good alternative to this ONLINE store to buy this kind of product.

References

Aiken, L. S. & West, S. G. (1991). *Multiple regression: Testing and interpreting interactions*. Newbury Park, CA: SAGE.

Anderson, E. & Weitz, B. (1989). Determinants of continuity in conventional industrial channel dyads. *Marketing Science, 8*(Fall), 310–323.

Armstrong, J., & Overton, T. S. (1977). Estimating nonresponse bias in mail surveys. *Journal of Marketing Research, 14*(3), 396-402.

Assael, H. (1992). *Consumer behavior and marketing action*, Boston, MA: PWS-KENT.

Atuahene-Gima, K. & Li, H. (2002). When does trust matter? An empirical analysis of the antecedent and contingent effects of supervisee trust on sales performance in selling new products in China and the United States. *Journal of Marketing, 66*(July), 61-81.

Bagozzi, R. P. & Yi, Y. (1988). On the evaluation of structural equation models. *Journal of the Academy of Marketing Science, 16*(Spring), 74–94.

Bain & Company and Mainspring. (2000). *The value of online customer loyalty and how you can capture it*. Retrieved from http://www.bain.com/Images/Value_online_customer_loyalty_you_capture.pdf

Bart, Y., Shankar, V., Sultan, F., & Urban, G. L. (2005). Are the drivers and role of online trust the same for all Web sites and consumers? A large-scale exploratory empirical study. *Journal of Marketing, 69*, 133–152.

Berry, L. L. (1993). Playing fair in retailing. *Arthur Anderson Retailing Issues Newsletter, 5*(March), 2.

Chen, C. & O'Brien M. (2005). An integrative model of consumer trust in an e-tailer. In *Proceedings of the Annual Meeting of Society for Marketing Advances*, San Antonio, TX.

Cronin, J. J., Jr. & Taylor, S. A. (1992). Measuring service quality: A reexamination and extension. *Journal of Marketing, 56*(July), 55–68.

Doney, P. M. & Cannon, J. P. (1997). An examination of the nature of trust in buyer-seller relationships. *Journal of Marketing, 61*(2), 35.

Dwyer, F. R., Schurr, P. H., & Oh, S. (1987). Developing buyer-seller relationships. *Journal of Marketing, 51*(April), 11–27.

Ganesan, S. (1994). Determinants of long-term orientation in buyer-seller relationships. *Journal of Marketing, 58*(April), 1–19.

Ganesan, S. & Hess, R. (1997). Dimensions and levels of trust: Implications for commitment to relationship. *Marketing Letters, 8*(4), 439–448.

Garbarino, E. & Johnson, M. S. (1999). The different roles of satisfaction, trust, and commitment in customer relationships. *Journal of Marketing, 63*(April), 70–87.

Gremler, D. D. (1995). *The effect of satisfaction, switching costs, and interpersonal bonds on service loyalty.* Unpublished doctoral dissertation, Arizona State University, Phoenix, AZ.

Hair, J. F., Jr., Black, W. C., Babin, B. J., Anderson, R. E., & Tatham, R. L. (2006). *Multivariate data analysis* (6th edition), Upper Saddle River, NJ: Prentice Hall.

Jaccard, J., Turrisi, R., & Wan, C. K. (1990). *Interaction effects in multiple regression*, Newbury Park, CA: SAGE.

Jacoby, J. & Chestnut, R. W. (1978). *Brand loyalty: Measurement and management*, New York: John Wiley and Sons.

Jarvenpaa, S. L., Tractinsky, J., & Vitale, M. (2000). Consumer trust in an Internet store. *Information Technology and Management, 1*(1–2), 45–71.

Joreskog, K. & Sorbom, D. (1998). *LISREL 8.20 for Windows*, Lincolnwood, IL: Scientific Software International, Inc.

Keller, K. L. (1993). Conceptualizing, measuring, & managing customer-based brand equity. *Journal of Marketing, 57*(January), 1–22.

Luhmann, N. (1979). *Trust and power*, Chichester, UK: Wiley.

Lusch, R. F., O'Brien, M., & Sindhav, B. (2004). The critical role of trust in obtaining retailer support for a supplier's strategic organizational change. *Journal of Retailing, 79*, 249–258.

Mason, C. H. & Perreault, W. D., Jr. (1991). Collinearity, power, and interpretation of multiple regression analysis. *Journal of Marketing Research, 28*(August), 268–280.

Mayer, R. C., Davis, J. H., & Schoorman, F. D. (1995). An integrative model of organizational trust. *Academy of Management Review, 20*(3), 709–734.

McKnight, H. D., Choudhury, V., & Kacmar, C. (2002). The impact of initial consumer trust on intentions to transact with a Web site: A trust building model.
Journal of Strategic Information Systems, 11, 297–323.

Moorman, C., Deshpande, R., & Zaltman, G. (1993). Factors affecting trust in
market research relationships. *Journal of Marketing, 57*(January), 81–101.

Moorman, C., Zaltman, G., & Deshpande, R. (1992). Relationships between providers and users of marketing research: The dynamics of trust within and
between organizations. *Journal of Marketing Research, 29*(August), 314–29.

Morgan, R. M. & Hunt, S. D. (1994). The commitment-trust theory of relationship
marketing. *Journal of Marketing, 58*(July), 20–38.

Nunnally, J. C. (1978). *Psychometric theory* (2nd edition), New York: McGraw-Hill.

Oliver, R. L. (1997). *Satisfaction: A behavioral perspective on the consumer*, New
York: McGraw-Hill.

Ostron, A. & Iacobucci, D. (1995). Consumer trade-offs and the evaluations of
services. *Journal of Marketing, 59*(January), 17–28.

Pan, X., Shankar, V., & Ratchford, B. T. (2002). Price competition between pure
play vs. bricks-and-clicks e-tailers: Analytical model and empirical analysis. In M. R. Baye (Ed.), *Advances in microeconomics: E-commerce economics*
(Vol. 11), Burlington, MA: Elsevier, pp. 29–61.

Parasuraman, A., Zeithaml, V. A., & Berry, L. L. (1994). Reassessment of expectations as a comparison standard in measuring service quality: Implications
for future research. *Journal of Marketing, 58*(January), 111–124.

Pavlou, P. A. (2002). What drives electronic commerce? A theory of planned
behavior perspective. *Academy of Management Proceedings & Membership
Directory*, A1-A6.

Ratchford, B. T., Pan, X., & Shankar, V. (2003). On the efficiency of internet markets. *Journal of Public Policy & Marketing, 22*(1), 4–16.

Reichheld, F. F., Markey, R. G., Jr., & Hopton, C. (2000). E-customer loyalty-apply-
ing the traditional rules of business for online success. *European Business
Journal, 12*(4), 173–179.

Reinartz, W. J. & Kumar, V. (2003). The impact of customer relationship characteristics on profitable lifetime duration. *Journal of Marketing, 67*(January),
77–99.

Rousseau, D. M., Sitkin, S. B., Burt, R. S., & Camerer, C. (1998). Not so different
after all: A cross-discipline view of trust. *Academy of Management Review,
23*(3), 393–404.

Shankar, V., Urban, G. L., & Sultan, F. (2002). Online trust: A stakeholder perspective, concepts, implications, and future directions. *Journal of Strategic
Information Systems, 11*(December), 325–344.

Silverhart, T. A. (2002). Commentary: Questionable metrics and unfair comparisons. *Limras Marketfacts Quarterly, 21*(1), 23.

Singh, J. & Sirdeshmukh, D. (2000). Agency and trust mechanisms in consumer
satisfaction and loyalty judgments. *Journal of the Academy of Marketing
Science, 28*(1), 150–167.

Sirdeshmukh, D., Brei, V. A., & Singh, J. (2003). The Web of trust: Joint influence of online, frontline, and company policies on consumer trust, value and loyalty. In *AMA Winter Educators' Proceedings*, Phoenix & Tucson, AZ.

Sirdeshmukh, D., Singh, J., & Sabol, B. (2002). Consumer trust, value, and loyalty in relational exchanges. *Journal of Marketing, 66*(January), 15–37.

Srinivasan, S., Anderson, R., & Ponnavolu, K. (2002). Customer loyalty in e-commerce: An exploration of its antecedents and consequences. *Journal of Retailing, 78*, 41–50.

Sultan, F., Urban, G. L., Shankar, V., & Bart, I. Y. (2002). Determinants and role of trust in e-business: A large scale empirical study. Working paper. Northeastern University, Boston, MA.

Urban, G. L., Amyx, C., & Lorenzon, A. (2009). Online trust: State of the art, new frontiers, and research potential. *Journal of Interactive Marketing, 23*, 179–190.

Voss, G. B. & Voss, Z. G. (2008). Competitive density and the customer acquisition-retention trade-off. *Journal of Marketing, 72*(November), 3–18.

Williamson, O. E. (1981). The economics of organization: The transaction cost approach. *American Journal of Sociology, 87*(3), 548–577.

Wind, Y., & Mahajan, V. (2002). Convergence marketing. *Journal of Interactive Marketing, 16*(2), 64–79.

Yoon, S. J. (2002). The antecedents and consequences of trust in online purchase decisions. *Journal of Interactive Marketing, 16*(2), 47–63.

Zeithaml, V. A., Berry, L. L., & Parasuraman, A. (1996). The behavioral consequences of service quality. *Journal of Marketing, 60*(April), 31–46.

13

Toward a Theory of Consumer Electronic Shopping Cart Behavior
Motivations of e-Cart Use and Abandonment

Angeline G. Close
The University of Texas at Austin

Monika Kukar-Kinney
University of Richmond

Timothy Kyle Benusa
University of Richmond

Electronic Shopping Carts (e-Carts)

How do online shoppers use their electronic shopping carts (e-carts)? Also, why would an online consumer be motivated to place an item in his electronic (e-cart), only to abandon it? e-Cart abandonment refers to "consumers' placement of item(s) in their online shopping cart without making a purchase of any item(s) during that online shopping session" (Kukar-Kinney & Close, 2010, p. 240). It is a million-dollar concern to businesses, and a perplexing online consumer behavior to explain and predict. Industry studies note that 88% of online shoppers have abandoned an online cart (Forrester Research, 2005). Even more telling, online shoppers abandon their shopping carts approximately a quarter of the time (Tarasofsky, 2008).

Consumers' motivations and ways in which they use the electronic cart (e-cart) are different from shopping in a traditional brick-and-mortar setting. Although abandonment is not as noticeable in the traditional retail setting, e-cart abandonment is a substantial concern for online retailers, as it may be considered a lost sale. As e-commerce grows in its importance and quantity, scholars and retail managers alike seek a deeper under-standing of consumers' motivations for using e-carts. Unfortunately, understanding motivations for e-cart use is not enough, because consumers all too frequently abandon such carts. Thus, we explain reasons for abandoning the carts during the online shopping process.

Relative to how common this online behavior is, e-cart abandonment has been a relatively underexplored issue from a scholarly perspective. Thus, we examine this behavior, and synthesize the findings of our studies in this book chapter. Namely, we synthesize the findings from two of our studies on the topic (Close & Kukar-Kinney 2010; Kukar-Kinney & Close, 2010) and expand the findings by adding generalizations and insights specific to this book chapter. We work toward offering the start of a new theory, a theory of consumer e-cart behavior. In this chapter, we investigate the online shopping process, with a focus on the motivations behind the determinants of online shopping cart use and abandonment.

The chapter is organized as follows. First, we discuss the current state of e-commerce and the emergence of new forms of online retailing, such as the integration of social media and online shopping, highlighting the importance of findings and research in the field of e-commerce. Next, we discuss the process of online shopping, paying particular attention to the three main phases of online shopping relevant here: (1) accepting the Internet as a means of shopping and commerce; (2) understanding hedonic and utilitarian motivations for using an electronic shopping cart; and (3) the online checkout process. Then, we discuss the development of a framework that synthesizes the findings of our two publications along with the existing literature. We continue by outlining the variables that affect or influence the three possible outcomes of online shopping: a successful online purchase, complete cart abandonment or unsuccessful purchase, or a cart abandonment in order to purchase the item elsewhere, such as from a different e-tailer or land-based retailer. We then discuss the findings from our synthesized framework, focusing primarily on the difference between direct and indirect links of the framework. Finally, we conclude the chapter with a discussion of the findings, the managerial implications, and avenues for future research inquiry in the context of social media and online shopping integration.

Importance of e-Commerce and Emergence of Social e-Commerce

Here we provide some statistics on e-commerce's projected growth. The e-commerce and online shopping landscape has grown substantially in size and scope over the last decade. In a 2011 report, J.P. Morgan esti-mated that 170 million online buyers fueled e-commerce revenues of over 180 billion U.S. dollars in 2010. The report estimates the number of online buyers and e-commerce revenues will increase to 189 million and approximately 255 billion U.S. dollars, respectively, by 2013 (J.P. Morgan, 2011). This growth shows that the online marketplace has become a sub-stantial player in the world of retail and shopping. As e-carts are a neces-sary vehicle to enable the purchase at most e-tail sites, an inquiry into the consumers' use and abandonment of e-carts is crucial to understanding consumers' online shopping behavior.

The increase in the number of online shoppers, increasing revenues, and emergence of new forms of e-commerce and shopping (both social and personal e-shopping) highlight the growing need to understand the online shopping process and variables that have an impact on online con-sumer decision-making. The online marketplace is no longer a niche mar-ketplace; it is a substantial player and, as such, a deeper understanding of the variables that affect the consumer's decision making during the online shopping process has the potential to affect millions of online consumers who spend billions of U.S. dollars on e-commerce goods. Additionally, a deeper understanding of the online shopping process will help online retailers fine-tune their Web sites to attract more shoppers and extract more revenue. Thus, we move to the focus of the present chapter, which is to investigate the online shopping process. We pay particular attention to the motivations behind the determinants of online shopping cart use and abandonment.

Process of Online Shopping

Online shopping is a unique process that can be broken down into three essential phases: acceptance and use of e-commerce, the hedonic or utili-tarian use of an e-cart, and the eventual checkout of the online store.

Phase I: Acceptance and Use of e-Commerce

Consumer participation in the online marketplace is predicated upon the consumer's acceptance of e-commerce (i.e., the Internet as a means of shopping). With the proliferation of e-tail, e-tailers have become ubiq-uitous, and most goods are now available in a virtual marketplace (Lee,

Tsai, & Lanting, 2011). The ubiquity of retailers and items indicates the acceptance of online shopping for nearly all goods (and increasingly, service vouchers), and not merely as a means to acquire rare and hard-to-find items.

A primary concern during the nascent stages of the online marketplace was security over payment and personal information. Some studies showed that Internet users of varying types struggled with online shopping due to privacy fears associated with transmitting personal and financial information (Warrick & Stinson, 2009). However, fears and concerns over the risks associated with online transactions seem to have been allayed. A prime example of consumers' acceptance of the security of Internet transactions is evidenced in consumers' use of online banking. According to an industry report, the percentage of consumers who transferred funds online nearly doubled in a recent five-year span (34% in 2005 to 67% in 2010; *eMarketer*, March 2011). Furthermore, the percentage of bank customers' checking account balances online jumped from 44% in 2005 to 75% in 2011 (*eMarketer*, March 2011). The increasing popularity of online services such as banking is indicative of a growing acceptance of the Internet as a safe place to conduct both social encounters and business. The proliferation of online retailers and products available online, the growing use of the Internet for financial transactions, and the emergence of new forms of e-commerce, such as the previously mentioned social shopping sites, not only indicate greater acceptance of, but also increased reliance on, the Internet as a virtual marketplace.

Phase II: Hedonic or Utilitarian Use of e-Carts

The use of an electronic shopping cart, here e-cart, is the stage following the acceptance and use of the Internet to shop. The e-cart must be viewed as a distinctive tool from the traditional tangible shopping carts from which they received their name. e-Carts are similar to traditional shopping carts in that they assist customers in gathering and storing items for imminent purchase; however, e-carts differ in that they are more versatile. e-Cart use extends beyond pure utilitarian functions. In light of the fact that existing literature recognizes both utilitarian and hedonistic motivations for online shopping, buying, and general Internet use (Arnold & Reynolds, 2003; Bridges & Florsheim, 2008; Papacharissi & Rubin, 2000), Close and Kukar-Kinney (2010) acknowledge that online carts may provide additional utilitarian and hedonistic functions in contrast to traditional carts.

Hedonistic Motivations for e-Cart Use

Hedonistic shopping motivations are defined by the online shopper's assessment of the experience-based benefits and disadvantages. Consumers may shop for the experience that accompanies the process of shopping above the goal of purchasing the item. Thus, the hedonistic aspect of shopping consists of the fun and enjoyment of the shopping experience itself (Babin, Darden, & Griffin, 1994). Such motivations to shop online are related to various shopping types, such as adventure shopping, gratification shopping, idea shopping, and value shopping (Arnold & Reynolds, 2003). For example, as a form of entertainment, adventure shopping recognizes that shoppers seek sensory stimulation while shopping for escapism, stimulation, and adventure. Gratification shopping is often done to overcome a bad mood, to relieve stress, or to indulge in a self-gift. Idea shopping entails shopping to seek out innovative products, and the latest fads, fashions, and trends, generally to gather information more so than products. Last, value shopping is associated with the thrill and rewards associated with finding a deal and acquiring a product on sale (Arnold & Reynolds, 2003). In short, consumers may use online shopping carts to obtain some form of entertainment value, which fulfills consumers' needs for hedonistic pleasure, aesthetic enjoyment, and emotional release (McQuail, 1987).

In our motivations study, we originally thought that the search for entertainment would lead consumers to place items in their online carts more frequently; however, data from our survey of 289 online shoppers did not provide support for this hypothesis (Close & Kukar-Kinney, 2010). Interestingly, a direct examination of the correlation between entertainment purpose and frequency of online shopping cart placement discovered a significant and positive correlation ($\rho =.12$, $p < .05$; Close & Kukar-Kinney, 2010). The discrepancy between findings can be explained by the use of structural equation modeling methods, which account for multiple predictor effects at the same time, any correlations among the predictors, as well as any measurement error. We concluded that above and beyond the other investigated predictors, entertainment purpose is not able to contribute individually to an increased shopping cart use; instead, entertainment-based motivations result in a decreased consumers' use of the cart. Hence, consumers who are shopping for fun, entertainment, or to escape boredom may be content merely browsing from page to page, rather than actively engaging in putting items into their virtual shopping cart (Close & Kukar-Kinney, 2010).

Utilitarian Motivations for e-Cart Use

Electronic shopping carts by their very nature are utilitarian inasmuch as they serve as a storage space prior to purchase; yet, their use also entails experiential hedonistic aspects (Close & Kukar-Kinney, 2010). Utilitarian factors are wide-ranging assessments of functional benefits and disadvantages (Overby & Lee, 2006). Utilitarian motivations for Internet shopping use (Noble, Griffith, & Adjie, 2006; To, Liao, & Lin, 2007) may include purchase intent at the given online shopping session and financial incentives such as online price promotions or sales. Utilitarian motives for e-cart use may be largely goal-directed and task-based, such as using the cart to make a purchase or saving time and money by purchasing online.

An example of a utilitarian function for an e-cart is using the cart to organize products of interest. In our abandonment study, we define the organizational use of the e-cart as: "the extent to which consumers place items in their online shopping cart for reasons such as creating a wish list of desired items, bookmarking the product for a potential future purchase, and narrowing down items for further evaluation" (Close & Kukar-Kinney, 2010, p. 987). Online shoppers may use their e-cart as a virtual place where they can temporarily store or view items they are interested in or are considering for a possible purchase in the future. Other consumers may like to place various items of interest in their carts, with the intent to narrow down alternatives in their consideration set for further evaluation. This utilitarian use often affords the online shopper the ability to return to the cart later without having to search for the products again. These examples can all be classified as organizational use of an e-shopping cart. In our research, we found that the greater the consumers' organizational use of the cart, the greater is their overall frequency of placing items in their online shopping cart (Close & Kukar-Kinney, 2010). Once the consumer places an item into the e-cart, the checkout phase begins.

Phase III: Checkout

The checkout phase is the third and final essential stage of online shopping. The checkout stage occurs when consumers move beyond placing items in their e-carts by clicking on the link to "purchase" or "check out" the items in their carts. It may be successful (the items in the cart are purchased), unsuccessful (the cart is abandoned and the customer does not come back), or neutral (the cart is abandoned because the shopper decides to buy the item from a different seller, such as a brick-and-mortar store).

In order to complete a purchase and check out, online shoppers are most frequently required to enter payment information, such as credit card and billing information. Additionally, online shoppers may be asked to indicate their shipping preference. The checkout phase of online shopping and traditional shopping differ due to the manual entry of credit card payment information by the customer and the customer selecting shipping information. The transaction inconvenience associated with the checkout phase has the ability to influence shoppers' experience and decision of whether to abandon their e-cart. A study conducted to focus specifically on the transaction completion stage discovered that perceived transaction inconvenience associated with the transaction completion process results in a higher propensity to abandon the shopping cart (Rajamma, Paswan, & Hossain, 2009). Any reduction in the inconvenience of the transaction phase is assumed to decrease abandonment rates.

Converting e-Shoppers to e-Buyers in Checkout
In order to address this problem, e-tailers and stores have recently begun to introduce programs to shorten the length of the checkout phase. For example, Amazon.com uses "One-Click Ordering." One-click ordering allows customers to bypass the lengthy process of entering billing and shipping information, by storing their credit and billing information. Upon clicking the one-click link, the online shopper immediately purchases the item using the credit and shipping information stored by the e-tailer (i.e., Amazon). Amazon has introduced an additional initiative to allow customers to bypass the lengthy process of checking out. Amazon calls the initiative "PayPhrase." PayPhrase uses stored information to decrease the time and hassle of entering payment and shipping information. The entry of a certain pay phrase, previously entered in conjunction with checkout information allows online shoppers to check out by simply entering a string of words. Online shoppers can then identify the payment and shipping information that they would like to complete the order. According to the e-tailer, the introduction of the PayPhrase allows shoppers to combine the ease of use and speed of one-click shopping with the versatility of a full checkout.

To stay competitive, Google recently launched a proprietary initiative, called "Google Checkout," with a view of decreasing the hassle and security issues of online shopping. An advertisement for the program begins by saying, "Online shopping seems quick and easy, until it's time to buy." Online checkout often entails forms for the online shopper to fill out, not to mention the necessity to recall usernames and passwords. According to the search engine giant, Google Checkout is a "new service that makes online shopping more convenient, more secure, and a lot faster" (Google, 2011b). Google Checkout stores credit and shipping information and acts as a liaison between online sellers and consumers. Merchants/sellers who accept Google Checkout have links on their Web site that allow consumers to purchase the item via one-click shopping through Google. Google Checkout retains all credit, shipping, and e-mail information for security and aggregates a customer's online purchases for reference. According to Google Checkout's Web site, their "fast, convenient checkout process helps Google Checkout users convert 40% more than shoppers who have not used Checkout before" (Google, 2011a).

Amazon and Google's programs are examples of initiatives designed for the purpose of converting online shoppers to online buyers. The programs are based on the belief that a hassle-filled checkout process will discourage purchase. Therefore, the goal of the programs is to convert shopping to successful purchase by decreasing the hassle of checking out. A successful completed purchase indicates that a consumer fully completed the checkout phase of online shopping by entering credit and shipping information and finalizing the purchase for delivery.

Alternative to a Successful Checkout
Simplistically, there is only one alternative to a successful purchase at the time of measure: an unsuccessful purchase or, rather, a nonpurchase. However, we do note an existence of a possible third outcome: that an e-cart abandoner may go to the e-tailer's brick-and-mortar store to complete the purchase in person; thus, the sale is not necessarily lost to the company. In online shopping terminology, an unsuccessful purchase is deemed as "abandonment." Consistent with the industry studies, indicating an abandonment rate of about 25% (Tarasofsky, 2008), our abandonment study finds that on average, online shoppers abandoned their online carts 26% of the times they put something in it during the same Internet session (Kukar-Kinney & Close, 2010).

Online cart abandonment is typically viewed as a lost sale to the retailer, and thus as a bad thing. To view all e-cart abandonment as an unsuccessful or uncompleted purchase would be to avoid a third outcome, separate from complete abandonment: abandonment of the online shopping cart in order to purchase the item from a land-based retailer. Online cart abandonment only results in lost sales when the shopper decides either not to purchase the item or to purchase the item from a competitor. However, the shopper may merely use the Internet as a shopping tool, instead deciding to make the purchase through a different channel, such as at the land-based store of the same retailer. For this reason, any application of our analysis of shopping cart abandonment must take into account that abandonment may not result in a complete purchase abandonment or loss in sales, but rather may result in the purchase of the item from the land-based component of the retailer. In order to capture this aspect, our discussion of online shopping, and subsequently our developed framework, includes the purchase of the item from a land-based retailer.

Theoretical Framework

Through the application of existing literature and the synthesis of our previous research, we develop a theoretical framework outlining the variables that influence the three main outcomes of online shopping: successful online purchase, complete cart abandonment or unsuccessful purchase, and cart abandonment in order to purchase the item at a land-based retailer.

Constructs

Based on our two studies (the cart use motivation study and the abandonment study), we include the following constructs in a new, synthesized conceptual framework: consumers' concern over cost, entertainment value, organizational intent, price promotion, privacy/security concerns, current-purchase intent, and frequency of use. We base these variables on both Kukar-Kinney and Close (2010) and Close and Kukar-Kinney (2010). All of the selected variables are either directly or indirectly related to the extent of shopping cart abandonment.

Tendency to Wait for a Sale
Online shoppers may be particularly sensitive to the total price of all the items in their online shopping cart, or to other costs such as shipping and handling costs, tax (if applicable), or additional fees. Although online shopping should be no different than traditional shopping in terms of the role of cost in consumers' decision making, the online context has specific implications with regard to cost. The calculated total of online carts may increase consumer's sensitivity to cost, as prior research has indicated that the overall cost of the final order may discourage or inhibit shoppers from completing their purchase (Li & Chatterjee, 2006; Lueker,

2003; Magill, 2005; Xia & Monroe, 2004). Furthermore, the addition of shipping or handling charges (which do not exist in a traditional retail setting) may make customers more sensitive to total cost. These additional costs are even more of a turn-off to potential buyers who see them as extreme. For example, a set shipping cost to mail an item intrastate, or a handling fee to place a ticket in an envelope and mail can insult the customer and trigger her to abandon the cart. Thus, the online shopper may place the desired item in her cart, but decide to wait to complete the purchase because of the additional costs and rather wait for a sale, presently abandoning the cart.

Online Price Promotion-Proneness

The online shopping context provides a unique setting for selected price promotions, such as discounted shipping costs. As such, price promotion proneness as a variable merits attention in our framework. For some, shopping entails looking for discounts, sales, or promotions; such monetary incentives have been found to have significant positive correlations with Internet use (Arnold & Reynolds, 2003; Charney & Greenberg, 2001; Flanagin & Metzger, 2001; Wolin & Korgaonkar, 2003). In our framework, *online price promotion proneness* is defined as the extent to which shoppers place items in online shopping carts in order to view or take advantage of price promotions, such as discounts or free shipping (Kukar-Kinney & Close, 2010). A positive relationship between the consumers' desire to wait for a price promotion or special deal and subsequent cart abandonment is expected.

Entertainment Use of e-Cart

In light of research suggesting that consumers shop online with hedonistic experiential motives, such as searching and shopping for fun, to alleviate boredom, or as a medium for entertainment or escapism, as well as goal-oriented motives, we define the *entertainment use* of the online shopping cart as the extent to which consumers place items in their e-carts in order to entertain themselves or alleviate boredom (Kukar-Kinney & Close, 2010; Mathwick, Malhotra, & Rigdon, 2001; Moe, 2003; Novak, Hoffman, & Duhachek, 2003; Wolfinbarger & Gilly, 2001). A positive relationship between the use of the cart for entertainment purposes and consequent e-cart abandonment should exist. In addition, the e-cart serves other purposes, such as helping the consumer organize his shopping items.

Organizational Use of e-Cart

The nature of the online shopping cart, in that it displays individual item prices, colors, sizes, number, and so on, allows consumers to use their online shopping carts as a research or organizational tool during the shopping process. As a utilitarian variable in our framework, we refer to *organizational intent* as the extent to which shoppers place items in their carts for the purpose of creating a wish list of desired items, bookmarking a product for future purchase, or narrowing down their items for further evaluation (Kukar-Kinney & Close, 2010). In recognition of the potential organizational intent of online shoppers, some online retailers such as Amazon and BestBuy provide "Wish List" tools, allowing shoppers to use their online shopping services to organize items. A positive relationship between organizational use of the online cart and subsequent shopping cart abandonment is expected.

The requirement of providing personal and financial information over the Internet, as opposed to providing the information in person, further distinguishes online shopping with shopping in traditional brick-and-mortar retail stores. Existing literature and studies have indicated that privacy and security of personal and financial information are noteworthy concerns of online shoppers (Horrigan, 2008; Miyazaki & Fernandez, 2001; Zhou, Dai, & Zhang, 2007). Concerns over privacy and security cause enough concern with some consumers that they avoid Internet shopping altogether (Laroche, Zhilin, McDougall, & Jasmin, 2005; Xie, Teo, & Wan, 2006). Due to its ability to influence consumers' decision making, we include privacy and security concerns as a variable in the framework and anticipate a positive relationship between the extent of consumers' privacy and security concerns and consequent shopping cart abandonment.

Current Purchase Intent

Acknowledging the potential goal-directed nature of online shopping, we include a current purchase intent construct in our model. The *construct* is defined as an online shopper's intent to use an online shopping cart as a means to purchase the item of interest in the current online shopping session (Kukar-Kinney & Close, 2010). The more the consumer intends to make the purchase during the current Internet session, the lower the proposed shopping cart abandonment likelihood.

Frequency of e-Cart Use

The final construct included in the framework is a consumer's frequency of online shopping cart use. The construct refers to the frequency with which a consumer uses an online shopping cart when shopping online. Consumers who use the carts very frequently are likely using the cart for purposes other than immediate purchase; hence a positive relationship between the frequency of online cart use and subsequent cart abandonment is expected.

Discussion

Synthesis of Research

The synthesis of existing literature, with a particular focus on synergizing and expanding our e-cart motivation and abandonment studies, results in a general framework for understanding the two basic outcomes of online shopping: successful completion of the process through buying and the abandonment of the online cart, either in full or to purchase the item at a land-based retailer. The framework distinguishes these two broad outcomes into three essential results: online cart abandonment, frequency of online buying, and the decision to purchase from a land-based retailer. We overlap the positive findings of our studies to highlight both the direct and indirect relationships of the seven aforementioned variables with the ultimate fate of an online shopping experience or purchase process. In short, we combined the variables of previous studies to formulate a joint framework of the relationships of online cart use and abandonment. The conceptual framework is graphically depicted in Figure 13.1. The following discussion separates the framework into direct and indirect relationships.

Direct Relationships

After synthesizing our studies, we found that there are three direct relationships between the aforementioned variables and e-cart abandonment. The propensity for a consumer to wait for a sale or price promotion is positively related to online cart abandonment. In addition, the proclivity of consumers to derive entertainment value from using an online shopping cart is positively related to abandonment. That is, the more an individual uses the cart for entertainment, the more likely she is to abandon the cart. Finally, the more likely the consumer is to use the cart for organizational purposes, the more likely he is to abandon the shopping cart (Kukar-Kinney & Close, 2010).

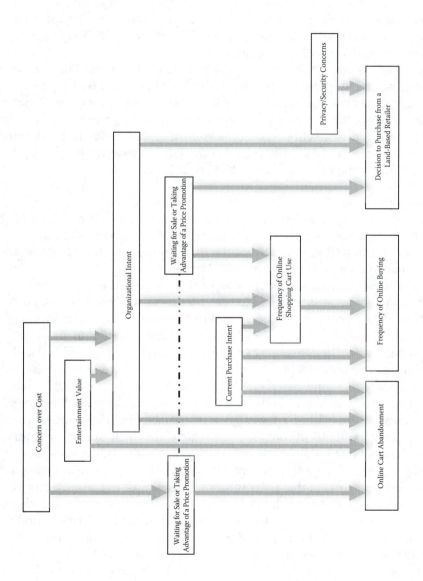

Figure 13.1   Conceptual framework of online shopping cart use and abandonment.

The frequency of online buying is positively related to the frequency of online shopping cart use and current purchase intent. The more frequently a consumer uses an online cart, the more frequently the consumer buys items online. A greater intention to purchase the item of interest during his current online shopping session is positively related to the frequency of online buying (Close & Kukar-Kinney, 2010).

The third outcome, the decision to purchase the item from a land-based retailer, is directly related to the consumer's inclination to wait for a sale or price promotion and the tendency to use an e-cart for organizational purposes. Also, the greater a consumer's concerns over privacy and security, the greater the likelihood that the consumer will decide to purchase the item from a land-based retailer as opposed to proceeding with their acquisition via the Internet (Kukar-Kinney & Close, 2010).

Indirect Relationships

Although the direct relationships provide a rich and interesting narrative of online shopping cart use and abandonment, the indirect relationships indicate an interesting notion, that the three eventual outcomes are not necessarily isolated and exclusive of one another.

A consumer's concern over the cost of the item is indirectly related to all three outcomes as it is related to the consumer's inclination to wait for a sale or price promotion and organizational use of the cart. Concern over cost is positively related to waiting for a sale or price promotion and organizational intent. The consumers' organizational intent is positively related to online cart abandonment, frequency of online cart use, and the decision to purchase from a land-based retailer (Kukar-Kinney & Close, 2010). The more consumers are concerned about the total cost of the order, the more likely they will wait until a lower price is available. Instead of using the cart to purchase items of interest immediately, they will rather use it for organizational purposes only; hence, there is a greater likelihood of abandoning the cart during the current Internet session. These relationships highlight the argument that these three outcomes must not be looked at as fully competitive and mutually exclusive. The three outcomes may interact and intermingle. We discuss this notion further in the managerial implications section. Examining how the total cost concerns affect shopping cart abandonment (even if indirectly through the above-discussed constructs), our findings suggest a positive correlation between concern about total cost and consequent online shopping cart abandonment ($\rho = .45$, $p < .01$), as well as a moderate total standardized effect (.30) of consumers' cost concern on abandonment (Kukar-Kinney & Close, 2010).

The entertainment value of placing items in the online shopping cart is shown to be indirectly related to both the frequency of online buying and the decision to purchase from a land-based retailer. This link is through its relation to organizational intent. Organizational intent, although directly and positively related to online cart abandonment and the decision to purchase from a land-based retailer, is also shown to be indirectly and positively related to the frequency of online buying by positively influencing the frequency with which consumers use online carts. Similarly, the inclination of a consumer to wait for a sale or price promotion is shown to be indirectly and positively related to the frequency of online buying by way of its relation to a consumer's frequency of online shopping cart use (Kukar-Kinney & Close, 2010; Close & Kukar-Kinney, 2010).

To examine total standardized (direct and indirect) effects of the variables in the framework, findings in our abandonment study indicate that the key drivers of online shopping cart abandonment are: (1) consumers' preference for using the cart as an organizational rather than a purchase tool, (2) using the cart solely for entertainment, and (3) consumers' concern about the price of the order (including all the incurred costs). By far, the two most important factors affecting the decision not to purchase online, but rather at the e-tailer's land-based store, is the consumers' concern about the total cost of the order (including shipping) and their desire to wait for a lower or sale price.

Discussion of Findings

Observation of the findings of our synthesized framework highlights the tremendous overlap in motivations of online consumers. Concern over cost, entertainment value, organizational intent, and waiting for a sale or price promotion are both directly and indirectly related to all three outcomes of our framework. The three outcomes of our framework then are not mutually exclusive.

Our findings highlight the contrarian viewpoint that abandonment need not be viewed as a negative outcome of online shopping. Conventional wisdom suggests that electronic cart abandonment is a bad thing because it lowers shopping transaction conversion rates or it may imply a nonconsumer friendly site (Hoffman & Novak, 2005). In addition, some scholars have also used online cart abandonment as a measure of consumer dissatisfaction (Oliver & Shor, 2003). Therefore, many e-tailers and scholars alike have made an assumption that the abandoned items represent a lost sale (*New Media Age*, 2002). However, consumers often leave items in their e-cart for reasons other than dissatisfaction with the product, the online retailer, or the purchase process. The findings of our abandonment study indicate that online shoppers are accustomed to using their cart as an organizational tool to hold or store their desired items, a wish list, and as a means to track prices for possible future purchases (Kukar-Kinney & Close, 2010). Our synthesized framework highlights this as well. E-cart abandonment does not necessarily indicate that the consumers will never purchase the items in their carts; rather it may merely indicate that consumers decide to delay their purchases or purchase the item from a land-based retailer (Moe, 2003).

Managerial Implications

The implications of our findings are that online retailers must tailor their Web sites and carts to encourage customers to use the carts in a way that suits customer needs. The traditional shopping cart analogy does not directly apply in the virtual world. We find that online shoppers tend to use their e-carts as a tool for entertainment, organization, and as a means to decipher cost issues. As shoppers use their e-carts for purposes other than merely storing the item for purchase, e-tailers need to make sure that they provide customers with persistent shopping carts, carts that continue to store the items even after the consumer has left the Web site. This finding highlights the importance of e-tailers ensuring a convenient way for their customers to return to their previously filled carts. Additionally, online retailers should be sure that their online carts update the availability and cost of the items and the associated transaction fees, such as shipping costs, and reflect the current promotions. Such updates would combine customers' use of the cart as an organizational aid with its ability to help consumers take advantage of sales and other price promotions.

Our synthesized findings show that those consumers who are motivated by sales or other price promotions have a higher frequency of placing items in their online carts compared to those who are not motivated by lower cost offers. This may be because some sites do not disclose the total price of the purchase, including the tax and shipping/handling fees, until the item is actually placed into the cart. Also, sale- or deal-prone consumers may desire a convenient way of monitoring prices for possible future price reductions. This finding indicates an importance of e-tailers maintaining promotion programs in place to stimulate consumers' online cart use and consequently, buying. Retailers can use the information on the items that sit in the shopping carts for a period of time to create sales as a way to move merchandise that a consumer is holding while comparison-shopping competitive sites or rethinking the purchase (Close & Kukar-Kinney, 2010).

Many online shoppers who use their e-carts intend to make an online purchase at that time. For managers, this finding highlights the importance of making it convenient for shoppers to easily place in their cart those items they intend to buy. Then, it is just as important to offer increased convenience at the checkout phase to enhance the conversion rate from online shopping to online buying. Once the consumer has placed an item in the cart, the purchase process, such as checkout and payment, should be as simple and hassle-free as possible (e.g., availability of one-click buying for returning customers) to better guarantee a successful purchase. Although it may be tempting to use this time to collect complete customer information for a customer database, it is recommended to acquire only the basic information needed here, so the customer is less likely to abort the purchase and abandon the cart.

E-cart abandonment should not be necessarily viewed as an undesirable result and, as such, e-tailers must shift their focus away from preventing e-cart abandonment. Instead, we encourage managers to increase the frequency of online buying by way of the indirect variables of our framework, which are in managerial control. E-tailers may increase the frequency of buying by increasing the entertainment value and the organizational aid of their online cart. To encourage consumers to buy online rather than switch to land-based stores, low or free shipping costs (including return shipping) should be implemented. Consumers should be frequently informed about price specials or price reductions of items they have left in their cart on a previous shopping trip. That is, the e-cart can be a managerial tool to help cater to the customer.

Future Research: Social e-Commerce

We conclude this chapter by noting an e-commerce trend and area for future research in online consumer behavior: social e-commerce. There is little research in this area, and we propose future research to test if more social e-commerce sites will have less cart abandonment or a higher online/offline conversion rate. Not only are the revenues of traditional online retailers increasing, but also the emergence of new forms of social e-commerce is adding to the growth of the online marketplace. We define *social e-commerce* as online shopping and purchasing with a group (online or onground) component.

This category entails online group discounts and digital coupons (e.g., Style Mint, Groupon, Living Social, Facebook's coupon program). In these social e-commerce sites, online shoppers join an online community in order to receive deals. For instance, Style Mint, an exclusive T-shirt e-commerce site, is shared via electronic word of mouth, with referral points for discounted merchandise going to the unofficial brand ambassador. Where Style Mint is more of a viral social e-commerce site, Groupon is a bulk social e-commerce site. One catch for bulk sites such as Groupon: in order for the deal to be unlocked, a set number of consumers must accept the deal. That is, the deal is off if the prespecified sales figure is not met by the end of the promotion. Thus, there is a new social motivation to buy. If a consumer purchases the deal, they are one person closer to making the deal available for others. In addition, seeing the number of other consumers who have already made the purchase may enhance the perceived attractiveness of the deal and lead to a faster decision to purchase. This group component may thus lessen abandonment instances.

A third social online shopping example, Living Social, is a site that offers one deal daily with major discounts to local restaurants, spas, bars, and other entertainment venues. The site sends a daily deal for consumers to buy a voucher. After purchasing, the customer receives a unique link to share the deal with friends. As an incentive to share, if three people also buy the deal via your link, you (i.e., the original customer) receive the deal for free. Hence, there is a social motivation and a financial motivation behind Living Social. Last, but not least, is the social media giant Facebook, which is a proper social media site with over 600 million members, however, the company realizes the power of using "your network" to obtain shopping deals. Facebook Deals offers a coupon, and once the coupon is purchased, the item is instantly posted on their news feed (which goes to all of their Facebook friends and networks). Although Facebook Deals does not have the group component needed to "unlock" a deal such as with Groupon, certainly, the social media giant is integrating a social, more personal component to online shopping. It will be interesting to see if these social e-commerce sites integrate an e-cart.

The emergence of social shopping sites highlights the increasing shift in online consumer behavior and the way that commerce is conducted online. Simultaneously, these emerging trends indicate the expansion of e-commerce beyond the traditional online retail marketplace. The consumer buys in cyberspace, but the services and products are redeemed in the on-ground market. Consumer spending on this new form of e-commerce, sometimes called "deal-a-day" sites, is poised to grow by more than 35% to reach $3.9 billion in the United States by 2015, according to a March 2011 forecast by BIA/Kelsey (*eMarketer*, March 2011). Although this chapter synthesizes research on online shopping/cart abandonment in general (versus specific to social shopping sites), we see this emerging trend of social e-shopping as one that is important to address up front. Adding the community/social component can help with consumer acceptance of the Internet as a shopping medium, which we discussed as Phase 1 of the online shopping process. As e-carts and e-commerce technology advance, there are more opportunities for individual, and now social online consumer behavior research.

References

Amazon (2011a). Retrieved May 20, 2011, from http://www.amazon.com/gp/help/customer/display.html/ref=hp_rel_topic?ie=UTF8&nodeId=468480

Amazon (2011b). Retrieved May 20, 2011, from https://www.amazon.com/gp/payphrase/claim/whats-this.html

Arnold M. & Reynolds, K. (2003). Hedonic shopping motivations. *Journal of Retailing, 79*(2), 77–95.

Babin B. J., Darden, W. R., & Griffen, M. (1994).Work and/or fun: Measuring hedonic and utilitarian shopping value. *Journal of Consumer Research, 20*(4), 644–656.

Bridges E. & Florsheim R. (2008). Hedonic and utilitarian shopping goals: The online experience. *Journal of Business Research, 61*(4), 309–314.

Charney T. & Greenberg, B. S. (2001). Uses and gratifications of the internet. In C. A. Lin & D. Atkin (Eds.), *Communication technology and society audience adoption and uses.* Cresskill, NJ: Hampton, pp. 353–378.

Close, A. G. & Kukar-Kinney, M. (2010). Beyond buying: Motivations behind consumers' online shopping cart use. *Journal of Business Research, 63*(9–10), 986–992.

eMarketer (2011, February 28). Consumers continue switch to online banking. Retrieved June 1 from emarketer.com, using University of Richmond database. http://newman.richmond.edu:2082/Article.aspx?R=1008255&dsNav=Ntk:basic%7cconsumers+continue+to+switch+to+online+banking%7c1%7c,Rpp:50,Ro:-1

eMarketer (2011, March 16). A bright future for daily deal sites. Retrieved June 1 from emarketer.com using University of Richmond database. http://newman.richmond.edu:2082/Article.aspx?R=1008283&dsNav=Ntk:basic%7ca+bright+future+for+daily+deal+sites%7c1%7c,Rpp:50,Ro:-1

Flanagin, A. J. & Metzger, M. J. (2001). Internet use in the contemporary media environment. *Human Communication Research, 27*(1), 153–181.

Forrester Research (2005). Rethinking the significance of cart abandonment. Carrie A. Johnson, Charles P. Wilson & Sean Meyer, (Eds.)

Google (2011a). Retrieved January 12, 2012 from https://checkout.google.com/buyer/tour.html

Google (2011b). Retrieved June 3, 2011 from https://checkout.google.com/buyer/tour.html

Hoffman, D. L. & Novak, T. P. (2005). Beyond the basics: Research-based rules for internet retailing advantage. Vanderbilt, TN: eLab Press.

Horrigan, J. B. (2008). Online shopping: Internet users like the convenience but worry about the security of their financial information. *Pew Internet and American Life Project* (February). Retrieved January 12, 2012 from http://www.pewinternet.org

Howard, J. A. & Sheth, J. N. (1969). *The theory of buyer behavior.* New York: John Wiley.

J.P. Morgan (2011). Nothing but net 2011. Provided to *eMarketer,* January 3, 2011. Retrieved March 25, 2011 through University of Richmond database. http://newman.richmond.edu:2082/Article.aspx?R=1008162&dsNav=Ntk:basic%7cnothing+but+net+2011%7c1%7c,Rpp:50,Ro:-1,N:498

Kukar-Kinney, M. & Close, A. G. (2010). The determinants of consumers' online shopping cart abandonment. *Journal of the Academy of Marketing Science, 38*(2), 240–250.

Laroche, M., Zhilin, Y., McDougall, G. H. G., & Jasmin, B. (2005). Internet versus bricks and mortar retailers: an investigation into intangibility and its consequences. *Journal of Retailing, 81*(4), 251–267.

Lee, K. W., Tsai, M. T., & Lanting, M. C. L. (2011). From marketplace to marketspace: Investigating the consumer switch to online banking. *Electronic Commerce Research and Applications, 10,* 115–125.

Li, S. & Chatterjee, P. (2006). Shopping cart abandonment at retail websites – A multi-stage model of online shopping behavior. Working paper. http://sloan.ucr.edu/profiles/blogs/working-paper-li-and

Lueker, T. (2003). Abandonment surveys help boost sales. *Marketing News, 37*(24): 16–21.

Magill, K. (2005). Building a better shopping cart. *Multichannel Merchant, 1*(8), 18–19. http://multichannelmerchant.com/mag/building_better_shopping_120105/

Mathwick, C., Malhotra, N., & Rigdon, E. (2001). Experiential value: Conceptualization, measurement and application in the catalog and internet shopping environment. *Journal of Retailing, 77*(1), 39–56.

McQuail, D. (1987). *Mass communication theory: An introduction* (2nd edition). London: SAGE.

Miyazaki, A. D. & Fernandez, A. (2001). Consumer perceptions of privacy and security risks for online shopping. *Journal of Consumer Affairs, 35*(1), 27–44.

Moe, W. W. (2003). Buying, searching, or browsing: Differentiating between online shoppers using in-store navigational clickstream. *Journal of Consumer Psychology, 13*(1–2). 29–39.

New Media Age. (2002). Online store layouts confuse shoppers. December 19, p. 14.

Noble, S. M., Griffith, D. A., & Adjei, M. T. (2006). Drivers of local merchant loyalty: Understanding the influence of gender and shopping motives. *Journal of Retailing, 82*(3), 177–188.

Novak, T. P., Hoffman, D. L., & Duhachek, A. (2003). The influence of goal directed and experiential activities on online flow experiences. *Journal of Consumer Psychology, 13*(1–2), 3–16.

Oliver, R. L. & Shor, M. (2003). Digital redemption of coupons: Satisfying and dissatisfying effects of promotion codes. *Journal of Product and Brand Management, 12*(2), 121–134.

Overby J. W. & Lee, E. J. (2006). The effects of utilitarian and hedonic online shopping value on consumer preference and intentions. *Journal of Business Research, 59*(10–11), 1160, 1166.

Papacharissi Z. & Rubin, A. M. (2000). Predictors of internet use. *Journal of Broadcasting and Electronic Media, 44*(2), 175–196.

Rajamma, R. K., Paswan, A. K., & Hossain, M. M. (2009). Why do shoppers abandon shopping carts? Perceived waiting time, risk, and transaction inconvenience. *Journal of Product and Brand Management, 18*(3), 188–197.

Tarasofsky, J. (2008). Online reservations: Increasing your site's "look to book" ratio. *Hotel Marketer*. Retrieved October 30, 2008 http://www.hotelexecutive.com/bus_rev/pub/001/757.asp" \t "br_article"

To, P. L., Liao, C., & Lin, T. H. (2007). Shopping motivations on the internet: A study based on utilitarian and hedonic value. *Technovation, 27*, 774–787.

Warrick, C. S. & Stinson, T. A. (2009). Increasing online purchasing: A study of web assurance and web insurance. *Review of Business Information Systems, 13*(4), 51–58.

Wolfinbarger M. & Gilly, M. C. (2001). Shopping online for freedom, control and fun. *California Management Review, 43*(2), 34–55.

Wolin, L. D. & Korgaonkar, P. (2003). Web advertising: Gender differences in beliefs, attitudes and behavior. *Internet Research: Electronic Networking Applications and Policy, 13*(5), 375–385.

Xia, L. & Monroe, K. B. (2004). Price partitioning on the Internet. *Journal of Interactive Marketing, 18*(4), 63–73.

Xie, E., Teo, H. H., & Wan, W. (2006). Volunteering personal information on the Internet: Effects of reputation, privacy notices, and rewards on online consumer behavior. *Marketing Letters, 17*(1), 61–74.

Zhou, L., Dai, L., & Zhang, D. (2007). Online shopping acceptance model – A critical survey of consumers factors in online shopping. *Journal of Electronic Commerce Research, 8*(1), 41–62.

Author Index

A

Ayers, M. D., 102

Aaker, J. L., 39, 102
Abraham, L., 240, 243, 245
Abratt, R., 92
Achrol, R. S., 273
Acquisti, A., 159, 209, 214, 222–223
Adelson, J., 6, 7
Adjei, M. T., 209, 248–249, 328
Adler, P., 122, 123, 124
AdReaction, 222
Agarwal, R., 246
Ahn, T., 241
Ahn, W., 191
Ahn, Y., 190
Ahtola, O. T., 245
Aiken, L. S., 311
Akerman, A., 58
Aksoy, L., 224
Alba, J., 239
Albinsson, P. A., xxix, 101, 102
Alch, M. L., 4
Alexander, N., 133, 137
Alix, A., 57
Alreck, P., 240
Altman, I., 159, 161, 167, 178
Alwitt, L. F., 218
Amit, R., 240–241
Amyx, C., 297
Anderson, E., 299
Anderson, J. C., 143, 145
Anderson, R., 304
Anderson, R. E., 92, 308
Anderson, T. W., 104
Andreasen, A., xiii
Ankutse, E., 246
Anthis, N. J., 135
Appiah, O., 46–47, 49
Arington, M., 83
Armstrong, A., 221
Armstrong, J., 307
Arnold, M., 326, 327, 332
Arnould, E. J., 125, 143
Arsenault, N., 58
Asch, D., 240
Ask, 217
Askegaard, S., 59, 73
Assael, H., 240, 304, 310
Atuahene-Gima, K., 297, 299

B

Babbie, E. R., 276
Babin, B., 92, 245, 250, 308, 327
Bagozzi, R. P., 145, 311
Bahl, S., 157, 159
Bailey, S., 221
Bain & Company and Mainspring, 297
Bakan, D., 249
Baker, J., 40, 40–41
Bakewell, C., 238
Bakos, Y. J., 239
Bal, A. S., xxix, 185, 195
Balasubramian, S., 216, 217
Balazs, B., 241
Baldassarri, S., 38
Ballantine, P. W., 110
Banister, E. N., 15
Bao, J., 244
Barber, N., 250
Barger, J., 134
Bargh, J. A., 37
Barnes, S. B., 209, 212, 224
Barros, S., 97
Barry, T. E., 223
Bart, I. Y., 303–304, 310
Bartle, R., 57
Barwise, P., 214, 217, 218
Batra, R., 39, 245
Batts, S. A., 135
Baudin, H., 44
Baudrillard, J., 188
Bausch, S., 209, 222
Baxter, L. A., 161, 162
Beatty, S. F., 36
Becerra, E., 58
Belanger, F., 240
Belisle, J. F., 58
Belk, R. W., 4, 6, 15, 59, 73, 165, 277
Bell, D. R., 283
Bell, M., 56
Bellman, S., 240
Belz, F.-M., 102, 107
Bem, S. L., 249
Bendixen, M., 92
Bendoly, E., 269, 274, 275
Beniger, J. R., 222

345

Subject Index

A

Abandonment, *See* Consumer electronic shopping cart behavior

Adolescents, 4

girls' mobile photo sharing study, 8–30, *See also* Mobile photo sharing by adolescent girls

discussion of findings, 28–30

identity-oriented characteristics, 11, 12–21

identity-oriented motives, 11, 21–28

identity performance through social media, 6–7

Millennials and online authenticity, 151

mobile technology use, 3–6

Advertising, *See* Online advertising

Amazon.com, 272, 329

Antibrands, 103

Anticonsumption, 15

Association for Consumer Research (ACR), xiv–xv

Attractiveness perceptions of avatar representatives, 41–43

Audience feedback motives for mobile photo sharing, 21–24

Authenticity in online communications, 133–134

authenticity types and definitions, 137

conceptual framework

authenticity, 136–138

interaction quality, 138–139

model of communication, 135–136

trust, 138

data analysis and interpretation, 145–149

discussion of findings, 149–150

future research directions, 151–152

managerial implications, 151

measures and confirmatory factor analysis, 143–145

Millennials and, 151

study hypotheses, 140

study limitations, 151

study methods, 141–143

Auto driving method, 10

Avatar (film), 35, 49

Avatars, 35–36, 56

body/appearance-related consumption desires, 69–71

researcher-subject interactions, 62

Second Life choices, 68

Avatars and consumer online interactions, 36

buyer-avatar ethnic match effects, 46–47

buyer-avatar similarity effects, 43–46

expertise and attractiveness, 41–43

hedonic and utilitarian values, 47–48

interactivity and responsiveness, 37–38

outcomes and managerial implications, 47–49

perceived socialness effects, 40–41

personality, 39–40

social cues and, 37

social response theory and, 36, 49

theoretical implications and future research, 49–50

voice capability, 38

Awareness raising online activism, 106

B

Banner advertising, 209, 212–213, 214

Bayesian conceptual mapping software (Leximancer), 191–193

Behavioral intentions and consumer trust, 303–304, 314, 317

Behavioral targeting, 213, 218, 220

"Big Five" personality traits, 39–40

Blair, Tony, 196, 201

Blogs, 85–86, 134–135, 215

activist use of, 105

advertising and, 215–216

authenticity issues, *See* Authenticity in online communications

consumer activism study data collection, 110

consumer trust and, 138, 149–151

model of communication, 136

online authenticity study data collection, 141

socialization and, 136

types, 135

Bluetooth marketing, 217

Bootstrap mediation test, 145–149

Boycotts, 102, 103–104

Brand authenticity, 137

Brand invertising, *See* Invertising

357